Becoming Ruth

The Diary of
A World Citizen

DESTINY FRIENDSHIP

Ruth Kaufman

Order this book online at www.trafford.com
or email orders@trafford.com

Most Trafford titles are also available at major online book retailers.

Printed in Victoria, BC, Canada.

ISBN: 978-1-4251-1574-6 (Soft)

*We at Trafford believe that it is the responsibility of us all, as both individuals
and corporations, to make choices that are environmentally and socially sound.
You, in turn, are supporting this responsible conduct each time you purchase a
Trafford book, or make use of our publishing services. To find out how you are
helping, please visit www.trafford.com/responsiblepublishing.html*

*Our mission is to efficiently provide the world's finest, most comprehensive
book publishing service, enabling every author to experience success.
To find out how to publish your book, your way, and have it available
worldwide, visit us online at www.trafford.com*

Trafford rev: 01/07/2010

www.trafford.com

North America & international
toll-free: 1 888 232 4444 (USA & Canada)
phone: 250 383 6864 ♦ fax: 812 355 4082
email: info@trafford.com

Praise for Ruth Kaufman's *Becoming Ruth: The Diary of A World Citizen*

"Congratulations on a beautiful job of capturing the feeling of escaping with a couple of your kids for a whirlwind trip encircling the globe on a tight budget.
I love your book! It is so fresh and openly honest."
Mary Echols, PhD. Art History.

"Ruth Kaufman chronicles with dazzling detail her 14-month journey through Europe, Africa and Asia in the late 1960s with two of her children. Her collection of journals and letters provide a multi-sensory wellspring of observation, allowing us to share the cultural and political vistas of a world gripped in Cold War.

This story of her travels with David and Nita, two of her children, gives face to the struggles, hope, love, courage and loyalty of the people and communities they visited.

Nita uses chess as an international language; David illustrates the ebullience of youth, adaptability and community the earth over; and Ruth personifies the determination of a woman hungry for the truth of the world, directly from the minds and hearts of its people.

Ruth shares her decision to start NOW, traveling cheaply and with local people, finding friends and resting places in the most unlikely spots. This adventure is one to be savored slowly, perhaps with a map nearby."
Pat Patterson, educator.

I enjoyed seeing the world through your family's eyes. The details of life in these exotic locations are a delight to read about. You breathe more life into the story than a basic travelogue would. I much prefer to learn what food and shopping is like, even toilets, than to hear of people's airline adventures, hard beds and tourist traps.

I think you did a fine job of including details and giving personal insight into the trip. The fact that you left me wanting to know more about your relationships proves that you did the job of portraying that goal in the book. It isn't just about a bus ride, but who is on the bus with you.

These days people are more afraid of travel than ever before. People are more liable to stick to the small circle of relationships they have rather than take a chance and smile at a stranger on the street. So perhaps the books will inspire people to travel, and make new friend while doing so. This is the goal, no?"
Heather Froeschl, editor

DEDICATION

This book is dedicated to Adam, who was the catalyst that started me on this expedition. Fortified by his affection, I found the strength to challenge society's mores.

Adam gave me the spark of his love for travel. He brushed aside my fears and trepidation and sent me forth with courage and a spirit for adventure. He proved dependable and considerate. A letter from him arrived at every single mail stop along the way, keeping us in close touch throughout my journey.

TABLE OF CONTENTS

ACKNOWLEDGMENT

I am eternally grateful to Gladys Vogel, who worked out an itinerary for us for a two-month camping trip across Europe. Her inspiration resulted in a trip incurring the least amount of expense and the most fun.

This book could never have been published without the efforts of some very key people. Many thanks for Heather Froeschl, my editor, for her clear thinking and creative problem-solving. She took top honors as Freelance Book Editor in the Preditors and Editors Book Editor category.

I am grateful for the time and energy generously offered by my son, David, who spent days editing hundreds of my photographs.

I am indebted to Nick Patler, who gave me support and attended to the administrative needs when I felt discouraged.

Without each of you this book may never have come to fruition.

AUTHOR'S NOTE

We all have dreams. My mother was a social activist who talked and dreamed of a trip to Europe. By the time she finally was able to go, she was in her 60s, and suffered from arthritis so badly that she ached constantly. Her shapely legs flared with excruciating pain whenever she walked any distance. It spoiled the trip for her.

I learned a lesson from my mother: Don't wait. Don't put off travel for the future. Do it now while you have health, stamina and go power.

I took my first trip around the world with my daughter and son in 1968. I was 45 years old and on sabbatical from teaching elementary school. The 14-month trip opened my mind and heart to new people and ideas all over the world. This book is a diary of my adventures in Madrid, Malaga, Barcelona, Andorra, Rome, Florence, Greece, Russia, Germany, London, Turkey, Iran, Pakistan, Afghanistan, India, Nepal, Mombasa, Nairobi, Poona, Goa, Ceylon, Indonesia, Thailand, Hong Kong, Taiwan and Japan.

Our journey was an unusual and glorious experience from start to finish. We made many friends in each country. We realized people are more outgoing, friendlier and much less fearful in other areas of the world.

Today, at 85, I am still a social activist and still curious about life.

PROLOGUE

Where does one start in the planning, organizing and thinking that a trip around the world involves? I had 14 months are ahead of me in which I abdicated the responsibilities I'd carried for at least half my life. I became a new woman, dropping the roles of wife, mother, housekeeper and teacher. I could become ME.

The seeds of travel were planted long ago. Those anthropology courses in college 25 years earlier had whetted my taste for travel to other societies. New Guinea, India, Africa, Indonesia … countries with magic in their names.

When we married, Jack and I decided we would rather not invest in furniture or expensive belongings. We would save our money for travel. When Nita, my eldest daughter, was 9 months old, we sublet our apartment, and for three months we toured the United States. My aunt challenged me to do it inexpensively. I proved to her we could make the trip for $500. This marked the beginning of my frugal travel.

I made up my mind to "sweat out" the Plainview, New York, school district where I worked as a teacher for seven years until I could apply for my sabbatical leave. By the time I applied for the leave I was earning $12,000 a year. By taking only half pay, I would have $6000 to spend for the trip.

Through the grapevine, I learned that less than the accepted four percent of teachers had applied and the chances were that I would be granted a sabbatical. This was important to know as a bracer for my final meeting with Dr. Savitt, the superintendent of Plainview Schools. He liked the letter I had written to him.

"Dr. Savitt," I said during our interview, "I promise you I will not enroll in school during my sabbatical."

He looked at me in shocked surprise. It was expected.

"I have been attending school nights and summers every single term since I began teaching in Plainview in 1961. I need a change now."

"I agree with you," he said. "But you must be out of the country for at least seven months. I don't want you seen at the local beauty parlors as some of the teachers have done."

"I promise you."

It was a pleasant, relaxed interview and I came home that night spilling over with happiness.

As soon as Jack, my husband, walked in I announced, "Dr. Savitt has recommended my leave to the school board."

"You are not serious about taking it, are you?"

"Jack, my sabbatical is all I've thought about for the past year."

"Are you planning to desert the family?"

"Yes," I replied.

"You are not! I will tell Dr. Savitt not to give you your leave."

"O.K. then, I'll take the children with me," I said.

"You will not. I won't let them go," Jack stood his ground.

"What would you have me do then?" I asked.

"Wait until the children are grown up and out of school."

My son David had five more years before he would finish high school. I had been teaching for 22 years.

"You want me to teach five more years without a break? Jack, I've been a mother to our four children, homemaker, a full-time teacher and a student taking courses and studying at night. I'll land in a mental institution at this rate. I need a rest from the children and from teaching. I must get away, now."

Jack and I did not see eye to eye on most issues during our marriage. It had not been a happy marriage for me.

I considered Jack's request that I not go unreasonable. But I would not take off and desert the family. I was a mother with responsibilities and I would not forsake that role. David is my youngest. I thought that perhaps during a year of travel he would mature and become a better student than he had been. I resolved to take 13-year-old David with me.

Knowing Jack, I knew I must leave a daughter to be his housekeeper. So Wendi, his protégé and companion, would take on my role during her senior year in high school. Wendi related well to her father. She discussed her schoolwork with him and they saw plays. They enjoyed television, flew kites and rode bikes together.

When I first asked Wendi how she would feel if I took Nita with me but did not take her, she accepted it and said she understood. I said, "When I return and work another year to earn more money we can go on a trip together."

Nita, at 18, was about to graduate from high school. Marlboro College had already accepted her for the following year. I knew that as she trotted off to college our relationship would change in a way I was not ready for yet. She was so independent that there would be practically no need of me during her college years. She had been my "right hand" all her life. She played the role of mother and cared for and helped her siblings when they needed it. She helped them get better grades in school. She stood by my side when I had guests and gave me a hand in the kitchen when I needed her.

I wanted to give her something more. She had a driving quest for knowledge and would find this year of travel an enriching experience before college.

I included Lori, my third daughter, in my original plans and hoped to take her to Europe during the summer. She was 15. "Mother," she said. "Travel is not what I want. My interest is drama." So we scouted around and found theater workshop camps. I took her to New York City for interviews and even an audition.

It was Lori's choice not to accompany us. However, as the weeks of planning went on, Lori let me know that I was making a mistake to leave her.

"I need you, Mother, and I'm upset that you are deserting me in my time of need."

This perspective was in direct contradiction to the unhappiness she felt when she learned her father didn't want me to go at all. She was willing to fight for my right to go then.

She'd pointed out, "We aren't children any longer. It isn't as though we don't run this household by ourselves most of the time."

Lori was my true concern. Nita had been her confidante. I tried to line up substitutes, people who she could turn to when she needed them. She resented my interference.

"Make up your mind Mother, if you are leaving — leave. Don't try to run my life while you are away."

The beginning to our trip was a most unusual one. I was having dinner with my friend Adam one evening when the conversation turned to travel, as it often did during this period. Adam looked at me and said, "Ruth, you have a big enterprise ahead of you and you are not prepared for it."

I interrupted with the plans we'd made and the shots we'd taken.

"That's not what I mean at all."

"What else should I be doing?" I asked.

"I've known you a long time, most of your life. When you think back, it has been a rather sheltered life that you've led. Your home and family absorb most of your time. For 22 years, you have been teaching school, and that is a small world. You haven't had any experience getting out among people you do not know, meeting new people and opening yourself to new experiences. My advice to you is: get out and meet people."

I took that advice.

At my next dinner with Adam I couldn't wait to share my new approach. It whetted the appetite of this voyeur, and from then on he encouraged me to continue meeting people and enjoying them, and then to return to him to relate the experiences.

This made an indelible imprint on my personality. Trying new ventures without fear was to become a big part of my life during the next year. Willingness to befriend new people became a necessity as the trip unfolded. Talking about what happened to me with someone who cares and loves me is a trait of my personality even today. I realize that being open and honest in my dealings with people is nothing to be ashamed of. Yes, "get out and meet people" was a very important beginning for me.

Two different sources recommended the same travel agent, Gladys Vogel from Trips Unlimited. I walked into her office and told her, "I have a husband who has never taken me to a hotel. We camp on our vacations. I have no idea how to go about taking a trip abroad."

"I have been waiting for someone like you to walk into this office. I have just the trip for you. It is a camping trip from London to India, 12,000 miles, and costs $400. It will take about two months of travel in a bus during the day, and you will camp out in tents and sleeping bags at night. This tour was made for you," Gladys said.

Gladys mapped out an itinerary in Europe with a stop in London, from which we would leave on our camping trip. By September 22, 1968, we would be ready for the Indiaman camping tour.

"I don't want to go to France," proclaimed Nita. "I want to go to Russia where they play chess."

So I returned to Gladys saying, "I understand Russia is a very expensive country to visit. Nita wants to go there instead of France."

Gladys took out her books and said, "We can get around that. You will go to the Soviet Union as students to study Russian. It will cost you $6 a day for three weeks and it will have to be paid in advance."

Together Gladys and I planned a trip that would take us around the world for 14 months.

DAVID   JACOB   LORI

NITA   RUTH   WENDY

PART I

A TASTE OF EUROPE
With
NITA, DAVID and RUTH

ONE

Portugal

Ruth's journal begins:

I'm holding a ticket to go around the world. The clouds envelop me and whisk me away to a new life. My adventure is beginning.

Tuesday, July 2

We began our voyage by waiting. Our flight, #154, scheduled for 10:30 p.m. left at 1:10 a.m.

The Dramamine threw me into a hazy sleepiness. Between naps I recall waking up for a cocktail. Then chicken a la king was served in a pastry shell. The wine in the sauce was delicious. It was a good snack. I looked out at mountains of snow. Nita claimed they were clouds and I was wasting my film.

Pam Am had no movies, music, lighting or air conditioning. The seats did not recline far enough for comfort. There were not enough pillows or blankets for each passenger. But the ever-cheerful stewardesses and the scrumptious food compensated. Breakfast was a crepe with scrambled egg inside, sausage and roll. The coffee had a strong aroma.

PORTUGAL

The plane dipped a wing and abruptly slipped beneath the clouds. We had hoped to see Lisbon from the air, but except for a few scraggly palm trees, we landed too soon.

David wrote home:

"What, a letter from me? Portugal is wonderful. The plane ride was fun but I wish it were over more land. When we got over Lisbon we came down so low I could read the street signs. At least the ones I could understand. I was scared stiff the plane would bump into a lamp post."

There was the usual chaos as impatient passengers departing the plane jostled each other. In the airport friendly, almost recognizable faces surrounded us. A kind of conversational undertone hung in the air, untranslatable. Even the familiarly shaped corridor signs had a disorienting effect because we could not read them.

Our New York travel agent had arranged for a hotel in Lisbon, Portugal. It was

1

our first stop on our "round the world" voyage. We registered and settled into our hotel room. This first pension, Residencia Mucaba, was unsurpassable — three double windows and a spacious room with a bathtub and shower. Our first accommodations were inexpensive. For a clean and airy pension containing three beds and a couch we paid 180 escudos, or six dollars a night.

There was one problem. Our brightest light shown feebly from a 25-watt bulb and we looked forward to identifying socks by flashlight.

Since Nita was a mature woman of 18, she wanted to limit any time she spent with her younger brother and her "immature" mother. Nita settled down and announced, "I'm staying here. I'm tired and I'm resting for awhile."

Nita had adroitly developed winning chess ploys throughout the night. Now she slept away the day. David and I fidgeted, finally abandoning her. David was raring to go. I gave him some escudos and we started our journey. We decided to get on a bus to see the sights of Lisbon.

We rode atop of a double-decker sightseeing bus under Lisbon's brilliant skies. We rode to the end of the line and saw all the churches, parks and interesting buildings. The bus turned around and we stayed on for the return trip. Still, nobody wanted any fare.

Someone finally told us that the bus and trolley workers were on strike against the British owners. Since Portugal had a non-strike ordinance, striking workers continued to provide the same services, except for one. They simply neglected to collect passenger fares. Workers put in the normal workday without the demeaning spectacle of a picket line shuffle, and the public continued to get to and from work. Therefore, all the buses were running and were free. They worked regular hours, but didn't collect money. Great for us!

We rode the full round trip on bus #31 for an hour and one half. We got out, bought some snacks for pennies apiece, and then rode for another two hours. We were like two butterflies, free and uninhibited.

After a couple of hours we found ourselves near our hotel. I suggested that we go to the room and rest after our long trip. As I stepped off the bus, David yelled from the window, "Hey Mom, I'm not tired so I'm gonna go on."

His voice got smaller as the door slammed shut and the bus drove off. I stood there with my mouth hanging open, feeling somewhat disoriented. He was gone and on his own on the first day of our arrival. He was 13.

When he finally returned he relayed his adventures to me.

"I walked up and down Avenida Libertad. That's Lisbon's Main Street. I popped into a little shop and bought a potato pancake. It was only a measly six cents. The funny thing was I fooled everybody and made them think that I was Portuguese by talking the little Spanish that I know.

"Then I discovered the open trolley cars. Mom, they were more fun than the double-decker buses. I could hang on the outside and ride along without paying. That was fun.

"I got a little lost because I forgot the name of the hotel. I did come back to the room and poked Nita to see if she was still breathing, but she was asleep. Some sister! She's no fun.

"I sneaked out again and bought a lobster for 180 escudos per kilogram. Figure that one out."

I was impressed with my son in more ways than one.

After that we went to bed but the rest of Lisbon was just waking up. They are night people.

Tuesday, July 2

Nita writes:

I am now in Lisbon and I feel hopelessly lost—helpless, strange. What is the real purpose in traveling? I don't know the language. I don't know a soul. I don't even know the money system. I feel like a buffoon.

Mommy and David are out eating and adventuring. I have just woken from a lovely sleep. From the window I can see the city, very much in the style of old San Juan. But with beautiful trees I have never before seen with the bluest, most cloudless sky in the world, with the freshest, most playful breeze in the universe. Lisbon doesn't smell like a city — only the sounds of the rumbling double-decker buses give the city secret away.

7:30 p.m. Portugal was very frustrating for me. This was because the Portuguese language is so close to Spanish that I felt I should be able to understand things, but then find out that I can't.

Lisbon was built on seven hills and was surrounded by houses of white stucco and red tile. Each, with its own small garden, blended into the hillside.

Coming down out of the hills, the cobblestone streets were lined with palm trees. The contrast between the verdant green lawns and the creamy stucco was accentuated by the deep blue, cloudless sky and the fresh, clear air. The hills and ocean breezes contributed to spring-like weather most of the year.

One was aware of a European flavor immediately; there were very narrow streets, steep hills, tile roofs, tile buildings. David noticed a bright purple building. The very old nestled next to the very new apartment houses.

In the street, traffic was about 50 percent modern vehicles and 50 percent mule carts. To me, women's dress styles were reminiscent of the 1950s, while men's wear had advanced to the conservative mode of 1968; still, the overall impression we had of Lisbon was of a vibrant city.

In the center of town, alongside a modern boutique, we found the local marble shop, where an artisan, elbow deep in chips, made sinks and counter tops. We found no chess club for Nita. The lack of grocery stores seemed strange to us. The city was full of pastellieres, outdoor coffee and pastry shops. Most often the people we saw were sipping coffee or milk.

3

The milk we drank was delicious. Lisbon had apparently not yet discovered the profit to be made from skimming off most of the cream. Compared to America's milk theirs was like sweetened, condensed cream. As good as the milk tasted by itself, milk in coffee was a peculiar experience. It was always served piping hot, usually in pewter pitchers. When this milk was added to the coffee it was too hot, too sweet and too thick to drink.

Portugal's college town, their equivalent of our Boston, was Coimbra, but in just a day's touring on Lisbon buses, we passed three universities, a huge hospital and a palace where fancy uniformed soldiers paraded passed a candy-striped guard-house. We saw several photo opportunities. A woman carried a wash basket on her head and a boy had long steel pole three times his height, which he walked with balanced on his shoulder.

On one of our trolley rides we witnessed a uniquely Portuguese incident. A woman boarded our trolley after the conductor had said, "No more!" The woman refused to get off. The conductor, equally stubborn, refused to close the doors. Another passenger gave up her seat, stepped off the trolley and began waiting for another trolley. It was a lovely gesture.

Wednesday, July 3

Every floral park came equipped with one navy-blue uniformed policeman, who in shiny leather boots, directed traffic. On some days there might be no traffic, but there he stood, either at attention or at parade rest.

The oldest section of Lisbon is the Alfama. Here many of the streets were too narrow for traffic. We watched as a second floor resident leaned out his window, reached across the street and shook hands with a neighbor. Where traffic was allowed, it was at the suffrage of another policeman, who with a red and green colored paddle, acted like a street light.

Three and four story stucco houses lined the sidewalks. Many of these had balconies with cascading flowers or cages with canaries. The whole section was alive in scent and sound. In the streets we saw open-air fish markets and old women selling bread or silk scarves. Fish in wooden trays stared through unseeing eyes, their mouths agape, as fish hawkers dragged wooden sleds up the streets, bouncing tangles of squid and ice. In spite of the fish, the area was clean.

Every morning before seven a city fire truck drove into the Alfama, and with huge hoses, washed down every inch of street and sidewalk, while kids pestered and teased, until a close squirt sent them running.

Nita writes:
The parts of Lisbon we saw seem very unamericanized. There were no Coca-Cola ads and we saw no television and we heard no English spoken. I understand that if we had done what most Americans do, and stayed at some of the better hotels, we would have had little need for Portuguese.

The most confusing part of our first travel adventures had been the problem of monetary conversion. A centavo is .00e cents. One escudo is .03 cents. 100 centavos equal one escudo.

A bag of plums costs 4 escudos or about 12 cents. A glass of delicious milk was 5 escudos or about 20 cents.

It was David's turn to miss a day. While he slept, Nita and I visited the National Students Association (NSA) at the university. We ate a cheap, filling lunch there. Nita was reminded of the prison in Puerto Rico where she had worked the previous summer. This building was an old, run-down place, quite unattractive indoors.

The next day Nita announced we were moving out. "This place is far too expensive for us."

We searched in another area of Lisbon for another room that cost less. Nita found a pension, Pensao Estrella dos Anjos, that was half the price we were paying. The total bill for the three of us was 91.30 escudos, or about three dollars.

Nita continued in the role of monitoring our finances throughout the entire trip. It was thanks to her penny-pinching that we were able to continue to travel as long as we did.

In the late afternoon, we took a bus and then a train to Casavales Beach. On the way, we were bumped out of the first class section because we had second- class tickets. The beach had crystal white sand and clear, but very cold, very blue water curling onto the shore in three-foot breakers.

David writes:

The next day we went to the Casavales beach. What a beach! It had Jones Beach sand, but not Jones Beach water. When you go out beyond the breakers it is as calm as a swimming pool. The breakers themselves were half the size of the Jones Beach waves that I am used to.

At first it was too cold to go in so Nita and I played on the beach for a while. We were unsuccessful building sandcastles. We went in swimming, but it took half an hour to get used to the coldness of the water.

I decided to make friends with some girls on the beach. I was speaking in my halting Spanish. Since I'm totally unable to understand Portuguese, I really didn't expect to be able to understand them, but I couldn't understand why they didn't understand me.

Nita finally unraveled the whole problem. While I spoke Spanish to them, they were responding in French to me. All very confusing.

While we were thigh deep in the water, the girls suddenly ran towards shore. Before I could become curious, a 15-foot wave knocked me down, and ground me into the sand on the beach. It didn't have to wait until my back was turned.

It had been a bad day for Nita. I suspected none of us had quite recovered from jet lag, from no sleep one night, to sleep all day one or two days later. But Nita's greatest frustration was that she seemed unable to communicate with anyone. She spoke fluent Spanish, and since the languages appear to be so similar, she couldn't understand why she should be having such difficulty with Portuguese. In a pique, she ridiculed my problems with the language.

"Mom, didn't you just ask that man if he understands English?"

"Yes, I did."

"Didn't he tell you that he doesn't understand English?"

"Yes he did."

"Then why are you still speaking English to him and expecting to be understood? Why don't you at least switch to French?"

"Because rusty as I am, French is as much a mystery as Portuguese is to you."

Ordinarily it would be Nita who was most sensitive to beauty, to the cleanliness, the wonderful riot of scent and color in Lisbon, but she was also most hopeful of meeting new friends. She was the most frustrated by her inability to communicate with anyone.

That night we planned to see Lisbon's nightlife. We would visit a Fado house, or nightclub; but first, we wanted to see the Alfama by night light. It was beautiful. The sections of narrow lighted streets sparkled as they twisted off into the hillside, high above the quiet harbor. In the tiny, tiny rooms of these houses, lived most of the city's blue-collar workers.

We also stopped at the Castle of Saint George, perched on Lisbon's highest hill; it is one of Lisbon's most beautiful areas. Old castle walls, complete with cannon and green moat, surround a park, enclosing both visitors and hundreds of albino birds. There are pure white roosters and turkeys. We expected to see swans a-swimming, but would have liked to see white peacocks.

Later we asked two young boys to show us a Fado house. We walked in and out— too expensive and with a minimum charge to boot. We asked a taxi driver to take us to a less expensive club, and after arrival, all had a good time.

Nita and I had clams and fish, served gourmet style in a spicy tomato and onion sauce, along with olives, rolls and milk. David ordered nothing, in an attempt to keep the bill down, but he still enjoyed the place. While I hummed along with the mournful songs of the Fado singers, Dave played drums and tambourine with the guitarist.

Everything was fine until the bill arrived. We were each charged a 180-escudo minimum. The place we had first visited would have been cheaper, only 100 escudos! The kids were furious, first, because the place had not listed a minimum, and, second, because we hadn't eaten our allowance, but mostly because I paid the bill.

On the way home, we groused that our taxi driver must supplement his income by acting as a shill for the club, receiving a commission for every tourist he steered there.

Though it was one in the morning, people still came into the club. Lisbon is

6

definitely for night people. A man on the street, noticing our mournful procession, took us by the hand, and led us to an electric streetcar. He was kind and was able to communicate with Nita in Spanish. He helped cheer us up after spending more money than we could afford. All in all, I thought, I'm not discouraged. I will read the small print more closely before abandoning myself to the next club, but I will not be scared off by this one experience.

On reflection, we had many wonderful and inexpensive experiences in our first new country, especially the initial trips that Dave and I shared atop the double-decker buses and trolleys. The only physical adjusting I felt was an inability to quench a thirst brought on by clear, low humidity, and a confusion of sleep schedules.

Each of us slept at different times, none quite recovered from the all night flight. David seemed to recover the best and Nita the least. She never really came off her grump throughout our short Lisbon stay. But by far the most disappointing adjustment we had to make was that we accepted our inability to talk to people. I had dreamed of new adventures, making new friends, but instead, I found it a chore to find the ladies' room.

Friday, July 5

All Nita wanted was Spain, "where I can understand them." We waited in the Lisbon airport for our flight announcement to fly on TAP Portuguese airlines to Madrid, Spain.

So many adjustments — to time, money, language.

Perhaps the truth was that we were all too new to traveling and had not yet mastered the mystical language of love and friendship, the language that needs no words.

TWO

MADRID, SPAIN

Saturday, July 6

How could Nita and David still be asleep? I checked to see if they were breathing. It was 10 a.m. and half a day was shot already. Street noises did not bother them. Madrid is similar to New York City with its rushing, noisy atmosphere.

It is no wonder they have a drainage problems here. The cardboard toilet paper doesn't dissolve, so they resort to bidets. They have to wash after using a toilet. Every place has a bidet even if there is no toilet. But bidets have faucets and drains and do not flush as a real toilet. We understood that Spain is one of the countries with NO toilet paper in most places. We carried our own.

Nita and I decided to go to El Prado. David let us know he would not accompany us. I got us good and lost. We asked many people for guidance. Finally, two boys Nita's age, Jose and Louis, took us there. Before they left they made a date to meet us at the El Rastro, the flea market, the following day.

Nita and I spent the afternoon at El Prado viewing Goya, Valasquez, El Greco and other great art. We discovered Dali, the surrealist painter. When we walked out of the museum David was sitting on a bench on the Avenue of Jose de Antonia waiting for us. He arrived after we did and went through the museum. He got there on his own without asking questions; he bragged that he had left the map in the room. Nita and he discussed the art.

We visited Galerias Preciados, a department store with inexpensive merchandise. But we were tired from El Prado and not in the mood for shopping. We had eaten no food yet and it was 6:30. The stores were open for shopping, but restaurants were closed until 8 p.m.

In the evening we went to Restaurant Real. I pondered the menu, trying to find the items in my dictionary, and Ignacio and Josefina, also customers of the restaurant, came over and helped us order our meal. We became friends. We walked and talked and played chess together.

Ignacio was from the Basque province and spoke fluent Basque, French, Spanish and Esperanto (an International language) and a tiny bit of English. Josefina spoke only French and Spanish. She was from France.

When we finished our meal they gave us a pitcher of "Vindo de Cahia." I became high on it. From then on Nita and David ordered milk for me.

Sunday, July 7

Jose and Louis, the two young boys who'd helped us when we had gotten lost, met us to take us through El Rastro, or the flea market, which is open all day Sunday. There were blocks and blocks of pushcarts with every imaginable item. We saw so much. It was a fine day for taking pictures, but I'd left my camera home.

We saw a block of original paintings, a block in which colorful birds were singing in their cages, the usual displays of clothing and of used car parts, rows and rows of antiques and junk. We saw an ancient typewriter Jack would have liked. We kept pricing mantillas of lace and handicrafts, sculptures and embroidered cloth for Wendi. We couldn't learn the price on the only sombrero we saw for Lori. We passed up all the items and didn't buy anything.

Nita proved a hard taskmaster with the budget. If we spent $10 a day she yelled "extravagance!" All hostelries are regulated by law to list prices. All restaurants have the menus posted outside.

We did not eat much in Spain. We mostly drank. We were thirsty all the time. Nita was a leche addict. All she did was cry "I'm thirsty." The milk was sometimes condensed and sweetened as in Portugal and sometimes slightly sour. In Spain it was mostly frio. Once it was caliente because Nita forgot to add frio when she ordered it. This day Nita asked for leche and got horchata, which is a spiced milk drink.

David ate helados, fresh cut ice-cream sandwiches. You chose your own flavors. They sold for 3, 4 or 5 pesetas (less than 10 cents) from stands on the street.

We located the chess club, but it was closed except Mondays at 5 p.m. We decided to take a bus tour to El Escorial and "Valle de Los Caidos." Despite promises, we had a non-English speaking guide. El Escorial is a picturesque town similar to Portugal's Alfama.

We met very unusual people. On the tour was a Philippine Jesuit Priest named Rafael. Both Spanish and English are spoken in the Philippines. He was 37 years old but looked about 20. Rafael was one of the most outgoing, friendly guys I ever met. He spent a year in the states and time in Europe trying to get good books for his church's library. Since the guide refused to speak English, Rafael was guide all through "El Escorial."

What impressed me most was "El Valle de los Caidos," the Valley of the Fallen. It was a memorial to the Nationalist, Fascist soldiers who died during the civil war. It had a fantastically huge cross on top of the mountain, and into the mountain was built an equally huge church-like building. It was about the ugliest structure I have ever seen in my life. The builders tried to mimic the gloomy, dark, monastic-type structures of the 1300s. Unfortunately, they almost succeeded, but not quite, because theirs was worse. All over the place were monstrous angels carrying swords and there was a stiff Madonna. In the center was a glorified tomb of the founder of the Fascist Party, Jose Antonio.

While the tour people ate in a restaurant, Nita and David sat on a wall eating fruit. I sat nearby listening to Nita give David a history of Spain, with emphasis on the Spanish Civil War up to the present government. It gave us all a better understanding of what we were viewing.

The land was sandy and dry as we drove by bus through the countryside. We saw olive trees and pine trees, but no lush grass. I did see cacti.

We had no complaints about the food, but we were always thirsty. We ate some strange but good food, including tripe and fried octopus sandwiches. I had mussels with chopped onion for dinner the previous night.

This night we bought half a kilo of tomatoes, two for each of us for 4 pesetas, and half a kilo of apricots, 9 pesetas; three for each of us. We also bought a container of milk, six glasses for 10 pesetas, and a loaf of bread for 4 pesetas. It added up to 27 pesetas or about 45 cents for good nourishing food for the three of us. Can't beat that!

TOLEDO

Monday, July 8

We decided to take the bus to Toledo to see the town of El Greco. At the bus station we met Dinesh and Suli, an Indian couple, and Juanita and Charles Taylor, Americans from Atlanta, Georgia. We traveled all day with Mr. and Mrs. Taylor, a very pleasant, but rather typical young American couple. She was a pretty stewardess.

Suli and Dinesh were a rather atypical Indian couple who absolutely made the day.

On our bus ride Dinesh sat with me and outlined the tour we should take when we arrived in India.

Nita sat with Suli and found out about her. Suli was a Jain, which is a strict Hindu sect. She wore a sari. Dinesh was a religious non-conformist. They were in America for three years and were on their way back to India. Dinesh, for fun, attended Northwestern College for a post-graduate degree. He got straight As and graduated with honors.

Meanwhile Suli, who left her newborn baby in India, was sad and restless, so she went to the Boston School's superintendent to ask if she could teach. After much futzing around, she finally got an illegal job teaching all about India in the depressed area for the Title I program. She must have been a great teacher, but after two or three months the government caught up with her and made her stop teaching.

Suli said that most Indians are influenced by astrology. At birth a child's complete chart is made up. Then his lucky numbers and letters are derived. The child's first name must begin with one of his lucky letters. Every name has a meaning. Suli's lucky letter is M and her name was originally Malte, which is a white flower. But Suli's grandmother was old-fashioned and thought that any name ending in an "e" was improper. So when Suli was 3 years old her name was changed to a beautiful long one beginning with S and ending in "a." This was very proper. The name means "beautiful eyes."

Dinesh's name means "King of the Poor People." When pronounced with the accent on the last syllable it means "Child of the Sun." Suli had a 17-year-old cousin named Nita. It was a usual name in India.

Our Indian friends were not permitted to travel to Portugal, as that country was not on friendly terms with India. Visas were not available.

We toured El Greco's home and museum and visited a couple of synagogues. There were many tourist shops. We saw a stool, hand carved, that women sat on while in labor to deliver their babies. It proved to be more comfortable than our chairs.

David liked the fencing swords and wanted to buy one for $2.50, but it was too clumsy to carry or mail. We priced sombreros and matador hats for Lori, who loves hats.

We were impressed by the Cathedral de Los Reyes, which took 260 years to build. Through ignorance we had failed to buy round trip tickets and there were no available bus tickets home. So we took the train back to Madrid.

It was 7:30 a.m. We had just come from the room of our friends. We woke them out of a sound sleep to ask them to keep our excess baggage until our return to Madrid. They're remarkable! I loved them both.

I dumped my pocketbook. Unbelievable what what in it:
1. A black scarf for head or shoulder coverings when we enter a church.
2. Our lunch menu — gazpacho soup, paello , clams, meat and rice.
3. Sunglasses, a necessity.
4. Franc coins the Taylors gave me because I wouldn't be going to France.
5. Paper napkins to use for toilet paper, wipe off perspiration and for Nita's bloody nose. She had three already.
6. Instructions from our travel agent.
7. Book: "Spain on $5 A Day."
8. Berlitz: "Traveler's Spanish," a small phrase book in constant use.
9. Nita had her dictionary, David had his dictionary, and both spoke Spanish constantly.
10. Book: "French-Without a Teacher."
11. Book: "Un Dia En Toledo." We sat next to a monk from Seville and he gave David this little book in friendship. David was forced to converse with him in Spanish on the train home.
12. A train ticket as a reminder next time to buy round trip bus tickets.
13. A map of Madrid and a map of Spain, which Suli gave me.

14. American stamps I hoped to exchange for Spanish stamps.
15. Four unmailed letters and six postcards.
16. AYH conversation phrase book.
17. A tour of India made out by Dinesh while we rode in the bus to Toledo.
18. Wash and Dri.
19. Tickets to the house and museum of El Greco. We saw a synagogue from the 1500s in Moroccan style.
20. Ticket for Santa Iglesia Caterdral. This was awe-inspiring. It must be larger and more ornate than both Notre Dame and all of the Vatican in Rome. We saw sculpture and gold work that was so remarkable as to elicit disbelief. It took 267 years to build.
21. Card for Hostel Mairu where we stayed.
22. Wallet with the last 800 pesetas in it, about $14.16 left.
23. My change purse.
24. Passport with health and student cards.
25. List of expenditures for the day.
26. List of errands to do the following day.

My pocketbook was filled again. This day I would organize the next segment of our trip, to Malaga, resort and seacoast town.

Wednesday, July 10

Our pace was not the fast one of the "tourist on tour." I read tour literature and they jam-pack too much sightseeing into one day. If we went to one place a day it was exhausting and we returned to read, rest and write. Dave and Nita relaxed and played cards.

We had our exciting moments. I sent the children to the American Express freight office with a locked valise to ship ahead to England. Meanwhile I went to Iberian Airlines office with our tickets to verify the reservation to Malaga.

I also investigated five pensions to find a new place to live when we returned. We couldn't stand our proprietor in our current pension; Nita called him "a dirty old man." He was so friendly and wanted to be helpful, but he was very difficult to understand and not at all bright. He walked in and out of our room and interfered in our life. Cheap as the room was, and pleasant and large with a phenomenal private shower, we would find other quarters on our return.

A gentleman picked me up and walked along while he talked to me. He spoke Spanish and French. I had too many other things on my mind to concentrate on understanding him. He invited me to dinner and I explained I was leaving Madrid. He gave me his phone number and said to call when I returned.

I went into the Metro at 5 p.m. to get to the children at American Express. The train was stuck; it was hot, crowded and miserable.

At 6:30 I arrived. Nita was very excited. She explained to me that the suitcase would cost $30 to send by airfreight — too expensive for us. It would cost $10 by slow freight and it would take two months. That was okay; we had the time. But we had 15 kilos and they would only allow 10 kilos. Five kilos (eight pounds) had to come out of the valise. However, the suitcase was locked and the key was back in our room.

Nita said the freight office closed in half an hour.

So I hopped in a taxi, raced home, got the key and drove back in the same taxi — just in time. They closed at 7 p.m. and I just made it with a tote bag to carry back the excess eight pounds. Now we had more luggage than before, with eight pounds to disperse in various bags.

In America I tried so hard to bring as little as possible. It proved to be too much. I hoped it reached England. If not, no great loss, four rolls of film and our winter clothes — underwear, sweaters and heavy jackets.

Thursday, July 11

David writes to Lori:

We just got off the bus to get to the plane. Now we are on the plane. Spain is marvelous, my favorite country so far. The day before yesterday we went to Toledo, which is a favorite city. We were going to buy you a matador hat there, but Nita said you would rather have a sombrero.

I saw a beautiful sword, and with a little bargaining I could have it for 150 pesetas or about $2.25. But mom said it was too big to carry and too big to send home. We are spending way under $5 a day per person. It is more like $10 a week.

The view from the airplane is beautiful even though the man next to me won't let me sit next to the window

I hope the play you are in, "Destry Rides Again," gets a good review. We've made lots of friends, but none my age. Now our plane is descending. The ground is all red. Fasten your seat belt. Put out your cigarette. We're landing. The steward just came around with a piece of candy. I wish it were the stewardess.

We took the plane to Malaga. On the plane we met Peter Visson, a Dutchman who married a woman from Bogata, Columbia. He works as a stockbroker. We have his number to call on our return to Madrid.

We had more excitement at the Malaga airport. Nita asked a woman to telephone for a pension for us. We finally found one, only the bus driver was having fits holding up the bus just for us. We ignored all the taxi drivers who hung around and offered us cheap pensions. We lugged our own suitcases. Even though we know we shipped off pounds. Now we have more than before. Figure that out.

Finally took a taxi to the Pension Del Sol, Malaga, where we found a pleasant room with sink and balcony and three separate beds. We paid 140 pesetas, less than we paid in Madrid.

We looked for a beach where we could swim.

Whenever Nita and I see American tourists we pretend we're Spanish.

Love, your brother David.

Nita writes:

The plane is in the air now. Spain is a patchwork of colors. Everything is in nuances of browns and gold except for the few dots of green trees. Every once in a while there is a glob of civilization; then bare fields for miles and miles. Surrounding the edge are green and brown mountains and the rivers are visible because they are thick with green algae. Everywhere else are rectangles, squares and triangles of tilled land. Sometimes there is a polka-dotted triangle. This is part of Spain's revegetation program. The civilized globs are far, very far, from each other.

I am going to miss Madrid. I really loved that city. Actually, it was very similar to New York City with much activity, and places to go, but it was friendlier.

Malaga, I am told, is a resort town. We will at least get some swimming there, I hope.

We are now in the airplane passing over patchworks of red — must be clay — very beautiful.

Haven't played chess with any one, except David, and I miss it.

Love and I miss you, Nita.

Friends Mentioned in Chapter 2:

Ignacio and Josefina. We dined with them. They held our baggage for us in Madrid.

Jose and Louis. They guided us to El Prado and walked us through El Raspo, the flea market.

Rafael. A Philippine Jesuit Priest, a very friendly man on our tour to the Valley of the Fallen.

Dinesh and Suli. An Indian couple who studied in the states. We met in Toledo.

Juanita and Charles Taylor. Americans from Georgia.

LITTLE GIRL ADMIRING
HERSELF IN MIRROR IN SHOE
STORE

NITA EXPLAINING THE SPANISH
CIVIL WAR TO DAVID

THREE

Malaga

Thursday, July 11

Nita writes:

Our first day in Malaga the heat was emanating from the sidewalks. So we decided to head for the nearest beach. Everyone told us these were some of the worst slums imaginable.

We walked along the seashore watching the tiny kids swimming in stagnant mucky water, smelling the manure and rotting animals. We passed one dead dog and three dead cats and looked at the endless piles of garbage in which the kids played. It was about a three-mile walk to what could be considered a beach. The water had an odor of sewage, but David and I jumped in for a quick dip.

We found the most miserable hovels I have ever seen. In Lisbon, Dave and I saw a few hovels and, of course, Alfama is a poor district — but this was the lowest poverty-stricken level imaginable. Pigs, roosters, people all lived in one room. Filthy children and the beaches covered with garbage, huge piles of it. Our shoes covered with feces from our delightful walk along the water. We were dressed in bathing suits, but when we saw the sewers emptying into the seas —well, not for me.

I missed getting a few good photos of the washerwomen and a nude child. They wanted dinero and we didn't have any at the time. The best pictures I never got; I was too slow and self-conscious still.

The narrow streets and busy nightlife of Malaga were interesting. The day began very early because of the unbelievable heat. No wonder the town shut down all afternoon. We konked out.

I went to the bus station alone for tickets to Nerja.

A gentleman at the bus station asked if I spoke English or French. I said, "Yes, a bit of both."

He was Mohammed Barchid. He came from Morocco, was 24 years old and was a French teacher. He was a Moslem. His friend, Mohammed Malha, spoke Arabic, French and Greek, because he was a Greek teacher. They were tourists deciding on an excursion and they wanted us to join them. We bought tickets and walked together back to Pension del Sol.

We went to the Cathedral and David roamed on his own. We took a knapsack with us to Nerja. We left all our other bags at the pension; we were to return there the following day.

As Dave said, "One valise is en route to England. Two valises are with Josefina in Madrid, and one valise and two airplane bags are left in our room in Malaga. They told us to travel light and we are!"

On the bus Nita sat with Barchid and got her first French lesson. She discussed politics, hippies, American tourists and the Kennedy murder. She found out that Barchid was a Communist. My partner, Malha, gave me a refresher course in French vocabulary.

Nita writes:

We are now in Nerja about 30 kilometers south of Malaga. We made friends with two Moroccans. Once again I am frustrated because although one of them speaks good English, the other man speaks nothing but French, Arabic and Greek. I keep wishing Wendi were here to translate the French.

NERJA

Friday, July 12

Nerja? A clean, pure, white town. Blinding white sand contrasted with the deep blue of the Mediterranean Sea. There were rows of attached houses. The white washed walls hid most of the homes. Sometimes we could see through the doors in the walls to view the colorful, flowered courtyards. One house stands out in my memory because of the flowerpot arrangement and color. It resembled a child's drawing.

The two Arab boys we met in the bus station accompanied us to Nerja. The first thing we did when we arrived was to locate the beach. It had beautiful, transparent water that was clean and refreshing and we swam for hours. It was the perfect temperature, not frio, just right. We spent the afternoon in water play and conversation and planned the next few days of our trip.

We found a bright room overlooking the Mediterranean Sea. We met Adrian Fernando, proprietor of Hostel Florida, a delightful guy who collected stamps. Nita and I were in a double bed in Hostel Florida and David joined the Moroccans in Pension Monte Sol.

A visit to the caves was a focal point for visitors to Nerja. We enjoyed the trip into the innards of the earth with the stalagmites and stalactites and sculptures formed by nature. Our guide was one of the five boys who discovered the cave eight years ago in 1959 as a youngster of 14. It meant a new life for him; he got 400,000 pesetas from the government. He had been studying archeology and languages and spoke Spanish, French and English fluently.

The caves are much grander and more impressive than Carlsbad Caverns. It was a worthwhile trip.

We returned to Nerja and Adrian, our friendly proprietor. There we changed into our bathing suits. This time our sun exposure was longer and earlier in the day; Nita sunburned her front. I slept on the beach and my legs became striped red.

Later Mohammed II taught Nita Arabic and French. In two days she learned two languages. That's all we did at a fast pace. Otherwise, we were slow and lazy. Mohammed Barchid bought a bottle of wine and we both drank it. He was high and romantic all day. We sang American, French and Arabic songs. The boys danced for us and we all enjoyed ourselves.

The boys reminded me of Iraj and Asghar, Iranians who lived in my home while I attended college. One was the romantic playboy, and the other, the deeper more serious person.

Nita told our Arab friends she was Jewish. They fought the Israeli war all by themselves while David swam. We made plans to meet in Seville.

Nita slept from 7 p.m. on with a short break for food I brought from the farmer's market.

We flew to Malaga and found a pension.

As we settled in our room David saw a Ferris wheel. "Wow! Must be a carnival there. I'm going to it."

I could almost see his heart pound with excitement. He ran out before I had a chance to stop him. Off by himself, he found the fair two blocks away. Wild rides, lots of noise and confusion and many, many people. Cars drove smack down the center of the fair to further confuse the situation.

That night I paced the floor back and forth, back and forth, anxiously waiting. "What could have happened to him?" I kept repeating to Nita.

Sunday, July 14

Finally, after midnight, he barged into the room.

"Look everyone! Look what I won. A bottle of wine!" Proudly he proclaimed, "I won this wine by tossing a peseta into a plate. The funny thing was that it was not the dish that I was aiming for. Oh, I had such a good time. All those rides and I stuffed myself. Who thinks of time when you're having fun?"

At 9 a.m. both children were still asleep. Our bus for Algeciras was scheduled for noon for the three and one half hour ride. Real tourists would have been on the 7 a.m. bus and 11 a.m. ferry to Gibraltar. Mine sleep away days at a time. We lost a day. We spent much of our time in our rooms sleeping The afternoons in Southern Spain are fiercely hot even in the north and everything closes at noon. So we had no choice but to sleep.

We left most of our baggage at the hostel and took the bus for Algeciras, the port of entry to Gibraltar. We took the bus along Costas del Sol, a beautiful ride along the Mediterranean Sea. It was similar to the coast of California, with the sea on one side and mountains on the other. I spent the hours writing letters on the bus from Malaga to Algeciras, telling how delightful everything was. We landed in Algeciras at 3:30 p.m. It was a grubby, horrid town.

We knew there was a ferry from Algeciras to Gibraltar that runs on Sundays. It was hot! We were thirsty. The conductor of the bus decided Nita was pretty and he sat next to her. She did not want his "guide" remarks! Nita asked where to get "La Feria" to Gibraltar.

We were told to take a bus saying "La Linea." We took it; it was crowded. David had to stand. I gave the conductor 4 pesetas he wanted 14. Why so much? I got sore. It couldn't be that far away.

We rode for a long time and most people got off. The bus stopped at La Linea finally. We asked for the ferry to Gibraltar. Two people sent us to the left. We went through paper-strewn streets, past overhead lights, and stand after stand after stand of sweets, torrone, citrus candied fruits and nuts.

We came to a Spanish Coney Island — rides, more rides and food stands. Where was our ferry? We came to a correra de toreros — a bullfight ring. We saw hats being sold, mats to sit on. Where was the ferry?

Nita asked a policeman for Gibraltar.

He sent us back toward the bus. Unbelievable. The heat was terrible and David was cranky. We had only one light knapsack to carry, but Nita had sunburn and David had a mood. He dragged his feet and lagged behind.

We knew the ferry left at 7 p.m. and it was only 5. We weren't worried. As we retraced our steps Nita theorized.

"Gibraltar is a hot spot. Spain hates it, so people are deliberately sending us wrong."

Now we got angrier and angrier. We inquired about taxis. "None. This is Sunday."

Finally we spotted a ferry landing. People were passing through a gate and boarding.

"We've made it! Hooray!"

Now the guards asked, "Do you carry passports?"

We answered, "We do."

"Then you cannot go to Gibraltar from this area," they replied.

We had to leave from Algeciras; this was a port of entry for Spaniards only.

They sent us back to take the bus we got off an hour before.

While we were waiting, we sat at a restaurant table. We asked for cold milk.

"No."

"Soda water?"

"No."

"Aqua? Plain water."

"No."

"De Nada."

19

Now we added this waiter to the list of people who gave us a hard time.

Finally the bus arrived. I tried to explain to this conductor that our being there was a mistake.

"Pay anyway."

Another 14 pesetas each; 42 and 42 is 84 pesetas — for nothing. Nita figured out what happened. This was the Gibraltar Fair. "Where is the ferry to Gibraltar?" They thought we wanted the fair! Feria means FAIR, not ferry.

In France "bateau" would not have gotten us into this trouble. We never got to Gibraltar. We had planned Gibraltar for the night and the following day. Then we would take the bus to Seville. Right next to the boat that left for Gibraltar was the ticket office. We bought three tickets to Seville for 7 a.m. This was the earliest we have ever planned a bus trip.

"A good hotel and a good meal will put us in better spirits," I told Nita after our miserable experience.

It was a complete day wasted! We paid more than 300 pesetas to come to Algeciras, when we could have gone directly to Seville from Malaga and saved that money.

"Cheerful Nita" appreciated seeing Costa Del Sol — a famous resort area. Robert Kennedy's son was staying there.

I tried Hotel Victoria. "375 pesetas." They said, "Since 1966 prices have changed."

I found two rooms in Pension Sanchez for 150 pesetas, one with two beds overlooking the canal. The other room was a single with sink and hot and cold water. I went back to get the children, deciding to give grumpy David his own room.

As I lay on the bed Nita and David planned to play cards. Dave enjoyed the view. I told Dave to switch and give me the peace and quiet of my own room, which he did.

I now had the single, and I was hot, tired and filthy. I stripped, washed and was beginning to calm down and relax. I admired the green roof gardens.

As I began writing, 16 kids started playing rock and roll outside my window and dancing on a tiny roof area. Nita and David came in.

First we laughed about my "peace and quiet," and then Nita reminded me that at least I did have my "solitude."

Later, we met two American boys whose father was a Lutheran minister stationed in Frankfort. We ate dinner with them, but had an inefficient waiter. We started the meal at 10 p.m. and finished after 11:30.

Monday, July 15

In our pension I found only one ticket for Seville. The "worrier" got upset. I found the other two tickets in the wastepaper basket with scraps and scraps of paper from the day before. The scraps were all old bus tickets that I'd tossed. We rescued the good ones in time. I vowed to put them in my change purse next time.

Then, on the bus, "the worrier Nita" saw that other people had first class tickets and we had second class. As the conductor checked each one, Nita was ready to be tossed off the bus. I figured out the front half of the bus was first class and they paid 168.50. The second half, the back half of the bus, cost 150. Both parts of the bus reached Seville at the same time.

A monk was wearing a brown cloak with hood and rope belt. He had a small beard. He was in his 30s. We conversed, using David as interpreter.

The bus ride to Seville was through mountainous terrain. Oxen and mules were at work; it was haying time. Most of the cattle were beef cattle, not dairy cows. There were no visible barns. We also saw herds of goat and sheep. We saw horses and herdsmen, but no dogs to help them round up the animals. Storks stood in the field among flocks of turkeys.

The dry land was undeveloped. The cacti grew best; they were large and healthy. Whole cacti became fence rows. The corn was growing but I didn't see any cobs. There was sugar cane in Andulusia, with acres of sunflowers for seeds.

The trees shapes are different from those we know. There is some vegetable growth, but it doesn't seem sufficient. We were still driving along the coast. They needed a desalting processing plant for seawater and they needed irrigation.

There were camping areas but we passed them. Gladys said they were not for us because our rooms were cheap enough in Spain.

Most of all I loved the courtyards. They were colorful arrays of flowers with such a contrast to the stark, white plaster exterior of the houses.

SEVILLE

Seville was our trysting place with the two Arab boys, Mohammed I and II. The two Mohammeds were due in the early evening. David met a Mohammed III.

We located Hostel Del Prado on Calle Malaga in Seville, one block from the bus station, and took it for 180 a night, but no shower. Nita didn't feel well, so she went to the room to rest. I went to Alcazar, where I had a personal guide. The Alcazar palace is a magnificent example of carvings and mosaic artistry. Beware of museum guides! They guide visitors into dark passageways or blocked off areas.

As I walked home a workman, carrying his lunch box, introduced himself as Luis Lopez. He showed me wallet photos of his wife, son and mother. We walked through the Santa Cruz area. Finally, he took me to his mother's home. His sister was delicate and feminine. No one could comprehend that I traveled without my husband.

Tuesday, July 16

Nita writes to her Grandma:

I am now in Seville. The weather is hot, but the town is lovely. Mommy made some friends last night, and we spent an enjoyable visit in the home of Luis Lopez. Mrs. Lopez is very sweet, but her rapid speech makes it difficult for me to understand her. Young Luis, 9 years old, played games with David. They are very poor and live in a brand new housing project. They pay 150 pesetas a month. We pay 180 pesetas a night for the cheapest hotel room. A peseta is worth 1.6 cents. We have been doing fantastically little sight seeing, mainly spending time with people.

I have been to the Cathedral of the Venerables in Seville. I have never seen so much gold and silver in my life. There were ornate crowns and capes sewn with gold and silver thread. Magnificent! There were two statues of the Virgin Mary crying tears of diamonds.

Spain is really a great country despite its awful government. The people are "muy sympaticas," very friendly. Even on a short bus trip everyone talks to us and makes us feel that Spain is our home.

Of course Mommy has a lot of trouble because she cannot speak Spanish well and always gets it mixed up with English and French. David is able to get along fairly well using some sign language when he can't remember a word. I am the official translator, and my Spanish has been improving, but my accent is pathetic.

Most people think I look Spanish, Venezuelan or English. No one mentions American.

Please tell us what is, or isn't, going on at home.

Lovingly, your Nita.

Wednesday, July 17

This was only our second day here, but the next day we had to return to Malaga. I would have loved to stay longer, but unfortunately time was not on our side. I was in the Alcazar Palace, sitting under one of the very simplest arches. It was painted red, blue and gold. Every statue had intricate designs in different colors. No picture could possibly do it justice. It took 600 years for the Moors to complete this palace. Alcazar means "fortress palace." Its walls are yards thick, so even on a blazing day it was fairly cool inside.

In the Alcazar garden there was a pool with bright orange gold fish. The garden benches had inlaid mosaic patterns. The green commanded attention. This is not usual because Spain, at least in this season, is very dry.

Both Mohammads arrived in our room, but the boys could not continue their journey with us. They had to end their vacation. They met an Arab friend who was en route to France to work. He needed money for transportation. They gave him all their money — 4,000 pesetas. The generosity of these boys was admirable.

David stayed with them, ate and played cards and drums by pounding on the drawers.

Nita and I returned to the home of Luis Lopez. We brought the family a bottle of wine. A meal was prepared for the two of us. Nita noticed that the family ate before we arrived, a different custom from ours. Nita liked the family, even though she was forced into the role of translator.

We had to leave Seville by bus to go to Malaga. It was a miserable, hot ride that took five hours.

To my chagrin the carnival was in progress. What could I do this time? I figured I would outsmart David by giving him only a few coins. Maybe this time he would be forced to return home earlier.

It didn't work. By midnight, when he hadn't appeared, I cruised the fairgrounds looking for him, but in vain. Then I returned to the room and paced the floor. Waiting and waiting. Back and forth, back and forth, opening the door, looking for him, and closing the door in dismay. No David in sight. What could be keeping him so late? At two in the morning he burst into the room, exploding with excitement.

"I made a friend, Miguel. We are like brothers under the skin. I spoke Spanish with him. His parents work at the carnival. We went on ride after ride all night long. They fed me until I nearly burst. I had such a good time."

We took the plane back to Madrid, which was home to us now.

Funny, regardless of the direction we flew into Madrid we never flew over the city.

If people need land, Spain has it. There are miles and miles between houses, miles and miles of dry soil with no trees, no grass. All the riches have been poured into the Cathedral — the pure gold statues, gold thread, gold sculpture. All this elaborate work in cathedrals. But "pobre" Spain.

MADRID

Thursday, July 18

Nita writes to Wendi:

Hi ya again from Madrid. Just flew in from Malaga. I'm glad to be "home" again. I do feel that Madrid is home. I love it despite the noise and business, which is lacking in most other parts of Spain.

La Costa Del Sol was beautiful, but I hated Malaga, "King of the Resorts." Hah!

Nerja, a quiet little village, about 50 kilometers from Malaga was a million times better. I really would love to live there.

Ruth writes home:

Dearest Wendi,

Now we are sitting in an outdoor café waiting for Josefina and Ignacio to return home. I haven't eaten a meal yet today. We hope to eat together. It is after 8 p.m.

Yes, you'll love traveling and the change of environment. There are so many ways of going about it. We have met kids who do it on $2.50 a day. They live on bread and cheese and sleep in dorm arrangements.

There are schools you could go to. One girl went to London University for a while for the experience. She regularly attends University of Arizona.

However, one very important thing: Learn French well! Mine is so pitiable. I have difficulty speaking it and now it emerges as a hodge-podge of Spanish, French and English because I hear so much Spanish these days. The strain and effort of carrying on a conversation French is great; don't depend on learning it here.

Of course the trip can be taken on many different levels. We discussed that before we left: The Peace Corps working in one locality for two years, the American tourist tour with fast paced schedules and the goal of seeing many museums and historic sights in the company of fellow Americans. We are not doing either.

We hear practically no English spoken except at airports as I purchase my tickets. We take the 2 p.m. plane instead of the 8 a.m. plane because of the time pressure. We sleep a lot, rest and relax. No constant push to go or to see. This, of course, is due to the knowledge that we are not on a 21-day tour but have a year ahead of us.

I think all of us have different responses and seek out different things. But we all agree that making friends is foremost. There are good friends all around, intelligent and responsive.

David expressed it last night about Manuel. "Mommy, it's like I've known him all my life."

With your effervescence and wit, Wendi, traveling would be a delight. It doesn't seem to matter where. It is much more the question of how and whom you meet.

I finally stood next to two gentlemen of a type I'd like to meet. Rich, right age, dignified, but they travel first class on airplanes and take taxis, not buses.

In Madrid, there is a bus on the airport ground to take passengers to and from the plane. That is where I saw them. But we did not speak. On the bus trip from Seville to Malaga I promised Nita I would not talk to anyone because I had complicated our lives with two dates in one evening.

Poor Nita is dragged along because I need her to translate. So I tried hard not to speak, but soon my neighbor with a baby on his lap began. I wrote down answers for him and I don't know if he ever realized I could not understand some of what he said. He had three children and a wife and he was going to visit his mother in Malaga. He had a jar of water and shared it with us. It was a hot trip over and through the mountains with different and dramatic scenery.

By the way, each bus trip we took offered different kinds of scenery. Spain deserves far more than a month to do it justice. We whet our appetites and know we will return another year.

Our next experience should be with young people at youth hostels in Barcelona and Ibiza. By the way, we should pick up our first mail here today. Something else to look forward to.

All my love to you,

Affectionaly, your Mom

Nita writes:

We met two Moroccans who traveled around with us. Both decided they wanted to marry me. I told them I was Jewish, so Mahla, a very strict Muslin Arab, decided he would marry one of my sisters instead. Mohammed still insisted on me, and offered me all kinds of riches. We finally left him swearing he would get drunk, which is forbidden in the Muslim religion, and kill himself for love of me. If he sends a letter home for me it means he didn't. Mother had the most fun with the boys and thought Mohammed B's lovesickness very amusing.

At any rate, I'm not bored.

Your loving, Nita

Friends Mentioned in Chapter 3

Mohammed Barchid and Mohammed Malha. A French teacher and a Greek teacher. Both are from Morocco.

Manuel. The friend David made at the Carnival in Malaga. "It's like I've known him all my life."

Luis Lopez and Mrs. Lopez. We were guests in their home. Young Luis, 9 years old, played games with David.

FOUR

BARCELONA

Friday, July 19

We arrived in Barcelona. I was very organized, but what good did it do? We had problems finding a pension in our price range.

The youth hostel was a 50-peseta ride away. It didn't pay for us to go there even though I had written ahead for reservations. We could not get help from the girl at the information booth at the bus station. She wouldn't list pensions in our price range, nor give us a map of the city.

The "helpful" girl said, "There are no pensions in your price range."

However, we insisted. Finally she gave us a list and we set out. We located the tourist bureau and left David sitting there. Nita and I spent from 5 p.m. to 8 p.m. hunting for a room in our price range. I became discouraged.

Eventually we found one for 120 pesetas – 40 a person – the cheapest in Spain so far. Less than $1.00 a person! We were on Les Escauldiers Street and it was full of nightclubs and prostitutes calling out all night long. Finally, by 5 a.m., the street was quiet.

Taxi drivers are leeches, parasites – horrid people! We will never trust one.

The first day in Madrid we had to pay 75 pesetas for a taxi ride. The previous night we took the same trip for 20. The second taxi on the first day charged us 50 pesetas and drove and drove and drove. Later I walked and found it was about four blocks from where he picked us up to where he left us off. Cheat! But yesterday was the limit. We knew Malaga; we had stayed there three different times.

We said, "Airport bus station, por favor."

The taxi driver stated, "There is none."

We said, "We took it to Malaga."

He said, "Only in one direction."

Of course we didn't listen and our bus was standing waiting for us. It cost 15 pesetas each. He did not get away with not putting his meter on. But I paid him 54 pesetas, less than the first taxi in Malaga.

Lesson #1: Don't listen to or trust taxi drivers. Ever.

Lesson #2: Travel with no luggage. As soon as they see you with luggage they know they can take advantage. We wish we could have rid ourselves of all our bags. They were so heavy and caused us so much trouble when we landed in a new place.

Another lesson learned. The day the children went to American Express office to ship our bag to England, it cost $10 for 20 pounds. The American Express man told us Spanish airports would hold luggage only for $7 a bag.

So we woke our friends Josefina and Ignacio early in the morning to leave our bags with them. Then we had to spend a day in Madrid to get them back. From Malaga I found a "left luggage" room and parked our valise and knapsack at the Madrid airport. It cost us pesetas to get it back, but less than $1.00.

It was a great idea. I planned to leave luggage at Barcelona airport and live out of one bag for a week. In Rome we did not need all that luggage. We learned a new method of traveling lighter.

Saturday, July 20

Grandma Kaufman was dead. Grandma Stern and Aunt Minnie mentioned it. The family didn't write at all. Grandma, with her sparkling eyes and deep wrinkles. Grandma, glistening smile, but not too often. Grandma is dead. We ate her meals of tuna fish and salmon, her blintzes and cookies. Grandma is dead. Just like that. Someone wrote it in a letter and it became a fact.

In Barcelona, six flights up, it is greys and browns, dirt, depression. Dirt. Far, far away. Grandma is dead.

I wondered what I was doing when she died. Was I exploring a strange new place? Swimming in the sea? Walking around looking for a pension to sleep in? I, oblivious to the world, lived on.

Ruth writes:

Dearest Jack,

Olga wrote us about your mother. It is very difficult to find words to express our feelings. We each reacted to the news. I'm sorry you were alone at this time.

Did the whole family get together sitting Shiva? I have confidence in Poppa to remain his usual self-contained person. We know Momma has had a good life. She has been as happy as all of us could make her – in the past few years.

It was disappointing that there was no mail from home at our first mail stop. However, we go and come through Barcelona several times in the next week, and we should hear from you before we leave.

Nita writes:

We just heard that Grandma Kaufman died. What can I say? I mailed a letter to Grandma and Grandpa a few days ago. I still cannot believe that Grandma is dead.

We are all depressed now because of the news. I'm glad that it was so fast. How is Grandpa? Is he going to live alone or move in with Aunt Ann? We are in Barcelona now, and we are sorry to leave our friends, Josephina and Ignacio, in Madrid.

We are going to Andorra in a few days.That is Josephine's true home. We will stay with Josephine's godmother, who owns a pension there.

I want to come back to Spain another year. I love it.

I miss you all and please write soon. I can't write more now.

Love, Nita

I got a letter from my mother telling me Jack's mother died. It was very unreal. I felt remote from the entire U.S. and family. I found words of solace difficult. How could I say I wish I were with you during this difficult period? I didn't. I was very glad I wasn't.

I wanted to remember Momma alive. We spent time together and I drove her home from my house.

I think she had a considerate husband. I feel she had a good life. She experienced years of poverty, but in the 20 years I knew her, she did not want for anything material.

She needed more love and devotion from her children. The reasons she did not get it extend beyond the time I knew her. I felt Poppa could make an easy adjustment to his life. He had always left the house and gone out with his friends.

My first mail and contact with home in three weeks was upsetting. The fact that Momma died was heartbreaking. But the "Jack's upset he can't reach you" bit was strange. Jack reach me for what? Why was there no mail from Jack, or Wendi or Lori? Would they break down and write? I was ready to write only to my diary.

The most important thing that day happened when we picked up our mail in Barcelona. We liked the more modern fashion of Barcelona, compared to the dowdy old-fashioned apparel of Madrid. Nita had to have her dress over her knees in Madrid. She shortened it in Barcelona.

We went to American Express and found out we could leave our baggage there for 10 pesetas a day, half the price we paid at the bus station. While there we were given a first communication from Jack, a brief note. We had only walked around a bit; no real sightseeing yet. We had the Gaudi work to see and we visited the Picasso museum and home.

The Goya where we stayed the previous night gave us dinner and agreed to lower the price on our room. You get your room rent raised when you don't accept their meals. I moved to a cheaper place, but we climbed up high to get to our room.

The café con leche was delicious. Real coffee flavor. I drank a lot of beer, too. I thought I liked Barcelona better than Madrid. It was much cooler.

I should have taken the Argus C-3 camera. I have a new camera with a broken aperture. It cost 500 pesetas to fix, but after the man fixed it he explained the lever to advance the film did not work. No wonder I had all that film left over from roll #1. On roll #2 I had taken about 46 photos. The camera mechanic told me I was on picture #12.

In Berlin, I would buy a new camera. But Spain, Italy, Greece and Russia … no camera.

I wondered if other people missed home when they traveled. I felt no pull, no desire to return. I wondered if I would tire and want to go home later on.

I was glad I took these two children because they got along. However, I would have liked more consideration from them. I think most of our trip was quite painless and well organized. I always wanted to share with them.

I was disappointed David would not read and learn about the place he was in or where he was going. He was so proud to get along without a map. I didn't think this was so smart.

Sunday, July 21

We visited the Picasso museum and Nita and I enjoyed it.

We went to the Cathedral Plaza to see dancers. We took buses to the funicular over the harbor to Monjuich Park. The park had a good amusement area. Nita enjoyed the Pueblo Español, Spanish village, watching the folk dancers perform. We ate snails and squid.

David and I went to the bullfight. Nita wanted no part of viewing one.

BOAT TO IBIZA

On the dock a fellow passenger offered me a cup of coffee and room in his bed in his Ibiza house. He was willing to put up with my two children. In French, our mutual tongue, I chased him away.

We found ourselves in one cabin in the boat, even though a big fuss was made at the ticket office about how many girls or boys were in our three-person party. We were put into one room with a German girl about 20 years old. Did they think Dave, in long hair, was a girl? Qui sait?

The trip took 12 hours at sea. On deck in the morning, we made friends with Pauline and Marion. They were two English girls looking for work.

Monday, July 22

We finally arrived in Ibiza at close to noon. We waited for second class ferry tickets to return on Wednesday, but there were no beds available. We would have airplane chairs for our return trip.

Someone at the boat agency told us to go to the San Antonio Abad campground, so we took a bus there. The proprietor gave us a tent and three sleeping sacks. No mats. We slept on the hard, hard ground for 30 pesetas a night in a double tent with insulated air space between. Most tents have a two or three- room arrangement. The proprietor had large tents available that had bunk beds with foam mattresses. He supplied the linen, all for 35 pesetas a person.

David commented, "He supplies the linen, big deal. He wouldn't change the linen. Kids who were there two weeks had the same dirty sheets."

Hitch was a boy who got sick on wine and threw up on his sheets and Nita tried to get clean sheets for him.

Finally the proprietor said, "Yes, but I will charge extra for them."

The swimming pool was emptied and refilled with pure transparent water and no chlorine. We swam there. Ibiza is known for its beautiful, sandy beaches. We three lazy bums were too happy and comfortable in our country club with the convenience of the pool.

The young girls in G-string bikinis swam and sun bathed around the pool. They were of all nations – French, Spanish, Dutch. The strum of guitars was almost continuous. I joined in the singing. These campgrounds are different from ours back home. They're usually in open, sunny fields and very seldom in a shady grove. There is no wood chopping at all nor camp fires; they cook on tiny stoves. The smell of smoke and food cooking is missing.

In the evening Nita and Dave ate at the campground restaurant, which had no menu. They charged 70 pesetas and served a five-course meal – soup, egg, meat or fish, salad and a fruit for dessert. The kids ate there two nights. I like to choose my menu and found the meal limited.

I went to town. I met Jerome, from the camping area, and joined him in an excellent restaurant, which had a meal for 35 pesetas. I got picked up on the way home and had another invitation to stay the night and share an apartment, but in French I refused. Though buses stopped running two hours before, I managed to hitch a ride

Ruth writes to Wendi:

I went into the city of Ibiza from camp and climbed in the morning. I spent a morning thinking of you, Wendi; this is your town.

This mountain has a cathedral and archeological museum at the top. What an experience, walking those cobbled stone streets with art galleries and ceramic studios all along the way. There were such interesting nooks and crannies to browse in. The studios are a nice size and I can't describe the view of the harbor overlooking the island. Remember, you come up high on a mountain to reach this old section of town. You'd love it. This is an international area. People from every country live in this art colony. It is also a hippie set, but they go off to a smaller island called Formantera. This place has a young crowd. In summer, they camp and carry rucksack and guitars. It has a large winter group who work as artists and writers.

The first night I joined a camper for dinner in Ibiza. Then, on my own, I searched for the La Tierra Bar, as per the instruction of Gladys, our travel agent.

I met Arlene, who was 24 years old when she decided to quit teaching in Brooklyn, New York. She traveled and bought this bar and has kept it as a second

home for hundreds of people who lived the year round in Ibiza. It has a lounge and attracts many English-speaking people. Arlene had an extensive record collection. While I was there she played folk music, jazz and Calypso.

People made requests and she knows what her regular customers prefer. She has a remarkable memory for the customers who frequent her bar. She knew people by their names. She was only 29 years old, has had the bar for five years and was planning to sell. I sat with her for a couple of hours.

She said, "You are the first person that Gladys has sent to this island."

Well, it is one place for you, Wendi, to come and enjoy. You'd be happy here off-season.

I understand Lawrence Olivier is coming to act here soon in the local theater.

Tuesday, July 23

Nita writes in her diary:

We mingled with French, Spanish, English, Dutch and German youngsters who were 24,23, 21 and 19 years old.

Why not me too? Why can't I include myself? Why don't I become part of youth? Why do I feel estranged with a group of laughing, playful kids? Why can't I join in, laugh, become carefree, become young? It's just not in me. Maybe when I'm old I can become young.

We spent all day at the pool in the camping area and then at 4:00 hitched to town in a free taxi. We spent over 300 pesetas for odd bits of salami, chicken, bread and chocolate. It lasted us until a meal on the ship with the two English girls, Pauline and Marion. They had a cabin and we only had chairs. On the return trip home Nita and I slept in their cabin all night. David slept in a canvas chair on deck.

We continued to spend time with our friends in Barcelona, visiting Gaudi Park and other tourist attractions.

Wednesday, July 24

David writes to his father:

Everything is so beautiful in Spain. The boat ride from Ibiza to Barcelona was fun but sometimes I got seasick.

When we were embarking everybody held one end of a roll of toilet paper. When you stood back and saw all of those rolls of toilet paper unrolling, about 300 of them, it looked very colorful.

The camping ground we stayed in was beautiful. The pool was just what we needed. Can you do a swan dive standing at water level when the water is barely over your head? I almost did.

Everybody there was an intellectual snob. That is, some of them were intellectual.

There were tremendous chess players there, some even better than Nita.

Almost nobody spoke English. The few that did were the biggest bitches I have ever known. However, two girls were very nice to me. Their names were Susan and

31

*Mary Joe. They got an unfurnished apartment for 35 pesetas a night. The only dis-
advantage is that it was one hundred percent illegal. What they do is go into a bar
and pickup a man for the night. He pays for the meal and drinks and when they've
had enough they just end the evening.*

*Susan spent a night out on the town with Mary Joe and they had five dates in
one night. The last date was with some Spanish boys. When they left they gave Mary
Joe and Susan permission to ransack the apartment. They got plenty of good things.
Neither of them slept at all that night.*

Love to you all, David

We spent the day with the two English girls we met on the boat to Ibiza. They
were in their early 20s and were traveling around Europe looking for work. They
had already spent a year on an Israeli Kibbutz and loved it, but they didn't have
enough money to go back. They were absolutely marvelous girls.

We found we couldn't sleep because it was the noisiest street in Barcelona, with
prostitutes and nightclubs.

At 5 a.m. it became quiet, but a knock on the door told us we needed to get up
in time to make our 6 a.m. bus to Andorra.

The first hours in each new place overwhelmed me. So many adjustments. Well,
it was all adventure. We loved it.

Friends Mentioned in Chapter 4

Arlene. I met this 29-year-old at her bar in Ibiza. She quit teaching in New York
and opened La Tierra Bar.

Pauline and Marion. We met them on Ibiza boat. These English girls spent time
with us in Barcelona.

Susan, Mary Joe and Ina. David knew them in Ibiza.

FIVE

ANDORRA

Friday, July 26

We slept a good part of the five and one half-hour bus ride. Off we went to Andorra through the Basque area of Spain. We had the usual passport and custom check as we crossed the border. This small province set in the mountains is as picturesque as Switzerland before modernization.

We arrived in Andorra and took the bus to Los Escaldes. Our "Madrina," Lina, owned the Hotel Auberge.

Lina was Josefina's Madrina and was all we thought she would be. She had a room and bath for triple for $5 and breakfast. That was expensive for us, but as friends we had to take it.

We saw folk dancers in the town square in costume, less than an hour after we arrived.

A three-day festival of dance and songs entertained us for hours.

Lina telephoned Pan Am and got reservations for noon on Monday, July 30. Right on the nose of our planned date.

Nita pushed me. "Speak French, it is your language." I tried, but no one understood me at all. Nita, resorting to Spanish, was understood. Finally, Lina explained that it wasn't French, but Cataluna the natives were speaking.

The town uses francs and pesetas and people speak both French and Spanish here. But Catalan is the Basque language. Nita and I bought a French loaf of bread and cheese and planned to climb the mountains the following morning.

David bought snails and a potato salad. We liked calamari and David loved snails.

Saturday, July 27

The healthy fresh air and clarified mountain air invigorated us. Nita and I climbed a mountain and watched the funicular. We sat by a stream reading and letter writing and munching on fresh fruit and French cheese and bread.

I read Carson McCuller's, "Clock without Hands," a worthwhile book about the south.

Andorra is a fairy-tale Swiss village with sloping mountains and rapidly flowing mountain streams. My foot was in one of these streams, turning blue from the cold.

I took a bus to Ordina, a tiny village. The smell of cows permeated the atmosphere. Farmers loaded hay on the back of mules. I walked along. Finally I resorted to taking the bus. My Ordina bus driver didn't plan to return to Andorra La Ville. But he switched the signs on the front of his bus just to return me to my hotel. He was a young happy fellow who sang all the way home. I had an enjoyable time.

Sunday, July 28

Nita writes:

I cannot describe the beauty and simplicity of this country. The streets are narrow and curving. The houses are mainly of stone and the mountains and streams are everywhere.

These are festival days. In a few minutes the villagers will dance through the streets of Les Escaldes, the town we are in. I found a chess club here. It seems a good portion of the population plays and plays well. There is even a champion here. Chess clocks, sets and books are sold in the Andorra stores. Whoopee!

On Monday we're off to Rome. I absolutely don't want to leave, and have no desire to see Rome, but I can't wait until Florence. Everybody who has been there loves it.

Now we are going back to our room for the midday siesta. It is a custom worth doing.

Andorra was a good visit. We were sorry to leave.

Missing you, Nita

Monday, July 29

Later, on the bus back to Barcelona, we learned there were sightseeing attractions nearby, but no one told us about them. Inhaling the atmosphere rather than seeing sights absorbed our time. The crafts and folk art exhibited in the small shops stole much of our time. We bought a pocketbook for Wendi.

Back in Barcelona we lived on the street of the Red Light District and it's active, noisy atmosphere gave us a rather sleepless night.

We went for our final visit to American Express for mail.

"This is all the Spanish money we have," I told the taxi driver. "Would you please take us on a tour and show us some of the places we have not seen? Then drive us to the airport."

The driver agreed. He took us to Gaudi's Sacred Family Church. Gaudi was a mad scientist who concocted a potpourri that must be seen to be believed. It was never completed, but left in an unfinished state because Spain's taxpayers did not appreciate Gaudi's modern approach to art and architecture.

The taxi driver was a delight; he reversed some of the ill feelings I had against taxi drivers. He also helped Nita like Barcelona a little bit more.

He was the first Spaniard who actually talked to us about serious matters concerning the government and what was happening as a result of the Spanish Civil War. People refrained from discussing politics with us throughout our month in Spain. We noted the lack of schools while we rode the many buses and we saw no health facilities.

So the last person to spend time with us, our taxi driver guide, was the most vocal and enlightening person we met. He discussed the "brain drain," people relocating to Mexico for more money and freedom.

You wouldn't believe our economy. During the month of July I cashed $310. It was July 29, so you can see how close we were to $10 a day for all three of us.

At the airport we forgot to save enough money for our airport tax. A friendly woman paid it for us. The plane was delayed and we had hours of waiting, but we were busy reorganizing luggage that we had put in the left luggage area during our stay in Barcelona.

We met Jean, our stewardess from Kennedy airport, on the Pan Am plane to Rome.

Friends Mentioned in Chapter 5

Madrina Lina. She owned the hotel that was our lodging.

SIX

ROME

Tuesday, July 30

David writes:

At the Barcelona airport our plane was delayed for four hours from Kennedy airport. Because of this, everyone on the plane got a free meal ticket. Naturally we thought that the meal ticket was for a meal on the plane, but much to our surprise it was for an airport meal. When we found this out it was already too late to go to the restaurant because then we would miss another plane. So we switched to a meal at the Rome airport.

We hung around at the Rome airport until suppertime. We ordered the most expensive things on the menu and it would have easily run up to eight dollars each.

Rome was magnificent. You would die at all of the money thrown in the fountains of Trevi.

The coliseum was amazing. The Christians not only fought lions there, but the coliseum was filled with water and they fight crocodiles.

At St. Peter's Cathedral everything was gold. We saw the gold-plated body of Pope Pious I.

We slept at the youth hostel using our hostel pass. Mom and Nita shared a room with about 20 other girls, but I shared a room with one other boy, named John.

We toured Sistine Chapel with Michaelangelo's arched effect done by him lying on a flat surface. He had to lie on a platform for days to paint that ceiling. Saw the Raphael rooms also. Went to Capuchin church and looked at the skeletons of the persecuted Christians in the basement.

We spent time at the Trevi Fountains, the Pantheon, and the Soldier's Monument. My feet became blistered! This was a real sightseeing day.

Wednesday, July 31

We hitched to the Coliseum.

"I don't want to see the boring Forum," cranky David said and wandered off by himself.

We went to the Trevi fountains and the Pantheon so Nita could see them.

Rome has many restful areas where we made friends.

Raffaele from Germany and I spent hours with our feet in the Bernini fountains while we learned about one another.

Cathy Baker, a New Yorker with mutual friends in the neighborhood where we lived, helped me to catch up with some of my friends there.

Evu, a Danish girl, who learned English in London, sat in Piazza Navana and ate "Tartuffe," a pastry. We shared our travel adventures.

We bumped into David by accident and took him to the Capuchin church boneyard, which was in the church basement. It had rows upon rows of skulls of the martyred Christians.

David discovered 100 pesetas in his blue pants pocket, so we walked to a restaurant and David ate macaroni and cheese.

I had a restful, satisfied feeling. There were some wonderful people around and speaking with them was great.

Thursday, August 1

Ruth writes:

Dear Mom,

We received the letter you sent to Barcelona. We're happy to hear that Lori was pleased with both plays she acted in. Sorry Wendi hasn't been able to get work yet. I'm glad you speak to the children on the phone often. Good of you to have invited the family for dinner.

Too bad that Jack says he is too busy to make a date with you.

Getting painters in your home can be traumatic. You have so many books to take off your bookcases. It is an awful chore.

Your loving daughter, Ruth

Friday, August 2

Nita writes:

I met a girl today who is very much like myself, very much. And you know what? I like her! Yes, she is another me, but still I like her. Oh, the reassurance. Maybe those laughing kids at Ibiza, those cliquey kids at camps; maybe they are at fault, too. Maybe it isn't only me.

David writes:

Now comes the grand fiasco. I met Nita and Mom at the Spanish Steps.

I complained. "I don't feel good. I have a pain in my belly. Mom, I think I have a hernia."

This made sense to my mother because I had a hernia operation when I was 4 years old. I have been carrying heavy luggage.

After mom learned the address of the American hospital in Rome, Nita said, "Mother, if David is going to be sick, let it be in Florence, not in Rome."

Nita was dying to spend time in Florence.

We decided to hitch to Florence and go to a hospital there. We got a ride from a very nice woman named Mimi.
Your friend, David

Friends Mentioned in Chapter 6

John. David roomed with him.

Raffaele. She was from Germany. We spent afternoon with our feet in Bernini fountain.

Cathy Baker. A native New Yorker, we had mutual friends.

Evu. A Danish girl, she spoke English with us.

SEVEN

FLORENCE

Mimi wanted company for the four-hour drive. Since Mimi spoke French, I sat in the front seat with her and conversed in French. She was my age and had two sons 15 and 16. Her husband was a traveling journalist. She taught nursery school in the morning, made jewelry with a friend in the afternoon and was a wife and mother in the evening. She had traveled extensively in Europe. She spoke a tiny bit of English, French and Italian.

Later David remarked, "Boy, did we need Italian at the hospital."

She was a go-getter. She stopped and bought coffee and chocolate for us. She made a scene when I insisted on paying the toll for the car on the autostrasse. Florence was her hometown.

She drove us to the hospital that does emergency operations. She made all the arrangements for us. David was assigned to the room with 32 Italian patients. She decided that would be more pleasant than being in a room by himself.

David got anesthetic by injection in his backside. That was preferable to a mask over the face. A woman doctor operated on David.

After David's operation, at 6:30, he was wheeled back to his bed, and was asleep and resting quietly. A pillow was put on the chair by his bed. I was expected to keep vigil that night. I left him sleeping and took a walk.

David writes to his friend:
It turned out that I had acute appendicitis. Two hours later I was operated on. I was miserable lying in the hospital when I could be having a good time in Florence.

I am staying in the surgical ward. There are two hospitals in Florence, the new one and the old one. I am in the old one.

Rome was magnificent. You would die at all the money thrown in the Trivoli fountains. The coliseum was amazing. The Christians not only fought lions there, but the coliseum was filled with water and they would have to fight crocodiles.

At St. Peter's Cathedral everything was gold. Even the body of Pope Pious was gold plated.

The thing I dread most is mealtime. I watch everybody eating spaghetti while I get cold meat and potatoes.

The aids here are supposed to help me. They are more hindrance than they are help. Whenever I get up ready to walk, they tuck me back in. When I do need the aides for something they are never available. When they finally come around they can't understand me anyway.

It is impossible to get any sleep because when I start dozing off the nurses come by and pinch my cheeks. They think I am adorable.

Visiting hour is great. Mom visits me every day. Only I never see her. She wanders off and visits everybody but me. I'm always surrounded by at least five people by my bed, including Nita. Complete strangers come up and give me gifts.

This morning my stitches came out. As soon as I get out of the hospital, we will fly to Greece and find an island where I can recuperate.

I wish you could come on the rest of the trip with me.

Your friend, David

When I went for a walk I saw Sherry and Hitch. They met each other on the boat to Ibitza. She was from Philadelphia and he was Canadian. They traveled together and intended to marry. We spent time with them in Ibiza. They said they would visit David the next day.

I stepped into a tobacco shop for stamps. I helped a boy who needed writing paper and envelopes and we walked out of the store together.

As I was telling him about David, a car swung around the corner and glanced off the wall. It crashed into the store window and jammed us into a corner. The car missed us by inches. I realized as I released the boy's arm I must have held him hard. It was a terrifying experience.

I'm a little overwhelmed. Nita had a reaction of great tiredness. Leona, a Seattle girl rooming in our house, met us. We talked. While I was in the hospital she took Nita shopping. Nita bought a llama hat for Lori. It was a good diversion for Nita, who is a worrier like me.

In the evening, Nita hung around with Leona until she left town. Leona was an interesting girl who found herself as she discovered the world. Travel seemed to be good for everyone we met.

I rested at home for a while and returned to the hospital at 5 a.m. The door was locked so I climbed in the window.

I needed long afternoon naps every day after visiting David. I decided it was the emotional reaction to Dave's operation.

Dave spent our eight days in Florence in the hospital. While there we befriended Gino, who had been a prisoner of war in England and learned to speak English. He was in the bed next to David.

Gino was a great help to David. He washed his face and translated for him.

Gino needed a blood transfusion before he could have his operation. I donated my blood to Gino. We made a life-long friend. Antoinetta, Gino's wife, was grateful.

She took us to their home. She fed me rare steak and red wine to restore my blood. Antoinetta made dolls and she presented me with one in appreciation.

Saturday, August 3

We spent the mornings visiting David and in the afternoons Gino's youthful daughter, Marietta, guided us through the museums. She had a lively step as she taught us about the artwork we viewed. She was knowledgeable and we learned a lot from her. She proved to be a good friend to both of us.

The original David should never be copied. Yet I saw two copies in Florence. We visited a whole Academia of his statues. He rarely finished one. I wondered why.

He sculpted David when he was 28.

I visited many churches and admired sculptures by Donatello and Cellini.

Thursday, August 8

Ruth writes:

Dear Lori,

The Etruscan archeological museum was very large, complete with Bronze Age tombs, and vases taller than I am. I visited this one alone, setting myself up as victim perhaps. A guide pushed away a chair and shoved me into a closed off section. He was too quick with his hands. But I moved out of there faster.

The Medici Riccardi Palace is resplendent with gold and objects d'art. I enjoyed these sights. I paid a visit to the hospital to see David. And then was blessed with another filling meal at Mariella's home.

I went off to Michaelangelo Plaza across the Arno River. What a magnificent view of the city! I walked, and then accepted a hitch home. Wish these "great Italian lovers" would go slower. I'm still in control.

I was taken on a personal tour of the foundling home. Lori, there are 250 babies below the age of 6, all outfitted identically. There are no toys or equipment in the back yard, only beautiful flower gardens.

My guide took me into the gardens. We could see the tremendous flood damage in the water lines on the buildings. Water pushed in huge wooden doors supported by iron. Four cars floated in the gardens. The waters flooded in the morning. If it had happened at night, 100 babies would have died. Expectant mothers reside here, too.

Lori, you have a home at Gino's house if you want to learn Italian and live in Florence and work at this baby home.

We resided at the Student Cassia and paid very little for a beautiful spacious room. Our windows looked out on a courtyard. We loved it.

Gino waited on David, washed his face and interpreted for him. When I heard that Gino needed blood, it was my pleasure. Now we are blood brothers.

Afterwards, I had to eat rare thick steak and drink red wine at their home to restore my blood. It was delicious Italian food. Better we became good friends.

Love and many kisses, Mommy

Friends Mentioned in Chapter 7

Mimi. She was our driver from Rome to the Florence hospital.

Gino, Antoinette and Mariella Barontini. I donated my blood and afterwards was fed in their home.

Leona. A young woman from Seattle, she kept Nita occupied and distracted during David's operation. Later we met in Germany and assisted her getting a ride with the hitch we abandoned.

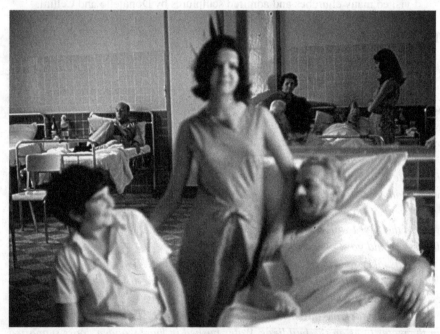

GINO, MARIELLA AND DAVID IN HOSPITAL.

MOSES

GIRL FEEDING PIGEONS

STOCKING SALESMAN

EIGHT

GREECE

Friday, August 9

We took a free airport bus to Athens, then a taxi to the hotel. It was a long day for a kid just out of the hospital. David was a doll.

As we entered the tax, Nita said, "Put the flight bag on your lap, Mom."

I didn't. It went into the trunk with the three suitcases. The driver dropped us off and as the taxi drove away we yelled that our airplane bag was still in the trunk.

The hotel landlord said, "The taxi driver is my friend." I didn't worry then, because the landlord said he would get the bag back for us.

The stolen bag had my toiletries, toothbrushes, soap, all the items we bought in Spain and money. It had our new sandals, a book and Dave's new sunglasses.

In retrospect this day equaled the frustration of our "Non-Gibraltar Day." I awoke from a night of no sleep. I hated that room and that house.

We were staying near two outdoor cafes in the Praxes region. It was a miserable, noisy night. During the night some upstairs neighbor "watered" the balcony outside our bedroom twice.

Saturday, August 10

Landlord Karkas kept promising he would get our airport bag back for us.

First he said, "The taxi driver is sleeping." Then, "Come back at 8:00 tonight."

Then he explained how he "searched" for the taxi driver and he said he called the police. It was a bad beginning for Greece.

We went off to American Express for letters. My mother, my friends, my love, but none from the family. What game were they playing?

I was sent to Intourist for our Russian visa. The visas we had were for Finland and the USSR. But because we spent extra time in Florence we never would get to Finland.

I met an obnoxious and officious young man. We hoped he didn't represent others we would meet in Russia. He gave me one address for the Consulate but I found another one in the newspaper. I didn't know which address to use.

I was sent to Sabena about a ticket to Brussels. Indiaman, our tour, went from

London to Brussels. I tried to figure out how I could send the luggage to Brussels to await our arrival.

I went to the train station for information on train schedules.

I found out the time schedule for our train.

"I want to buy the tickets."

"We are closed," the person behind the counter announced. "Come back at 4."

"I am in the office now. Can't you sell them to me?" I asked.

It didn't work.

For two-hours I walked around. That was Saturday afternoon.

I spent hours and hours in Pam Am trying to switch an unused Athens ticket to Brussels to something else to get me closer to Russia. Three hours lost Saturday. Viking Agency tried to organize my trip differently. We considered a boat to Odessa and a train to Vienna and Warsaw, but all in vain. Gladys Vogel's trip plan to Sofia turned out to be the best.

I returned to David, who I had left in an air-conditioned Air France office.

Nita found a good triple, 120 drachma in Cleo's Guest House. I vetoed it because it was in the same district as our accommodations of the previous night.

On a quiet street we found a rooftop, Fanti's House, for 20 drachmas each. Too much, but I figured it was close to the bus that we would take in the morning. After resting for an hour at Fanti's I went with Linda, a California girl living in New York who was a social worker. She was traveling alone for three months. She shared a great deal about the history of ancient Greece.

We walked to the Acropolis together and watched the sunset on the roofs over ancient Agora.

At 7:00 p.m. Nita and Dave went back for our bags. They paid Kakara 100 drachma and left. He still did not have our flight bag. I went back for it at 9 p.m. and it still was not there. He was using the language barrier to give me a hard time. He said something about the man coming five times. He said two men looked in the square for the driver for an hour. He called the police. What a phony. He promised to bring the bag to Fanti's House for me.

That second night we slept well on our roof. It was cooler than the previous night.

During the night I woke. The full moon shone in my face and lit up the hands of my watch at 3 a.m. It was a romantic night, lacking only love.

Sunday, August 11

We rushed out early in the morning. In Athens I noticed a rude aggressiveness on the part of the women. They stood in line for hours waiting for buses. When our bus arrived they pushed and shoved with no regard for those who were on line in front of them. We would be first on line and still remained there after the bus left if they had their way. In the other countries people were respectful while waiting in lines for buses.

We did board the bus from Athens to Pireus. Then we took a taxi to a boat. We rushed to make a 9 a.m. boat to IOS Island, as listed on the schedule.

The kids were angry. "Waking us up so early and rushing us and then no boat."

Nita was upset. So I bought tickets for a day on an excursion boat to Aegina. A Greek girl, Anna, in line for a ticket, spoke English. She helped me purchase our tickets. She told us to go to Saint Marie Beach.

We meandered around the port town. It had only restaurants and one hotel. We bought fruit and discovered fresh pistachio nuts. They tasted good when eaten with lemon.

The bus trip to San Marino was wild. The driver sat on his horn. We nearly collided with another bus, which forced him to drive in reverse back down the street. The streets are so narrow two buses could not pass one another.

We met a lovely girl named Nadine and spent the afternoon with her. She was the editor of the Columbia University's house magazine and was traveling alone. She appreciated the fresh fruit and vegetables that were plentiful on the islands. She spent most of her time on Aegina. Nadine's face was tanned and she had a robust figure.

We swam a little bit. Then I found a room facing the sea. It had two beds for $3 a night. Nita wanted to sleep on the beach. She was studying the constellations before she fell asleep in a cradle between two rocks.

A young Greek couple on the beach commented on the "Peace" button that Nita was wearing.

"We would be thrown in jail if we wore that," they whispered, "There is no democracy in Greece."

Neighbors, also Greek, saw the peace button and pointed to it and shook my hand. It is forbidden to wear it in Greece.

"Your CIA put Papadoupolis in power," they said to us. People seemed anxious and willing to talk politics, unlike Spain.

Monday, August 12
Nita writes:

Dearest Wendi,

I am in the pistachio nut eater's paradise, Aegina, an island off Greece. I have tasted my first fresh raw pistachios. They look almost like almonds, but reddish and greenish, and they have a soft outer shell. The inner shell is white and smooth and sometimes has the crack in it. The inner-inner shell is red and is paper-thin. The nut is a pure, rich green, unusual, but delicious.

We just arrived from Athens, where David and I did absolutely nothing but run back and forth from the old sleeping place to the new one trying to get back the gray airline bag we left in the taxi, but it was closed.

I found a chess club, but it was also closed.

The most striking thing about Greece is the light – white, white brightness everywhere.

I have just tasted my first fresh fig, also fantastic. The bright red seeds just melt, really melt in your mouth.

Considering everybody says Greece is such a cheap country, I think it is expensive, at least compared to Italy. We are spending 100 drachmas ($3.00) for a room with beds. I was going to sleep out on the beach

We haven't discovered quiet Greece yet. We hear singing on the rocks by teenagers late into the night. Colorful, and described as lush, but this place is drier than Spain.

Hey, Wendi, how about a letter? Greece is hot, hot hot.

Your loving, but hot sister,

Nita

On our walk along the sea I saw a beautiful large green lizard, 18-inches long, race madly into a burrow. The birds sang sweet, unfamiliar melodies.

Often the Greeks broke into charming folk songs, which I was determined to learn.

The air was filled with the scent of the yellow broom and rosemary hedges that bordered the terraces where the olive groves were.

We decided to stay for three days so David could rest. Dave was loggish. He hung around the room and ate the grapes we picked in the hotel gardens.

He finally took off the bandage and was about to brave his first shower in weeks. But he saw the hole in his scar.

A Greek maid showed it to a French woman. She dragged Dave into the big hotel to Room 11, a German couple's room. A man came to the door in shorts. They laid David on the bed and felt the reddening area and were quite upset. Infection was starting. The woman put hydrocortisone on the wound and redressed it.

At 11:00 a.m. and at 4:00 p.m. the German woman returned with antibiotic powder and put that on the wound and redressed it.

In German she worried all day about David. She wanted what was best for him.

She ordered David to "Stretch out in bed all day. No swimming. Rest in bed."

No water so we lost in trying to get him into a shower. We had all kinds of special attention because of him. We brought food from the restaurant to him.

"Heck. I have no fever. I'm not sick," he complained.

We thought we might be able to fight pending infection with cortisone and antibiotic pills and powder.

The German lady redressed David with antibiotic powder.

A Greek couple from next-door taught Nita the alphabet and we sat together in the evening.

Nita slept on the beach cradled between two rocks. She said there were no insects. She knew some astronomy and contemplated the stars.

Tuesday, August 13

The grapevines surrounded our room, so we snacked on bunches of huge green and purple grapes for our breakfast as we sat on the rocks at the water's edge.

I got tired of my "grape bellyache" and we searched for fig trees.

Nita and I took a bus to Aphia where a Doric Temple stands to the Goddess. It is a lofty sight from on high and a magnificent view of the island. I always get pleasure in getting away with things, and the man let me in for 2.50 drachmas on Nita's student card. She had told me to bring mine, but I forgot.

We picked succulent figs from trees and filled a big bag. Then we hiked until we came to a pistachio tree. It was a long, hot walk. We finally reached a tree with a few fresh nuts.

We took a bus up hairpin curves to the top of the mountain we had climbed down. On to "fig bellyaches."

My solitude on this romantic spot had me imagining, desiring and bursting with the need a lover. The thrill is to swim and return and make love with the wonderful feel of cool flesh. That's my favorite time. I lay on the rocks dreaming my own fantasy life.

Nita tried diving. We swam together.

A handsome Greek joined the two of us. We dove off the rocks together. Leftaris' blue eyes sparkled. I relaxed and sun bathed. Nita returned to David, who has been left alone most of the day.

Leftarius motioned me to swim and off we went to swim in the Mediterranean Sea. There was not another soul in the water. He swam into a cave, speaking Greek all the while. The caves are deep. We kissed but I halted further activity.

Leftarius managed the Club Café next door to us. There, he fed me pieces of dried octopus, Greek salami, beer and baklava. People were dancing.

Chris and a barber, two friends of Leftarius, and I discussed politics all evening. Chris lived in London and spoke excellent English. He owned a house in another section of Aegina, and he also owned land in Phoenix, Arizona. He was a marine engineer in his early 60s. He had a love of life, bronzed skin and handsome features. He was admittedly wealthy. He traveled for his work. He had been married, but was now enjoying his freedom. He lived with his sister and they both respected the "live and let live" sentiment.

We discussed politics like mad. He didn't like everything about the United States. He spoke of Negroes as second class citizens and he didn't like Nixon.

He said, "The CIA put Papadopolis in power. The Greeks certainly didn't."

That day there was an attempt to assassinate Papodopolis.

We spoke of Greece, now a police state. Later he mentioned how the "Club" had 200 people every night during the last year but now had only a handful. People lived with a daily fear of loss of their civil service jobs. They stayed home and saved their money. With no spending, businesses were going bankrupt. What a vicious cycle. Because Leftarious and the barber both were known radicals they were constantly harangued and had to pay off the police for minor infringements- like playing the jukebox too loud.

Chris was a political leftist from way back. He said his wealth had not changed his political views. Later on Leftarius gave us both hell for discussing politics in his place. He permitted it only because it was in English. His guests included a minister and Fascists.

It was a great evening.

Chris drove us to another club after Leftarius closed his club. Here, a crowd of young folk danced. One, an Italian girl, was a wonderful dancer. I danced the tango with Chris. I could still feel his graceful movements the next day. He wore a pastel blue embroidered shirt. I wanted very much to continue spending time with him, but he respected that I was the friend of Leftarius.

ATHENS

Wednesday, August 14
We took the boat back to Athens to Omonia Square and found Helmos Hotel, 85 drachma for three, or less than one dollar per person. There was not an English speaking person in the building.

Thursday, August 15
It was a holy day and everything was closed.

At Hotel Helmos, we appreciated the clean marble floor, a sink in the room and free hot showers.

I brought David to the hospital and was reassured that his scar was healing. The doctor redressed David's wound and convinced us the hole would close in a few days. There was no sign of infection. I had been giving him antibiotic powder to fight it.

We met Mary, who spoke 16 languages. She lived in New York. She was a Ph.D. in psychology and she interpreted for us. She drove us around in what used to be "the car of the King," a Ford Imperial. It needed someone to push it now. She fought the black market in babies in New York. When she was in New York there were three attempts to murder her. So she was running the office here. She was a journalist for the newspaper and quite a character. She drove us home after a midnight dinner.

We spent the evening at one police station and told the story of the stolen bag. They sent us to the traffic police station. They took down all the information with Mary as our interpreter.

They sent us to the tourist police station. Police were unsympathetic. I hoped our missing grey airplane bag would show up, but we had no help from police.

49

The Russian Consulate was closed; no visa.

American Express was closed; no mail. The post office was closed; couldn't send package. The sandal maker was closed; couldn't buy sandals. The barber was closed; no haircut for David.

So we walked to Plaka and found the location of markets on Athena Street. Viking Agency tried to work out our trip to Russia again. At Pam Am, I left tickets for them to switch our Scandinavian flight to a Vienna flight.

I ate souvlaki all day.

I swore I'd never eat another fig.

We had become adjusted to the "continental" ways of doing many things. We adjusted readily to new manners and new customs, but in Athens I found I was angry with the people for their lack of manners.

Our companions could be poor, but they had to be interesting. Nita ran off to watch dancers all evening. We saw nightclub entertainers in one restaurant at the festival and Greek folk dancers in another.

Farouch, from Libya, spoke to the Russian consul for us. Then we went to the opening night of the Daphne Wine Festival. It was a wonderful feast for wine lovers.

Farouch paid our bus fare and our entrance fee to the festival. He was so polite; he wanted to buy us everything. We could have had anything we wanted, but he had nothing to say. I blamed it on his inability to speak or understand English. He worked for a British petrol firm in Libya. He had no wife or children, but he had a great deal of money that he kept pulling out of his pocket.

It wasn't our type of festival. We each had a glass and tasted wines from the big wine barrels. Then we chose one and filled a carafe to drink all night. I drank sweet wines. I tasted retsina and liked a muscat from Fix. Nita enjoyed watching Baccus take over gradually. David roamed the street and ate souvlaki by himself.

We were aware of military police everywhere, even at the festival. But in my mean mood I felt if Greeks were more organized and less rude and pushy and inconsiderate of everyone else, maybe there would be no need for the military police.

Athens put me in a lousy mood. I became a prejudiced person and it bothered me. I gave Athens two different chances and both times I wasted an entire day on errands, which never brought satisfaction.

We planned to return to Greece in October with the Indiaman tour and hoped things would be different then.

I felt ready for Russia to take over for me. Let them make my decisions, find lodging; take me to places to see. It might be a horrible thought to Nita, but I thought I would enjoy it if the pace wasn't too strenuous.

Friday, August 16

The Russian Embassy gave me a hard time. I couldn't locate Nita's visa. New visas were needed for each different entry point.

"Rush to consulate. Visas are given only on Friday and Monday. You're lucky. Today is Friday. It closes at 1:00 p.m. Hurry and you'll make it."

I say, "I lost Nita's visa."

"No problem. Call Intourist and tell them. You paid for it. It will be waiting for you at the Kishenev border."

I returned relaxed and happier.

Nita had her visa, so that problem was solved.

I was at the end of my drachmas. I went to the bank and tried to cash my Italian lire. It did not work.

Nita writes:

We just left Greece. Mommy was most anxious to leave Athens. She developed a prejudice because of all the official type people she encountered there.

Me? I went crazy over the Plaka, the old section of Athens. The markets there surpassed even Florence. I bought a pair of great sandals for $2.50 and a red Greek dress at Plaka, which I will send home because of the luggage problem.

The main thing I discovered in Greece is that the Greek people hate their government. The CIA by general acclaim was behind the coup, and a civil war is bound to break out.

Love, Nita

Friends Mentioned in Chapter 8

Leftarius. He owned a café.

Chris. He was a graceful dancer.

Faroch. He was from Lybia and was generous to us at the Daphne Wine Festival.

NINE

TRAIN TO BUCHAREST

Friday, August 16

Our train trip was incredible. I learned that reserved seats were a blessing. We were in second class and had no berth. It was a compartment for eight people. A smiling lady, soft and round with a pretty, pleasant face, was about 55 and had a young son and a 23-year-old son with her. There was a soldier, 25, and the three of us. The mother laughed often.

As they stretched out to sleep I stood by an open window watching the orange moon rise and admired the Big Dipper. A man came over to me. He saw me in the station and sought me out on the train. He knew I spoke English and deliberately found me. We stood in the corridor for hours and hours conversing.

He was Michael, an American citizen, born in Romania. His mother was Romanian and his father was Greek. They had moved to Athens. He had been working and studying in New York for eight years, and was to become an electrical engineer. He was en route to marry a 20-year-old Romanian girl. He was 30.

He had the identical feelings I do for Greeks. It was like meeting a fellow Southern Democrat.

Mike found a place for David to stretch out in another compartment, so David slept most of the night.

"I'm hungry," I said.

Mike handed me salami and bread at 2:00 a.m.

We strolled back into our compartment. Smiley Lady lent me her sweater to wear. We laughed and shared drink and food and language into the morning hours.

All night, from 12:00 midnight to 4:00 a.m., our car was a ball. Everyone was awake, having fun laughing while the rest of the train was quiet.

Smiley Lady giggled, smooched up to Mike and later slept on his shoulder.

Mike spoke in both languages. The young son could read our English books, but did not understand the spoken language. Mike rewrote the Greek alphabet for Nita in her notebook.

We passed bottles around. First, a bottle of homemade cherry brandy, sweet, strong stuff. Then at 5 a.m. we drank peppermint brandy instead of using toothpaste. It's great for that "clean morning taste." Then we had rose-flavored liquor. The fourth bottle was Anisette. By now it was noon and we were still on the train.

I helped Mike drink because I didn't want him too drunk. He still had to buy tickets for us at Thessilonika to continue on to Sophia.

On awakening in the morning I opened my eyes and Mike handed me a shish-ka-bob. When the train stopped at stations people sold food and handed it in through the train windows.

Our passenger train now had only an engine and one car. Later on one car and a long freight were behind us. We would go forward and backward alternately. It is a wonder that we got anywhere.

At Thessolonika there is a one-hour stop at 7 a.m. I tried to buy train tickets for Kishenev. They wouldn't sell me any. They told me to buy them in Sofia. Mike said our train ended in Sofia and we would have less than 10 minutes to race to the other train. Mike said it was a far walk and NO time to buy tickets. Athens only sold me one half of my trip.

They sold Mike the entire trip to Bucharest. The train master said only Sofia could sell me the ticket. What a mood I was in when I returned to the train with another wait.

Mike kept asking Dave how he felt. He bossed everyone around, but considered us his family.

Around noon we came to the Greek border.

Our relationships were established, and we had merriment and fun! Great fun. But I had had liquor and was in a mood. So when the ticket man came by for the fourth time I raised hell.

The passport official came through. He was the Bulgarian authority, a big man with thick hair and a black, bushy mustache.

I said, "No. You can't have it. Look at my passport, but don't take it!"

I was a smart alec, a tea-totaller who has been drinking all night.

I gave him my passport

Later a young boy came to our compartment.

He said, "The passport man wants to see you."

I was afraid something was wrong with our passports. But it wasn't anything serious. He just wanted me to keep him company while he inspected the huge pile of passports. I joined him in his first class car. He had the pile of passports on the table in front of him and he was examining each one. I went back and fetched the others. If I was going to enjoy the first class car Nita and Dave and Mike should also.

Mr. Passport man affectionately held my feet as I stretched out. There was a complete language barrier, but he had a pleasant, smiling visage. We could not talk, but we smiled as the others joined us.

We spent our morning with Mike, who hadn't slept a wink — no food — only drink.

But who had my nerve? I got on a train, set for three or four days travel with less than $1.00 in Italian lire and about $1.00 in Greek drachma.

When the Bulgarian moneychanger lady came through the train, I asked, "Will you take my Italian lire?"

"No."

"Will you take my drachmas?"

"No."

"Then I won't exchange any money now."

She refused to give me money for those coins. I refused to get any Bulgarian money. She wouldn't take mine. I wouldn't take hers.

Mike brought out a pack of cards and suggested that the men and boys play poker. Dave borrowed money from Mike to play. Mr. Passport man's eyes were bulging out of their sockets as he handled his cards. The cards were nude bare-breasted women in various poses. David won all the money. Despite that, everyone loved Dave.

The train stopped. We bought yogurt in the café and listened to Greek music. We watched backgammon being played; it's *the* game in these parts near the Bulgarian border. A was a pleasant interlude.

Saturday, August 17

A Mohammed IV wanted to marry me. He was an Arab from Aleppo, owned a hotel, and was in the fruit business in Greece and Bulgaria. He offered to put me up in Sophia. He bought fruit for all of us at the stop. He was a "feeler" and kissed my arm.

Later in the day he got to me. He had hands, but lovemaking and kissing arms, hands and ears in public is not for me. I didn't encourage him. "I love you," he insisted.

Mike bought us drinks, solicitous of us all day long. We had a first class compartment most of the day.

The stern-faced Bulgarian conductor kept chasing Nita out of the first class compartment. She kept going back. This went on all day. He never got angry or upset. First class had three compartments and two were empty. My family took one over all day despite this Bulgarian conductor. I told him to smile and we stood by the window together. He pointed out the flax that was used for linen and the fields of tobacco and the mines. We conversed and ignored the language barrier.

The baggage car man gave us peaches. Mike shared his bread, Greek salami and Romanian salad with us. Then, of course, came the cold wine. Mohammad dashed out of the train to get us fresh, cold water. They bought us peaches and ice cream. All day we ate.

Though we had no money, people couldn't do enough for us. I loved every minute of it.

I ended the day by stretching out in a dark compartment and slept for a couple of hours. Glad I did.

And then Sophia!

Mike took over. "Don't worry, I'll take care of everything," he said.

"O.K. We won't."

We had less than six minutes between trains. We stood poised at the exit. Mike helped me get luggage off the train. He grabbed our valises and gave them to a porter. The porter ran with them to the next train. It was a long run. We jumped on. As soon as we threw our luggage on, the train pulled out.

Mike shouted, "I'll find a place for us," and disappeared in the new train.

The conductor yelled in Bulgarian—"billets" (tickets)? We gathered this was the sleeping berth section, mostly empty.

I yelled back at him and he went away and left us alone. Mike came back. He found no seats for us. We had our luggage between the cars. The gate was up and we climbed over. We stood in the corridor. I went to see if I could find an empty berth. Our car was full but the next car had some vacancies. I came back and reported.

I ran to get the conductor and hauled him back to Mike. There we were, situated outside the toilet, our luggage in the hall, as the conductor took out pencil and paper and drew pictures for us.

The first two cars would travel to Bucharest, while all the others went somewhere else. It was much too far to haul the luggage through the train. We had raced to reach the train and just jumped on the last car. Now we were told we had to be in the front of the train.

Next, the conductor asked for tickets. Ha! Ha! I laughed in exaggeration and he laughed, too. Then I revealed my tickets and his face changed.

"You want to go to Bucharest and these tickets go to Sophia? Yes?"

"Athens would not sell me tickets to Kirov. Thessolonika would not sell me tickets to Kirov. We had five minutes to get from the Sophia train to this one. No time to buy tickets. O.K. We'll buy them from you, Mr. Conductor."

Next shock! As I gently drew forth my traveler's checks I discovered we had only drachmas and lire. DOLLARS. Inspiration! I had a few dollars left from the original pocketbook money. "Dollars are good everywhere," I recalled people telling me. I located $11.00.

The conductor said, "But I can only sell you tickets to Ruse."

Later, the conductor explained why, but made no sense. I figured 9 p.m. to 8 a.m. for three people for a $10.50 ticket is a bargain. We let him keep the 50 cents in change.

We slept on and off all night, fitfully with our stiff necks.

We still had to move up to the front two cars. Mike and I ran with the luggage. The train jerked forward and we were separated. I started to walk back and found locked corridor doors at the sleeping car. I located a conductor to unlock them and in two more cars met the gang hauling the rest of the luggage. Whew! The passport inspector woke us at 3 a.m., 6 a.m. and again at 7 a.m.

At the border he requested Romanian visas. We had none. I was told, "Get out of the train and cash a traveler's check and pay $1 a person."

Then he must have changed his mind. The passport man gave me three visas and I paid no money.

In the morning the other passengers had liver paste spread on bread with to-matoes. They did not offer me any. So I returned to Mike's spot for breakfast. He gave us fish, cooked peppers, bread, salami and cake. We shared it with the friendly people from Sophia.

Arabs believed flesh was to be patted and kissed. This experience I missed dur-ing my twenty years of marriage.

Nita's writes:

Passed through Bulgaria yesterday by train. The people on the train were fantastic.

Another Arab fell in love with me. He didn't speak anything but Arabic and Turkish. He was from Syria. He taught me the Arabic-Syrian alphabet. It was dif-ferent from the Moroccan. Two other boys taught me the Greek alphabet. Alphabet and learning numbers were about the only means of communication I had in other languages.

Friends Mentioned in Chapter 9

Mike. He took care of us on our train trip to Romania.

TEN

ROMANIA

Sunday August 18

We arrived in Bucharest at 8 a.m. We parked our baggage. While Nita and I went to the toilet we lost Mike. We never saw him again. We didn't have his Romanian address to thank him for all he did for us. We expected to tour Bucharest with him for the day. No proper "Good-bye" and "Thanks."

Because we were to cross the Russian border, our tickets had to be purchased somewhere else, not at this train station. I cashed a $20 traveler's check.

The 11 p.m. train was an express and was a through train. First class was 210 lei, which was about $17.50. Second class was 127 lei, or $11.00.

But the 8 p.m. train has second class seats available at 82 lei or $7.00. which was four more lei. There was a big difference

We purchased our reservations for a train to Kirov at 8:00 p.m. That gave us the entire day to roam around Bucharest, Romania.

This was the city where my mother was born. She arrived in the United States when she was 3 years old.

We dropped cranky David with 25 lei in his pocket at the station. He would spend the day by himself. Two different guys picked him up, thinking he was a girl. One bought him soda, and the other man, candy. He did need a haircut.

Nita and I rode a bus round trip and circled the city. We saw parks with beautiful gardens and colorful flowers. It was peaceful. We spoke with people on the bus, friendly people who were interested in learning about us. The sky was lemon yellow.

When we rode back on the return trip we got out and spent our afternoon in the Park Gradina Cismigiu.

Nita brought over to a woman who spoke French. We conversed for a while. It was delightful.

She sent us to a restaurant that had very good food. In the restaurant I was aware of the quiet tone, despite the crowd. Pails with ice and various bottles of water, beer and soda were available to take what you wanted. For soup we ordered cold borscht and they brought us hot chicken soup, but it was good. Then stuffed cabbage and pastry. The meal cost about 60 cents each.

Nita and I separated for the day. We both spent it in the park, but in different areas. Fifty men, in army uniforms, followed Nita and spoke in Romanian. The young men were flirting and trying to make friends with her.

There were several lakes for boating, black swans and flamingos. Gaily-costumed girls, so picturesque in their embroidered dresses, strolled the park. Young girls wore huge bows in their hair. Herdsmen and gypsies wore costumes.

Most of the men looked like the pictures of immigrants to the U.S. in the 1910s. This was the only place men wore the flat-brimmed black hats and baggy pants. But, on the whole, neat, well-groomed people strolled in the park on this Sunday afternoon.

Venders sold syrup on ice cream at corners. Many pastries with rich gooey topping were for sale. I couldn't resist the chocolate with whipped cream.

The town had several cinemas. There was a "Broadway" with many theaters.

I was most impressed with the quiet of Bucharest. In our filled and crowded restaurant the noise level had been low. In the park the only sound was the creaking of the soldiers' boots as they passed. I slept on the park bench for nearly two hours. It was quiet enough for that.

We liked Bucharest. It had a dignity I admired. The people waited in lines for what they needed in stores. There was a "niceness" about all the people we met. We did feel frustrated at the language barrier, but we found people were anxious to be pleasant and helpful on Sunday evening.

Back at the train station, a woman in the toilet collected money for entry and toilet paper. A Bucharest station guard made Dave go into the ladies room for toileting.

ELEVEN

TRAIN TO RUSSIA

Sunday, August 18

It was evening when we boarded the train. On the train Stefan was alone in his compartment, so I joined him. He was Nita's age and a personable young man. He didn't even have a beard. He slept very little all night. I conked out as soon as I settled down.

When I woke up Stefan pulled everything out of his valise to show me photos of his family. He lent me his perfume. I needed it by now. Our deodorant was in the case stolen in Greece.

A family, Ross and her husband and mother, moved into the compartment with us.

The husband rose to let me sleep stretched out. We were able to reach across our language barrier and become friends. I gave them stamps and coins. We exchanged addresses.

Every time we fell asleep someone woke us and asked to see our tickets or passports. At 2:00 a.m. Nita found the bread in her pocketbook from the previous day's restaurant meal.

The family shared their food with us. They split up their chicken for all of us and we munched on bones. Later we tasted their home-made marble cake with nuts.

After our conductor opened an empty locked compartment for me, I gave him some cake too. Later he gave me three rubles for 29 lei. (This was a crime. I told Control a friend gave it to me.)

Nita writes:

When Stefan reluctantly left, he called me into the corridor and kissed my hand. I would love to know more about him, if only we could speak together.

I wish I could speak every language in the world. It isn't fair that so many people are completely lost to me because there can be no conversation.

Crowds of boys, gaping boys, laughing boys — at me? Why? I don't know, I don't know. I can't understand them. Understanding language is so important to me. Why? We're all people, aren't we?

Crowds of boys, friendly, asking. Me, alone — silent, dumb. Leave me alone! I want peace. Peace, solitude, now precious, how impossible. People supposedly need people. Not me! Am I not human? Stupid, stupid world. Why do there have to be so many languages? Why, why can't I speak them all?

Monday, August 19

At 7:00 am., after our passports and visas had been collected, we rolled into the station into CONTROL.

It's true! We met the stereotype, regulation-minded official.

He insisted on rummaging through all our valises. He took out all the printed matter. Of course I had trouble getting it all stuffed back in.

I signed the papers declaring I had no gold and no arms. I admitted I had 19 lire and approximately $600. This was the amount in my billfold. I had completely forgotten the $700 hidden away. He found it. When he counted all my traveler's checks there was $1,310. So why did I declare only the $600?

We were made to sit on a bench in the corridor for three hours, sweating it out. We felt like punished children on the bench in front of the principal's office.

We watched these officials draw tears from two different women. Over what? Their fruit from Romania was thrown in the garbage pail.

What could they do? Confiscate my traveler's checks? I would get new ones. Obviously this clerk didn't know how traveler's checks were used. Throw me in prison for perjury? Forbid me from entering USSR? What? I sweated it out.

The official was impressed with his own position, inflated with his own importance and control over people. He counted my money at least 20 times. I thought that perhaps he got his orgasms this way.

They were surprised I didn't know how much I had. But I kept track of what we spent, not daily accounts of what was left.

I explained over and over that I hid the money from myself in order to be more frugal, that we divided what we needed in half and planned to live for six months on the money I admitted I had. It was my psychology. It was impossible for them to comprehend.

I offered to change the declaration as soon as they counted the money. They wouldn't let me.

I raised hell at the indignity of it all. It did not happen to us in Lisbon, Barcelona, Rome, Andorra or Greece, only at the entry point of Russia. I said I was sorry. I came wanting to like Russians and their ways, their government. But I was angry at their rudeness.

We had traveled three nights on trains. We were dirty, cranky and tired. Intourist could not get us an airplane but that plane flight and shower were enticing thoughts.

I explained that David's operation made us change our entry point from Finland to Romania. I would have liked to push the fact that David needed a new bandage because of possible infection.

Finally Big Chief handed me my $610, saying, "These you declared! I am giving them back to you because you are a mother." As he returned the rest of the money, he said, "You will need this; you have two children to feed."

They issued us tickets to Moscow. We had another day on the train. Now we would be a day late for the seminar. Intourist got us a berth. It cost the same $100 I would have spent on a two-hour plane trip.

Cashing money was another ordeal. Each time it had to be registered on a certain form and I had to declare it at the end of our stay in Russia.

As the Intourist lady took us to the train she said, "I hope you enjoy your stay in Russia."

I replied, "Thanks. It didn't start out in a pleasant manner."

Enough of passports and visas. Abolish them all. On trains, passport agents wake people all night long. It shows a lack of respect for humankind. Instead, work on better means of transportation. We moved along at a pace where I could count the tits on the cows and the bulbs on the telegraph poles. In the states I couldn't even count the telephone poles.

I'm sure the toilets caused a great deal of sickness. Flies carried disease. These toilets did not flush. The floors were wet and stank. It was so unnecessary.
How about a "better toilet" campaign around the world? Bidets are grand, but we should spread the idea of soft toilet paper abroad. Trains without water, there was your crime. Bad enough having no drinking water on trains, but no water to wash hands after toileting and before eating is unhealthy.

Where was the air-conditioning? Why not have it in every bus and every train? Couldn't each country make one army tank less a day and donate the money for a better cause?

I wrote my anger out of me in the diary.

On the train David and I tried the restaurant food. We paid three rubles, over $1.00 apiece. Cookies and pears were left on a table by departing first class passengers and I took them. David was embarrassed, but he ate them.

Dave's occupation was card playing. Somehow, I felt he should be experiencing more than that.

This was an excellent chance to learn geography. He read nothing about the countries as we traveled. He read no travel folders. He could not relate the history or politics.

He promised he would wash his own clothes. But he didn't. Nita and I set a good example for him but it didn't seem to help.

He refused to get his hair cut.

I got upset when he wandered off by himself. Moping around the Bucharest railroad station for a whole day was a waste of time. We saw part of the city and enjoyed the fresh air in the park. But he just hung around all day.

I wanted to see Dave a polished polite, gentleman, not a cranky, dull, demanding child. I expected that we would be separated during the seminar. We needed to be away from each other for a while.

I loved to watch Nita in action. I enjoyed her loveliness. I took David on this trip to help him find an interest, some direction and a goal. He had a flair for language. He was good in Spanish and the Greek teacher said his accent was better than Nita's. I would have been thrilled if he'd applied himself and learned a few languages. Nita was an excellent role model. Each time she met someone from a new country she learned the alphabet and numbers and money system. She learned the pronunciation. It pleased the person who taught her and increased her knowledge. But Dave didn't pick this up. I wished for him to gain so much more from this travel experience.

Was it enough that he traveled around in a foreign city alone? Was it enough that he learned to handle foreign coins? Was it enough that people liked him? When would he mature? Did I expect too much?

On Train to Moscow

Monday, August 19

Boys in the next compartment gave us apples. I spoke to them. Lucien had approached me in the evening using French, but I was too weary and upset to speak with him.

Lucien and I communicated in French for a couple of hours. I brought Nita and David in. They spoke Spanish, which Lucien understood, and I translated his French. It was a three-way dialogue.

Lucien was a mature 18. He came from a middle-class, educated Romanian family. At departure, I met his young, pretty mother and his father. He had a 12-year-old sister who sat with us

Lucien was finishing lycee (high school) and would study literature at the university. The last three years he had studied the humanities, literature, philosophy and psychology. Next year he would study math, physics and chemistry. We discussed Romanian politics. He told us Romania was more democratic than America, despite the label of "1 million Communists, 20 million people."

We spoke of religion; his family was orthodox Jewish. He considered himself an atheist.

He had an uncle in Russia and one in Romania. One of them would leave him an inheritance. He expected to be well-to-do.

I told him about my morning Control experience. I apologized for rebuffing him on entry and explained I had been tired and upset. We were fortunate to befriend this intellectual, intelligent, personable, polite, handsome young man. Nita played chess with him.

A Russian girl was brought into our compartment to sleep. The conductor woke David up and put the girl in his bed. The conductor was very solicitous of her. All night we had no contact with her. I realized she made no effort to be friendly. I couldn't stand her silence so Nita and I discussed how to change the situation.

I took out our Russian alphabet and showed her our names, Nita and Ruth. You? Tanya. She read the alphabet and contact was established. She spoke a tiny bit of English. She was 19 and pretty, with a pleasant round face, but reserved. She attended a technical school. Eventually she began to speak more freely and initiated conversation. She gave us a pear and candy. This is how it is done. Everyone can be reached. Except Control.

MOSCOW

We arrived at the Moscow station.

Tanya told us, "You must take a taxi to another station to get the train to Leningrad."

We were ready to leave when an Intourist representative walked up to us on the station platform and said, "My name is Yuri. A car is waiting for you."

He located a porter and paid for our luggage to be carted to the taxi. As we got into the car, he announced, "There is a room for your family at Hotel Berlin."

"We don't want a room. We want the train to Leningrad. We are late now."

He said, "Tell it to Travel Services at Hotel Berlin. They'll take care of everything."

I said, "Please stop off on the way and let us pick up our mail."

"No. I can't. I have other errands to run."

It was a busy day for him. We were quite unappreciative at the time of Yuri's ability to speak English.

As we drove through Moscow streets Nita and I thrilled to the magic of it all. Yuri pointed out several buildings and the Kremlin. We saw blocks of people standing in a line leading to Lenin's tomb. I wondered: who stands in that line, the Russians paying honor to Lenin or curious tourists?

Yuri deposited us at Hotel Berlin, where I spoke to a motherly woman.

"It is a mistake for us to be in Moscow. Please help us go to the Leningrad station. We're a day late for our seminar now."

She spent the next two hours in an agitated state, making one telephone call after another, all in vain apparently. Intourist had made arrangements to meet us at the Helsinki border. I had fouled everything up by coming in from the south instead of the north. I explained that David had had an operation in Italy and that changed our plans.

She said, "Well, you see, I have tickets to Leningrad, but no seats. You will have to go to a special place where they will sell you a reservation."

"Can't we buy them at the station?"

She could not do anything without instructions from Intourist. They closed from 12 to 2.

The travel office was closed from 1 to 3. We missed our train. The afternoon train was an express but no seats were available. The evening train was more expensive and we would need a sleeping berth.

I was furious about the whole affair. I was anxious to get going. The clerk insisted we eat dinner.

I told her, "Our meals are already paid for in Djuny. I haven't much money."

She wrote a note so we could have a cheap meal in the hotel restaurant.

An Intourist woman arrived with an attaché case in hand.

"She will take you to get those train reservations."

The Intourist woman walked fast through the streets, dodging people. She did not notice the trouble I had keeping up with her. Nita and Dave gave up the race and returned to the hotel lobby. I tried to communicate with her, but it was impossible. This robot spoke only Russian and made no effort at any human contact. She held herself erect, straight-backed. She was in her early 20s. She wore unbecoming glasses and was unattractive in face, dress and manner.

After I purchased the tickets, I begged her, "Please take me to National Hotel for my mail."

She located a man who spoke English.

He asked, "What do you want?"

I explained that Intourist said the woman had to return to Hotel Berlin. I explained that I did too. But would she point out the National Hotel so I could pick up my mail? She raced me through the streets, pointed to a hotel and disappeared down the steps of an underground passageway.

I was astounded. How could she?

While I stewed about her disappearance, I picked-up my mail. There was nothing from the family. Now I had something real to stew about.

On the way I stopped into Pan Am to pick up a money exchange slip. Who should be there but the robot. I walked out. I found my way back to the Hotel Berlin.

I arrived in the hotel lobby fuming and asked Nita, "Are there any English-speaking people around?"

She answered, "Everyone here is Intourist. That man is going to take us to the train."

Lady Bountiful, Service Soul, arrived and when I told her what had happened she said, "You should be thankful that girl arranged for this gentleman to take you to the train. Now hurry."

We loaded the car and left.

Our agent said, "Your porter knows your train and car and he will take you."

Evening Train

Tuesday, August 20

The passengers ate from the time they got on the train to arrival in Leningrad six hours later. They saw we had nothing to eat during the trip. They had more food than the people in other countries. It was a friendless trip, six hours and not one contact. It was quite disturbing to me.

The woman sitting next to David was noisy, with a bratty kid. She had large packages she pushed under David's feet and blocked his passage. She ate and ate and ate, but offered him nothing. David was miserable and said, "Mom, ship me home."

When we arrived in Leningrad a porter came on to the train and carried our luggage to the platform. We had gotten used to this and did not question it. We would not move from the platform, though. We stood there surrounded by our luggage.

A man approached me. "Kaufman?"

"Yes," I answered.

He walked over to the conductor and spoke while we stood there.

He came back. "Give me your passports."

I did. A gleam of intelligence passed over his face

We were the Kaufmans.

A large black sedan waited for us. Luggage was thrust in and we were told to get in. Our large Intourist man vanished. We sat and waited and sat and waited over half an hour. Someone's radio blared music.

A woman popped her head into our car and asked, "Are you going to Djuny?"

I showed her our card, as I had showed the driver previously.

She said, "The driver was afraid to drive you there. He wasn't sure you were the right passengers."

We were tired and hungry. We finally relaxed as he drove off. The city at night is magnificent with blazing lights. We passed over many bridges. He drove fast.

Our comments to each other were, "Perhaps we're headed for Siberia after all."

It was a weird feeling to be brought to a car where no one spoke our language and we didn't know the destination. We were getting used to it.

I said to Nita, "I wanted someone to take over the responsibility of traveling and it's happening. Relax."

We arrived at Djuny after midnight. Everything was quiet. We said we were hungry and asked for fruit. We were served a meal of ham, tomatoes, bread and butter, buttermilk and an apple. Then it was off to House #3 and to bed. We were so happy to have arrived.

Friends Mentioned in Chapter 11

Stefan. He befriended us on the train to Russia.

Lucien. He was an intellectual, intelligent, personable, polite and handsome young man that we met after our episode with Control.

WOMEN CLEANING STREETS

FOOD VENDOR.
STANDING IN LINE—CAMERA
INCIDENT

TWELVE

DJUNY

Wednesday, August 21

After breakfast a bus drove us to school. Class had begun by the time we arrived. A tour group of 28 people from Los Angeles were in this language seminar. We learned our classmates had spent nearly 10 weeks studying Russian in a town in Southern Russia. Our brilliant classmates impressed us; they knew so much already. We had a unique class with many unusual personalities. No one dominated, but we all enjoyed one another.

Debby was a concert pianist from Los Angeles. Margarite was a French and German high school teacher, who intended to study Russian so she could teach it. Hannelore, a German girl, was fluent in several languages. There were two Finnish boys, who had less knowledge of English, but befriended David for days. There also were two 15-year-old girls and their mothers and we three Kaufmans.

In one day we had to learn the Russian alphabet. No easy task, but we arrived two days late to our class. We three were beginners.

After class the first day I asked Sophie, our teacher, "Could we please be moved to the kindergarten class?"

"This is the kindergarten class," she responded.

Most of our class was capable of simple conversation. I was the exception because I spent time, which should have been spent in study, socializing.

Debby, Elsie and I took a walk and we discovered a children's sanatorium. The children made a fort around a lagoon. I spoke to a teacher and learned there were 12 buildings and 3,000 children ages 3 to 7. They could remain for three to four months.

It was entirely free for the families. It was not for sick children. The woman who spoke to us had worked there for 37 years. Parents left their children while they went on holiday.

We spent three weeks in Russia. Because our stay was all paid for in the states, we felt like honored guests. I thought: I'll get fat on good Russian cooking, black bread, fresh butter and three meals a day. That's more than we had eaten on the trip so far.

We were happy to have two separate rooms. I was by myself and could leave my light on when I wanted. We had slept three in a room most of our trip.

We spoke of our family to everyone, proud and always hopeful. We mailed them 17 letters plus large envelopes and packages. Not a single word!

Sharing our experiences was essential for our enjoyment. We wanted to buy many beautiful things we saw for the family. We wanted them to learn languages and travel and enjoy another enriching, way of life.

Friday, August 23

This was a time of close friendships, communication and introspection. The talks with Debby were satisfying because we both looked into a mirror as we talked. We had similar attitudes towards life, men and sex. We both had neurotic personalities, which still existed despite many psychological probings.

We picked up that we had many similar interests and enjoyed relating our experiences to one another. Debby was a good friend with a zest for living.

Saturday, August 24

I could read the printed word, but could not translate it. I could write Russian already. We could speak with the Russian guests any time we felt brave enough to attack the language.

This night I spoke with Eva, the actress. I told her a little about Wendi and Lori's interest in the theater. We spoke about our travels. We shared our mutual hitchhiking experiences.

We enjoyed being together. She reprimanded me every time I denigrated myself. She mentioned my many interests.

Her parting remark was, "I like the way you are. I agree with everything you say. You have a direct, honest way of saying what you think and feel. When I am older I hope I am like you."

This was better than the dismal, unhappy days at home. There I was, day after day, made to feel worthless. No matter how hard I tried I could never achieve a feeling of doing right.

I could not return to that life again. I could not! Away from that atmosphere I regained a feeling of self, of having achieved success in my job of motherhood, of being a person enjoyable to know.

I wanted so much to make a new life for myself.

Sunday, August 25

What was happening to the days?

Yesterday, Intourist returned our passports and offered us tickets to the ballet. David didn't want to go.

"Would you like to look around Leningrad then?" I asked him.

"What do I need it for? I have chess, checkers, ping-pong, volleyball and swimming here. Why would I want to leave?" So he remained behind.

Ruth writes to Lori's ballet teacher:

Dear Eleanor:

They call them "Palaces of Culture" where they present opera, ballet and drama.

Intourist handed us ballet tickets at no additional cost. We sat in boxes in the Kirov Theater in Leningrad.

Kolpakova performed in the Norse myth, "Magic Land." What a distinguished actress and dancer. She was limp, fragile, most of the time. She was warm, tender in her love scenes — and her blind scene was magnificent! I have never seen such exciting dancing. I enjoyed the male sword dance also. The stage sets were artistic in design. They managed a fire and a waterfall on stage during the ballet. It was dramatic.

I realize now that Russian ballet is an experience, not just a few hours spent in the theater.

Love to you, Ruth

Monday, August 26

Sophie left class and took me to the clinic in town. I had a water treatment for my ear. Hunks of wax tumbled out. We learned that our flying in airplanes caused wax to accumulate.

In class I began to respond to and follow Russian. I felt ready to learn Russian now.

Tuesday, August 27

After class, Elsie King and I took the bus to Leningrad. We met friends of my mother at the hotel where we ate lunch.

The Museum of Ethnography had dioramas of folk tales and told the history of the country's independence. In the rest of the museum were clothing, pottery, homes and tents of various Russian areas, as well as displays of the crafts in Russia.

I walked to a department store, my first in Russia. It was quite different from what we had known in the states, a glassed-in walkway with people selling on counters along the way and square rooms inside with merchandise displays. The prices were much too high.

Shopping was more complicated. At one counter you said what you wanted. You got it at another counter. Then you went to a different place to pay for it.

After dinner in Djuny we had "girl talk." I loved these "Djuny Days." They were full and wonderful because of all the special people.

Wednesday, August 28

The dining hall manager joined us for our walk along the sea. She earned 180 rubles a month. Her flat in town costs 7. Room and board at the resort while she was working cost 5. All the rest of her salary was hers to save or to spend. She had three children aged 23, 26 and 30. All three went to summer camps and to the university. They spent their money because they had nothing to save it for.

We discussed differences in our countries. They said, what we don't have now, we will eventually. Many of the professional people had left the country. Peasants, farmers and workers were left, so that set back Russia until these types of people could be educated. The government paid for all education, for health and for most vacations. There was no income tax. It was hard to find fault.

The people we talked to were happy. They all worked hard without the incentives we have in the states.

Our waitress was anxious to please us and tipping was not permitted. Our teacher was concerned about each one of us and gave hours and hours of her free time.

Where did those other stories about the miserable Russia come from?

Nita shared her talents with members of our class.

Eva asked her to help her win at chess. So Nita taught her chess notation and how to win her game.

Nita was the director of a teenage play for David and Maria.

Nita beat the person who taught her how to play Russian checkers.

"Please ask Nita to cut my hair." Request from Elsie.

Nita wrote and painted the scroll we bestowed on Sophie as our parting gift.

Everyone was pleased to look at her. She was beautiful, charming, talented and intelligent. She had so many abilities that Sophie thought she was a marvel.

Sophie wanted her to come live and study in Leningrad. I thought Wendi would have gotten much from the experience also. Sophie could share their love of literature.

David looked good in his blue suit dressed for the opera.

We got tickets for the opera, "Queen of Spades," written by Chekhov, libretto by Pushkin and music by Tchaikowsky. The stage sets were elaborate and artistic. But it was a student performance, since the regular cast was on tour in the United States.

The highlight so far had been the Kirov Ballet, the Norse myth, "Magic Land," which was absolutely the greatest dance performance I had ever seen.

Sophie said, "David could learn the language. It would open many areas for him. With Russian and Spanish he could get a position in the diplomatic service, as interpreter, or work in the United Nations."

Dream on, Ruth

Our class was special, with an extraordinary teacher who was also a great human being. We sauntered along the Baltic Sea every evening. It was poetic and beautiful. We asked questions to learn about Sophie, her family and the people of Russia.

She told us that three percent of her salary was for rent. Twenty-five percent of ours was for rent. She had no health bills. She didn't worry about insurance or income taxes. The money she earned she could spend. She didn't have to save to send her children to college. It was free education. She didn't save for old age. They took care of the elders.

Sophie knew all about our family, Wendi and Lori, our Unitarian religion back in the states, and our Russian community in our home town of Sea Cliff, with two Russian Orthodox churches. The warmth and understanding she displayed was satisfying to us. We were indeed fortunate to have the experience of Sophie for our teacher.

Nita and I lived apart from one another, but we compared notes and said, "Yes, this is a great country."

Thursday, August 29

We had a program that we called Amateur Hour. Various members demonstrated their skills. There were piano pieces by Debbie, a concert pianist, and songs by youngsters from different countries, as well as a Ukrainian folk dance. The HIT was what David and Maria did, which they called "These Kids Today!" They sat in rocking chairs and commented on teenagers. They were hysterical.

A member of the audience called out, "He is the good chess player."

Dave spent the night dancing with the Russians in the dance hall. He made a hit wherever he went. Everyone was fond of him.

Friday, August 30

It was the last class. We gave Sophie a fishnet full of presents, including books, boxes of chocolate, a wallet, traveling kit and stationary. Very touching.

The poem on the scroll read:

Poetry is the silence of a rising moon...
the heartbeat of a budding flower...
the laughter of a child's first spring...
the melancholy of a lone song bird.

Poetry is the understanding of
another language...
another way of life...
another person.

Poetry is saying good-bye to a
newly found friend,

but knowing that really,
it is impossible to say good-bye.

Nita writes:
Dear Lil,

Guess where I am! Yep, and furthermore, I'm trying to learn the language! We've spent nine study-filled days at Djuny, a resort on the Finnish Sea, and now we are at Leningrad, living it up in a hotel.

After the nine days of lessons, four hours of lessons each day, not counting homework, I was able to compose a simple composition in Russian.

We started out on July 2 in Portugal. The language was so confusing that I couldn't wait to leave, even though Lisbon was very beautiful. Then we spent a fun-filled, friend-filled month in Spain. What a great country! I particularly loved Madrid and Nerja, a tiny village on the sea.

We met two Arab boys who were dying to marry me, but finally we left them, swearing they would commit suicide.

In Rome, David developed a stomachache. Because I was not crazy about Rome we raced to Florence just in time to get him to an operating table with acute appendicitis. Luckily, this lengthened our stay in Florence.

We became best friends with an Italian family (the father spoke English and his bed was next to David in the hospital) with a girl, Mariella, just my age. We spent almost every day with them.

Finally, David was released. His hospital stay was delightful. He was the only child there and everyone waited on him. Even the patients! And we rushed to Greece. We settled on the island, Aegina, so that David could recuperate.

After a couple of sun, swim, beach-laden days we boarded the train to Russia.

I think we made more great friends on the five-day train trip than ever before in our lives. I am now committed to writing to 10 more people, all boys, really nice.

The funny thing is, none of them can even read English! Oh well, we got along anyway.

The most fantastic experience was during the one day-stop in Romania. Romania is a country that I immediately fell in love with more than any other country so far.

It was Bucharest, and I went off alone to the Botanical Gardens to spend a pleasant, solitary afternoon. And what happened? The second I step into the park a friendly Romanian boy steps up and offers me a movie. I push him off and a second later another wants to take me to the museum. I run away and the next thing I know another boy is walking and talking to me in Romanian as if we'd been friends for years. This was too much. I wanted to be alone! I ran away again and sat down to write letters and watch the black swans. Honest to goodness I'm not exaggerating, but over 25 boys in what formed a group came up and invited me to come walking with them. I wouldn't have minded so much but not one in the group spoke anything but Romanian. After hours of explaining to them that all I wanted was some peace and quiet I left, and they followed me all around the park at a respectful distance. They really wanted to be friendly. Finally, since I was completely lost, two of them walked me back to the station. One of them was deaf, but a terrific lip-reader. To make a long story short, I am writing to them, too.

On the train from Romania to Russia was the greatest friend, Lucien, a Romanian, who speaks fluent French, Romanian, German, and Latin and understands Spanish perfectly. The only language he lacks is English. That didn't matter because between French and Spanish we talked for hours. He is 18, brilliant, beautiful, mature, and has his first novel published, for which he got a lot of money.

As you can probably tell, I have been having the most fantastic time of my life. I came abroad to meet different people and learn different ideas, and believe me, I am!

After this trip, I realize that I can never, never live in America. I would never be able to settle down with an American boy. The world is too full of exciting people and things to just settle with what one knows.

I am deciding that after one year at Marlboro I would like to study in Romania or here in Russia. The atmosphere is so different, so intellectual as compared to that in the United States. People are respected, talents are cultivated, education is a way of life, not just a few hours in school.

There can be many negative things said about Russia, but I think the positive things much out-weigh them. The only things that are not paid for by the government are food, clothing and travel. Also, the chess playing is out of this world. Everywhere I turn chess, chess and more chess. This is the life!

Friends Mentioned in Chapter 12

Sophie. Our teacher devoted many hours beyond our class work to befriend us.

Eva. She was an actress who said to me "You have a direct, honest way of saying what you think and feel. When I am older, I hope I am like you."

Debby Greene. A concert pianist, she was compatible with my personality, which mirrored her own.

Elsie King. She was a psychologist.

Elizabeth Bay. We became good companions in our language seminar. We traveled to Germany together. She thrust money as she descended the train. It was Sunday and a Godsend.

THIRTEEN

LENINGRAD

Saturday, August 31

Good-bye Djuny. We left Sophie at 8:30 a.m. and 14 of us rode in the bus to Leningrad to the Vyborgskaja Hotel. After breakfast we left on an enlightening bus tour of the city. I liked the patter of Natasha, our Intourist guide.

In the morning we went to Pushkin's last home. He lived there four months. He was a political figure and a poet who was killed at 37 in a duel over the honor of his wife.

Sunday, September 1

We had three days in Leningrad with hotel, meal and tours. We had great experiences everywhere. We made friends wherever we went.

Here, we broke down into separate groups for the buses — the Los Angeles group, the English group and we 14 individuals for whom they provided a special bus all morning.

We had a tour of Petrohof, Peter the Great's Summerhouse. He had 10,000 people a day working to make his home resemble Versailles. It had fountains and gardens. The Nazis used it as stables and destroyed most of the palace, but it was being restored.

We saw the Hermitage, with the most famous painters' works.

Then the two tour groups left and we stayed on for three days in Leningrad.

Then it was flying to Moscow for three days.

All the bus tours and guides were there if we wanted them. We were relaxed and happy. The children were in room 243 and I was in room 550. We were floors apart and it was good for a change.

I befriended Elizabeth Bye, a German woman close to my age.

In three days I had the opportunity to know her. It was thanks to Elizabeth that I can now spend time with a German without hostility. With all her progressive ideas, she instilled by example, and this is the way she brought up her four progressive children.

Our lives were similar in some ways. Our discussions gave me some insight into what living through Hitler's time was like.

She was frank about her marriage. Her husband was a doctor. Both of us had self-involved husbands who neither recognized our special qualities, nor praised us for them.

We both struggled through the raising four children. She was 14 years older, so she had passed my stage and established good relationships with her children. Better than that, she had worked out a pleasant relationship in which she could live with her husband, even enjoy him, and every once in a while he did something thoughtful to keep their love alive.

She was relaxed in the "friendly companionship" of this period of her marriage. The couple owned a chalet in Switzerland and she spent time there for relief from the pressures of family responsibilities. We bonded when we had our personal talks. Her warmth was obvious.

Cathedrals were now museums. We saw one cathedral that was still functioning as a church and people attended three masses a day. The stock exchange building was also now a museum.

A great deal of restoration was taking place. They set up a special school of arts and architecture where students learned about restorations in order to work on buildings. The Russians were not obliterating history, but placing it in perspective as history.

We were getting our first review of Russian history. I had forgotten so much. It all made sense now. Each day we better understood these people and what they suffered.

We criticized. One cannot avoid it, but it was always the material comforts the Russians lacked that we complained about. They had aims. I thought: give them more time and they can achieve these goals if the forces against them leave them alone.

Monday, September 2

Intourist gave us a tour of Pushkin, where Catherine the Great's Palace was. There was a remarkable restoration in process. Mother of Pearl was inlaid in the floors. Germans took many works of art, which were not yet returned.

It was the first day of school and we watched the uniformed children. Girls wore white aprons over brown dresses and had bows in their hair. A few wore the red ties of the Pioneers. All paraded to put fresh flowers on the memorial for the dead.

In the afternoon Elizabeth, Eva from Austria, and Wilhelm all visited Peter and Paul Fortress and the St. Isaac's Cathedral.

Tuesday, September 3

7:00 a.m.: knock on doors for luggage.

8:00 a.m.: On bus en route to the airport.

I took a seat in the rear of the plane. The plane quivered when we started. It sounded like a tin toy.

Who said Airflot was the best? And I believed them!

The noise of the engine made it impossible to carry on any conversation. We hit and buffeted clouds like they could fight back.

Dave said, "How noisy it is up here."

We saw the communes, very straight roads, rivers, farmlands and many forests.

On arrival in Leningrad, an Intourist representative said, "I have been waiting a long time for you. Why are you so late?"

Boris was a short man, in his 20s. Pompous!

When Joel heard we were to stay at the Ostankino Hotel, he raised hell. It was a bus and three metro stations away from Red Square. It would be 45 minutes riding time.

"Move us to a hotel on a metro stop."

We liked this idea. To eat all our meals at National Hotel, including breakfast, was the final decision. Rooms were distributed. Everyone in the group got a single room. I requested one and got a triple. I objected.

The proprietor put us on the top floor away from everyone. I complained. Finally, we were put in a room near the others. Later, I found out we were next to the kitchen and all night long heard the rattle of dishes being washed.

We were supposed to go on a bus tour of the city. Our bus driver disappeared.

We waited around all afternoon for another bus. We waited around for an English-speaking guide.

At the airport Joel told Boris he didn't speak German and Boris still insisted on speaking German.

We got our tickets ordered and hung around.

Finally Elizabeth Bye and Stan Hale showed up. They had a nap in their rooms.

We arrived at the hotel around noon and we had to wait until 5.00.

Finally, we said, "We're hungry."

Our Intourist guide led us around the entire hotel, looking for the restaurant.

When we had to go to the bus he asked us where it was located. Apparently he wasn't very bright.

We asked him to stop at Intourist headquarters on the ride to the hotel. We could have settled everything there. He refused.

Our English speaking Intourist guide was Irina, a blonde. It took her a while to understand why we didn't speak Russian, since we had just come from the language seminar. We were very tired on her tour.

We could have had naps if we had known how long we would have to wait. We finally had a bus tour. Eva left because her visa ran out. Thirteen were left and we had eight on the bus with us.

Wednesday, September 4

We took a morning bus to National Hotel for breakfast. Irina met us and took us to the exposition grounds. Then we had lunch at the National Hotel.

In the afternoon we went to Hotel Russia and then to the Lenin Museum.

During dinner Boris proclaimed, "May the ice cream be cold and our friendship be warm."

In the evening the group went to Boris Godenov but David and I went to the circus in Gorki Park instead. The circus was excellent. The bears were on roller skates and jumped rope and stood on their heads. The acrobat clowns made us laugh. The clapping was rhythmic, different from the way we clap in America. There was no selling food or eating in the arena.

We met Natasha and her father, who bought us ice cream.

Irina took us to the Metro. We were impressed with the beauty of the stations.

Nita was boiling mad. She returned after dinner to sleep and couldn't get the key because David had it in his pocket.

Thursday, September 5

We had a tour of the Kremlin and Lenin's tomb.

We saw Stalin's tomb too but there was no statue. His name is on top along with the words "Died 1953."

The Tretekov museum was slated for afternoon. Irina took us into the Metro stop for the museum and we said goodbye to her.

Nita writes:

The most amazing incident happened to us this afternoon. We were on our way to the Tretyakoff gallery.

Mommy put film in her camera for the first time in Russia and decided she was going to finish the roll in two days. That meant a lot of picture taking. So the first thing we came upon on our way to the gallery was a long line of people waiting to buy fruit.

Mommy wanted a picture of this, since it is probably the most typical scene. She took out the camera, snapped it.

Immediately the whole line in one angry wave fell upon us. They started yelling and screaming in Russian and snatching at our camera. One man in particular came raging at Mommy, grabbed her by the arm and started dragging her off somewhere.

It was an absolute nightmare. Wilhelm, our German friend, stood aside silently throughout. Eva, our Austrian friend, who spoke some Russian, tried desperately to explain that Mommy meant no harm.

The man paid no attention and kept pinching and hurting Mommy. By this time there were hundreds of people gathered. A man came to our rescue and tried to pacify the other man, who insisted on confiscating the camera.

Meanwhile, a different guy blew a whistle for the police, who never did show up, we found out later.

Our protector finally pacified the crowd to an extent and shuffled us off in the direction of the gallery and, after a few blocks, disappeared.

Immediately, the other horrible man was upon us. He had followed us all the way. He was swearing that he would destroy the camera or Mommy. He almost did, too. The whole scene was repeated again, with people yelling and screaming and pounding on us.

We were terrified, to say the least. Our protector arrived again and finally saw us safely to the gallery.

However, in the gallery a man came up to us asking if we wanted to buy some Icons, which a friend of his had.

This is normal black marketeering and we said, "No thanks." But he insisted that his friend show them to us later and he left.

Due to the extraordinary beauty of the paintings we forgot about him. But when we went outside who should we find with a huge newspaper package under his arm?

Our protector! When he found out that we really did not want icons he went to find that other horrible man, who wanted revenge. We were terrified and ran to the bus, but nothing more happened.

Doesn't it sound like the 1950s anti-Russian propaganda stereotype? Even though that happened hours ago, we still haven't fully recovered, especially Eva, who had the burden of translating. Wilhelm spoke Russian, but he was afraid and wouldn't open his mouth, much less help Mommy when that horrible man was attacking her.

Wilhelm is a lawyer-librarian and a fantastic photographer. He explained to us that we weren't allowed to take pictures of food lines because they could be distorted into "Look at all the starving people in Russia waiting on line to get their small ration of food" type propaganda. I don't know why he didn't tell us before.

Our feeling were mixed, fear and the humor at the situation at the same time.

This experience came out of the blue, because until this time all the people on the street had been very friendly. Eva was glad it happened.

Another interesting incident. Funny because Irina left us a couple of minutes before, after two days of being our guide.

Funny because we only took one roll of film in Russia and attempted to take more in the two days left. Others have been taking pictures all day long.

Ruth writes:
Dear Mom,
Moscow was twice as big as Leningrad. It was not beautiful, but it was exciting.

The theater is elegant here. But I missed "Boris Godenev" when the group went because I took David to the circus. We saw Cinema in the Round and the MetroPushkin Museum with French Impressionists. Yes, the Moscow subway was as beautiful as you heard, with paintings and sculptures of marble, and every station different. It had the longest, fastest escalators in the world.

We had many discussions on all subjects. Most of our conversations were with our Intourist guides. We were quite fortunate. We had knowledgeable, pleasant guides except for one, Boris.

One particular thing I've noticed about the Russians is their fantastic interest in politics. Everybody, but everybody, at the first opportunity, asks us about the United States government, American attitude towards communism, etc. The only other place we encountered this was Greece. But the difference is that in Greece there was a damper on all conversation that leaned left. The Greeks were scared stiff, lest they be overheard by someone who might report them to the regime. The Greek state of affairs is really bad, and there is sure to be a civil war there soon.

That's all for now.

Love from your daughter, Ruth

At the end of our stay in Russia, Intourist arrived, ready to drive us to the train. Our visa had expired. September 5 was our date of departure. Nita and I were waiting in the hotel lobby with bags all packed. We waited for David, who was nowhere to be seen.

The Intourist man asked sharply, "Where is your son?"

"I don't know."

"Are you the mother?"

"Yes."

"Why isn't your son here?"

"I don't know."

This he could not comprehend. He harassed me and further upset me. We waited and waited. No David. We waited some more. Where was that boy?

Our train was at 7:00 p.m. I was ready to hand in my tickets to get another train just as David arrived. At 6:40 he raced into the lobby. The Intourist man thrust him into the Intourist car. The driver sped the car through the streets of Moscow as they do in chase movies, frantically.

The train slowly chugged from the station. We were shoved in and our luggage was thrown after us. We just made it.

I never found out the penalties for overstaying our visa.

Hours passed before I could calm down enough to speak to David.

"Mom, I forgot the name of the hotel. I was lost on buses since three this afternoon. A man helped me find the hotel."

What a nightmare for him. Waiting for David became a theme for this trip.

We were aware that U.S. newspapers reported events where we had traveled; Basque uprising while we rode through Northern Spain, an attempted assassination of the Greek Premier as a reward for our arrival in Athens, invasion of Czechoslovakia to make our stay in Russia more intriguing. We had newspaper articles on the Czechoslovakia invasion, but except that we knew about the attempt to overthrow the reactionary forces, we did not know any more than people in the states did.

People buzzed in excitement at each new rumor. Now I wished I spoke and could read Russian. I hadn't the patience for this slow learning.

We were on the train now. Border tomorrow morning and Berlin tomorrow night.

FOURTEEN

RUSSIA TO BERLIN

Thursday, September 5

We were ensconced in a second-class compartment for eight people and had it all to ourselves. This was without a reservation. We felt fortunate.

We secured our visas for a train to Hoek von Holland, where we would take the boat to London. All night long German uniformed men turned on our light and woke us up to see our passports. Only once did they ask for our tickets. We had no idea what borders we were crossing. Only one stamped our passport.

I had a new Carrie Nation campaign: do away with all passports and visas. Put a stamp in a person's hand and watch how important and obnoxious he becomes. He loses all sense of humor and proportion. The guard looked intently at the photograph, then at my serious face. I gave a wide smile as in my photo. I got a laugh from some men.

I thought, as long as these hundreds of men and women are employed in this asinine job and until we substitute some other hand stamp job that will allow them to maintain their importance and phony dignity, we will continue to have their inhumane indignities thrust on us.

I met the first obnoxious stamp artist before I left in Mineola, New York, and since then I had met them in every country. Put a uniform on anyone and anyone can be nasty and unfriendly.

I handed the guard the tickets as he started to put on the light. I stopped him. He could see in the well-lit hall. "Schlafen" could see the two children sleeping. He told me in German that the next car was the sleeping car and this was a sitting up car. After he finished talking and punching the tickets I said, "Nicht verstehe." I wouldn't give him the satisfaction of knowing I understood his German.

FIFTEEN

LONDON

We got off when the train reached the Berlin station. There was a restaurant near by and we trooped in.

There I met Ullrich, who recommended the soup to me. I moved from the kids' table and we sat together. I told him I wanted to buy a camera and he told me he knew places and would take me.

Ullrich took us to a couple of discount stores. We finally bought my Voitlander camera. I hoped it would take fine photographs for me.

I made friends rapidly again. We already were special people to each other. Ullrich offered to take us to a teahouse where he played chess. After he said the magic word Nita and he became friends. We spent nine hours together and parting was not easy.

He played chess on Nita's level. They had good games together. We spent all evening with his friend, Ilona, who looked and acted mature, but was only 16. She had traveled and was so politically aware that she was a delight. She was taking German, Latin, French and English in school, but was a math major. She was an amazing young girl. She had a good social life and many boyfriends. She wanted to become a veterinarian, Nita told me. She wanted people to write to her and inform German students about what goes on all over the world.

Ullrich directed drama in the theater and wrote. He was 24, with a handsome, vibrant face and delightful smile. He spoke English fluently. His father was French, his mother, German. Both parents were dead.

Imagine nine hours of continuous discussion on politics mostly, each of us trying to better understand the other's country. McCarthy, student uprisings in our two countries, police in both countries, anti-Vietnam feelings in both countries, trying to figure out the size and force of reaction in each.

Ullrich was thinking about emigrating to Canada to live and teach art. They needed teachers there and he thought the politics might be more reasonable.

We spoke of marriage and boy-girl relationships "since the pill." We discussed the reaction of the clergy to the Pope's "anti-pill" speech.

We saw Berlin a bit on foot but we experienced little of Berlin sights or museums. Berlin was most like New York of any city we had seen so far. The stores carried beautiful items. Clothes were well made, with high style. The shoes Nita loved were beautiful and inexpensive.

The high buildings were built in a modern, New York style. I missed the Van Mies gallery. We saw the tourist section, with restaurants of all nations. Dave discovered the ice skating rink and we watched a youngster dressed in a red skating costume show off her Olympic figure skating.

So we did it again; we spent two whole days in a city and saw only an iota. Ruth and Nita won. Ulllrich was shrewd in his appraisal of people and depth of understanding. He enjoyed us both. I would have loved to see him again. Why, oh why, did I have to be over 40? I kept meeting these eligible, delightful men, who were so much younger. It wasn't fair.

I searched and searched for the right values. Had this visit helped erase my blight of prejudice against Germans? Could I now recognize Nazis are Nazis and Germans are people?

Dave had had it. We all recognized it. I saw it as a lack of interest in political or historical things. I saw it as lack of cooperation

I continued to wonder what he got out of all of it. Was he too immature for it? Was sending him back home and back to school the answer? I hated to do it, but neither Nita nor I could take his moods any longer. When we were down and needed a cheerful soul, he always fell into the deepest moods and misbehaved.

At some point I would not be able to keep the group motivated and maintain my good mood. I was amazed at the amount of stamina I had and my spirit throughout the trip. I was becoming disgruntled and angry, but still tried to maintain a good feeling, despite all negative experiences.

Ullrich suggested a farm for David, a peaceful life, few demands and a place to put his world together and find himself. I would have loved it for him. There he would be helped to search within himself and discover his own values.

I did not think our Sea Cliff home or the Sea Cliff school would help him achieve these goals.

Money continued to be a challenge. Ann, of Switzerland, thrust rubles and dollars into my hand. She had too many. I counted them and stacked away $30 in my own traveler's checks under our chocolate bar wrapper. She had given me 37 American dollars.

On the train in Poland I met Jill Watts, a speaker from England. Her vouchers never arrived and she had to pay cash for everything. She needed money so I gave her $35 cash.

That left me with American traveler's checks, 25 rubles in Russian traveler's checks, $4 cash and 15 marks from Ann.

The visa lady from East Germany took my 15 marks, but was ready to ship me back when I told her all I had were traveler's checks.

They collect visa money on both sides of Berlin. At first this lady said she wanted 15 German marks from each of us. That was when I told her I did not have it. Later she accepted my 15 marks and said it was enough for all three of us. Qui sait?

Of course we arrived after 11 p.m. We had to show our passport three times to get through "Checkpoint Charlie."

At the station they gave us the address of the mission. We took our luggage and bus 90 to the mission. It was after midnight when we arrived.

It was Sunday. All money exchange places were closed. We needed the 50 marks that our acquaintance Elizabeth gave us for sleeping Saturday and Sunday nights and food, the zoo and carfare. How considerate and thoughtful Elizabeth was.

We had made the decision to stop in Berlin. We should have gone on to Koln with Elizabeth. It would have been easy to avoid the East-West-East funny business.

What if we had? We would never have learned about border controls and how they work. It was an experience to see that human beings can be shut into a country and not permitted out. West Berliners are allowed into East Berlin in a limited zone area for only one day.

It was an education, being stopped, no visas available, and then obtaining them.

The five-mark duty as you entered East Berlin had to be spent there, we were informed. It was another way of obtaining revenue, all for the want of the second visa. We learned that a visa is an important document. But if we had gone straight through and not gone to East Berlin we would have missed seeing Lydia from Moscow, and becoming acquainted with Ullrich, Illona from Germany and Michael from Biafra. They were worth the experience. There were also our Kenya fellow hitchhikers and we met Leona again. No, it was good that we stopped in Berlin.

Ruth writes:
Dear family,
Crossing the street involves different cautions in each country.
There are people-first countries and car-first countries. This also determines the character of the people.
In Spain people wait patiently before crossing the street.
In Greece people jump the gun on lights.
In Russia the name of the game is "chicken." Each waits until the cars go. People dart in front of buses and somehow don't get killed. We learned as we approached each country.

Monday, September 9

The Mission was another new experience. I woke up looking at a young face.
"Speak English?"
"No."
"Sprechen Sie Deutsche?"
"No."

She was Russian.

Immediately "Dauber Auto," Nita and I said excitedly.

Lydia, big, blue eyes shining through her 23-year-old-face, smiled at us. She also spoke French and Spanish.

So we sat together and drank the ersatz chicory coffee. We met her husband from San Salvador. We exchanged addresses and invitations to our homes.

Speaking all our languages was a big thrill. I even managed essentials in German under stress.

The women kept their belongings in lockers. They were all unshapely humans and unkempt. They took hours in their toiletry. The bathroom had no showers, so they stripped to the waist to wash.

No towels were given to us, nor any softer pillows.

The cost for us was 10 marks, or $2.50 for the three of us.

Breakfast was included with the bed. It was a cup of undrinkable coffee. The color looked right but it had no taste. We ate a piece of bread with apple butter and a liverwurst sandwich.

In the afternoon we went to the zoo with David. The monkey house had glass-enclosed cages so there were no odors and we couldn't feed the animals. It had a slanted floor so everyone could see the monkeys. In the park we found the largest aquarium in the world. An orchestra was playing. The audience sat at tables in the garden drinking tea or beer.

That night we had our first meal in two days, foot long wieners for 25 cents.

We took a long walk back to the mission.

We hauled our luggage to the nearest autobahn.

While we were waiting for our hitch, we met two young people on the road trying to get a ride, Philip Ndehi and Jedidah Karanja from Kenya.

"Oh, we are going to Kenya," I told them. "We expect to be there in February."

We exchanged addresses. They were our contacts when we got to Nairobi. We learned Phillip was attending the University in Nairobi and Jedidiah was studying catering.

"I'll get you a ride, " I said confidently. And I did. We piled our luggage and their bags on the back of a truck and all five of us got a ride to the border. We had hitched to the border from Berlin. Passport Control again. We were stopped and couldn't continue because we did not have the right visas. We had no stamped visas in our passport. They sent us back to East Germany to get them.

At the passport control point we met Leona, our friend from Florence. She was fortunate she could continue her journey, using our ride with Scott from Minnesota.

Hildegarde, a young blonde German woman, gave us our next ride in the opposite direction. Instead of heading west we now were going east.

Hildegarde worked in an office getting hitchhiking Americans temporary jobs.

We were off to East Germany for our visas.

We passed the Marx-Engels museum and the memorial to Fascism, with two guards out front.

We picked up loads of propaganda there, especially on Czechoslovakia, to send to New York.

We visited the Pergamon Museum and saw art from Babylon and Mesopotamia. The walls were covered with Egyptian paintings. There seemed to be much more than in our Metropolitan Museum in New York. The Greek temples were impressive and large rooms were needed to contain them.

On the street, we saw bombed out buildings and took a photo of one.

The train appealed to us more than hitching.

From a train window we passed through Holland. Now I know why they call it the lowlands. It is flat, flat country. Lush green fields are everywhere. The cows walking in marshes chomped on the bright dewy, sparkling grass. There were top-hatted, tall haystacks. (There were also haystacks in the shape of houses from Rome to Florence.)

Holland farmers appeared to live in better homes.

Did I mention the flowers in Russia? They were everywhere, in the streets. Growing and cut flowers gaily decorated every monument throughout the country.

Even East Berlin had more flowers in the streets than West Berlin.

Friends Mentioned in Chapter 15

Ullrich. This 24 year old directed in the theater and wrote. He had a vibrant face and delightful smile. He took us to camera stores and helped me buy my Voightlander camera.

Ilona. She looked and acted mature but was only 16. She was politically aware and a traveler.

SIXTEEN

LONDON

Tuesday, September 10

I spent one and half-hours and 10 six-penny coins on telephone calls looking for lodging. We settled on the Shelbourne Hotel for a pound each.

London is a metropolis. We had many errands to do.

Wednesday, September 11

After breakfast the kids did the laundry. I went to Garrett-Fisher in Kingston-on-Thames to find out about our Indiaman tour.

Thursday, September 12

We moved to the bed and breakfast of the Greatbatch family on Penn Street in the suburbs.

Sylvia Paley, a long-time friend of my parents, had given me the address of her son Tom in London. We called him. We knew Tom from our summer vacations.

We spent the evening in Tom Paley's home. He was a fantastic person of many talents, a math professor, an established folk singer and a professional photographer. Nita and Tom spent hours playing 4D chess and discussing topology.

Friday, September 13

I purchased new eyeglasses and I picked up the Afghanistan visas.

Nita loved the geological museum. David got a great deal out of the mining exhibit at the science museum. Madam Tussard's Wax Works was a must on the tourist lists.

It was a busy day.

On the bus heading home, David announced, "I want to see Piccadilly Circus." And he jumped off.

That began another frustrating evening for me. This time we were staying at a bed and breakfast. I didn't want David ringing the bell and waking up people. So I paced the floor, watching for a lone figure approaching the house. I was getting desperate. Where was he at this ungodly hour? He didn't know London. What happened

87

to him? All sorts of tragedies went through my head. I kept opening and closing the door looking for him, pacing the floor in frantic worry.

After two in the morning he arrived, as always, excited and happy. He rushed over to the bed. He emptied one pocket and poured coins out on to the bed. Then he reached in his other pocket and out streamed another mass of coins.

"Where have you been? Where did you get all this money? I've been worried about you."

"Oh, I had a good time. I went into a penny arcade with all those machines that have prizes. I asked a man, 'Would you be my father, so I can play here?' The gentleman said yes.

"Mom, I kept winning and winning. I couldn't stop winning. So I couldn't stop playing. I kept winning money and played until they closed the establishment."

In London the trains stopped operating after 11:30. He had to locate a bus. Then he walked a distance to the house. That was his explanation.

"You're going home!"

The next day I made arrangements for him to fly back to New York.

When I tell people about our Round the World adventures, I suggest that they make friends they meet on the trip and miss the kids, who they will have left at home.

Saturday, September 14

Nita writes:

Dear Grandma,

We are in London, the swinging city. The weather has been "delightful," rain, rain, rain. This afternoon was so foul that David and I stayed in our room and played cards and chess with Chris Greatbatch, the landlord's son, who is David's age. It became a pleasant afternoon.

Yesterday was wild. In between running around for our Arabian visas, we managed to scrounge around the geological museum. Oh, those precious gems were magnificent, especially the black opals in the science museum.

We succumbed to the touristy Madam Tussard's Wax Works. Some of the figures, John and Robert Kennedy and Sammy Davis Jr., were not realistic enough, but others like Ghandi were terrific.

David was educated regarding the history of the Royal Family by me.

The famous part of the exhibit, the chamber of horrors, was too much for me to take. Bloody people being knifed, beheaded, and otherwise maimed, give me nightmares. So I stood in one corner and waited for Mom and David to come out.

Tomorrow before we take David to the airport we will go to Hyde Park and hear the "soap box revolutionaries" speak.

I love you all, Nita

Sunday, September 15

Ruth writes:

Dear Jack,

We saw a world clock today in the science museum. We figured out it was 2:00 a.m. when I woke you up. It was 7:15 p.m. here. It was fun hearing your voice, indistinct though it was.

The decision to send David home was made after I visited our tour guide at Garrow-Fischer, the agent, for the Indiaman tour. I perused the passenger list. There are no children on it at all. David would be bored by this trip. He is happiest when he stays in one place more than in the "on the road" type of travel. He does not respond well to schedules, and he likes to sleep late in the morning and stay out late at night. Tours operate on tight schedules. The tour leader told me I could use the insurance and get back a full refund for medical reasons, since he had his operation only last month. This is obviously a rugged tour. I sent this information to our insurance agent.

Dave has mixed feelings about it. He had a great time. He enjoyed himself, made friends and became an independent soul in each country. He would like to go on, meet his pen pal, Niren, in India. He is ready to settle down and digest all he has seen and done. He misses his family at home.

Nita and I will miss him very much. Remember, we have eaten all our meals together and slept in one room most of these 10 weeks. I think he looks well and has slimmed down a bit. His face doesn't look as pudgy now.

Everyone loved him everywhere he went. I hope he catches up in school, and the two weeks he lost does not throw him.

It would be good if you took him to the chess club in Sea Cliff. He plays well and could improve his game. Perhaps some Russian friend could continue his lessons.

We put a Playboy centerfold on top of his suitcase. It was to divert the attention from the propaganda material included in Dave's valise. I'd like you to read the propaganda and see what you can make of the Czech situation.

Please pass along the material to my mother. My theater program is in the package from Russia. It is a weekly listing of the events in the four Leningrad theaters.

Our coin collection is in that package

I'm sending another itinerary for the Indiaman addresses and mailstops. I should take the hint and give up.

At 11:00 a.m. we took David to the airport for a 2:00 p.m. flight. He would arrive at 4:20 at Kennedy. The rain was so bad we couldn't even see his plane leave. A steward promised to look after him on the flight.

At 4:00 p.m., dripping and sopping wet, we arrived at Michael's house. There we met Comfort and Robinson, who became our good friends. They were African

Ibos and were returning to Biafra the following year. I read about the Biafra struggle. I think the Ibo story in Nigeria had close parallels to the Israeli struggle.

Robinson was a surprising fighter. He was the only Negro in his job, and he was in a high position. The men under him resented his color and set a bomb in the printing machine he used to kill him. It almost did, too. The prejudice in England was generally subtle, but very intense.

We had our first African meal. It was a mound of ground rice pudding made into balls and dipped into a stew sauce. We used our fingers. The whole meal was eaten without utensils.

It was an entertaining evening talking with brilliant, conversational people.

I spoke to Allen Silitoe on the phone and did not know he was the author of "Loneliness of a Long Distance Runner," and "Saturday Night and Sunday Morning." He is a friend of Michael's.

Monday, September 16

We finally got our visa from India House.

The bookstores are large and we enjoyed browsing and buying books.

Nita returned home to read them. I went to the theater and saw "Spring and Port Wine."

Tuesday, September 17

I went to High Street in Kensington for the Iran visas, discovered a market and bought a pocketbook that would last throughout the trip. I went to Garret-Fischer in Kingston with Nita and returned David's ticket.

I managed to exchange my 25 rubles for $1.10 in English money. It was always difficult to cash the loose coins we were left with as we left each country.

On the Tower of London tour I was impressed with all the jewels the king and queen owned.

Wednesday, September 18

I saw the play "Canterbury Tales." What they did to that classic poem was a terrible sacrilege. We spent the evening in Tom Paley's home and didn't leave until 2:00 a.m.

Thursday, September 19

I went to the university casualty hospital for an ear check. No satisfaction.

Nita went to the Kenya embassy for the visa. They gave her a hard time.

We both visited the home of Jill Watts. I lent her 15 pounds when we were on the train in Poland so she could go to Czechoslovakia. She returned the money. Then she served us lunch. She was a vital woman with varied interests. She refurbished old homes with antiques from Czechoslovakia, Poland and Bulgaria. She taught physical education. She gave us a picture of the Russian invasion of Czechoslovakia.

We wandered through Westminster Abbey, the Parliament and St. Paul's Cathedral. Nita returned home to read and sleep.

I purchased a theater ticket and saw the play "Hotel in Amsterdam," with Paul Scofield. It is a John Cabernet play. I took standing room.

Friday, September 20

I picked up my film. The photographs of Florence were good. The picture of Sophie in Russia was not clear. Many of my pictures were out of focus. Was it the camera or me?

I went to Middlesex Hospital with Nita. She received a shot of penicillin for her ear infection. Nothing was the matter with my ears, according to the doctor. Why did they ache?

The British Museum was our next stop. We saw the Elgin marbles and the Parthenon statues. Later it would be on to Greece to see the temples where they belonged.

At Shepard's Bush we visited Comfort, Robinson and Tony. That evening Robinson related the bomb incident at his employer's. Tony proved to be delightful company. We arrived home around 11:00 p.m.

Saturday, September 21

Laundry was done. Nita repacked but still had too much.

I received a letter from Jack. Each letter had some problem he hasn't been able to solve.

We spent hours in Shepards' Bush markets. There were shops with Indian food, palm reading and cold cures. It was fun. I wanted to see London at night and now I had. We went home to a hot bath and hair wash and final packing.

Nita writes:

This trip has been one dream. I still cannot believe that it is real. Traveling is a much better means of education than a million hours at school. I have learned that ours is not the only way of life.

Traveling, and I don't mean just going to museums and cathedrals, I mean meeting people and becoming involved with new situations, is the best means, I think, of broadening one's outlook on life. I really would not miss this worldwide trip for anything.

London is as wonderful as you pictured it. We spent 12 days here. Unfortunately, there was no time to leave London and see other parts of England. We got visas for Afghanistan, India, Iran and Kenya.

We spent more time with people than in museums. But we did see El Prado, Hermitage, Repin's home, Pushkin's home, and Pergamon museum in East Berlin, as well as the British Museum with the Elgin marbles from the Parthenon.

We can read Russian print and write it. We had nine days of lessons, four hours each day. We made friends in Russian and then switched to another language for communication. We have met wonderful people all over the world so far.

Free health care, they took care of David and me free. And free education is a great security they have in Russia and I wish we had it.

David was a hit among the Russians. He beat them at chess and he danced with a Russian girl in a dance pavilion and he acted on the stage. No, he didn't learn much Russian, but he had a good time.

We tried hitchhiking in Germany, but did not have the right visa, so we were stopped at the German border. But we did meet two people from Kenya and made friends there.

Sunday, September 22

Ruth writes:

Glad to hear David arrived home. We would love details on his trip. Was there a delay? Any trouble with customs?

Blue Cross had no card for us. It was my social security number. I'll get a doctor's letter for you.

We saw "Spring and Port Wine," a light comedy. "Canterbury Tales had great scenic direction, but the play was a sacrilege against Chaucer. They could have done more, especially with music.

Paul Scofield and Osborne May were in "Hotel Amsterdam." It was all talk and not enough action.

We appreciate the opportunity to see so many plays in London at reasonable prices. I paid less than one dollar for the theater tickets.

We saw the Elgin Marbles from the Parthenon at the British museum. Now we can go back to Greece and see the Parthenon. Berlin also has floors of Greek statues. The temples are also in the Pergamon museum in East Germany.

Countries are resenting having their antiquities stolen from them.

Nita writes:

Dear Daddy,

We love receiving your letters. Please tell my sisters to write. I am on the train to Brussels. I was just taking to a boy from Japan, who is on my bus. An interesting man, a doctor. I am not a "tour person." I have forebodings about the trip, but I am hoping for the best.

I have been reading in England like mad. Oh, I miss books. England is the 'bookiest' country I have ever seen in my life. We will send home anther package soon. Have you gotten the others? I can't believe how slow the mail is, but we can't afford airmail too often, so be patient.

All the while I was going through the markets looking at the magnificent wild clothing I kept thinking of Wendi and Lori. They would go crazy. The satins and velvets and puffed sleeves are unreal.

Daddy, it was great hearing your voice again. I wish it wasn't so expensive to call. I wish you were here to share some of our experiences. You would go crazy over some of these people we've been meeting.

I hope we make it through the Arab countries. So far, out of four Arabs I have had four marriage proposals. One thing about them, they all have a nationality inferiority complex. Love, Nita

Friends Mentioned in Chapter 16

Comfort and Robinson. These were our African friends. We experienced new dishes in their home.

Tom Palley. He was a friend from our past, a photographer and a folk singer. Nita played chess and four-dimensional games with him.

Chris Greatbach. He was a friend for David in our B&B.

DAVID IN LONDON

PART II

NITA and RUTH
on
INDIAMAN TOUR

SEVENTEEN

INDIAMAN TOUR

Sunday, September 22

On the boat crossing the English Channel we met Fredrika and Claire.

Our first lodging on the tour was Hotel Ostend. Dinner tasted good, but there was no salad. The waiter refused to serve us water, but we had our choice of coffee or tea.

After dinner, we took a walk with Patrick and Diana, a delightful couple, newly married.

No evening activity was planned, so I went to bed. My roommate was Marya.

Monday, September 23

We woke up to a rainy Monday morning. Nita was assigned to the other bus, but decided to join me on mine. She regretted it later because her bus group was more spirited and younger than our group. The group leader in the other bus was more democratic. We would have had access to both groups had she stayed on the bus she had been assigned to, even if we remained separated.

The buses drove us 200 miles from Ostend, Belgium, to Luxembourg. The rain accentuated the green of the countryside. First there were very flat fields, then rolling hills. We drove through a couple of forests and passed the site of the Belgium World's Fair.

We were thrilled each time we saw the sun. Our first stop was for food. The second stop was for sightseeing. At the third stop we camped for the night. Marya, a nurse, and I were in one tent. Nita was with Fredrika. Tents were good sized and comfortable for two.

Wednesday, September 25

Breakfast was champignon (mushroom) soup. We arrived in Ulm about noon. We viewed the majestic cathedral and walked around a 500-year-old house and along the canals.

We drove along the farmlands in Germany and stopped in Munich. While Nita enjoyed the markets, I walked around town and visited the national museum. When I washed my face, I left my sunglasses on the sink.

At 6 p.m. in Salzburg, Austria, I mailed a letter to the museum to send me my glasses.

The first Christian Church was built into the side of a mountain. It is in a lovely, picturesque town made famous by Mozart. We saw his home and museum and a puppet theater. Fredrika raced us around, happy to be in familiar territory. The time was not nearly long enough to appreciate this town.

We were entertained the whole evening by Austrian folk dancers. After dinner, they encouraged us to join them in dance and song.

That night we were placed in three separate houses. Nita and I were together. I loved the huge comforters that enveloped us in warmth.

Thursday, September 26

We drove through Brenner Pass, crossing the Italian border for our first sight of snow-capped mountains. Most of the houses had colorful balconies with flowers. Farms had the fresh odor of manure.

Innsbruck was a colorful town. The house fronts had painted murals. There were delicate iron-work signs. The people wore Tyrolian costumes with waistcoats and splendid ruffled blouses.

In the dark, we set up our camp in Vipatavo, beyond the Brenner Pass. Fredrika and I laughed hysterically when the wet tent shrunk and we could not put the tent pole into the hole. The front did not reach the ground. We couldn't stop laughing. Fredrika went to the toilet but the doors were locked.

On the way back she helped a couple put up their tent, and in the process laid down her container of butter. A "gentleman" stepped on it. Now she had grass in her butter!

I thought avoiding liquid at night was a good idea and didn't to get up during the night.

Friday, September 27

We awoke to the 5:00 a.m. church bells.

For breakfast, we had soup, chicken and leek with blood sausage and cucumber, not exactly your all-American wake-up meal.

The bus drove off at 7:30 a.m. Nita sat alone and complained about the group. I walked around listening to the conversations. During the first days people asked: Where are you from?

Two English girls, Jan and Loris, had worked in New Guinea for two years. Kay had lived there for 16 years. I heard Nigel sing melodies from classical music. Cyril and Marya guessed which symphonies. Cyril discussed English literature, which he taught. A boy from Chicago related the fascinating history of the royal house of Scotland.

He claimed, "Not my line. Just my interest."

We had a good dialogue with Kasimir, in which he tried to explain that the

Communist countries had to work out their own economies. The West could not help them or rush them. Kasimir left Poland 20 years ago at age 21, as the country turned Communist. He admitted he had matured and has changed his point of view on how Communist countries should develop. He was intelligent and had a sensitive, delicate way about him. I thought he was effeminate. Fredrika thought not. She said, "He is sickly; he gets out of breath too easily." Kasimir shared his rose petal jam with us.

Michael Dunn and I exchanged teaching experiences. Most Australian teachers came from teachers' colleges. There were more primary teachers and a shortage of secondary teachers. It was two-thirds men to one-third women. Private schools (called public) included religious groups. A third of the students attended them, but these schools provided two thirds of the universities with students.

Teachers had no choice in where they were sent for their first jobs. They were graded on their work. Curriculum guides were provided and had to be followed, but teachers could not be fired, except for embezzlement or molesting their students. Teachers received steady raises. Michael taught 6 and 7-year-olds who were already reading. He had 48 children in his class.

Friends Mentioned in Chapter 17

Kazumi. He was a young Japanese doctor.

Fredrika. She was Dutch and in her 60s.

Kasimir. He had left Poland at age 21.

Claire. She was a fellow traveler.

Patrick and Diana. They were recently married.

Marya. She was a nurse and our tent mate.

Jan and Loris. They were two English girls who worked in New Guinea.

Kay. She lived in New Guinea for 16 years.

Michael Dunn. He was my seatmate on the bus.

Nigel. He sang classical music.

Cyril. He was an English teacher who liked composers.

INDIAMAN GROUP

EIGHTEEN

ITALY

It was 9:00 a.m. and the Dolomite Mountains lay ahead. There were haystacks on hedgerow racks. All morning we watched people haying on the sides of mountains. The Dolomites are sharp, ragged, limestone mountains, rocky with sparse trees, unlike the Alps, which have been rounded with age and are covered in greenery.

We bumped along in our bus, our home for three months. The previous night we had arrived at our campsite at 8:00 p.m. around mud puddles. The driver insisted that it was against company rules to sleep in the bus, but in the face of a rebellion, permission was granted.

We took out our sleeping bags and crunched up in the seats. We slept well.

Friday, September 27

Nita writes:

Dear Family,

It is now the fifth day of our Indiaman tour and things have begun to settle down. Last night we camped in Vipitano, a thickly wooded village high up in the mountains with snow, on the border of Austria and Italy.

It was our first rainless night, so everyone was happy despite the freezing coldness, darkness, and the sopping wet condition of all the camping gear. We were headed towards Venice, supposedly a beautiful city, but I will miss the green and white splendor of Austria.

Our friend, Fredrika, a woman over 65 years of age, who acts about 25, knows Austria like her own home. She guided us around Salzburg and Innsbruck. I have never seen such picturesque villages. Fredrika is Dutch, but has been living in Vancouver, Canada, for the past 20 years. She reminds me of my Aunt Becky with an accent. She has the same attitudes, curtness, independent spirit and energy. She is amazing.

Most of the people on the trip seem rather conventional-minded. Nice, but very conservative, both politically and socially. For instance, two of the women, Kay, older and gruff, and Jan, a wishy-washy young woman, are from New Guinea. They were discussing the "savages" in the interior of the island. "They are like children and we had to teach them how to bathe and eat properly. They are horrible ingrates who don't appreciate all the hard work Australia is doing trying to 'civilize' them."

Their attitude disgusted me.
Lovingly, Nita

Friday, September 27

We arrived at the camping grounds and made the decision to camp rather than find a hotel. Our tent became home. I discovered Fredrika had a sleeping bag that zipped all the way round. I made a real bed, sheet and all, with room to scrounge up, and slept better than ever before on the trip. I hoped Nita and I could find other sleeping bags, not mummy types, so we could be more comfortable.

We drove into Venice. Meztre was the name of the town near camp. We had a ride in a vaporetto (boat) into the city.

The architecture of each town was unique. One could admire the beauty and bewail the age. Did one look at how unique this city of waterways was and love it for its beauty? Or did one think of the stench of the smaller canals where sewage was dumped from kitchen windows?

Did one see only tourists roaming the streets and not a few thousand Venetians?

Saturday, September 28

Nita was snappy and cranky, so I went off by myself.

I wandered through the army quarters, until I saw signposts pointing to the synagogue. The synagogue was a large temple where women sat on one side, men on the other. It was the Sabbath. A few families gathered. I was present when the ark was opened. The rabbi walked around with the Torah, which the people touched with a kiss. The children knew the prayers by heart.

I thought of humanity enduring through time.

Later I walked past a shop where a man was working on glass figurines of Jewish characters. We spoke for a few moments. Only 10 Jewish families were left in this area. Herman Wouk in "The Source" mentioned that at one time there were 900 Jewish families in Venice. In his book, he described the methods used to eliminate them.

The stalls displayed those beautiful fruit and vegetable stands of Italy with thin, deep purple eggplants and brilliant orange and flame colored peppers.

I discovered the route signs for Rialto. All I could think of was Shylock's speech from "The Merchant of Venice."

I bought a pear and some concord grapes and ate as I strolled along. I was determined to get to Murano. Finally I took the boat. On the boat I became acquainted with Jean Peter and Bernard. Jean spoke English, but both men were French and Bernard spoke French and Italian. They were obviously homosexual. Bernard dyed his hair blonde and kept looking in a mirror and combing it. He posed, hand on hip. They were clothing designers from France with a room in Rome where they were selling their merchandise.

A gentleman on the boat assured us the glass factory was not working and guided us into a shop. We were given a glass blowing demonstration and the "hard sell."

I never experienced such rudeness. The guide made it obvious I was a fool for hanging around those two. I was not interested in buying his glassware. My friends decided to buy glassware and we were taken on a tour of room after room of gorgeous, detailed, artistic glasswork. We then walked to their appointment and I left them. I wanted very much to spend the evening with them.

Large Klieg lights illuminated the area. The police were keeping people from the Teatro Venice, where a movie was being filmed.

Chris and Willie joined me. We spent the rest of the evening together. I enjoyed this young couple, on their honeymoon from their home in Scotland. We laughed as they described their sleeping arrangements. They were both on one stretcher. No wonder they didn't sleep very well.

I was "home" at 9:00 p.m. A good day!

Nita was lying under the stars. She had a crowd around her talking. It rained during the night.

Saturday, September 28

Ruth writes:

Dear Family,

Do you appreciate the hours I spent choosing this particular set of stamps? Mail is getting so expensive I think we will settle on airgrams from now on. We each enjoyed Munich. Nita liked the colorful and cheap markets. I browsed through two museums.

Salzburg, Austria, Mozart's town, has the oldest Christian church cut into a mountainside.

The Alps displayed their magnificence to us for hours on end. But the Brenner Pass is an engineering feat. I'll send home the pamphlet on it for Jack.

The Dolomites are rugged limestone mountains, very different from the Alps.

Nita wrote about our camping. Marya is our tent mate, an Australian nurse, who is very intelligent. We have been in a different country every night of this tour except for a weekend in Venice.

All yesterday we passed miles of mouth-watering fruit trees, apples, grapes and pears hanging heavy on the trees.

We see many woman and children picking up potatoes. We rode along the Italian coastline much of the day. As it became warmer the fields changed. We saw alfalfa, garlic, vegetables and hibiscus flowers.

We took the boat at Brindisi to Athens.

Sunday, September 29,

We woke to the symphony of church bells early in the morning.

The need for male companionship was so strong it was tearing me apart.

For me, touching, holding and feeling was a necessity. I needed physical and soul contact with a man. The female chatter was not satisfactory at all.

I had had a "year of loving" with Adam, and I missed it desperately. I wondered how long this feeling would last. Would I find what I needed or would I sublimate the need?

I missed my son David. He had a special warmth about him; sweetness, deliciousness and those occasional hugs we shared gave us good feelings.

Monday, September 30

Robert, the bus driver, decided it was time to get better acquainted. We took a long walk and talked. He bought coffee. Unfortunately, he was only confident, and fluent, in French and Flemish. He thought in Flemish and had to translate into English. Since I struggled the same way in languages, I appreciated that he felt he could not carry on as deep a conversation as he would have liked.

His boss's rich sister wanted to marry him. This was a big decision for him. He was 38 years old.

He told me about his past fiancées. He said his 63-year-old father, who was a prisoner in Germany, objected to his German girlfriend. He was a good man with a sense of humor.

I asked him why he drank each night. He said, "To forget that I am a man." He had the same night frustrations I had. We discussed camping. He said, "It is difficult to work anything out. The girls all watch each other like hawks."

We made a date to get together in Athens. I was ready for a lost weekend.

In the evening Fredrika gave Nita a rough time.

"Where are the tent poles? Where are the pegs for the tent?"

Finally, they discovered they had some one else's tent. When they located their tent they discovered some items were missing.

Fredrika yelled at Nita, "Where is my pillow?"

I said, "Look in your sleeping bag."

Finally, she dumped the bag and found it. There was no apology to Nita.

I was not in the mood for Fredrika's domineering behavior. I stayed with Marya.

During the day we stopped at a Byzantine church with a large, mosaic tile dome. Dave related its history.

San Marino, a principality, existed only for tourists and stamp collectors. High up was a castle. But the town itself was a series of souvenir shops. Stamps. Stamps. Stamps. Granted they were beautiful. The tourist trade was the town's only raison d'être.

I couldn't resist and sent a card home. But I did not get my visa stamped. It cost 100 lire.

Tuesday, October 1

The showers were hot until I got in but there was only cold water for me. I washed my hair and felt clean and virtuous.

It was a beautiful day and the sun was shining. Kasimir was a teacher of the Polish language and Polish literature when he left Poland more than 20 years ago. He met a Polish girl in Australia. He had a son who was 22 and a daughter 20. They lived in a four-room house. He had a satisfactory home life. The family had little need for friends or outside social life. His wife wanted him to go home to see his mother. His mother had an operation and had half her stomach removed. She was 76 and still vigorous He had good feelings towards his mother, but he had been away for a long time. He owned a delicatessen and worked seven days a week. He was ashamed of it. He was my age, 44, and already a grandfather.

Our evening campsite under pine trees was in the town of Pescare. It was beautiful land but had horrid toilet facilities.

Many people walked to the sea and went swimming that night. I enjoyed a walk on the beach with Robert. My hands were icy, despite the sweater and my jacket. Robert had no warm covering, but warmth emanated from him. What a gentle person he was, sweet, affectionate and loving. Even putting on my slippers and wiping the sand from my feet he did gently. We stopped for a cappuccino, which was warm and delicious, and sat with girls drinking milk, and then had a good night's sleep.

Every day from September 22 to this day we had been in a different country — Luxembourg, Germany, Austria, Italy, San Marino. We camped in each. I found a weekend in Venice pleasurable. I appreciated the beauty of the city and architecture. But the commercialism was too much for me.

Touring was different than on the first part of our trip. There were hour stop-overs to see an entire town and the people. Those of us on the bus trip had lived together for one week now. Our companions were mostly likeable people, with some intellects among us. They were the hardest to get to know.

Australian men preferred male companionship and a beer in a pub to a good lay. So the men went off together. Nita went off on her own.

While we rode on the bus it was fun to listen to the lilting voices of the inhabitants of Wales, England, New Zealand, Australia, New Guinea, Switzerland and Belgium. It was a concert.

Nita objected to the reactionary points of view she overheard.

Dave, an American, knew all the details of the royal houses of England and Scotland. He also talked about the Byzantine periods. He enjoyed history and related the gory details. I enjoyed this trip. Companionship was good and it was there whenever we wanted it. Since the previous night, finding one warm person responsive to me, I thought things would look up in the one lacking area.

I asked Nita why she didn't get involved in conversations.

"If I have nothing to say, why should I talk?"

"How could you have nothing to say? You are constantly thinking."

"Not about the pleasant day, or what I'll have for breakfast. Not about the things I hear people talk about."

"What do you think about?"

"People, mostly, and me and why in the world am I here in Italy. I tell myself I do have a purpose — enlightenment. Yes, I push it all off on education."

October 2

In the morning Fredrika washed up and returned to bed. I washed, brushed my teeth and went in to wake Robert. Again, my hands were chilled. He was warm, delicious and sweet. It was hard to break away and face the reality of breaking camp.

We followed the Adriatic Sea and saw the varied colors of the water's depths. Grapevines and olive trees were still visible.

June commented, "You went for coffee with Robert last night. He's a nice guy."

Nothing goes unseen. Make up your mind to that. I tried to spend time with Kasimir to use him as a decoy.

Nita asked, " What do you see in Kasimir? He isn't worth the trouble."

"Who do you like?" I asked her.

"Robert is a good guy," Nita replied.

O.K. Nita approved of my choice.

We spent three hours in Brindisi, a port city. We bought a chicken. We changed our Italian lire into Greek drachmas and that stopped us from any further buying.

At 9:30, we boarded the boat and found out that Nick, the other bus driver, had been in an accident. A car darted out of a hidden driveway and smacked headlong into his bus. Nick swerved. Due to Nick's fast thinking, the driver of the other car wasn't killed. But his car was smashed badly. Nick's bus had one broken headlight.

The whole incident caused a three-hour delay, what with waiting for the Cabinari (police). Then we had to rush to Brindisi to make up for lost time.

On the boat I was settled in a four-berth cabin with Nita, Shirley and Ella.

We watched the boat leave the harbor and saw the buses squeezed into the hold.

Robert and I left the B deck bar as it closed at midnight. There was a beautiful moon that got fuller as it shone on the water. We stood by the railing, holding each other. I thought it was romantic.

I learned why Robert did not join us the evening before. He had become aroused from the kissing. He went to bed early.

I went down the steps and found Nick's bus. Everyone was sitting in a huge circle drinking. He pulled me into the group and I drank a beer.

One of the men bragged loudly. "Tomorrow I'm gonna plaster Wallace signs all over and, boy, when he becomes president, boy will America change. We'll kick out all you damn liberals and then finish the niggers off. Law and order and conservatives, but mostly order. America. White America."

He was kidding, of course — at least everyone thought so. But inside I cried. Filled with tears for all those Alabama lynchings and police-bashed heads. He meant it — with every serious fiber of his being he meant it, and I could do nothing but cry. Even abroad I could not escape America. My inside burned with fury, and I could do nothing but cry.

Thursday , October 3

I woke at a Corfu stop early in the morning. I ate a continental breakfast in the luxurious dining room. Then I went back to bed for a bit of sleep until the porter wanted to fix up our rooms at 9:00.

I ate lunch with Nita, after which she wandered off to find chess players.

I looked forward to Athens. Would Robert drink for hours before retiring, I wondered.

There was another problem. The biggest thing on my mind was the inflamed area. I had had it for days now. First itching. So I put foot powder on it and it burned. Then I found baking soda and used that. That also burned. But it did not clear it up. I tried two antibiotic pills to guard against internal infection. I asked Marya, the nurse, and she gave me an antiseptic pad.

It was driving me to distraction. What next?

1:00 p.m. We were packed and ready to vacate rooms.

I wanted more verbal communication with Robert, but no one man could be all things. I could always talk with Kasimir, or establish contact with Cyril, the stiff intellectual professor, unapproachable and unfriendly.

I returned to my room and relaxed, slept and read a bit. Near landing time a young porter invited me up to his room. He offered me a Cappuccino and we talked. He was a 29-years-old Italian, good looking with limited English.

Nita rushed me into the waiting line with my baggage.

We were off the boat into the bus. After we landed we had nine hours of driving. We made quick stops to buy food.

Writing on the bus was headachy and when on land we only had enough time and light to set up camp and plop into bed.

At the Patras camp ground we set up tents under artificial light. We were getting better at it all the time. The evening meal at real tables made us feel dignified, after a fashion. Nita cooked potatoes and sausage with cheese.

In the evening the crowd made a small campfire and started singing as they drank wine.

Hugh complained about the camping trip. He hated handling his tent. He liked the hotels better.

He said, "If I was smart I'd leave from Athens and return to London."

Robert said, "I could write a book about my adventures. I would include the first night we had to put up that tent."

They had no idea how to do it. I put up their tent for them. Nita couldn't believe they couldn't do it, and stood by and laughed.

I went back to my tent and thought: Hugh was a poor tour leader from the start. He weakened instead of strengthened our esprit de corps. He was indefinite about time schedules. He liked to sleep late in the mornings. He didn't get us on the move on time.

He was an "all for me" guy. He expected people to take care of his needs and his food. He certainly didn't overwork himself. His drunkenness at night was way out of line. He complained of headaches. He didn't speak civilly to his fellow passengers.

We made errors in routes nearly every day. One autobahn was missed completely and we were lost for an hour. If Fredrika had read the map and guided Robert, we would have been better off. Robert fell into the trap of Hugh's thinking. "I'm crazy to be doing this. I miss the comforts of my bed, food and women."

Each time Hugh drank, he panned our bus and admitted he liked the people on the other bus better. It had more people who drank.

I thought the way the two men pulled away from the group at every stop was not good. I thought Hugh ought to return to England.

He was not such a good driver. He was not a good tour leader. Robert was more capable and better at it and better liked. Hugh did not have the respect of the group.

Thursday, October 3

Nita writes:

Dear Daddy,

Oh, I'm chess sick. I haven't watched a game since Russia, and I miss it. I just found out that Nick, the other bus driver, who I almost never see, plays chess, but I have no idea how well.

How goes life with you? I practically don't even remember what home life is like. I feel so removed from it. We still haven't received that 12-page letter from England that you claim you wrote. We're hoping our friends have sent it on to Athens or Turkey.

You know, I'm discovering that most travelers I've met don't get too much out of their travels. They see a lot of buildings and pretty scenery, but not much else.

It's really a shame, because then they go back home and spout off all the places they've been and show the pretty passport stamps, but really they have returned knowing as little about the country as when they started out. It's sad.

We're camping now in Rion, a Greek port town, and we have just come from making a fire on the beach and singing. These songs are difficult, because everyone comes from different countries and common songs are rare. We are gathered around the outside bar and nearly everyone is drunk. They're having fun trying to do Greek folk dances, but, oh, will our bus be miserable tomorrow. Even the wine is wasted on me.

    Love, your daughter, Nita

Friends Mentioned in Chapter 18

    Jean Peter and Bernard. They were in Venice with me.

    Chris and Willie. They were from Scotland and on their honeymoon.

    Robert. He was the alternate bus driver.

    Hugh. He was the bus driver who liked hotels and bars.

    Dave. From Chicago, he was interested in history.

NITA AND CAT

NINETEEN

GREECE

Friday, October 4

Nita writes:

> *Dear Mr. Haulenbeck,*
>
> *Corinth today, Athens tomorrow, Delphi next, and how are you?*
>
> *This is our second trip to Greece. In August we went to Athens and Aegina, and Greece changes with the season. The reds and greens are richer and the land, though still dry, doesn't cry for nourishment. As we pass the heavy-laden vineyards and olive groves, we can see leathery old men in worn, baggy pants and wrinkled women wrapped in shawls and long, heavy skirts gathering the harvest.*
>
> *We imagine "The Golden Age" as we pass these people, as we pass the rubble ruins, as we pass the small gray white buildings, blending with the gray dust. I find that Greece is a country for imagination, for myths. Little is left to remind me of Athens, the great.*
>
> *It has been dispersed into the Pergamon Museum in East Germany, the British Museum in London, the Metropolitan Museum in New York and hundreds of others.*
>
> *Greece has been picked apart and now it is but a whisper of its past. But the people I have talked to, they remember. They have ingrained in them the philosophers, statesmen and poets that I read about.*
>
> *A government can suppress their activities, they say, but not their minds. Being in Greece makes the military take-over even more tragic. Evidence is everywhere. The civil war, I think, will be horrible. In my spare time I am trying to learn modern Greek. So far I have only conquered the alphabet and a few words. What a difficult language.*
>
> *Forever, your student, Nita*

We had the hardest stretch ahead of us. If we had to bear Hugh's weight and attitude it would be even it harder for us.

Fredrika planned to write to Garrett-Fisher and I also wanted to. I wished that Hugh could save face and quit before that happened.

We all sat at the tables in the local restaurant.

The owner danced Greek dances. It was a pleasant, but late drinking evening.

In the morning I woke up at 6:00 a.m., energetic, in good spirits and restless.

We visited a museum. I still think these pitiful, headless statues should be exchanged for the better ones already off Greek soil.

A castle on a hill sounded fascinating, but there was no time to visit it and buses couldn't make the climb.

The town had a few shops, so we bought milk, yogurt and apples — good hard, green ones. A half-hour later, we stopped by a water pump. We had to carry our own water.

I located a dentist and let him smooth the rough spot from my chipped tooth.

Then we arrived in Athens. Nita went off with Mike. I hoped all would go well with her. She wanted to find her own place to sleep in Athens.

I was left in the lurch. So I could go off as I pleased, I thought. Only my bag was too heavy now to lug around. I found June's room and dumped my bag there and went to Helmos Hotel around the corner. Beryl and June R. agreed to let me join them. Only Miriam did not agree.

So, I thought, I'll stow away and see what happens.

Beryl's bath water flooded the room. I scooted out as they called for help.

Off to the hospital at 4:30 p.m. The nurse was studying French, but she didn't know "le medicine." Finally, she told me the doctor was sleeping and I should return at 6:00 p.m.

I bought souvlaki and sat down in the restaurant for the hour. It was raining.

I returned to the hospital at 6:00 and waited in the doctor's office. A nurse came by and said in English, "I will get a doctor for you."

About 6:30 a doctor showed up, but he didn't speak English. He withdrew and later he returned at 7:00 with an old man who spoke French. I said a few words in French, but realized I couldn't say "itch". I tried pantomime. I sat down and showed the doctor my inflamed area. He pulled up my panties. He rushed me through the hall to an English-speaking doctor. I explained about the diarrhea and dysentery in our crew and the need for a prescription for them.

I was taken into the room where babies were delivered and again I showed the red area. The doctor gave me a prescription and instructions: Wash out the area with this one. Wash and put these heart-shaped pills into the vagina. Smear the cream on.

I had no money. I missed the time the bank was open because of the three hours I spent waiting in the hospital. I needed some relief immediately. He gave me two heart-shaped pills.

The doctor disappeared and I spoke to a woman in labor. She was crying and carrying on.

"How long has this been going on?" I asked the nurse.

"She has about three hours more before delivery," the nurse said.

Gosh. How could she last? She already was acting like she was about to deliver.

111

It was her second baby. We talked for a while. It calmed her down and she relaxed and stopped bemoaning her fate.

The doctor returned. He made out the prescription for dysentery.

He pointed to the Peace button and told me, "You should wear it under the lapel of your jacket. You can get in trouble if the people in authority see it."

I told him about our trip.

I came home, wrote and went to bed. Room 44 was quiet. Were they all out drinking?

I recalled Robert saying, "I drink to forget I am a man."

When the girls came in they decided I was to move to the single bed and sleep alone. Beryl and June shared the bed.

Saturday, October 5

Miriam gave me notice to get out. I paid my share, 50 drachmas, for the room. I visited Hotel Helmos, where it was 60 drachmas per single instead of Achillon's 115.

Beryl and I hiked to the Parthenon and listened to an enlightened guide. His review of Greek history and mythology was educational. I taught Greek history and was familiar with some aspects of it.

It was an exciting place, very beautiful. I'm sure that all who came wished they could be alone to meditate.

I met Nita and arranged to spend the afternoon with her and sleep in her Hotel Carolina. Beryl joined us and we wandered around the Plaka, where we saw great bargains.

I bought $8.00 worth of drugs to clear up the yeast infection and fight dysentery.

I learned that I had a fungus that forms internally, and as it leaks out it itches. I was told it is very common among women.

I went to the police station to see about the stolen suitcase from our last visit. They sent me to another station far away.

I met Nita and she bought a lovely pair of handmade sandals. We walked around the stalls as they were closing. I bought a knapsack. I would like to have left our valises in Bombay and to have traveled around India with a light knapsack.

I found salesmen who refused to take our money for the produce.

"Finis. Ferme." Pantomime for key closing in lock. Why wouldn't they sell to us?

We picked up my nightgown. Nita was in a dormitory with five double-decker beds and one sleeping girl.

When she woke up she told us about a hotel in Istanbul where we should stay.

I wrote a letter to Arthur, the clerk, there. We were set, June, Beryl, Nita and me.

We took baths. Our friends in the room I just vacated couldn't bathe because the bathtub had leaked and flooded the room.

I had an afternoon nap and then went to the exhibition so highly recommended by Dave, Michael and Keith. It started out with Greek mythology. The entire exhibit was a history of war in Greece, period after period. There was nothing else, only photos, uniforms and guns. It went from the Persians to the Turks to the Communist revolts that needed squelching. There was nothing about the beginnings of democracy — Solon — Justinin, etc., nothing of the contributions of the historians, philosophers and mathematicians, but only photos. No explanation of the most famous Greeks' contributions to the world.

We both became weary and trudged home to bath and bed.

Sunday, October 6

As Nita surmised, the boys had played one big joke on us. We saw them later in the lobby of the hotel.

"How did you like the exhibition?" They queried and broke into laughter.

Damn Dave. Sometimes he could be a despicable character. He wasted an evening for us!

I left Athens without checking my mail and also before checking the police precinct for the lost airplane bag. I felt moody and uncomfortable the entire weekend because of my failed rendezvous with Robert.

Back at the bus, Hugh told Nita to sit next to Kay so two new American girls could sit together. It was upsetting because of the way it was handled. He did not ask her, as he claimed to have done. He told her to move. Nita stewed all day, upset.

Delphi. Unfortunately. I would have liked someone to accompany me and bring the place to life for me. I read the "$5 a Day" book about it, but it was not enough.

Our student card worked again. In Greece, we consistently got in for half price with it.

The buses were driven to the top of the hill and all we had to do was walk down. We spent the time philosophizing about the place of religion in the world.

The Oracle is a peasant woman, half-starved, half-crazed, who mutters mumbo jumbo that is interpreted by priests. A country guides its people in this way? Skeptics? They are tossed off the cliff by the side of the Oracle's Temple. Aseop died in this manner. I thought about all the other imbecilities, including the crusades, the Inquisition and the witch hunts, all in the name of God and religion.

Does traveling, more than anything else, make people non-believers? Do we lose faith in God or in man? Who builds these edifices?

In Venice there were churches in every open square. In Greece, there were Byzantine churches every few blocks.

Who interprets a religion? Who collects the money from the poor people to place all the gold within those sacred walls?

By the time we paid our drachma for using the washrooms in the museum, we decided against paying 10 more to see the great chariot driver. They did not even have a postcard of the famous statue.

After a while, we had seen enough churches. I missed the one in Venice with the pictures of the Old Testament.

We had seen enough palaces and jewels, and we did not go into the armory at London Tower or the Palace of the Doges in Venice.

At the end of the day we sat outside the Delphi Museum until our bus picked us up to take us home.

Our campsite was a natural camping site. It was called Rocky Red Soil.

We had trouble putting up Fredrika's tent. We had to hammer the pegs in two and three times before they held the tent down.

Nita and Fredrika were not getting along well. They were snapping at each other.

Plumbing? Hide behind bushes. We had limited water in our plastic containers. It had to be used for cooking and washing for eight people.

Nita cooked the eggplant stew with olives and Kazumi added his rice.

I told Robert we had shopped and would prepare a meal for him, but he said Hugh and he bought food together and Loris and June were cooking for him. They had tinned luncheon meat and boiled potatoes. Our meal was gourmet by comparison.

We passed cotton fields, but the plants had skimpier balls than in America. We saw people bent low picking the cotton.

I had not figured out how olives were picked. One at a time?

Monday, October 7

The bus climbed high into the mountains. There were switchbacks for hours on end. Our bus stopped when we met a bus or truck coming in the opposite direction.

I considered buying a water bottle. We needed one.

We stopped by a farm for lunch at 2:30. Girls crossed the road for "bushes" and picked grapes. An hour later we arrived at the Platemon campsite.

On the beach the waves sounded out their rhythm. There were good, clean washing and toileting facilities in the restaurant and bar.

A beautiful castle was on a hill above the campsite.

We set up camp. Some of us went into the water, but it was too cold for me. I added layers of clothing as the evening wore on.

I spoke to Peter and Lynda from England, who bought an ambulance and in five months would be traveling to Australia to live for a while.

I brought Nita to play a game of chess with Peter, but he wasn't good enough. We sat around tables at the bar for the entire evening — from 8 to 12. I tasted wine and anisette. Finally, Leon the bartender, poured Drambouie into a glass for me. That was delicious.

Brazenly, Beryl and I walked out with the two men and the group called out, "Say goodbye at least," which we did.

We separated. Leon walked with me because Beryl decided Leon was too old for her. It was a delightful, romantic walk along the beach in the moonlight. We kissed, but I said no to the all night proposal. Leon was a gentleman, sweet and easily excited, even though I played a passive role.

He continually spoke French and I thought that I wanted to always have someone make love to me in French. He said he had his eye on me, that young girls are not as receptive as mature women.

But he respected my "no."

He became excited and satisfied himself. Afterwards he said, "That was the first time I did that in six months."

I woke Fredrika as I came to bed. During the night she reached over for me to be sure I was there. I laughed as I wondered what would happen the next night night, when I wouldn't be there.

Tuesday, October 8

I had a restless night, and thought how much nicer it would have been if I had said "yes" and enjoyed the warm and cozy night.

I left the tent around 7:00 a.m.

I was given a good morning kiss, a cup of coffee, jam toast — and a rose.

There were sweet, gentle words I could not comprehend, but I relished the thought.

Later, chestnuts were brought out for me.

For dinner Nita and I ate beefsteak and salad. Leon fed Nita as well as me all day. We ate creamy, sweet pastries for dessert, and shredded wheat baklava. Nita discovered she liked Cappuccino.

The most amazing thing was how skinny Leon was. He was loving and highly stimulating. Despite his skinniness I was amazed at the warmth of his body. My feet were their usual icy temperature and soon I was warm and comfortable. Unfortunately, he had worked too hard all day. We both fell asleep very soon.

During the day, Leon had pantomimed the crook of his arm where I would lie — and so I did most of the night. I had missed holding a man's body and receiving its warmth all night long. I did not sleep much after 1:00, but Leon did. I turned frequently and he turned with me — but in the morning he admitted he slept well.

The moonlight guided my way back to my tent.

Wednesday, October 9

After packing up the tent, I went to say goodbye. Leon offered me coffee, but I knew Nita wanted yogurt so we shared one. He made toast for me. He poured liquor and filled a bottle for me. As he presented it he said, "This is good cognac."

This was a typical gesture for this guy.

We got a good start. Robert drove and we got bogged down in the beach sand. Everybody had to get out of the bus. Dave dug under the tires. Rocks were put under the wheels. Everyone pushed! No luck!

With another grand push we were on our way.

We pulled into Salonika at about 12:30. We ate facing the water. Nita and I walked away. She was in search of oil for sun protection. We never found it.

We used the toilets in a small hotel and had a brief interchange with two maids who were crocheting. We admired their handwork and that made them feel good.

We saw a huge caldron of tripe soup. There were interesting foods in this restaurant. We met June, who was furious because the two drivers ate with her group, but did not contribute money for their food.

The campsite had a beautiful layout with a large area for each tent.

The beach area was sandy and clean. The people on the other bus raced into the water for a quick swim.

We headed for town and wandered along the waterfront among the boats. I wanted to go out in one.

Nita kept insisting. "They don't even understand you. You don't speak Greek."

I hung around while one man worked on the light in front of the boat.

"Fraulein, come!" a voice called out distinctly. I came. Nita still hung back in the shadows.

Three boys were working on the boat and invited us to join them. One pointed to the spears to show me what they intended to do.

I sat in front of the boat where the spearman stood ready with his long harpoon. Nita sat in the back of the boat.

The night was perfect, with a bright, full moon shining on the water. It was quiet except for the paddling. They paddled forward, opposite from the way we do it. The boys carried on conversations in Greek. The spearman caught three fish in a couple of hours. There was not much activity in the water. In some areas the water was transparent; in others it had a murky quality. The eels were very small and skinny and slipped through the prongs of the spear. We navigated close to shore so the spear hit the ground to secure the fish.

The first paddler had a broad grin and a pleasant, good-looking face. Later he switched seats and Nita and he carried on conversations in a mixture of many languages, Italian and Spanish mostly. He wanted so much to talk with her.

Two of the boys were named Giovanni and Yoni. The boy who smiled was Yoni. Curso was the third boy.

I spoke to Yoni, who spoke German. He wore a colorful sweater, which enriched his handsome face.

When we docked at 10:30 p.m. he said, "Nein ge schlafen. Essen und trinken."

The boys placed the three fish in my hands and I walked through the streets carrying them. They returned the spears and we continued on to the restaurant.

116

The fish were fried for us. We also had sausage, cabbage salad, tomatoes and chips. They put the large fish on my plate and we were told, "Mangerai."

In the course of the evening, we five people consumed three bottles of Retsina. Neither Nita nor I particularly liked it. We played games with "bottoms up."

Nita became flushed and giggly. "Mommy, you're not supposed to encourage me."

The boys walked us home to our campsite and said goodbye at the gate.

They were so decent and enjoyable and pleasant and generous. It was such a shame that we had a language barrier. Nita and I both had a good night's sleep and no hangover.

That evening is embedded in my memory as one of the most enjoyable times on the journey.

Thursday, October 9

"Photo stop" also means "bushes," I learned.

The lunch stop was on a beach. The other bus people popped out in bathing suits and swam before we were out of our bus. Obviously, they were prepared beforehand for this stop. The other bus had Nicky as the driver. He had made this run before and knew what to expect so he prepared his crew. We had two novices and never knew what to expect.

We changed scenery abruptly several times. We zigzagged through mountains along precarious roads. We passed people working in cotton fields. We passed goat herders and shepherds with flocks of sheep.

We slowed down most often to pass donkey carts on narrow roads. It was a bumpy ride and a few pages of reading made me sleepy.

At the campsite each bus took over one side of the road. Mosquitoes bothered us as we put up the tents, but they were not bad after we sprayed.

We sat in the restaurant and conversed with Peter. Swiss people met so many tourists. So Peter and his girlfriend left Switzerland and traveled and lived in other countries readily. Peter's girlfriend wouldn't mind relocating to New Zealand for a few years.

Later we talked with Elizabeth. They had a good leader in Nick. He was a happy fellow and enjoyed camping. He maintained a happy bus. There were the usual cliques.

One elderly woman was unhappy and wanted to go home. A couple of people were not well-liked, but on the whole there was a unity of spirit.

The people in the other bus enjoyed each beach for swimming and they loved to sing. I'm sorry Nita changed her mind and moved to the bus I was in. She would have enjoyed this crew more.

We fell asleep to the pleasant harmony of their singing. Marya and I spoke awhile before falling asleep.

Marya admitted she never could tent with Fredrika. She would have had a clash long before that day. She noted Fredrika's constant fault finding and blaming others at each raising and pulling down of the tent. This time it was a missing pin from the tent pole. After Nita did all the taking down of the tent, Fredrika came up to me to complain that Nita did not help her carry the tent back to the bus.

Fredrika was a vital, energetic person. She hiked at every opportunity. She swam in all the bathing water. She took cold showers every night. She made a fetish of washing. She bragged that change of temperature did not affect her badly. She could tolerate cold and heat. She bragged that after a good wash she managed to sleep well. She ignored the camp cot stretcher and slept well on the floor. All this was quite amazing for a woman who was 67 years old.

Fredrika worked on prodigious notes all year long that she read and reviewed each day. She knew the names of most of the flowers and of the insect life. She had traveled many of these parts before and sometimes was a guide for us.

However, Nita decided that her behavior was immature. She was completely wrapped up in herself, her needs, her demands. There was no give to her. One could not talk to her or share with her. She would not become involved. She said she had a lover, but was not anxious to marry him, though he wanted it.

Fredrika was a chronic complainer. I had never criticized her so had not gotten into an outright fight. But she was beginning to wear thin and I would gladly have relinquished her as a tent mate. Nita started out with her, but when they fought, I switched with Nita. All through the trip, I wanted to keep Nita happy.

Friends Mentioned in Chapter 19

Beryl, June R., Miriam and Elizabeth. They helped us find alternative lodging.

Leon. He was a generous bartender.

Peter and Lynde. They were Swiss living in England.

Giovanni (Yoni number one), Yoni and Curso. We fished with them at night.

A STOP TO FILL OUR WATER CONTAINERS 18

Al Preller, Insurance Agent
2079 Wantaugh Ave
Wantaugh, NY 11793

Mrs. Ruth Kaufman,
c/a Indiaman
Lourdes Hotel, P.O. Box 68
Mafeking Road,
Quetta, Pakistan.

Dear Ruth:

I have been enjoying your letters and your travelogue. I also dread them because of their usual claims.

1. When a claim occurs you must remember that I have to present it in a logical manner, with full details, to an insurance company. A full description of the incident, preferably on a separate sheet of paper that can be forwarded to the insurance company. That would be very helpful.

And now to our problems:

2. David's appendix operation is not a covered item under your travel policies. They are accident coverage for loss of life and any medical expense an accident would incur. An accident means something caused by violent and external means, such as a fall, blow, broken bone, cut, auto accident, etc. An appendectomy definitely does not fall into this category.

This matter has been referred to Jack so that he may collect this claim under your normal family medical policy.

3. The "Indiaman Travel Insurance" certificate is also being forwarded to Jack for handling. He has the extra copy of the Florence hospital bill. Without it I cannot do much in recovering any monies you have paid in advance for David.

It is just as well that Jack handle this. I believe Trips Unlimited would be able to handle this refund for him.

4. I checked into the possibilities of a refund of the unused portion of David's policy and was not successful. These policies are issued on a fixed charge basis, period.

5. Your August 8 loss of two bags while in Greece presents no problem, but I do need a detailed list of the items lost. Please show each item including the bags themselves, their original cost and when and where purchased. It is the items lost that is of significance, not your expense in replacing them.

6. Your camera presents the same problem. Was it the Canon automatic 35mm? The expense of the new Voigtlander camera has obvious significance as a possession after your trip.

I am adding it to your existing camera floater. That seems to cover our problems. I should have no trouble in recovering your lost camera claim and the lost airplane bags claim if you will forward me the details — mainly your description and values of the items taken.

Jack: I trust Ruth's letter and this reply will be explanatory. Enclosed is the Indiaman insurance rate.

Yours, Alan J. Preller

TWENTY

TURKEY

Friday, October 11

We parked at a camping ground. It was not attractive, no grass or trees, but I slept well. Even the convenient lights were turned off so we had a dark tent.

We packed, planning for the hotel weekend.

In Alexandropolis, we spent 50 drachmas on insect spray, a can of fruit, stuffed grapes leaves, melon, pomegranate and pastries.

At the Greek border I got 50 drachma for 23 lira. What a gyp. At the Turkish border it was 100 drachma for 23 lira.

I tried not to change money at borders.

We found out that only six people in the other bus planned to use the base hotel in Istanbul. Nita and I had been made to feel like outcasts because we had not gone along with the thinking of the passengers on our bus. We did not like Indiaman's choice of hotels. We wanted to save money by finding our own less expensive ones.

How differently the buses presented each situation. In Nick's bus, the passengers felt the choice was up to them. In ours, we felt like outcasts because we did not accept the options presented to us.

Where was the respect for individuality?

Mail stop. There were three letters from my mother and one from Aunt Minnie.

Adam mailed four letters on 9/26, 9/27, 10/2 and 10/8.

Beryl, June, Claire and Elizabeth joined us. For ten lira each night we stayed in one room. It was a three-bunk dormitory with sink and free, hot showers.

We saved 102 lira by sleeping at this hostel. We showered and dressed and looked for a place to eat.

We entered one restaurant where the waiter spoke English. We ordered salad and shish kebob. We paid for that. He also brought strawberry wine, apples, grapes, baklava and Turkish coffee, all free. There was such generosity on the part of the restaurant owner.

We thought: we must to go back and get the bottles of wine he said he would give us.

Ergoun, who studied English for nine months, took us for a walk to the Bosforus River. He paid our entrance fee to the park.

We met a family of three girls at the waterfront. They were dressed like dolls. Their father gave us creamy pastries. We conversed for a while.

We walked with Ergoun for a couple of hours.

Ergoun said, "I will meet you in the bazaar tomorrow. I promise to take Nita to the Chess Club on Sunday." So far, so good.

Saturday, October 12

I woke at dawn to the Turkish call to worship, which involved colorful chanting. I had had a comfortable night's sleep and we had a leisurely start to our day. I drank tea while writing letters.

We wasted time in a bank exchanging money. Then we were off to the Grand Bazaar.

We tried to buy a pair of earrings for Nita but had no luck. We did see a pair in antique, 24 karat gold, in an ancient setting for $20. Nita said no.

However, she did persuade me to buy a suede suit for $23. I hoped to mail it off soon.

Jewelry, copperware, carpets, furniture, material — we saw only a small part of the bazaar, though we were there for three hours.

We sampled food and everything tasted superb. True Turkish cooking is delicious. We conquered the language problem easily. We walked into the kitchen and looked into the pots in restaurants. I pointed to food we wanted.

We traveled by bus to Dolomache Palace. The entrance fee was 15 lira ($1.50) each. Elizabeth decided to go in. She spent two hours there and liked it. Nita and I sat in the vestibule and waited.

Later we met Ergoun, who guided the four of us to the Sahara Restaurant. A huge tray of salads was presented to us. We drank Ouzo Rackquet wine. We each contributed money to Ergoun for our meal.

June and Beryl had dates and left us at 7:00 p.m.

We were home by midnight.

Sunday, October 13

Ergoun arrived at 8:00 a.m. as promised.

The first stop was the Blue Mosque. Meditation was lovely in this hallowed hall. It was a magnificent structure; the stained glass reflected blue and there was no gold.

We looked around the grounds of the archeological museum, and wandered through gardens waiting for the Topkapi Palace Museum to open. We traipsed around various rooms from 10:00 to 1:00, three hours, and I still missed the embroidery room, a couple of others and the harem rooms because of restoration.

As we wandered around the "Jewel" rooms, a guard came over and spoke to us. He volunteered information on the history of Turkey. Suddenly he appeared in another room and showed us a white ruby and black diamonds.

He let me know he was 43, unmarried and working until 5:00 that evening. He sent us off to see the summer palaces.

This was my idea of a palace room. I would have loved to live and make love in this room. Comfortable large pillows were arranged on the floor and gorgeous tapestries lined the walls.

As I was ready to head back, the same guard raced over to me. He had searched me out. We finalized the date for the evening.

Sababhaddim taught himself English years ago and was working on learning German now. He was a police guard, but he studied Turkish history and the palace relics so that he could become a guide in the Topkapi Palace.

He earned $100 a month as a civil service worker with a 9-5 workday.

He had held this job for 15 years.

Ergoun took us to a post office, but we could not mail packages on Sunday.

Ergoun, Nita and I ate rose-flavored jello at a pudding shop. Ergoun took us to a coffeehouse called the Flea House, where the game damar is played. There were hundreds of men in a large smoked-filled room. Nita and I were the only women in the place. Thirteen billiard tables were in active use. Damar, like checkers, is a tile game using cards. Finally, Nita found the chess players. She watched happily for hours.

Nita met a French professor who wrote a letter to Lucien for her. He discussed politics with Nita.

We arrived home close to 5:00 p.m. I had a hot shower before Sababhaddim arrived.

He took me to a restaurant where we ordered stuffed squash and eggplant.

We strolled to the river and took a boat up the Bosforus River for a couple of hours. We missed the last return boat.

On the way back we stopped in a teahouse and had chai by the river. We rode a bus back to the Hilton Hotel. He wanted to show it to me. I wished we could have gone to the top floor to see the view of the city.

He invited me to spend the night with him, but I explained to him that it was the wrong time of the month. I still wanted to be with him for the full night. So bravely I set forth the proposition that I would lie in his arms, but keep my dress on. He accepted! And bless him, I did just that. He was an unbelievable gentleman.

We took two buses to get to his home. We passed the old Roman aqueduct and the high, thick walls of the city. We walked blocks down steep cobbled streets, narrow streets with old wooden houses. I was determined to see the inside of a home. Now I could see his. In the entrance way he exchanged his shoes for slippers, walked up a few steps and ducked his head because of the low ceiling overhead. We passed through another hallway. Three bedrooms led off from this hall, and the toilet as well.

His room had a chest with blankets piled on top. His narrow bed took up most of the space. Hooks hung on the wall for clothing. There were pictures of his mother. There was a double set of curtains on the window. One window was broken and a stovepipe extended through the other. Books were piled high on the small table by the bed. His notebook was filled with German, which he was working hard on and learning by himself. The teacher in me admired his neat, careful, studious work.

He told me that most of his clothes and belongings were in the home of his sister, who lived in a bigger house.

When his mother was alive she lived in the large room. She had died six months ago in her 70s. His two brothers and sisters were married. He stayed home and supported his mother.

In the large room now lived "the old woman" who owned the house. Her son lived downstairs with his wife and two children, ages 7 and 10.

The toilet room had a squat toilet, water and brushes by it to keep it clean. The sink had a cold-water tap. He changed into wooden sandals in case of splashing.

There were rags and cloths hanging in the toilet room. No paper at all. Why? "We do not use paper. We wash," he told me.

He offered me tea or coffee, but I did not see the stove area.

When I returned to the room, clean sheets and a clean blanket were on the bed. I lay down and he asked permission to undress. It was a wonderful night. He was an affectionate and truly lovable person. It was unusual for me because I took a very passive role; I relaxed and enjoyed being there with him. His pleasure was in loving and he did get excited, but by some magnificent means of control, he managed to break away from me before spilling a drop. It was hard for me to believe it. I turned my back as he requested and he took care of himself.

He wanted to let himself go and love me and kiss me, but I was embarrassed in my state. He was embarrassed about how he achieved his satisfaction. But none of this put a blight on the warmth of the night or his ardor. Permission asked at each stage and granted. But I had to smile as I realized I had dress, pants, garter belt and stockings on all night. It was madness. This was a night of lovemaking I would long remember with good feelings.

He made me promise that I wouldn't tell anyone because it was blight on his manhood.

At 4:30 a.m. there was the call to prayer and for at least 30 minutes I heard the actual prayers.

We were close to several mosques. Each man said the prayers at a different pace.

Monday, October 14

We reluctantly rose at 6:00 a.m. My anxiety was that the others at home would worry!

We returned and I learned Beryl slept. Nita came in at 1:00 a.m., June at 6:00 a.m.

I packed hurriedly and forgot to pack my yellow nightgown. Nita and I met Sabab for a breakfast of sweet pudding and milk and hurried to our bus. No one was ready. We paced back and forth saying "goodbye" and "we'll write" over and over. It was a reluctant parting.

Nita had spent time with 25-years-old Ergoun. He ran the silver shop at the bazaar with his brother.

Nita met his family. She said they were great; parents, grandparents, sister, nieces and nephews. Nita admired a plate a small niece had painted so the generous little girl gave it to Nita.

Then Ergoun took Nita back to the same restaurant we had eaten at before and told her to select from a new menu. Nita enjoyed herself with a new choice of foods.

Ergoun took her to the Chess Club where Nita also enjoyed herself. Then he got bored and took her to first one nightclub and then another. She had a great evening. I'm so happy she had a good time. I had such a desire for all to go well with her.

Beryl told us she finally watched her belly dancers.

June R. met a student on the Bosphorus boat. She told him she wanted to try marijuana and he took her to a pot party of young college men. June had a high night.

I thought each one of us found what we were looking for in Istanbul.

Monday, October 14

Ruth writes:

Dear Mom and Minnie,

We are driving away from our three nights and two days in Istanbul. Nobody wants to leave. Each one of us had a fabulous time in her own way. The tour hotel was 44 lira a night. We found a six bunk dorm for ten a night, saving 102 liras nearly $10.

We found the Turkish people friendly, generous and anxious to please. Ergoun, speaking English for nine months, attached himself to us Friday night at dinner. The proprietor gave us shish kebob and salad and beer as ordered. In addition, apples, grapes, homemade strawberry wine, and baklava and coffee. FREE.

That was only the beginning. We walked through the park and he paid our entrance fees.

Back to the bazaar. No earrings for Nita, but not because we didn't try.

A great unique city. Very, very different in atmosphere from the continent. Men hauling atrocious sized packages on their backs. Foods are different and well-cooked.

That evening Ergoun surprised us and took four of us to another great restau-

rant with a huge tray of new foods. The men at the table next to us sent over melon and beer. We sent nuts to them. Singing music enriched our evening.

Ergoun gave Nita a puzzle ring, which occupied her all night.

Home at midnight.

Sunday we went to the Blue Mosque to meditate early. Nita had a short dress on and they gave her a robe to cover her up.

We heard the prayers at 4:30 a.m. At the Topkapi Palace Museum we saw the sword that was used in the movie. Three hours in there.

After giving me historical background and showing us white rubies and black diamonds a guard made a date with me.

My Sabab took me on a moonlight boat trip up the Bosphorous River. He was an unselfish, self-educated English speaking man. Nobody wanted to leave Istanbul.

Monday, October 14

Our bus friends went to the Pirlanta Hotel, our original Indiaman address. Only the water pump broke down.

We had a late start and were not on the road until after 9:00 a.m. I dozed most of our trip and made up for missing sleep the night before.

The scenery was, for practically the first time, boring, only plains and fields and occasional flocks of sheep, goats, geese and ducks.

We stopped in a village. A man washed his feet at the fountain. Women wore scarves around their faces and their flowery dresses tied between their legs.

The bus climbed up a steep hill studded with shops. We were searching for a place to have lunch. We bought nuts, half a loaf of bread, butter and yogurt.

A group of grubby boys with shoe shine kits stood gaping at the bus. We wondered why they weren't in school.

Our lunch stop had a roadside table. We listened to music from a nearby restaurant. It was a pleasant place.

We passed many donkey carts. Bullocks were working in the fields.

I wanted a picture of a family in a cart with children but I was too slow and missed it.

By evening we were on the end of the peninsula. The Royal Navy War monument was our destination. We passed miles of barbed wire and pillboxes and huge wall fortifications.

The Dardenelle Straits is an important waterway for many countries. This area was fought over many times. We passed the straits. We would have natural camping this night. Marya, a nurse, attended to Kay, who had tripped over a tent rope and broken her arm.

Mrs. Minister tented with Fredrika now.

At last, Nita and I were together as rightfully we should have been. We were both happy about it. Nita could not take Fredrika at all, and I was beginning to lose patience with her. I would have broken soon.

So tent #13 was now ours.

Tuesday, October 15

Nita writes:

Dear Family,

Too, too fantastic things have been happening. Too fantastic people I've been meeting. Yoni, Yoni and Curso on a midnight harpoon fishing trip and fish and a retsina party afterwards.

Ergoun and his family in Istanbul with "Oriental dancing" in two nightclubs. Many nameless people like the restaurant owner giving us homemade wine, grapes, apples, baklava just because he liked us, the people in the villages as we pass waving and smiling — I feel less like a monkey-watcher and more like a person.

I didn't go in to see the rubble of rocks called Troy. I didn't go wild over Corinth or Delphi. "What's wrong with you, child? Are you anti-cultural? Don't you get a spine tingling thrill every time you see a headless statue or a broken marble wall? Can't you revel in the glories of the past? What's wrong with you, child?"

So it goes.

Love to you , Nita

We went to Anzac Cove. There was no sign of war except for the many cemeteries. Further up the road we saw trenches. There were some pillboxes.

The New Zealand war monument was located at Lone Pine Sulva Bay.

It was rather moving to be there on the actual spot after all those years of reading about it. Anzac Day is celebrated in Australian schools. World War I was the first time Australian troops fought as a country. It was a terrible disaster. It was a massacre by the Turks. Kemel, the Turkish leader, led the Turkish troops here. It is a historic place for them as well.

Ataturk, as leader, became a war hero. When he formed his republic he moved the capital from Istanbul to Ankara because European forces occupied Istanbul until 1923 as a war punishment. He could control the country better because Ankara was more centrally located.

At 10 a.m. we crossed the Aegean Sea on a ferry to Marmore to go to Asia.

In Canakkale, horse and buggies were used for transportation.

At Troy, Nita and I refused to pay the entrance fee. We walked along the fence and viewed the area. I bought postcards. Some people bought maps and tried to follow life as it was in those times. Nine different periods of Troy have been discovered. Schlieman worked on this site and uncovered ancient relics.

Two different people offered to sell me ancient coins for only 5 lira, or 40 cents. I didn't buy them. A mistake? Were they real or fake?

The next stop was Pergamon at 5:00 p.m. It was worth stopping at this site. This archeological site had depth, height and interest. You could locate the rooms and see the stadium situated on the mountaintop. A view of another acropolis was visible in the city below.

Papers explaining these ruins were handed out. I hated this method of touring. We were told, "Get out and look around." I didn't know what I was looking at or why.

Michael saw grubby, dirty people in dusty towns. I knew they had a fetish about cleanliness. Five times a day they washed. It is part of their religion to keep clean. They washed their feet before prayer.

In the evening we camped at "Beauty Bath."

We were preparing to sleep out and set up our tents and were happy. Nita and I began cooking our hunks of meat over a charcoal grill owned by the restaurant. It was unusual for us to buy meat in this country. It was a treat.

We cut up potatoes and added a lump of butter and rolled it all up in tinfoil.

Then the lightning and rains came. All of a sudden, our tent was flat.

Nigel, an angel, arrived as we needed him and helped us get the poles up. We never did get all the tent pegs in. We jammed the bedding into the tent. It was a bit too late. Everything got wet. It was a mucky mess and my clothing was soaked.

Oh well, all the decisions we made couldn't always be right.

The waiter from the restaurant dragged our belongings into the shelter and we finished our meal.

People raved about the hot bath. I changed into my bathing suit and went there. First, we washed down in a room with a small waterfall of hot water, then on to the next room to a large pool. From 8:00 p.m. until 9:30 there were about 20 people splashing in the warm and comfortable water. This was a good example of the hot springs where Romans set up their towns, always where water was available and flowing.

Our moustached manager joined Ester, Beryl, Peter and Mattis, the Swiss couple, and me. We had some rough water play. We were lifted up and thrown back in. We drank bottles of Rocket and the manager brought in food, finally. It was a tray of grapes, cheese, halvah, bread and olives. I was fed the grapes like in a Roman orgy. Peter's rough play broke off the button on my suit.

The police came and watched us for a while. At 10:15, one showed me his watch.

By about 2:30 I could not keep my eyes open and the Turk rubbed me down with the towel and took me into the washing room to wash my feet. He sat me on the straw mats and tried one last time. "Eine Eine" "Quickie." No! No! No! At that moment he could have overpowered me. Luckily, he didn't.

He escorted me back to the tent like a gentleman. I was fortunate. Pure luck.

Later the Swiss came by, yelling "Up everybody."

We heard loads of noise. Later a scream: "I've got a bloody nose!"

I thought it was nothing, just three drunken blokes.

But the next day I learned that while Ester was changing, two men grabbed her face and gave her the bloody nose. Her husband was nearby. She screamed. It was an actual fight.

Wednesday, October 16

There was great excitement as we learned Ester's story. Our manager came by with the bar bill for the food and drink we had the night before. Ester refused to pay.

She said, "I felt he got his money's worth from his evening's entertainment."

The bar bill was not paid. The guilty party was discovered. He swam with us for a while the previous night. I didn't like him at all.

We heard that two guys entered tents of other bus people. Those in the tents were English folk, too, but they didn't scream. They efficiently rid themselves of the men who had intruded.

Riding on the bus I had my first hangover. My head ached and I took an aspirin. Rain was heavy at intervals during the day; sun, rain, sun, rain, and to vary it a bit, for a time in the town of Izmir we had sun during the rain.

I used a WC outside the mosque. I saw men inside and started to walk away. They told me to come in. One stood at the urinal, unconcerned as I walked into the booth.

I'm getting used to stand-up toilets and stoop rather comfortably. I still needed paper, but appreciated that the system of using water instead might be cleaner IF soap were provided for hand washing afterwards.

Pamukkle. This was a motel stop for many. Not for us. Pamukkle was another outdoor, no tent camp, where an earthquake left sulfur springs, pools of water in lovely patterns of rock. Romans built their cities where they found these warm springs. We spent only two hours in the natural-springs outdoor swimming pool.

Wednesday, October 16

Nita writes:

Dear David,

Why no letter in Istanbul? You know we looked forward to it.

We stopped last night at Pamukkle, between Istanbul and Turkey, and I think this is a place you would have loved. It is a volcanic mountain and on the surface are the weirdest formations I have ever seen. It looked like cement, but it was really sulfur. There are old Roman ruins everywhere, because this was once a major city. But the best parts are the baths. Everywhere were natural springs and pools of steaming hot water. Luscious colors were displayed. I spent hours just pattering around in an absolutely enormous natural outdoors Roman bath. I couldn't get out. I slept outside overlooking the magnificent ruins. It was too lovely.

In our last stop in Greece, near Alexandropolis, Mommy and I had the greatest experience. We went harpoon fishing at midnight. We were walking around the tiny village and three boys were preparing the boat to go out. They invited us to join them. So we naturally went. Their names were Yoni, Yoni and Curso, and none of them spoke English. But young Yoni spoke German and Curso spoke a little Italian. So we managed. After a couple of hours, we had three fish and a crab that was thrown back into the water. We sat in a little café and they prepared the fish and we ate them. I drank liquor called Retzina, tastes horrible, but boy did I get giddy.

So far I still think Mommy and I were better off on our own. Since the tour began we haven't made a single great new friend. Our routine prevents it.

We arose at dawn, close to 5 a.m. Our chores were taking down the tent, folding the sleeping bags, cooking breakfast and getting into the bus by 7. We ride in the bus until 10:30 when we shop for lunch. We ride in the bus for another two hours and then from 1-2 we eat lunch. We ride in the bus from 2 to 6 and hope to find a camping site by then so we don't have to set up our tents in the dark. At 6 we cook dinner, set up camp, maybe take a cold shower and then go to sleep.

Is this living? Remember and think about our invitation for the family to meet us in India.

Thursday, October 17

We awoke at 5:30 and watched the sun rise. For breakfast we had grapes and a sweet pudding similar to farina and halvah.

We were still passing cotton fields with colorful peasants working and grape vines. We saw many donkeys. The women carried children on their backs. Women sometimes had trousers on. When we stopped to shop for lunch, we settled for yogurt and halvah.

The lunch stop was by Edimir Lake. I wanted to take a picture of the mountains and clouds through the delicate bamboo shoots.

The bus water hose broke and we had a delay until it could be replaced.

Everyone filled the water casks by the town pump. Each container was for eight people. I saw a woman with a donkey, who had a hatchet in her arm and a scythe knife in her belt.

We camped in a natural setting by a stream. We didn't use the tent for warmth and it got cold at night.

The roads had deep ruts made by streams of water and it was a difficult driving day. It was my turn to sit in the front seat. But Hugh's conversation with Michael, which showed his attitude, was disturbing and killed much of my pleasure. All Hugh looked forward to was our Bombay stop and his plane ticket back to London.

The group spoke to Hugh about changing the route. We spent a short time in Konya, a sightseeing town. We rushed on to Goreme to see caves where early Christians lived underground to avoid persecution. Cyril and Keith were staying in a hotel in Konya, rather than rushing on. But our speaking to our leaders did not result in a change in our schedule.

We arrived in Ankara Sunday night; I couldn't go to the post office. We always managed to arrive in town — Athens, Istanbul and now Ankara — on weekends. Museums were closed on Sundays. Banks and post offices were closed and this was our official mail stop.

Friday, October 18

Konya. Medlava was the founder of the religious sect Whirling Dervishes. We learned about it in the Medlava Museum.

Nick had organized his bus so that his passengers were happy and compatible. He arranged two hours at Konya for a good stop and sightseeing.

He suggested that a person on his coach tell his passengers about the sight seeing tours.

Nick was interested in saving money. Leaders on Nick's bus pointed out inexpensive restaurants. The group made a kitty for meals. Four people were given the responsibility of shopping and cooking breakfast and dinner for the entire group. It was a rotating system. For lunch, everyone was on his own.

Seats on the bus were also a rotating system and were completely changeable.

The bus, under Nick's leadership, was far superior to ours. It was all young people, with only one woman over 40.

Nita was originally scheduled to ride in that bus. What a shame she changed to the one I was on.

Nick had made this trip before and he didn't mind driving. Robert didn't want the expensive bus used as a "bloody restaurant." Of course it was everyday, anyway.

We were up at 5:30 a.m. and there was no gorgeous sunrise. Cyril was asked to lecture us about Konya. He refused. He was a professor, capable, but only interested in himself.

Konya was originally was a monastery of Whirling Dervishes. Ataturk outlawed it, but people were still praying there. In 1927 it was made into a museum. It was different from anything we had seen so far. It contained manuscripts, a bookstand of inlaid pearl and gold incense burners.

But these museums did not offer knowledge of the religion. The museum included many colorfully draped coffins with headpieces on the top surface.

We still needed a post office to mail the suede suit, papers and pages with coins attached, two packages of slides and two undeveloped rolls of film.

We located a pizza house in Turkey. The dough was thinner, crisper and much better than ours. It was a meat and onion mixture and baked in an oven.

We bought a kerosene lamp. I was afraid that a candle could set fire to the tent. Perhaps we could read or write by our gas lamp.

There were no evening singsongs or group discussions at night; in fact, no activity at all. Nita and I both missed it.

So we headed for bed and the dark. There was nothing to do in the dark. Unfortunately. What a waste.

The people in this area grew loads of turnips, mostly as fodder for animals. Not many turnips were sold in the stores.

Where were the sesame seeds growing? Where did they get all the sugar for their sweets?

Sultanhac was a camel caravan stop. It hasn't been used for the past 80 years.

The first touch of autumn color appeared and made a beautiful scene against the mountainside. An eye-appealing blue sky framed puffy white clouds. Suddenly there was one house in vast nothingness. This day we saw mostly compounds of neat houses and grapevines in oases of greenery.

Our savory evening meal was oxtail soup, potatoes, onion and squash cooked in real butter.

I joined a long table of Turkish men at the outdoor restaurant. I bought a bottle of wine for the others to drink. There was wine and Rocky, but I recalled the last hangover and decided against it. We listened to the Saas, a sitar-like instrument, played by a professional teacher. Spoons were clapped together with singing. We danced with the men. They would have liked me to dance all night long, but my breath gave out.

My newest friend took me on my first motorcycle ride up and down the mountain road. I enjoyed it. I was tired and crawled into my sleeping bag under the stars. He tucked me into bed, fully clothed, and kissed me goodnight.

In the early morning my escort took me mountain climbing to see some church caves I had missed the night before. Paintings decorated the walls.

My friend took me back to his restaurant and he gave us breakfast. He gave Nita and me postcards, so I didn't take photos. He bestowed one goodbye kiss.

Then we boarded the bus to Ankara.

ANKARA

Saturday, October 19

Turkish cooking is the best in the world. Stuffed peppers and dolmas are what I ordered most of the time. I also had tripe soup, which was prepared in a huge cauldron with tiny chopped tripe with sauces and flavors added. I went crazy over the sweet flavor of it. It was a specialty in this area.

In town we stopped and a lady offered me a quince. We stewed it and then added grapes and sugar. There were plenty of quince and pomegranate trees around. We ate a lot of grapes, halvah and yogurt. They all tasted much better in this country.

Food was important. Good markets always were first on my sightseeing list in all countries.

We arrived in early afternoon and set out on our own to locate our own hotel, after getting our mail. I felt good because we received 11 letters.

Exploring the area for a decent low-priced hotel could be fun, if there was ample time. The group rate at the tour's choice hotel was 20 lira a night. We obtained ours for 8.75 lira, less than half of theirs.

Our hotel room was freshly painted pink and blue, and clean, clean, clean, with good sheets and a lovely, warm comforter on the bed. There were no bugs. We heard later that the base hotel had bugs and was dirty, but they had hot water and we didn't.

Sunday, October 20

Nita writes:

Dear Daddy and Siblings,

We only received five letters out of about 20 that we wrote. How ghastly. But it is good to hear that at least you write, even if we haven't been receiving anything.

Obviously, we reached Ankara and received your letters, Daddy. Thank you. Comfort and Robinson, our friends from Biafra, who live in London, wrote also.

Wendi, how is Mr. Haulenbeck? Watch out, he's an absolute writing disciplinarian and will probably be harsh on your laxity. But he will do wonders for your writing, if you don't get too discouraged. Please tell me the rest of your schedule and about your teachers and dancing.

Lori, how's school coming? Is the orphanage work very different now that you are getting paid for it? Probably not, you should have gotten paid for it years ago. How is your dancing coming along?

Dave, a caddy. How great. Isn't it hard work? Have you gotten used to home life and school yet? You wouldn't like this tour at all. We are always on the move.

Daddy, can't you tell from our letters what kind of times we've been having?

Don't you read? Before the tour we were having fantastic times, meeting people, going places, and seeing things. It was unreal.

Since the tour we have had to settle down to days of riding in a bus filled with dull, unpleasant people, with a few exceptions. Our nights consist of setting up camp, cooking and trying to keep warm in bed.

But during the hotel stops in the major cities it was like old times. We wander off alone or sometimes with Beryl and June, and, oh, the wonderful things we do.

We wandered around the market and bought olives and sweets. We were on our way to the Hittite archeological museum and didn't know the way. A woman, who spoke English, took us there. She invited us to her home afterwards.

The museum played mellow music, giving it atmosphere in the two rooms.

It had a good layout and interesting relics from before 300 BC. Well worth l lira or 8 cents.

We spent about two hours in the Ankara home.

We met the woman's beautiful 13-year-old daughter named Bouquet, and her 10-year-old son, Sadu. Her husband works in a bank. She is a teacher. Her family and home radiated warmth and happiness.

We understood Poppa's partial German. Mommy practiced her two years of high school German with him.

Momma spoke English.

She fed us cakes, sweet pudding and tea while we perused photo albums. He had been a soldier when he was 18-20. He was moustached, slim and very handsome.

At 6:00 p.m. he laid out his prayer rug and beads and prayed in front of us, davaning. Momma dressed in a scarf around her head and took her prayer rug into the bedroom out of sight. They have three bedrooms, one stand-up bathroom and a full bathroom with bath and shower.

The chairs were comfortable and there was a radio. They want a television set from America or England and need to know the cost of one. Can you send me shipping costs from some manufacturer?

These Turkish people are the kindest, most generous people we have met yet. I must be careful not to praise a possession of theirs too lavishly, or they will give it to me. This happened in Istanbul when I visited Ergoun's family and I am still carrying around a plate with a cat on it that I said I admired.

Ergoun also gave me a puzzle ring that, when I am in a sadistic mood, I will send home to frustrate you all.

Love, Nita

Turkey was a wild and wonderful place. In 1920 Ataturk outlawed Purda, seclusion of women, and the Moslem custom of veiling faces, but it obviously didn't stick. We were always the only women in sight in the villages. The occasional woman in the field always had a shawl covering everything but her eyes and nose. The dresses were bright reds and greens and at the bazaar we saw flowered patterns. The pant dresses, which people on our bus made fun of, I really liked. They looked like bloomers and were very practical, as well as good looking.

The school children wore starched, long black smocks with bright white collars that were made of satiny material.

The barrenness of the country made it uncomfortable for what we delicately called "bush stops." Not a single bush in sight. We tried resorting to hiding behind small hills, but often we merely had our back discretely turned away.

Nita writes:

Dear Family,

Guess what? I finally found someone on the bus that plays chess. Well, I wouldn't exactly call it plays, but his middle game isn't too bad. Maybe I can talk him into learning some openings from me.

By the way, it is Willy, half of the newly wed Scottish couple. His wife is Chris. They are absolutely dolls, and about our best friends on this trip.

Aha. We just made a bush stop, men on one side of the bus and ladies on the other.

Oh, we just came upon another unfinished portion of road. Occasionally, we had to stop and wait while the workmen made a road for us. It gives one a feeling of importance.

My feet were still frozen from this past night, even though it is now noon. We look up at snow-capped mountains and shudder. This is what we will camp in tonight.

Just think, not even a week ago we were swimming outdoors.

Please tell us what is going on in America. News is almost impossible to get. I probably won't learn who is president for weeks after the election. The two new ghastly Americans on the bus are both 'go-get 'em' Nixoners. Ugh!

Mommy and I are the 'brunt' of the bus because of our position on Vietnam; our refusal to disdain those "lazy no-good niggers;" and our view that these "uncivilized natives" in the countries we pass do not have inferior intellects. Woe to this bus. We love traveling in spite of them.

Affectionately, Nita

One fantastic place we stopped at Gorme, a city of caves. In the third and fourth century when Christianity was outlawed, people hid in the hills. The rock was soft from volcanoes and they tunneled into rock and carved homes to live in. Many of these homes became elaborate apartments. These were the first Christian churches and houses. They constructed churches with intricate architecture right into the mountainside. Many frescos still survive on the walls and ceilings. The landscape looked like we were on the moon. The atmosphere was like living in a science fiction movie.

Ruth writes:

Hello,

When do I stop calling you family?

Did the packages from Florence with the sweaters ever arrive? Have you been getting the heavy envelopes with coins from Rome? Do our letters embarrass you? Do you want them to stop? Do our letters bother your conscience?

David, how do you sleep nights? Don't you have nightmares about broken promises? Didn't all your experiences and disappointment at mail stops change your attitude about not writing? Do you want us to tell you about Niren when we meet him? Tell us why should we continue to write to you.

Olga and Minnie and other friends manage to write to every mail stop. Why don't you keep your promises?

And Lori, should we look for jewelry for you in Afghanistan? Should we continue to call you sister and daughter? Should we? Why?

And Wendi. Same to you.

In Ankara I had a letter from Adam, one from Jack, but not the kids, and five friends wrote from the states.

We decided against the hotel the tour arranged for us and found a cleaner room, even if it was non-English speaking management and clientele. It was less than half the price of the hotel the tour chose. It had freshly painted rooms, and clean. 8.75 lira is less than 70 cents a person for the night. Cold showers though.

Then the lady who showed us the way to the museum invited us to her home. We spent two hours with her family. The wife speaks English and her husband speaks German. We ate puddings and pastries and chai (tea) while we perused photo albums. There is a daughter, 13, and a son, 10.

At 6:00 p.m. they lay down their prayer rugs. The husband prayed in front of us. But his wife prayed in her bedroom. They were hospitable people. We liked Ankara, but we only had 18 hours there.

Most of the passengers in our bus spend the free hours in towns in bars drinking. We are the exceptions, invited into the homes of people.

We have our minor infections and Nita's foot is bandaged. She needed a "bush" stop several times today, but all in all, so far our health is O.K.

Look into our need for malaria pills. Some say yes, some say no. Some have started taking them. See about the once a week pills and send them to us, please, if we need them.

We are heading for Anatolia. The cold and snow region. Yozgat tonight. Erguzum has snow. Rain today as we drive. The food gets scarcer, the flies more plentiful and rougher days ahead.

We are warned, "Stay away from Persian men and buggy hotels."

Will we survive?

I could tell you about the school children we see, and the cotton fields with the small cotton balls compared to what we have in the states. It is not easy getting the photo shots I want from a moving bus. Our drivers couldn't care less about photo stops. So I take second-rate photographs and hope for the best.

Love, Ruth

Sunday, October 20

Ruth writes:

Dear Adam,

I wish you would think about dropping in on the family. We would love to hear from the children. Lori has a paying job at the orphanage now. Wendi is taking dancing lessons. David is caddying and baby sitting. He earned $17 one weekend.

Dogs brayed and barked all night long and I couldn't sleep. Two nights in a row without sleep. So far you're still my best correspondent.

I miss you, Adam.

Yours with love, Ruth

Sunday, October 20

6:30 p.m. We were camped in a natural setting high in the mountains. By the next day we expected snow. There were icicles hanging from the tent in the morning. This kind of camping was meant to be done in twos; even down sleeping bags remained cold.

We bought a kerosene lamp because our flashlight had been lousy. We bought a plastic container for water.

Dinner was a feast of onions, green peppers, tomatoes, squash, stew meat and rice. For dessert, we had stewed quince and raisins. I was fortunate that Nita cooked for us.

We were sitting in the bus because it was too cold out and too early to go to bed. Rising time was 5:30 a.m., only we hadn't seen sunrises that I could photograph. We told jokes and discussed movies we had seen.

We heard about the group that ate uncooked sheep's liver. Parasitic eggs of ticks reside in sheep's liver. Nice to be told after supper.

Water was boiled at least three minutes to sterilize it. All apples were peeled. This was rough country.

Monday, October 21

5:30 rising time.

Nita and I decided that in Lahore and Delhi we would go to the youth hostels. June and Beryl planned to join us.

A crowd of schoolboys surrounded the bus everywhere we stopped.

Nita used hot water in the water flask, but it leaked.

Tuesday, October 22

I had never been so miserable in all my life – any second, any second I would cry, my filled eyes would overflow and I would cry. Oh, this abominable self-pity! No, I would not cry. I would not let one of those horrid people see me weaken. I would be strong and hard. My hatred of this tour would carry me through. It made me miserable.   Why was I so unhappy? Couldn't I just envelop myself in the joy of traveling and ignore my companions? Couldn't I be the loner — the unmindful loner of old? No, this could not be! Not in Turkey, in Iran, anywhere where the men follow in groves and stare and laugh. No, I was not strong enough.

We saw Agri-Mount Ararat where traces of Noah's Arc were found. It was a volcanic mountain lake with ice all year round, 5,165 metric high, or 15,000 feet.

We saw women in fields collecting dung in baskets hung on their backs.

Police came with rifles. I was on the bus. One came on the bus, shook hands and said something in Turkish. Two policemen stood outside our tent. We fell asleep next to all the noisy tents. It rained all night.

Ruth writes:

Dear Jack,

You know how much we have written. We want so much to share the wonderment, our experiences with you all at home.

When you write, "I can't tell if you are enjoying your trip," I can't understand it. We both burst at the seams with our adventures, daily life changes, people, languages, and friendships. The only sore point is the fact that we don't hear from our family.

In Ankara I received 12 letters. Yes, I do have friends who do write. Received your three letters dated September 1, 10 and October 9. Now I will refer to them.

So happy to receive them. Sounds like you had a great and successful vacation. Glad. Yes, I got the letter from Canada in Russia. Yes, we are having fun. In the letter I received in London you refer to a 12 page Canadian letter. It did not come.

Deposit check from health insurance into my teacher's credit union to help pay off my loan.

Please, find out if Roslyn Savings can mail me a Letter of Credit to use from February to July. That's when I run out of money. I met a couple in the bazaar in Istanbul who use only that and never have to worry about getting or losing money. Traveler's checks are expensive to use. We lose money on every one we cash.

I wrote to Gino in Italy to get a letter from the doctor. I'm sure that it will reach you eventually.

Lori, I'm glad that the orphanage is finally paying you after all the years you have worked there. Do you work with Sister Carla? Now write and tell us the names of your teachers. Did you get the fur hat we sent to you?

Wendi, who are your teachers? Tell us about your dancing lessons. Did you get the fisherman sweaters yet? Like the grandpa doll from Russia?

Dave, great about your caddy job. Glad to hear about the money you earned. The photos of you in London are good. Nita goes crazy for a game of chess or cards. She misses you.

The last few days have been full of wonder. I don't know where to begin. Turkey is a magic name to Nita and me. We found all the Turkish people generous and friendly. People offer to pay for our taxis, pay for our meals and escort us every-where. The taxis are called dalmas and anybody can jump in and pay.

Imagine sleeping under a pearled bedspread or sitting on an emerald and ruby throne.

The mosaics on the tiled walls of the mosques and the ancient paintings in the early Christian churches are all unusual. So much to see and so much to learn.

Love, Ruth/Mom

Friends Mentioned in Chapter 20

Rabin and Hayati Uzuner. They were a bank clerk and teacher. We spent an evening with this family in Ankara, and enjoyed Bouquet, 14, and Sadu, 10.

Sabahaddin Telligoglu. He was the Topkapi guide in Instanbul and a good friend.

Ergun Oztuber. He was a silversmith who spent time and money on Nita. She visited his home.

Ester, Peter, Beryl, and Mattis. We played together in the hot baths.

FOOD VENDOR 19

MAKING SHOES 20

WEAVER

GOREME-EARLY CHRISTIANS LIVED UNDER-
GROUND FOR 300 YEARS

TWENTY-ONE

IRAN

(From Gladys Vogel, our Travel Agent)
 Dear Ruth and Nita,
 Sorry the tour is not working out to your liking. You have obviously become very sophisticated travelers since you left home as greenhorns. You have learned a lot in a very short time. Nevertheless, you are now faced with camping in out of the way places in Iran and Pakistan where it could be disastrous on your own. So don't champ at the bit, and go along with it. There's still a long way to go across deserts and hinterlands, where you will be glad to have company at hand.
 The places where you sleep are up to you, anyway. You know that you don't have to take Indiaman's recommendation on that.
 The places you are going to are a lot more primitive than anything you have encountered so far. You will be completely on your own in India.
 Your encounters sound like you are taking advantage of meeting all the people who come across with complete trust. Making friends has proven to be a major theme of your voyage. I hope they have all proven worthy of your confidence.
 So far as I can see, your unpleasant experiences have been with officials, not the average local people.
 I have sent $911.68 to the Valley Stream Teacher's Federal Credit Union and they have credited your account. The hospital bill for David — I sent a copy to Garrow-Fisher with a letter asking for refund of David's tour price. I know the Garrow-Fisher insurance was cancellation insurance.
 Your letters are wonderful. I feel your reactions as clearly as though I was there with you. I hope you can continue to enjoy the trip — even with the shortcomings of the Indiaman Tour. If I had known of a better tour, I would have arranged for it.
 I will call your mother and Jack to tell them that I heard from you.
 Love from Gladys

Tuesday, October 22

The evening camping stop was mud, mud, mud. It caked on thick on our shoes as we tried to walk.

Heck, another evening already and dinner finished, dishes washed and it was only 6:00. What to do all evening?

Wednesday, October 23

This day was difficult. Mud was everywhere. The tent was difficult to clean. Nita was tired of the tour and wished it were over.

We had one more month to go. I was the one who separated us in two different buses. She made the decision to come together, not me. Why should I be punished for her decision, I wondered.

For the first time I had to pay for the articles we bought. Suddenly she wouldn't handle the money. I had to mail her letters.

I refused to continue traveling with her like this. She had gotten a free ride all along and when she made me unhappy, who needed her?

Mud continued. The streets were miserable. This was the first town that was so dirty and disgusting my stomach actually felt queasy. We shopped for food and bought onions, peppers, tomatoes, bread and tangerines.

At 1:00 p.m. we came to the Iran Border. The Turks made the English boys cut their hair.

In our hotel we had to fight for towels from the proprietor and finally received dirty ones. We managed to take a hot bath and wash our hair. Somehow I had clean sheets, but the others didn't.

Thursday, October 24

Barzargan was an interesting town. But we only had half an hour there. People were working in the streets.

For the first time we saw chapati breads made. They are delicious hot, but not good cold.

There were open ovens on the street where they baked them.

Tabriz was a city of 350,000, a low, sprawling town.

I went to the John Kennedy library and asked about Asghar and Iraj. These two men lived in my home while they attended Queens College. I looked forward all trip to spending time with them in their Iranian homeland.

The librarian said, "I don't have Asghar's last name and Valipour (which was Iraj's last name) may be in Tehran. There is no phone book listing for Tehran from Tabriz."

I went to a tourist agency for tourist pamphlets about Iran. Then we walked through the bazaar and bought dried berries. I tasted hot sugar beets cooked in syrup.

We arrived late to the bus and Hugh deliberately pulled away as we neared it. We had to walk further. Nice guy!

We found a good camping spot, but it rained while we were cooking. The rice paste did not turn out good. It rained all night long. The tent gathered puddles and I did not sleep well. My feet would not warm up. I even wrapped a sweater around them.

I spoke to Nita. It was the tour that she wanted to junk. She wanted to be on her own, but she wanted to continue the trip.

I told her if she couldn't be a loving daughter, or a good companion, then to heck with our continuing together. I told her I would not give her money to travel if she continued to make me unhappy.

Friday, October 25

We traveled along the barren, eroded mountains. Here and there were rocky outcroppings, but on the whole the desert was colorful countryside. Occasionally we saw the brilliant emerald green of a small patch of cultivation.

The houses were flat-roofed, and had the cubist look of little walled villages.

It was blowing and dusty, but it dried up our tents, which were sopping from the night before.

Saturday, October 26

Nick's bus had a party last night. They woke us up.

When I went out at night to "spend a penny," the Big Dipper was standing on end.

Tehran? What would my memories of it be? When we arrived we decided this was the crummiest hotel so far. There were dirty sheets on the bed, so we remade it with our own bed sheets. We could not reach our sleeping bags in the bus.

I tried to locate Iraj Valipour and Asghar Mallahoshy. I made several telephone calls, but to no avail. I felt low and depressed because I had fantasies of a great re-union. I was in college at the time when these two young men were borders. Iraj and I became good friends. Asghar played chess with my father.

Hussein made the calls and promised me he would make efforts to call again later on. Meanwhile he took me to his room and explained he was a guest there. Later, while we were doing our laundry, he met Nita and spent the rest of our time lauding her beauty. We spent all day in his room. I read and Nita beat him at chess.

He told us he had been an opium seller for his father after he spent eight years in the air force. He was an expert shot and stamped his silver medal to the ground when they bestowed it on him because he felt he deserved a gold medal. His imitations and sense of the dramatic were amusing.

He walked out on his father and became a coin dealer. It was still an underground activity and not permitted in Iran. He was the biggest talker I had ever met. He had loads of pictures of females and told us how they all loved him. He fed us beefsteak in his room. We thought we were his guests. But later we learned he put the meals on our bill. He proved to be the most scheming man we met on our entire trip.

He took Nita and me to the Habib home. The mother, Mary, a second grade teacher, served us tea. She read our fortunes in our teacups. She spoke English, but we had a dull evening. We watched television and saw Peyton Place in Persian. We also saw the Shah coronation that took place the previous year. The Shah had three wives because the first two wives couldn't produce children.

Nita played chess in the parlor with the 19-year-old son, Khos. Veeda, 17, had a sweet face when she smiled. She was a quiet child, with no sparkling conversation, just like her mother.

We walked home and saw an electrified city. All the government buildings were lit up like Christmas in the states.

Sunday, October 27

I was lazy and got a late start. We went off to the bazaar. Hussein arrived and made a pest of himself. He announced he wanted me to babysit the "old woman" so he could be free with Veeda. To hell with that! Nita played challenging games of chess. Hussein was bored and dragged her away and she became angry. He was stuck with Momma.

We met a dentist who gave me the address of a dentist in Isfahan who could repair my broken tooth. Another Hussein who knew everything. But he was a less obnoxious person.

Hussein gave us a large ceramic pot as a gift.

In Tehran men pinched and poked girls in the streets. Nita hated it.

Monday, October 28

Our only stop was Qom, an historic city with mosques and shrines. It had to be a tourist town because there were rows of candy stores with cases of mustard-colored slabs of candy. We watched the men making it.

We found a ke-bob place and had one skewer of meat and one of skewer of tomatoes broiled over charcoal.

The day was weird. We drove along desert land most of the way and I finally saw one area with camels. The mountains were eroded and had no growth on them at all. There were very few areas of habitation and then always behind high walls.

June R slept and made a '"sick stop." She had too much heroin the night before.

A coke bottle exploded and made a gash in Shirley's leg. The road was bumpy and shook up the gas in the bottle.

Then a wine bottle fell from the overhead shelf and we had to stop and clean up that mess.

No "bush stop" in Qom. So Chris begged for one. A long troop of girls had far to walk for some hidden spot along a wall out of range and sight of the bus and field workers. Ella grabbed her camera and followed us, thinking it was a photo stop.

We arrived in Isfahan at 4:00 p.m.

The room arrangements were organized with some people in the Cyrus Hotel and some in the Saaid Hotel. June, Nita and I were in the Annex. We slept there one night to keep June company. But we didn't like the room and set out to find a better one.

I met the Swiss couple and dined with them in Jahan restaurant. Less than $1.00 fed Nita and me.

Tuesday, October 29

We moved to the Jahan Hotel. It was cleaner, and had a window with a much nicer view. It was 20 rials cheaper for each of us.

We took the bulky package of pottery that Hussein gave us to the post office. They told us to go to customs and it would cost about $8. It was too far away and we decided it was not worth it and that we would sell it.

I located an English high school teacher who explained our sale to a shopkeeper. The shopkeeper didn't want it and we gave up.

We searched for Dr. Hakami, the dentist. Instead we met Dr. Hakimi, a surgeon. He spoke English well and invited us to his home. He had a stunning courtyard. He served us tea. He knew Iraj Valipour's ex-wife.

We went to Iran Air where Shala Valipour Norissi, the ex-wife, worked. We made a date for the evening. She located Asghar Mallahasshy's phone number. I telephoned him in the afternoon.

I went to the dentist, who was a cheerful person. He didn't want to take money, but I insisted. I made an appointment for Nita the next day.

We visited with Shahla in the evening and gave her the pottery. We were happy to get rid of this bulky parcel. We met Perouz, her boy friend. Her brother, Esis, popped in. He gave Nita a "Ban the Bomb; Make Love not War" button. We learned about his life in the army. There was six-months of compulsory training afterwards and he was in the teaching corps. He would go into villages and educate people how to read and he also would teach people how to bathe.

We were fed all evening long, and we were invited back the next evening.

Wednesday, October 30

I called Asghar and arranged to meet him. He was perky, still good looking, and he had a remarkable memory.

He was the dean of Harati high school. He was also a director of hunting for 14 provinces. His wife, a teacher, was a relative of the Shah.

He had been married for 15 years and had a daughter 14. He drove us to his hunting office. Then he drove us to Harati high school and we met Ahmad, 19, who spoke English. Asghar told us Ahmad would be our guide around the city in a Land Rover.

While he drove, Ahmad told us he wanted to study law in California. He did not like Persia and wanted to marry an American.

We saw Pol-e Shahrestan Bridge, built with rooms for entertaining under the road bed. The Ali Qapu Palace was being restored and we saw plaster chipped off the paintings.

We were also shown the Maidan–e-Shah mosque, Mardan Shar, the Royal Square, Masjid–e-Shah mosque, Masjid-e-Sheikh Lulfollah Mosque for Shah Abbis. 1603-1618, Chehel Sotun Palace, with faceted mirrors and restored paintings.

We returned to the hotel to rest.

Asghar was called out of town in the afternoon and said he would call us in the evening. Asghar did not call either in the evening nor the next morning. I was disappointed. I wanted to get to know him better and to go to his home and meet his wife and daughter.

We went to Dr. Hakami, the dentist. He cut open the gum over Nita's wisdom tooth. Nita went to bed in pain.

Thursday, October 31

Nita slept until 10.

I saw Shahla and said, "Goodbye," thanking her for her hospitality.

I called Asghar to no avail. He turned out to be the major disappointment on this trip.

We found an interesting bazaar where we watched men making felt hats. It was a fascinating procedure. We also saw shoemakers and dyemakers at work. Nita bargained like mad. She certainly knew the art of bargaining. She bought jewelry and miniature pictures.

When traveling, one of the greatest sensual pleasures was a hot shower.

Back at the hotel Nita undressed and got into bed. Then the telephone rang. Perouz was downstairs with a friend and wanted to see us.

"I want to speak English," he said.

So Nita dressed again. She wasn't sorry. It turned out to be an entertaining evening.

Nita beat his friend two games of chess. Then we said goodbye at the bus to Tehran. We walked to Perouz's room and had tea and talked all evening.

As we walked to our room we saw men sleeping on rugs in the lobby and hall upstairs.

I felt better as I went to bed. We both liked charming Perouz.

Friday, November 1

We went to Perouz's room for a brief time to get out of the rain.

Open sewers poured through the streets. People washed clothes in them.

Perouz told us, "The Shah puts his money in Swiss banks. He does not give it to his people. He took land away from people to keep for himself."

If the Shah was so great, why all the arid land? Iran needed trees and water projects, dams, irrigation and highways.

Why were so many children still working in the carpet factories and as shepherds in the fields? We passed villages and saw children in the streets and wondered why they were not in school. Why did the young men we met want to leave Iran? Why didn't they like Persian women and want instead American women to marry? Why did they claim Persian women were uneducated?

By Friday night we were at Persopolis. Many in our group slept outdoors with no tents.

Kasimir told us, "Their religion tells them to be charitable. So they say they need beggars so they can be religious. It is part of their social structure. Ataturk outlawed many customs. The Shah could outlaw this one."

A man took June on a personal tour in a minibus and then he took her to dinner. He apologized to her because "he was too old to make love to her."

Saturday, November 2

Persopolis. The city of Darius, the Great, from 500 BC. Alexander the Great destroyed it when it was a flourishing city. He burned down the libraries as he conquered cities. Tombs were constructed into the mountains.

We wandered through the garden of the Shiraz Mausoleum of the poets, Sa'ad and Haifa. Persia had many poets who Persians recognized and valued.

Isfahan had the cleanest stores that we encountered in the Middle East.

Surmaq. This was our first day of crossing the desert.

Our camping spot didn't have a bush in sight.

Monday, November 4

Abaragh. The word yazd means town.

Kerman. We visited carpet factories and witnessed the young girls working. Their excuse was that children had smaller fingers and could handle the threads more easily. It is still child labor.

Evening we camped in the mountains with no tents. It was Mike's birthday party. If the water had been in canals the heat would have dried it up. They made an underground water system called Quants.

All day long we saw deserts, occasional compounds and few villages.

Nita writes:

November 4, 5, 6

Dear Family,

I am now at the tombs of Xerxes, Darius, and Artaxerxes (son of Xerxes). We have just finished eating (in a dust storm, naturally) and we have a half hour to examine the tombs for 20 rials.

We came from an hour stop at Shiras, one of the major Persian cities, and during that time we had to shop for three days worth of food and sightsee.

We lunched at an oasis today. You cannot imagine the exhilarating joy of water, grass and trees – a momentary escape from the choking dust and dried rock reality all around us.

The Great Sand Desert is a hopeless stretch of barren mountains and plains of thistles with thick chalky air.

Next afternoon.
Oh, this driving heat! The entire horizon has changed from yesterday. Now there is nothing but parched sand and windswept dunes as far as the eye can see. My throat and lips are caked with dryness and even the sky is scorched white.

This morning was so cold that my hands were cracked and purple and swollen and when I bashed my numb toes against a rock they bled, but I felt nothing.

This morning seems like years ago. I can barely remember it. All time is meaningless here. The desert goes on, hours and years are the same. Only the heat, heat, heat of the sadistic sun is meaningful.

We went to a Persian carpet factory yesterday. That is, we went to a place where carpets are made. It was a small-impoverished village set up in typical complicated Persian style.

The beautiful-eyed, filthy children were crowded together and crying. A withered ancient grandmother with laughing eyes was coaxing her shy child to come out of the shadows. A hunched, year-worn woman with cracked, raw hands sat at the loom and with deft lightening movements made colors and patterns appear, covering the bare string. The room in which she worked was dark and small with only enough space for the two huge looms and two workers, one was a mere child. It would take eight months for the weaver to complete this complexly designed rug, if she worked constantly. Her children were ragged and almost starving. The rug will cost almost $300, but she won't get the money.

Next afternoon.
It's another desert day, through Baluchisan , a no-man's land, and Pakistan. The thermometer read 52 centigrade, which (you guys can figure it out in fahrenheit) means it's hot.

Outside the bus window is a lovely lake in the horizon. Everyone can see it and it taunts us, for the closer we come the further away it goes. It is a torturous mirage because our water supply is almost gone.

We stopped at the Pakistani border and tried to get some food for lunch while we waited for our passport to be returned. It was a minute settlement, sun scorched and filthy. As we alighted from the bus, we were met with a swarm of flies. The air was almost black with them. In the village, the men were eating sitting among the goats and dung heaps.

A little baby sat in the corner; his face so covered by flies that no skin was visible. The poverty and filth was appalling; we ate no lunch today.

The two American Nixonite girls were glued to the wireless all day today trying to find out election results. They could get no English or European–speaking channel. It merely fortifies the feeling that this desert is really not part of the world.

147

It occurred to me today that Dave, the Chicago Wallace-tie, is just like Kalev Pahme, my school mate, even in his behavior to me. Imagine having Kalev on your bus for two straight months!

Love, and write soon, Nita

Tuesday, November 5

Election Day, also, Guy Faukes Day

Mirjaveh. We saw our first date palms today. We passed a real oasis, an enclosed palm tree.

We also passed a camel tower high in the desert, midway, to show camel caravans the way.

A camel train passed. It excited me every time I viewed them.

We had a pile of rocks for a bush stop. Film was not advancing; camera trouble again.

It was a hot and dusty ride.

Election talk all day long by Dave.

No Man's Land. Iran, Pakistan and Afghanistan fought over this land. Wonder why? Nothing. Nothing. No usable, cultivated area. Gravel and rocks. No bushes, no greenery. I never knew there could be so many miles of unusable land. Why fight over this? No people in this area at all. I'll never understand war.

Border of Iran.

Had stew for supper and then a singsong with the other bus. It was a pleasant evening. Slept outdoors under the stars.

The next day election talk all day long by Dave. We received final results in the evening. Too bad.

Friends Mentioned in Chapter 21:

Habib Khorro and Mary. She was a teacher with a 17-year-old daughter named Veeda. The son, Khos, 19 played chess player with Nita. We visited in their home.

Shala Nassiri. She was Iraj's ex-wife. We visited with her In Isfahan.

Ali Asghar Malabashi. He was dean of Harati high school in Isfahan. He gave us a car and driver.

Iraj Valipour. I had known him when I was a college student.

Hussein. He did not help us locate my friends.

Perouz. He wanted to speak English with us.

IRANIAN PEOPLE WORKING IN THE FIELD

TWENTY-TWO

PAKISTAN

Tuesday, November 5

Pakistan passport control was a traumatic experience. We had an onslaught of insects. There were so many flies that the air was black. I tried to go out, but raced back into the bus after taking a photo of a colorful truck. The heat felt like a furnace door had opened when we stepped off the bus. The heat and flies disturbed me. I began to drink that miserable mixture of lemon concentrate and water. Luckily, it was diluted more each day.

At the passport control we found a few dingy restaurants. Our group saw chapati bread made and drank very sweet tea. Some bus people found apples and tomatoes. We didn't.

I located a post office and bought airgrams.

We had our lunch stop in an area of flat nothingness. We sat in the shade of the bus to shield us from the hot sun. No bushes.

We approached our first Dak Bungaloes, walled in areas that had rooms for the women. We used them for stripping and bathing.

We had a long wait for food, but dressed up for this occasion. We brought our own dish and fork. Rice, stewed chicken and dal (lentil curry) made our first decent meal in days. Afterwards we had a sing.

Thursday, November 7

Quetta was uniquely different from any other town we had seen thus far.

Friday, November 8

Quetta

We relaxed in bed until 11:00 a.m. Then we showered using a pail of water.

In the evening, Mike telephoned for us and we drove to the army club. We met Bob, a lieutenant major who was also a landowner. He stood for everything I was against. I drank a whiskey with orange juice. He fed us fish and meat.

Mike, Keith and Dave got drunk and went home. We met Sahib, who was a civil engineer and a decent chap.

At night we heard the men from India talking, then coughing. Dogs barked. We heard the Moslem call to prayer. Beryl and I conversed most of the night.

The taxis were painted in brilliant colors.

The red light district had signs that said the district was out of bounds for the soldiers.

Saturday, November 9

We arrived at the border of Pakistan about 11. We left Afghanistan Control after four. Five hours, most of it in Afghanistan. They looked through our passports and took out the paper visas. They stamped the visas and put them back into each passport and brought them to inspector #2. He switched papers, kept one and gave one back. He entered every detail from the passports into his book. Then two men signed the book.

There was a problem with Nigel, who had no exit visa, so Hugh married him off to a girl on bus #1, who also misplaced her papers.

Then an official came on to the bus and individually checked each passport, matching the photo to the person.

He asked if we had a camera or transistor radio and wrote that in each passport.

Robert took it all in stride. I boiled up at all the nonsense. We lost half a day of travel and missed the opportunity of getting to the bank.

We drove through deserts and mountains and one switchback pass. I became dizzy from all the turns.

There were many areas with camels. We saw nomad tents in the distance. We also saw small tornadoes and dust storms. We arrived at a desert camping spot for the night.

It was a cold night, but I had a good sleep and there was a lovely sunrise at dawn.

QUETTA –TAXI

TWENTY-THREE

AFGHANISTAN

Sunday, November 10

We traveled onward to Kabul. I finally rotated to a front window seat, which was convenient for picture taking. We saw hundreds of camels and colorful women and children with jewelry in their noses and in their hair. The women wore bangles of bracelets. They asked us for tooth medicine.

During our lunch stop Mike and I visited a school. There were only boys. Girls don't get educated in schools.

It was becoming cold and then it got colder. We saw snow-capped mountains.

In Kabul we stayed at the Metropolis Hotel for 120 afghans, about $1.70 each. I had a room with Beryl. We had a good view of a mountain with homes built into the side of it.

We ambled around town and located a good restaurant for 20 afghans each.

We watched how they ate with their hands. They kneaded the rice into a form that could be carried in the fingers to the mouth. We learned how to do it and returned home full and happy.

One man in the post office made a date for the next day. Another walked us around town and back to our hotel. We had a hot shower and finally felt clean and had a good sleep.

We heard Moslem prayers at 4:30 in the morning.

Monday, November 11

We walked from 10 a.m. to 5 p.m. I bought fur slippers, books, a fur hat, and a pendant and chain, all for $8.00. We crossed the Afghanistan border.

Tuesday, November 12

We camped in a crowded square at the border. Dogs barked and cats meowed all night long.

We were still lamenting the fact we did not stop in the animal market at the edge of Jalalabad. Tents were crowded together on one side of road. I saw sheep, goats and camels, and would have loved to witness the exchange and sale of them and to mingle among the people.

We had many stops throughout the day. As we went through the Khyber Pass there were good scenes. The bus stopped briefly at a waterfall gorge and at a sign that said: donkeys, camels one way, cars in the opposite direction.

I talked with Mike. It was no help to my ego. He was keen and observant. Nita read books, and made no effort at conversation with Nigel or other intellectual people. She would not take up the cudgel of Mike's challenge.

It all bothered me too. I couldn't forgive her for latching on to me this trip. It would have been a very different trip for me if she hadn't. I would have integrated and joined in, instead of always being on the periphery of the group.

If we had traveled in two different buses we would have gotten along better. My mistake was that I responded as a mother.

Her immaturity showed itself often and bothered me because I had gotten to regard her as an adult in so many ways back home. She made snap judgments about people; she condemned before giving people a chance. She was asocial, snobbish in attitude. I was sick of seeing the faults in people and would like to have observed the good.

Wednesday, November 13

Michael said I was an "affected pseudo intellectual." He said that I could hold no deep discussions; that my arguments were merely superficial emotionalism. He may have been right. It was true that I did not have a million facts at my fingertips, that I did not know detailed history frontward and backwards; that I could not cite causes of, for instance, the evils of colonial rule. It was also true that my arguments were mainly emotional. However, this emotionalism was not superficial. The reason, I think, that we could not ever have a satisfactory discussion was that Michael, although he considered himself removed from the "petty middle class," had the attitude that white-ism was the answer, and only white-ism.

It was the "white man's burden" to enlighten the non-western savages, to import western civilization, undamaged, to people so removed from the western way of thinking that it was simply alien to them. When they could not accept this way of thinking, he, and others like him, condemned them as stupid, shiftless lazy and no-good. (Of course, I realized that the phrases "western civilization" and "western thinking" were superficial, but how else could I express the attitudes so prevalent in America and, seemingly, England and Australia, attitudes of motherhood, love-of-money for its own sake, security, going to church, my house is bigger than your house, and other Babbit–like features.)

Without knowing any of them, he condemned three quarters of the world's population because they tolerated flies and pee in the gutters, could not speak English, wore tattered, un-western clothes, and did not eat fish 'n chips. He abhorred such people as the Australian aborigines, saying they existed solely because of the goodness of government welfare, that they were so lazy they would prefer to see their children starve rather than work for decent wages.

It went on and on. I knew it was wrong and bigoted of me, but I held nothing but contempt for his point of view. I considered it to be narrow minded to take no understanding of basic differences in civilizations. He thought my opinions immature; I thought his dehumanizing, or at least inhumane. Probably we were both right (or wrong).

Thursday, November 14

We saw Islamabad, or at least a quick perusal of a small area of it, including a modern mosque with sculptured plaster architecture, not especially spectacular. Box after box, row on row of houses. What a shame for a brand new city.

We arrived in Lahore about one p.m. The group stayed at the Park Luxury Hotel for 48 rupees. We paid 16 at the YW. We walked along the mall and into handicraft shops.

We ate supper in a sidewalk café, two eggs mixed with meat. I swallowed an entro-viaform pill as we ate it to prevent stomach upset.

When we arrived "home" we saw a note that Michael had invited us to a party. A fiasco night! We found out the next day the party at a wealthy Pakistani's home was loads of fun. There were Swedish girls and a person from Planned Parenthood. It sounded like a good party with dance and drinks. Oh well.

Friday, November 15

Nita and I trotted off to a bazaar. I bought a gray fur Karacel hat for 6 rupees.

We met Hoochinan, the Pakistani equivalent of George. He was a newspaperman, who was bald with a gray fringe of hair and a swarthy, suave face. He walked his bike as we talked. I wanted him to make a date for the evening.

He had a son who was an engineering student at the university, and another in the tenth grade. He went off before 2:00 p.m. to get home in time for prayer.

In the bazaar shops I saw saris I loved, yellow silk with embroidered flowers, for 135 R.

I watched men make rope beds. I wondered why they didn't weave them to the end.

I walked near the entrance to the walled city where there was an old bazaar, but it looked so scrungy. I was afraid of going in alone.

I rested from 3 to 7 p.m. while Nita, June R. and Beryl came in to talk. Each related her day's experience.

Nita met Steven, an English boy, and a Pakistani boy who accompanied her to the old and new bazaars and bought her lunch.

June and Beryl saw the Fort and Shalimar Gardens and enjoyed a horse taxi ride there and the bus ride back. I should have gone with them.

After tea and dinner with Pakistani women sitting with us, we dressed to go to the hotel and the dance there.

I wore my new hat. People laughed, but I liked it. They told me I got a good deal for my 6 rupees.

I met Arthur, an army lieutenant veterinarian. He danced with me. Then Basher Hussain Butt talked a while and we danced together. He was an industrialist and supplied hospitals. He had a wife and sons, 7 and 10. He was easy to be with and I enjoyed dancing with him.

We left. Bashi and I sat in the back seat of the car and we drove him home.

He had about five servants, a cook, watchman, gardener and chaffeur in a very large home.

Arthur drove me home to the YW. I was locked out. There was a chain and lock across the gate. I had to climb over the wall to get into my room at 2 a.m.

I didn't sleep all night. I was stimulated and excited. I looked forward to the following day.

I heard Moslem prayers at 4:30 in the morning and Christian church bells and the cocks crowing.

Saturday, November 16

I paid our 16.50 rupees after breakfast for our night at the YW. I had something to think about all day. With so little sleep the night before I dozed a great deal.

Friends Mentioned in Chapter 23

Hoochinan. He was a newspaper man.

Arthur. He was an army veterinarian.

Basher Hussain Butt. He was an industrialist who supplied hospitals.

CAMELS AFGHANISTAN

3 CHILDREN – BASKET ON HEAD

TWENTY – FOUR

NEW DELHI

Saturday, November 16

Crossing the border took more than three hours. The flies were not so bad this time and the heat was not as bad as at the last border.

India was different. We saw many trees and cows.

In Amritsar we spent a long time lost. The street was too narrow for the bus to go forward or backward.

The incredible Golden Temple, the jewel of Punjab, is the holiest of holy places for Sikhs all over the world. The city is more than 400 years old. The Pool of Nectar is holy water. More than 400 kb of gold were used to rebuild and cover the domes of the temple in 1803. The Golden Temple is one of the most beautiful religious structures in the whole country. There is a free kitchen and free hostel. No tobacco or liquor permitted, and no caste system.

The guesthouse for three rupees had rope beds. Dinner cost seven rupees. We didn't have enough to eat, but the food was good.

We drove all day to Delhi. I slept both morning and afternoon. The roads were lined with trees and we couldn't see much through them.

In the evening, the bus crew stayed at the International YMCA for 18 rupees a night. Four of us took a taxi to Mr. Singh's guesthouse. We used our own bedding for six rupees a night. We liked it there.

We met turbaned Mr. Singh and Tahitian campers.

French speaking Bernard and Jean Claude took us to Hotel Ashokar for Indian dancing. Then they took us to a Greenwich Village type of cold cellar. It had loud music so talking was impossible. The men in my group didn't dance, so I joined a German group and danced like mad with a young man. He played the guitar across the country for a living and this night he was high on pot. I had a good time, but it was a fiasco for the men who brought us.

Monday, November 18

When we arrived in Delhi, India's capital city, we saw a crowd of people gathered around. We nudged our way through and witnessed a snake charmer. We heard him making music on his pipe and the snake actually stood on end. We had never

157

witnessed that before. Then we moved to the other circle of people. There, a bear, all dressed up, was standing up and dancing. Now we knew we must be in India.

We decided to take a day tour in Delhi. We saw all the attractions: Red Fort, tombs, the tower, Gandhi's Memorial Park, two emporia, one for handicrafts and the other for saris. We didn't buy anything.

Shah Jahan's Red Fort entrance is through the imposing Lahori Gate, which leads to a roofed passage now lined with antique shops. Five times a day musicians play instruments.

The Gandhi Memorial at Kanniya Kumari has a representation of being Gandhi in stone. Spaciousness surrounds the memorial and gives the place a peaceful feeling.

The group divided up into nine taxis. We had a sick driver so the director, Anand Solomon, had to take over. One taxi ran out of gas. Another had a flat tire. It turned out to be a tiring day.

In the bazaar we ran into Anand Solomon, the tour director. I bought a wooden kangaroo sculpture for two rupees.

We drove off with Anand and his brother. We drove 20 miles to a place where I had beer and fried fish. Three of us were in a bad mood because of the mail. June heard her father was sick and Beryl and I received nothing from home.

We drove the girls home and I continued the evening with Anand.

Tuesday, November 19

It was a day of errands. I filled out forms at the Nepal embassy. I took photos for the visas and bought band-aids for Nita's infected foot.

The tourist office planned a tour of India for us.

Nita had a chess date with Anand. He enjoyed the game even though Nita was the better player.

Anand took both of us out for a chicken dinner. Afterward he took us to the Omar Khyam Room and he had four whiskies, even though it was a dry Tuesday.

He took Nita home. She enjoyed her evening.

He drove me to his home and I went to bed on the roof of his house under the stars. Anand realized he had to go to sleep because he hadn't had any sleep for two days.

I had to climb a precipice. I landed in Anand's lovely room. I was formally introduced to Anand Kewalramani. Anand K. is a chemical engineer and travels a great deal. He told me he was a 24-year-old virgin. He was always afraid to go to completion.

It was a very peaceful night without love making at all.

In the early morning Anand went down to buy fresh milk. At 6:00 a.m. he rode his motorcycle two miles away to get the key, so I would not have to navigate the wall climb again. He made tea and brought it to me. I soaked in the bathtub and relaxed. He had offered me the hospitality of his home.

Wednesday, November 20

In the bus we drove to Agra to the tomb of Akbar the First and then to the Taj Mahal. The Emperor Shah Jahan spent 22 years and had 22,000 laborers to build this memorial to his beloved wife, who died in 1631. The Taj Mahal is an example of a garden tomb. The photographs of this marble mausoleum did not do it justice. We were not prepared for the impact, which transcended the visual. It was an artistic masterpiece.

Thursday, November 21

Fatehpur Sikgi was Akbar's abandoned capital. This ancient city was worth more time. It was built well and was more than 400 years old. We saw the marble mausoleum with mother of pearl canopy. There was an elephant rug where elephants crushed the convicts.

When we were boarding the bus, someone threw out orange peels. Two little girls grabbed them and were chewing on them when I took their picture. It is one of the best photos I have of children in India.

We drove to Jaipur, Amber City. Vidyadhar, the architect, gave India the first planned city among the sprawling plains. The buildings were all red so it was called The Pink City. We stopped first at Divan of Amber and the Palace of Wind. It was magical, especially when lit up at night. We saw the hall of mirrors in the ceiling of the royal bedroom and the intricate mosaic work.

Amer Fort was one of the most beautiful palaces in Rajasthan.

The group took rides on the painted elephants. I enjoyed seeing the baby monkeys hugging their mothers around the waist as the monkeys wandered everywhere.

What we didn't do to save a penny! We arrived at the Jaipur youth hostel and found it closed. It was under repair. After hours, we got a ride to a cheap hotel, seven of us plus luggage in a tiny car to save taxi fare.

At Ashokar Hotel in Jaipur we sat on the porch waiting for two hours and then arguing and trying to get a good price for our room. We ended up in a large room with adjoining toilet bowl and filthy sink. There was cold water in the shower and no spray. Beryl saw a rat run down the drain. It was an odorous bathroom. We had three beds for the five of us, Nita, Magna, Beryl, June and me.

The hotel cost four rupees each, with our own scrungy bathroom attached. But would we take it? Oh no! We had to bargain down to two rupees each, two in a bed. Fine, except that the widest bed was wooden boards, very wooden. Except for the incident of the huge rat that scuttled through the bathroom and into the drain, it wasn't too bad. But so much trouble we went through!

Nita writes to Sophie, our teacher in the language seminar, in the USSR:

Dear Sophie,

It's been a long time, but I will give it a try. Actually my Russian, or lack of Russian, has suffered lately. While we were in Greece it was O.K. because the Greek alphabet is amazingly like the Russian. We had no trouble reading the street signs in Athens after we learned the Russian alphabet. But after we came to Turkey. Wham. A whole different world and not a drop of Russian anywhere.

Since Mommy and I have discarded almost everything but a knapsack, I could not carry a Russian dictionary. But I did manage to pick up a semi-conversation booklet, which keeps me remembering the alphabet.

I received your letter and I can't describe how happy I am. I was afraid the Russian postmen wouldn't be able to read my lousy writing on the envelope.

The actual tour has not turned out well. The people, mostly English and Australian, are not my type of people. For the most part, they are imperialistically inclined, with an attitude that white western people are superior. When we drive through the Asian countries they comment, "What horrible, filthy people. I'm glad I'm not Turkish, or Iranian or Pakistani, etc. I wouldn't live here for money."

This, as you know, is not Mommy's or my attitude toward other cultures. The atmosphere on the bus is like that of a tiny island in the middle of an ocean. Instead of trying to make friends and become a part of the country we visit, these people pull away and say how much better England is. They purposefully become more isolated from the country than the usual tourists.

Even though Mom and I don't particularly like the tour, we do have fun when we can get away on our own.

In Turkey we made friends with a family and spent the evening in their home in Ankara. I played chess for two nights with a really marvelous boy, who is not only a great chess player, but also had a huge stamp collection that Mom went crazy over.

Everywhere we went we met wonderful, wonderful people and we hated to leave them. It was meeting new people, not just visiting temples and monuments, that made our traveling so enriching.

Yours with love, Nita

Friday, November 22

We took a bike cart and rode to the bazaar. I took photographs of camels and cows roaming the streets and eating the produce on the food stands, of young girls carrying manure on baskets on their heads and a parade of women in saris.

Jai Keeshan, who escorted us last night, came to our room to show us his sculptures in stone. He made a date for us to go to his shop in the evening.

We already expected to go to a wedding. Jai was our only date for the evening. So I read, wrote and rested in the afternoon.

There was a telephone call from June and Beryl to bring us to the wedding. We never received the message.

Jai was a flop from our first exposure to him. He never found us a place to stay. We had a complete language barrier, but we let him take us to a restaurant.

We met an older man at the Rainbow Room and he gave Jai hell for bringing us to an expensive restaurant. He invited us to his home the next day. We had to refuse. We paid our 4.25 R, our last money, and started walking home. Luckily, Jai left us.

We met two young men who took us for rides on their motorcycles. It was fun.

Later, one went home to get his guitar. We drove to a rifle range, spread a blanket and sang together under the stars, with the city lights at the periphery.

The two young men took us back to the hotel. They told us they hunted tigers and enjoyed it. They were Toyota car salesmen. We had offers to come back with all expenses paid

Nita and I came home at midnight, June and Magda came in around two and Beryl never did return home.

Saturday, November 23

Orange was the predominant color for the turbans and dresses that people wore. The women wore attractive silver jewelry, large nose rings, bracelets and ankle bangles.

We passed a flock of peacocks and storks in ponds. We saw the bullocks pulling the ropes at the wells where the people get their water.

We stopped in Dak house at 3:00 p.m. We relaxed, and then cooked stuffed peppers and a suet pudding. It was a pleasant evening.

I spoke to Jill for practically the first time on the trip. She was a lovely person. She said that Maryra's sickness was psychosomatic and that Marya was enjoying her trip in spite of herself, that she was lucky to have Nigel's support.

She said Keith was narrow-minded and provincial. It was interesting to hear her perspective on our bus mates.

Monkeys were everywhere in the trees, and peed and shit on people. Not us!

Sunday, November 24

We had one photo stop. It was for a bridegroom on a horse. He was a young boy, no more than 15. He didn't look very happy.

India's problem: overpopulation. They could put in intra-uterine devices and loops into girls when they began menstruation. They could sterilize women after the first or second child. People could find other leisure time pursuits and de-emphasize sex.

Children needed nursery schools and kindergartens like those in Russia. There should have been childcare from birth. More education was needed.

The cities should have been cleaned up. All animals should have been put in one section of the city and fenced off from roaming among the food stands and eating food from the baskets that people purchased.

The streets had manure that was picked up by children and carted away on their heads in baskets to use as fuel in their homes.

Children had many eye problems. Did they put medicine in the eyes of newborn children? I saw a child without an ear.

Most of the begging was done by children.

It may have been built into the customs, the religion and society, but some reformer should work it out of the system.

Why, if in ancient times they could build such palaces, couldn't town planning be established in this epoch? The people needed substantial houses instead of huts, shacks and tents. I imagined planned societies, stores, schools, homes, animal corals, streets for cars and playgrounds for children. Other countries had these things. Why not India?

And food? Birds, dogs and rats ate up food meant for people. Better control was needed. Rats were a big problem on trains that transported grain meant for people.

We were in Bani, a city built within a fortress down in a valley and extending to a high hill. As we approached we saw the women washing clothing in the lake at the outskirts. The bright, colorful material dried in the hot sun.

The tour hotel stop in Indore was 30 rupees a night, including dinner.

We drove off to a rest home. Nita insisted on staying. Bed and supper for 8.50, or 17 rupees for both of us, was a good price.

We had mattresses and clean sheets, a pillow and a clean blanket, as well as peace and quiet and our own bathroom with a pail of hot water. Good service, good light and a comfortable chair and table. Thanks, Nita.

I felt badly for Beryl because Nita insisted we would no longer stay with Magda. Nevertheless Magda and Fredrika joined us. They both pushed in front and took over and suddenly we four took a back seat.

I would have liked to spend this last evening with June and Beryl alone.

Monday, November 25

Ruth writes:

Dear Adam:

Many times I start mental letters to you to try to share the visual excitement of this country.

Jaipur – Amber City where painted elephants carried us up to the Red Fort Palace. There we witnessed fairyland as candles reflect in the mirror-faceted ceiling of the king's bedroom. Camels stalk proudly through the dirt paths. The cows and bullocks push their noses into the baskets of grain designed for human consumption. A monkey sat outside my window this morning eating our banana peels.

A rat visited us during the night and nibbled our banana.

Young girls, rings and jewels in their noses walked down the street with baskets of camel dung on their heads. Every child holds a child. All babies are nude from the waist down for easier toileting.

There is music and parades signifying wedding processions, with women in gorgeous bright gold-edged saris. Women walk with clay or silver pots on their heads. The bride and groom sit royally on a colorfully draped elephant or horse.

Hindustani News: Friday November 22, 1968 Front page. Two photos of two foreigners caught selling contraband gold, our friends, Bernard and Jean Claude. They are now in jail.

In Delhi these two men were our dates. They took us to a Greenwich Village dance spot. We liked them both very much. Adventure? We don't miss much. But these brief letters leave out so much.

In Indore, Nita and I stayed in a rest house. Clean bedding and mattresses and we had a meal for 2.50 rupees or 50 cents. Nita couldn't finish hers, there was so much to eat, vegetable curry, eggplant and chapati.

Ajunta and Ellora are towns where there are caves.

Then we leave the bus tour at Bombay. I'll miss Michael, my seat companion, an Australian teacher.

Dearest, your dependability and reliability endears you to me more and more. I put two films in each mailer and I put your name to receive my slides. Thanks.

I hope some of the photos come out.

I witnessed the girls in "cages" lining the streets, hundreds of them. Who sold them? Were they kidnapped? Can they get out? They are young girls, a street for Africans, and a street for Indians. I did not see the street with Caucasian women. They are used in the slave market.

We met our Parikh family. Niren was David's pen pal. Beautiful people of the Jain religion.

Bombay, a big city, was overwhelming for me.

You ask how are we doing on money? Nita and I have had 5 months of travel. We had 12 weeks when we were three people. We spent exactly $1500. I have $500 left and hope it will last until February when I take out the last pack of traveler checks.

Yours with love, Ruth

We rode all day in the bus. The drivers did not stop for food; we had no food. The only trick not played on us this trip finally was.

We drank water, ate a couple of bananas and played scrabble to forget we were hungry. We gave our water to the Swiss couple, who made soup. It was all they had. Mike gave me some tuna fish he had saved. Good of him.

After "lunch," we stopped in Dhulia to shop. Nita bought tomatoes, cabbage and bananas.

I chased around to find a post office. People sent me a far distance, but it was around the corner from where the bus was parked. People misdirected us. Boys pushed against us as we stepped into the bus. Boys banged against the bus and adults didn't stop them. These were the most ill behaved boys we had encountered on our trip so far. Dhulia — never again.

On to the Ajunta rest house. We played cards. I learned Australian 500. I ate our last can of Donald Cook's potpie. It was ghastly, worse than dog food. Nita could not eat it. I spoiled the cabbage and tomato she had sautéed first. We also ate fruit soup and added bananas. Keith cleaned out Cyril's food box and donated a can of sardines. We asked four men to help us open our can.

Tuesday, November 26

In the morning we arrived at the Ajunta caves. We spent a couple of hours there. The frescos were more than 1,000 years old. The sculptures were fine, but the paintings were in disrepair. These cave houses or prayer halls were excavated from the second century BC to the seventh century AD.

We philosophized about the Buddhist monks and thousands of workers who spent hours carving stone for religious purposes. If this labor and time and effort were devoted to health, welfare and education, imagine how much better off Indian people would be today.

On to Ellora, which was 65 miles away and with more caves. There were large cut out sculptures in the courtyard. Two elephants in stone flanked the center building, which we climbed. We were rewarded with a bird's eye view of all the sculptures. I took a photo sitting on the Buddha's lap. The Hindu section had scenes from the Ramayama.

We climbed the mountains toward the "Jain section" and soaked our feet in the mountain waters. Dave, Keith and Elizabeth walked with us.

The rest house was the most elaborate and beautiful of the entire trip. It was situated high on a hilltop. The lovely rooms had beds with canopies. The large sitting room had enough light so that people could read and write letters.

We finally invited Chris and Willie to be our guests for dinner. We owed them for feeding us all along. Luckily, it was an excellent meal of rice, meat in a sauce and pieces of chicken in another sauce. There was soup and dessert of a delicious fruit salad with a custard sauce. The food tasted good and we had all we could eat.

The sunset was the most glorious of the entire trip, especially brilliant yellow orange sky with the silhouettes of the campers.

We all slept well. It was cold in the morning when we dressed. Our departure time was 7:00 a.m., people stirred at 5.

We drove past vultures eating the carcass of a cow.

Wednesday, November 27

Nita writes:

Dear Daddy,

We just finished seeing the Buddhist caves at Ajunta. Now we are on our way to the caves at Ellora. Naturally, guidebooks say two days are necessary for full appreciation of the caves. We were given one and a half-hours each place. The caves were huge, elaborate, richly decorated rooms carved out of pure rock. The the free flowing statues carved into the walls, ceilings and pillars were extremely detailed, even down to the individual ringlets in the women's hair.

The caves are really astounding, but somehow, even with the marvelous paintings on the walls and the intricate carvings, they don't give me the thrill that the roughly made caves in Goreme, Turkey did.

There was, however, one particular cave out of the 50 or more that was really outstanding. It was a huge Hindu cave at Ellora and within the cave were separate temple buildings and layer upon layer of carvings describing the feats of Siva and other Hindu Gods and Goddesses. The main temple was the Temple of Love. It was built on four different planes and all over were carved positions of lovers. The interior of the cave was opened and the mountain formed the two extreme walls. I guess its awesomeness was really indescribable.

We are not at Bombay. Last night we stayed with June and Beryl at one of our usual cruddy places, but this one seemed to be situated in the middle of a circus.

Thank you, Daddy, for your informative letter. We do so love to get them.

David should have a good time with Mr. Potter for science. I remember the trick with him was to get the work done the day he assigned it. He gives three week deadlines, but if you wait, the work piles up and you forget or just never get it done.

It's good that Lori dropped Spanish. Anything that creates problems should be dropped. She sounded happy at her job and with her English teacher. I'm so glad.

Today we're going to try to go down "Cage Street," where for centuries the slave market has raged. Since an unofficial slave market of white girls still goes on today, we will see it only from the windows of a cab.

Please tell me if the postcard was from Lucien. Could you copy it for me?

The next time I go around the world I'll have a ball. It'll be a "friend in every port." I'll just go from one family to another.

Love, your daughter, Nita

Dear Lori and Wendi,

Long time no see, or hear. At the moment a family of monkeys are frolicking in the trees above our heads where we were sleeping. They were adorable, with long grey haired black faces; pot bellied things with the skinniest, longest tails, which are used for balance. We were warned that at night we would get a shower of urine in our faces while we were sleeping.

In Jaipur, Mommy and I went motorcycling. Such fun. We were riding around for about three hours, then one of the guys who is in a band played his guitar and sang Western and Indian songs.

You guys would go crazy over the jewelry. Toe rings, ankle bracelets, arms bands and hair bands, buttons, nose rings and belts all in the loveliest silver. The trouble is, the effect is ruined if they are not worn altogether.

The Indian infants and young children are made up with globs of eye mascara, kohl, which is applied with a smooth stick of ivory or silver to the inside of the eyelid. Poor babies.

Saris are really fun. I have learned how to put them on and will probably buy one in Bombay or our second trip to Delhi. They are infinitely more comfortable and cooler than western type dress. I wanted to buy you guys a suttee — the pull-over Indian dress. It is a shift-type long sleeved, very short dress with baggy matching slacks underneath. They are magnificent in silk or satin.

The birds in India are brilliant spring green, delicate cranes with graceful sword tails. The vultures are, unfortunately, the most numerous of the birds. They are constantly gliding around the skies looking for carcasses. When they find one they swoop down, completely covering their meal and about one half an acre or more when the word spreads. They are ugly beasts, rivaling the spiny, long snouted slit-eyed boars that run around the streets.

Your loving sister, Nita

Ruth writes:

Hello Family,

According to my records we mailed a letter to you on November 11 in Quetta. My, we have been through a great deal since then.

Quetta was in Pakistan, then Kabul in Afghanistan with many camel caravans. The girls wear loads of bangles and jewelry. Nita spent four hours hunting for jewelry for you people.

Kabul is the capital of Afghanistan. Streets are mud and filth and sewers drain into the streets.

We saw a student demonstration. It was peaceful where we sat. But the people on the other bus saw buses overturned and burned along Peshawar near the border.

Kabul has the shops to go in with sheep skin coats and moneychangers.

Back across Khyber Pass we were told of the savage tribes in the hills. Khoti is the town in the middle of the pass with forts and pillboxes. Everyone must travel through the Pass in daylight because of the attacks.

In Lahore in Pakistan, we stayed at the Y there, and I went to a dance in the Park Luxury Hotel at night. Two men wanted me to stay on, or come back, all expenses paid. One was a rich industrialist.

Markets are great in Lahore. The fun in Kipling's story, "Kim." Read it, David.

We went to Pakistan, then Afghanistan and the back again to Pakistan through to India.

India was exciting.

Amritsar had a Sikh temple with gold inside and outside and it was situated in the middle of a lake of holy water. They fed thousands daily in a free kitchen. Hungry people, first they feed them and then they pray. They also have a hostel for sleeping. This religion has no caste system. There was a lot of good in it as we see it.

Delhi and New Delhi was a two-day stopover. First day we took a taxi tour and saw the sights — The Red Fort, temples, Gandhi's Memorial Park.

Nita got her chess game with the director of the tour. He also took us both to a good dinner.

A band preceded the wedding processions. The bride or groom sat on horse or elephant. They are all gaily decorated. The clothing was so beautiful we gasp and admire. It changed style and color as we traveled. Each scene from the window was a picture. Brahma cows were used for pulling carts, plowing fields, and pulling *water up from the well. I took pictures of women with silver pots on their heads or young girls with baskets on their heads filled with camel dung.*

So many children, young babies all carried by young children, their siblings. Bare bottoms on all. Animals, I never saw so many dogs and puppies, but the monkeys in the trees are the biggest thrill. At our rest home they made water and droppings on the cots and people below. Nita and I moved out, away from the trees in time. Others didn't.

One monkey came to our hotel balcony and ate our banana peels.

News: There are visible women in India. There weren't in Moslem countries.

Love, Ruth

Dear Mom and Aunt Minnie,

Yes, we received both your letters.

India? Camels are beasts of burden, along with donkeys, oxen and cows. The horses, used as taxis, are a thin, starved lot. The dogs are mangy. Animals— everywhere goats and cows are wandering in the streets.

We saw a couple of snake charmers, and dancing bears and monkeys entertaining people.

People? The saris are magnificent and we never tire of their beauty. The children are beautiful, some clean in neat braids, others with fly infested faces and many with pockmarks.

We see some women in purdah. We see young girls with baskets on their heads hauling away the camel and horse manure from the streets to use for fuel. We see youngsters at work everywhere.

We bargain over every purchase. Today it was a pair of slippers for Nita and fruit for our meals. We peel all the apples before eating and we don't buy cauliflower or lettuce because we can't wash them clean enough.

We spent one day in Delhi seeing palaces, Muslim temples, a fort, and Gandhi's cremation memorial.

We saw the Taj Mahal and it is as stunning as claimed. Emperor Shah Jahan built this tomb for his wife in 1648 A. D. His own son put him in prison in the Red Fort for the rest of his life. His room in prison looked out on the Taj Mahal.

All our love to you.

Ruth

In our restaurant they had little squares of fried dough.

There was a man in the street and he was beating his breast in some religious frenzy. It was the first time we had seen that.

We also saw fortunetellers and incense sellers sitting in the street. The barbers did their business on the sidewalks.

It was long day's drive, 260 miles to Bombay. We saw the worst slum district so far along the outskirts of the city. There were corrugated tin shacks cramped together. The pollution of the factory's chimney smoke filled the air. The approach to the town was an hour long, so it had to be a big city.

We saw a great deal of building. But the buildings looked shaky and old even before the construction was completed. What is a low cost housing project here? Who gets them? Why couldn't they be more substantial and graceful edifices? The houses along the main streets as we drove into town were all terribly run down. They could have used white wash and paint. Couldn't anyone give these people a sense of pride in their homes? The streets were all torn up.

Nita met Bob, the Argentinian, who said he would take us to the Salvation Army, Red Shield House. No luck. It was filled up by the people from Bus #1, who had phoned ahead and gotten there first.

We settled in Miramar for a night of no sleep. There were four hard wooden beds and a lumpy mattress with five women, and there was a dirty bathroom with a broken toilet chain. It was a horrid place and I wanted to get out.

Thursday, November 28

We had to get out. So we ate breakfast and packed. I handed the manager the 5 rupees for breakfast and 30 (6 apiece) for the night's lodging and left in a taxi for the Salvation Army.

The taxi driver gave us a hard time. He wanted 3.30 for each piece of luggage. I finally gave it to him and by that time he upped the price because he had kept his meter going.

The Salvation Army manager was a lovely lady.

She told us the rules: Pay the men who carry the bags upstairs. Water is scarce and must be used only in the morning and at night to wash. Get to meals on time. We had to leave December 1.

She gave us a 14-rupee room instead of the 12.25 one so we could have our own private toilet.

It was a Hindu holiday and the American Express offices were closed, as well as the banks.

We changed some money in a hotel and walked around a little bit.

I walked home for tea and took a sponge bath in forbidden water.

The Parikh family arrived. They were beautiful people, all of them handsome, and inner goodness shining from them like cleanliness.

They drove us around and spoke about the beauty of Bombay. The told us that the industries wanted the workers who flocked to the city for jobs and they set up the shacks. Some workers slept in the streets. They said people had peace of mind so sleeping in the street did not bother them.

They took us into a temple of Jain, the religion of non-violence.

Nita surprised me when she decided she wanted to play chess rather than spend time with the Parikhs.

In the evening, Nita stayed home to sleep. She has been run down and she told me she had felt sick for a couple of days.

I went to the Parikh home. The father and I conversed for three hours. The women sat silently in the room.

Mrs. Parikh served us cake and lassie, a milk drink, from the Chinese gooseberry. I was driven home near midnight.

June came in at 1:00 a.m. and Beryl at 3:00 a.m. They had an interesting evening at the Festival of the Arts. There was Indian dancing, singing and comic acts, and they met Indian film stars.

Friday, November 29

Nita discloses:

My point of view is distorted. After all, who would rather play a game of chess than spend time with Nita and Niren Parikh?

Who, but a fool, would travel a couple of thousand miles to get to know some Indians, and then play chess instead? So what if the players involved are really good? So what if I would be happier playing? It is correct to visit with the Parikhs. I must be social. Yes, Mommy, I guess my point of view is distorted because I'd rather play chess.

November 29, 1968

Dear Ruth and Nita,

We are all well and there is nothing new or exciting to relate. Your various packages have arrived by now, the sweaters, hat, dolls, pictures and coins.

The school picture has changed now from what it originally looked like. Wendi is very excited, and is working hard. She is taking one class and auditing a second with Haulenbeck, enjoys French with Mrs. Chub, and has English with Dr. Ross. She is doing sculpture; has dropped her bad cit. ed. and replaced it with an excellent Track 2 class with Dr. West that she finds exciting.

Lori had dropped Spanish. Otherwise she was doing well. I have an appointment at the Hempstead Consultation Service regarding possible therapy for her.

David gave me quite a jolt. I received a deficiency notice in science for him and had a conference with all his teachers. Potter is disgusted with him, feels he does the absolute minimum to get by. His other teachers felt likewise that he makes no effort to really learn — though he probably has the ability.

My impression was that his attitude is probably a response to things that are bothering him. I will ask that Mr. Wray see him.

Incidentally, when I spoke with David about his school behavior, he was genuinely shocked. He thought he was doing well.

We will probably have Thanksgiving dinner at my sister's this year.

Love, Jack

Dear Mom and Nita,

I'm making lots of money now. I can make an easy twelve dollars a week caddying. I work at the driving range for a dollar fifty an hour. You think that's hard work?

All I do is go around with this funny red contraption and pick up golf balls. The tricky part is that when I am out there picking up golf balls, the people are shooting more golf balls down there AT ME. The only protection I get is a ripped cardboard helmet and even that is cracked in two pieces. Dad lent me one of his helmets to use. Caddying is a cinch. One guy kept asking me if the bags were too heavy. Every two seconds he and his wife wanted to carry of couple of clubs themselves. At the sixth hole, we joined another couple who had a cart. They insisted on putting some clubs in the cart and there was nothing I could do

Now it happened that this guy couldn't play well and kept hitting the balls into the woods and blamed me for losing six of his precious balls.

Now I am not allowed to take two bags at once and only get three dollars for nine holes. The reason for this is that dumb guy said I get too tired with two bags and I can't find the balls.

I mentioned babysitting. Lori sits three Dixon kids for 60 cents. I have a job for one little girl, Bonnie Budd. It is easier than any of Wendi's and Lori's jobs. I make a buck an hour.

I've also got a newspaper route. That's getting all kabolized up with new and old customers.

There was a big mess up in school today. Because of it I won't go to school tomorrow. When I was out in the playground I vomited. Isn't that messy? Since dad has no job, he has no phone number. No way to reach him. I'm in the nurse's office.

I'm not in the mood to listen to Philip Knox taking chunks of glass out of his foot. Finally I fell asleep on the nurse's couch. The nurse called all of your references but no one is home. I guess listening to good ol' Philip would have to do for me.

Saturday, November 30

Nita and I saw the group off at the bus from 8 to 9 a.m. June and Beryl and Nita and I will miss one another.

Friends Mentioned in Chapter 24

Mr. & Mrs. Singh. They were our landlords in Delhi.

Bernard and Jean Claude. They were our French friends who took us dancing at the Hotel Ashokar.

Anand Solomon. He was our tour director.

Anand Kewalramani. He was a chemical engineer.

Jaikeeshan and his friend. They played guitar and gave us one of the loveliest evenings.

Parikh family. Mr. Parikh is a diamond merchant. His daughter, Nita, attended college.

Niren. This was David's pen pal. They chauffeured us around Bombay.

PART III

ON OUR OWN
NITA and RUTH

TWENTY-FIVE

BOMBAY

Saturday, November 30

Of course Nita and I had different feelings about leaving the bus. We took the last few things off, including Nita's chess set and our food tote bag.

Michael said his goodbye to me. He said, "I decided you were the only worthwhile woman on the bus after two months of being seated next to you."

We liked Mike, our Australian teacher. We celebrated his 30th birthday one night. I would miss Mike and the bus routines, and not having to scrounge all the time.

Nita was just glad to be rid of the bus schedules and most of the people on the bus. We would both miss June and Beryl.

Nita and I would be changed when we returned home to the states. Too much happened to us and too fast.

I was still not quick enough for Nita. I could not size up people or bargain hard enough.

We mailed a large box home, items we had picked up along the way, discarded clothing because we were on foot and had no bus to help us haul our stuff.

We had become hardened to mothers with nude babes in their arms holding out cups for bakeesh. All deformed people preyed on tourists for money. It wasn't easy pushing away youngsters who begged.

The Parikh family were our pen pals. Their son, Niren, was David's age and Nita, their daughter, happened to be Nita's age. The father was a diamond merchant and they lived well, but self-denial was their way of life. They practiced the Jain religion. They were vegetarians and they did not even kill insects. In fact, they wouldn't eat root vegetables because when the plant is pulled up it disturbs the insects living in the ground. Of course David's absence was a great loss to them. Niren was disappointed he could not spend time with David.

9:30 a.m. Nita P and two friends called for us. Nita P studied liberal arts and took us to her class at Jai Hind University.

The teacher read aloud to the class and interpreted every word and action. There was practically no class participation. Three pages were read in 45 minutes. This was an example of how to make a stirring drama into a boring lesson.

173

The second class Nita attended was English poetry and the teacher never showed up.

I sat in a logic class. At the end of the period the teacher asked me to say a few words. I did. The class was enthralled. I stopped, and the group asked me to continue, so I did. The period ended, and they sacrificed an English poetry period. I spoke about our trip for over an hour to a responsive group of 150 students.

In the afternoon, we saw a Hindu movie, an ancient Hindu story. The film had everything, excellent photographic shots in color, melodious songs, dances and comic slapstick scenes. A restless yearning lover's soul returned to haunt a young girl after 500 years.

Afterwards, our friends, Nita and Niren, and their cousins Nita and Bidu, took us to several restaurants for unusual cuisine. We ate sopardi on a betal leaf. Sopardi was a favorite dessert.

Sunday, December 1

We spent most of the day reading and sleeping.

Nita, Bidu and Niren called for us at 4:00 and we drove to a big park near the reservoir and water works. The fountain waters danced and reflected the sunset.

The Parikh family had a chauffeur who drove us places day and night.

We talked continuously and shared our lives. We strolled on a beach and sampled fresh coconut and sugar cane juice with lime and ginger.

Ruth writes:

Dear Jack,

Received your letter of November 20. Aren't the girls pleased with the fisherman sweaters? And Lori with her new fur hat?

Glad that Wendi's last year in high school was her first gratifying school experience. So Lori has her first "great" teacher also. I'm thrilled that Lori's true light is shining in the English Class.

David, of course, is no surprise to me. That was the reason I tried to skip a year in the hope that he would mature and care about school. Obviously, it didn't work. He is a playboy and has a casual, laid back attitude. I couldn't stir up interests even as we traveled. Nita also tried. He has the happier outlook and perhaps is much more adjusted than the people who drive themselves. Only he is in the wrong community to express his own innate personality. If he were in Ceylon or India, he would have no adjustment to make.

I am confident that all my children will come out on top, in the end. They had basic grounding, the stress in one society is very different from another, and they will have to find the one that suits their own personality.

You can plan to send a letter to Nairobi, Africa, for January. That is as far as we know. From now on we stay wherever we get a good welcome. No time schedule to hold us down. We are literally, " On Our Own."

I wish the children would spend more time with their Grandma Olga and Aunt Minnie.

Your wife, Ruth

Monday, December 2

In the morning we visited Kazumi in the hospital. After he departed the bus, he was admitted with Asian flu and it developed into hepatitis.

Our friend, Billy Rapp in New York, who was in the Peace Corps in India last year, gave us the information regarding Rohini. He enjoyed his time with her and encouraged us to do the same.

At noon, we met Rohini and Sharad, both dancers. Rohini invited us to her home, where we had our photos taken in saris. Rohini and her husband are lawyers. She owned a dancing school in Bombay and also one in Poona. We spent a delightful afternoon with her father and mother-in-law.

We spent the evening talking with Yasouha, Minka and Jenny Campbell. Nita Parikh arrived at 5:00 p.m. and joined us.

Yasouka received a telegram from Gray, her South African Englishman. "I love you. Will you marry me?"

Nita was always tired or sleeping. I called it sleeping sickness.

I did not know if I would ever get Nita out of Bombay. This family was wonderful to us. We lived at the Salvation Army for $10.00 for three days, for the two of us, for a room and all our meals. Can't beat that!

We were in India, the home of philosophy. I hoped to be able to find the peace of mind some Indians have attained.

India was absolutely the most colorful place in the world. Everything, even the food, was splashed with brilliant color.

Birds came up to the veranda in our room.

We took a taxi to see one Bombay sight, a street with many bright lights and rows of doors with bars, so men could look in and choose their own girl. "Cages," they called them and that's what they were. This system of slave trade and wide-open prostitution used young girls, too. I had a morbid curiosity; it was worth seeing and knowing about. It was a big joke in the "Modern Millie" movie starring Julie Andrews, but it really existed.

Tuesday, December 3

I took Nita to Breach Candy Hospital for blood tests. It cost 90 rupees. I went to the American Embassy for gamma globulin shots.

Nita P., Bindu and Niren took us to the aquarium and St. Xavier's doll exhibit. It was a worthwhile trip

Nita felt sick and we drove her home.

Nita P. presented us with three saris. We chose the most exquisite, blue with gold thread, and lovely jewelry to go with it.

I ate an Indian meal in their home. We perused a photo album of the family and the wedding pictures.

Nita's sickness dominated my thoughts and conversation. I hoped the doctors at the hospital would find a cure for her soon.

Wednesday, December 4

Nita had a urine analysis in the hospital.

I visited Kazumi at the hospital again, accompanied by Yaska and Daniel. I enjoyed conversation with them. I learned how Yaska met the Gray's family. She could not get a visa to South Africa. They did not write for one year to try to forget one another. They hitchhiked together as they traveled, and enjoyed each other in every aspect. He was a minster who was a progressive, understanding man.

Thursday, December 5

Ruth writes:

Dear Jack,

Our trip highlight is MAIL. Thanks for your letter. We received eleven letters. But we look forward to news about our family.

Did you finish the job on the Twin Towers building?

Tell us about Wendi's SAT results. Whose wedding did Wendi attend? What are Wendi's plans?

Relationships here in India were different. People appear to be more sincere and people give of themselves more readily.

In England and America "hold back" is the religion. Make the other guy prove himself first. This is not true of the East.

An example is the friendly way people find hostels, find restaurants, pay our taxi fares, takes us on tours, and ask nothing in return.

Love, Ruth

Dear Adam,

Days pass. Nita has been the "Sleeping Beauty." The blood tests in the hospital were negative. She sleeps most of the day.

We made friends in our veranda dorm at the Salvation Army. There were two Japanese women, one Australian swinger, Ursula, a German nurse and Jenny, who lived in our dorm. We had great talk fests.

I'm glad the slides I sent to you have arrived. Four more sets are en route. We have been in Bombay for a week now. I want to sell the camping equipment we no longer need and attend the Indian film festival tomorrow. We saw "Neel Kamal," an ancient Hindu story, and enjoyed that.

Evening. What a day! Jenny and I went to Nul Bazaar in the bus. We sold our flashlight, canteen, plastic dishes, gas lamp, knives and travel cup all for twelve ru-

pees. *Sold my sweater for five rupees. With the rupees we bought second hand silk saris, jewelry and pan (spices). We failed to sell our raincoat and sneakers.*

A Muslim boy led us around and we gave our air pillow to him.

We bought four embroidered saris.

We had fun, the color surrounding us, mingling among the beautiful people. Jenny's purse was stolen. It only had a few rupees, but all her keys.

Spent from nine in the morning until two in the afternoon at the bazaar. It was an exciting place.

Jenny is an artist and costume designer, so we visit art galleries. Jenny designed the costumes for the Sydney opera house. At the art exhibit we met the artist, Diddi Manoj from Delhi, who offered to give me a 500-rupee painting. He needs the money for his work. I could not accept his offer of a gift.

I saw him again in the school I visited. He has to hold down a teaching job to make a living. We also saw paintings of Mr. Sinha and like the work of both these artists very much.

Walked into a hall and watched a Hindu wedding. It was a wonderful day, full of episodes, stories and enjoying each other's company.

Love, Ruth

Friday, December 6

I had my hair dyed black and set in a very sophisticated style. No more gray hair.

I spent hours in the post office. Packages in India are sewed up in cloth, not wrapped in paper. It took a man two hours.

I experienced Indian routine, a grand run-a-round. Stand in one line for weighing the packages. Stand in another line to purchase stamps. Then stand in another line for insurance forms. Yet another line to check out printed material. They declared my package too heavy to send. Now it has to be made into two packages. So I took it home to sew it again.

I entered the room and I burst into tears, hours spent on nothing but frustration.

Jenny came home and said she had a date with the film director for that night.

The film director arrived with Jr. Executive.

I suggested, " Let's go to the film festival."

I sat in the back seat of the taxi with Jr., 24, a very quiet man. He put his arm around me and gently held my hand.

We sat in the movie and watched the film entitled "I Am Twenty." It was an excellent documentary asking such questions as: What is India to you? What do you want to be? Whom do you admire? What is the future of India?

"Marry the boss's daughter," was one response. In the documentary, "India 67," there were many scenes of places I recognized, and it had excellent photography.

Jenny and I were both willing to give the other one the film director. We both thought him personable, handsome and an easy conversationalist.

Jenny had a future with him and I didn't, so Jenny left with him and I said goodnight. Jr. Executive was hurt and whispered he would do everything to please me. But no thanks.

Daniel slept in Jenny's bed all night.

Ursula, a nurse, who worked in Afghanistan, told us that Nita needed salt in her system. She reminded us that it was the way they revived goldfish, too. We both started taking endovioform and salt tablets. Nita began to feel perkier.

Saturday, December 7

We were ready to leave for the railroad station when a man appeared at our door and asked us to become extras in the film they were making.

"Sorry, we are going to Poona now," Nita told him.

"Nita, have you ever been in the movies?" I asked her.

"No."

"Then this is our chance. We can go to Poona later on."

We drove to the outskirts of town to Joker Studios. It was confusion all day long. The English men guided us to the wrong make-up room.

I had my hair styled beautifully. The professional make-up man put cosmetics on me. I heard we were going to appear in a scene of a New Year's Eve party. We danced the European waltz. I danced with the dance director and he was smooth. I also danced with the star villain, Jeetingdar, who was a "clod." One, two, three, one, one, three. So clumsy. He was a nice guy and affable. The director asked Nita to teach the star, Abvas, the European waltz. She also had a close-up smile in the film and a flirting scene with the star.

But Mumtaz, the heroine of the film, got jealous and had to get back at Nita. Since the director admired Nita's smile, Mumtaz told Nita she had "black teeth." It was humorous.

People were friendly and talkative. It seemed to me they shot very little film.

Nita became friendly with the stars. Abvas and Mumtaz, the hero and heroine, were engaged in real life. She was patient and smiley and pleasant all day and never displayed any temperament.

The studios desperately needed air-conditioning. The stars and extras worked all week long and did not have weekends off. Why couldn't the stars learn to dance on their own time, not when 30 extras were standing round being paid for a day's work?

Extra's pay was designated as 100 rupees. But the man who made the contact and brought in the extras took the money. Foreign women got 35 rupees, Indian women got 30, foreign men got 30 and Indian men got 25.

We worked under the hot lights and sat around until 7:00 p.m. We received 70 rupees, or less than $10 for the two of us.

This system of payment was definitely unfair and caused bad feelings all around. Many people had to wait for their pay.

We were told food would be provided, yet we had to buy our own lunch.

There was no direction at all. Nobody knew what was going on and what was expected of us.

Who did they choose for the special dancing? The three worst dressed girls, who had no make-up on. Why did they put Jenny with the tall guy and want to substitute an Indian girl for the real camera shots? They changed their mind. Jenny was an attractive young woman.

We made friends with Henry, a young man, at the studio. He told us he would help find a place to stay at night. We worked to 7:00 p.m. and found a taxi. It cost 14 R because we had lugged our suitcases.

We landed at the YWCA. Henry obtained a good room with two other people.

Then he took us for a drink of sweet lassie and fruit salad. En route home he introduced us to Ronnie, an established guitar player.

Our plan to leave for Poona on the early morning train was postponed. We made a date to go to the Venice Room at the Hotel Astoria for a jazz jam session, a memorable evening for me. Henry accepted me and treated me as a young person, not Nita's "old lady." He danced with me and we had a good time.

We said thanks and goodnight to Henry.

Sunday, December 8

The Red Shield employees were not nice to us. We felt their attitude as they waited on our table. They deliberately made us wait for service and smirked as they served us, portioned food and refused to give any seconds.

Henry, our friend, was the lead of a street gang. His was a beautiful bearded face, his arm tattooed, and he was a Roman Catholic Indian.

Two more guys joined us at our table in the hotel ballroom. Now I had to Rock and Roll. This place was noisy and swinging. It had lights shining like stars around the room. I was in India.

The boys were taking Jenny to a festival and dance. Nita was tired and not enthusiastic. I thought I should rest and not run around all night.

We slept all night in the Poona station waiting room. At 3:00 a.m. a baby cried and the mother nursed it. The room filled with people. I wondered why all the people who slept on the platform didn't go upstairs to the waiting room.

We left Bombay.

Gladys told us she dreaded one thing in India — the trains. We would embark at 5:00 a.m. on the Deccan Queen, third class in the ladies' compartment. By the way, this train was faster than the express. It was crazy figuring it all out when buying tickets.

The train ride was over in three hours and I wrote the entire time. I stripped and washed in the lavatory. I sat in a wet dress and pants of necessity. The third class ladies' compartment was not bad at all. The seat wasn't padded, but it was O.K. People were pleasant.

Friends Mentioned in Chapter 25

Parikh family. Mr. Parikh was a diamond merchant. Nita attended college

Jeanette Campbell. She was an Australian companion in Bombay. I saw her again in Sydney, Australia.

Diddi Manoj.She was an artist

Mr.Sinha. He was an artist.

Henry Lobo. He was a gang leader, who we met at the movie studio. He was a very helpful friend to us.

Mark Mahadevia. He was in his 20s and a manager in his father's business.

RUTH

BEARS DANCING

SNAKE CHARMER

TWENTY- SIX

POONA

Monday, December 9

Tai-Vatsula Bahate, Rohini's elder sister, took us to Rohini's home. Rohini apologized for the "small room," as she brought us to a lovely room with two beds and two windows.

We had tea and conversed. Nita and I had a hot bath and washed our hair. After lunch we took a nap. We met friends all day long who came in and out of the house.

We walked to the dance studio where Rohini taught 25 students from 5:00 p.m. until 9:00. In the next two days she would teach 50 pupils.

I came home with Tai. We sat on the balcony and discussed the changing world and the difficulty older generations had in teaching about it. We discussed the attitudes regarding family unity in India and in the United States, the problems of old age in America, unrest in all countries.

We talked about Tai's own relationships with her family. Her father had died when she was 14 and Rohini was 2 and a friend sent all nine children to be educated. The mother was a friend to the big sister until her death five years earlier.

We had dinner at 9:00 p.m. and then retired.

Tuesday, December 10

We walked to the home of a newborn baby. The mother was a poet. All her children were talented. The youngest was an artist. The baby's mother gave us gifts of a doily and a handkerchief.

In the afternoon, we talked with Rohini. She married a dancer at 18. She gave birth to her son, Baba, and then they divorced.

All these years she had studied dancing, and her son was her life. Three years ago she married a cousin.

We spoke of the difficulties of a dancing career instead of one in a teaching profession.

Tai, as eldest, spoke of having to support the family. She had no time for marriage. Tai was the principal of a local school.

Dancing class was a world in itself. Rohini was an excellent teacher. She took the children for individual instruction. Nita and I learned different hand positions. It was not easy. We had a couple of lessons and I felt I got less coordinated each time. We put bells on our feet. Then we tried them on one foot. They were heavy. The foot stamping was fast and faster. This Nita and I could not do for 20 minutes, until the sweat poured down the face. From the youngest to the eldest, the dancers had grace all the way to their fingertips. The shape of their bodies was different from ours. The shape of their hands was different. We didn't have the slender fingers, which curved back, like they did.

An important ritual was the bow of reverence to the great masters of dance and to their teacher before and ending each lesson.

The class prayed to the God of Wisdom.

Guests arrived for the wedding — an aunt, uncle and niece. So we had to move out of Rohini's house.

We moved to Pawar's home. It was in Poona, not far from Rohini's house. Pawar's brother, Pratep, spoke English and entertained us until I thought of playing card games with the children.

Pawar's two young children were asleep. The three other children's parents worked on the farm and their children stayed in Poona because of more accessible and better schooling.

When Mr. and Mrs. Pawar arrived, we had dinner. It was 10 p.m. Then we went to sleep.

Wednesday, December 11

Nita arose at 6:00 a.m. and played badminton with Pratep. She learned a little about the game and came away impressed. A woman played in a sari.

We dressed for the wedding of Rohini's landlord's daughter and her nephew.

During the marriage ceremony there was a sheet between the couple. Then it was dropped. They drank coconut milk and a fire was made of the coconut husks. They walked around the fire three times. Piles of rice were placed around the room. The bride put her toes in each pile and then the guests threw rice. The bride and groom exchanged garlands of flowers and pearls.

All were welcomed and the meal was laid out. The wedding couple sat among cardboard cutouts and sand paintings.

The meal was rice with ghee, saffron rice, chutney, tomato salad, sweet-sour sauce with cashew potato, cabbage, fried cakes, pretzels, sweet jalaby, lassi drink and vermicelli pudding. As we finished each dish we were served more.

I rested and wrote in the afternoon. I visited Rohini at the dancing school and marveled once again at all the intricate steps committed to memory, Lord Krishna danced in pantomime.

Saying goodbye to Rohini was difficult. Even though we would try to contact one another in Delhi.

Ruth writes:

Dearest Mother and Minnie,

As each day passes we became more native in our outlook. We are now wearing saris instead of dresses, and walk around barefoot leaving our sandals outside the door. We eat all our meals with our right hand only, using fingers and not silverware.

I think how much easier each of these things is. Wendi would enjoy her meals without being told it is bad manners to eat with her fingers. Mushing the sauces or the yogurt into the rice, how children delight in doing this anyway.

The jewelry worn on everything, fingers, toes, ears, neck, nose and in hair on all children; and adults wear bangles of pearls and gold — as many as they feel like wearing.

Dresses have all the gilt and splash and frills little children love, happily dressed up. They wear uniforms to school, though.

We participated in a wedding today. Observed the many Hindu rituals. We learned of the fertility rites, garlands of flowers on each of the bride and groom. Became friendly with both sets of parents. We met many people and admired the gorgeous saris and faces. The hundred guests were fed. Food was varied, spectacular and as much as we could eat. We went with Tai and Rohini. We wore beautiful saris with gold thread and jewelry.

We moved to Pawar's house because Rohini had her relatives from Bombay visiting for the wedding.

There were five children, two belong to Pawar. The other three belong to another brother who lives on a farm. School is more accessible here for the children.

Pawar had a room on the roof for privacy.

Yes, people sleep on mats or mattresses on the floor. We have done that. They also sleep on beds. We each had a couch in Pawar's home.

Pawar told us we need the experience of being in the country. Most of our time we spend in big cities. Tomorrow we go to visit the family farm. The days are never without new experiences. All wonderful.

Love, Ruth

Thursday, December 12,

It was the end of Kasha's fourth year and Meena conducted some rites. There was a candle and they put tikka's good luck symbol on his forehead for him.

Mr. Pawar, Shema, Kasha, Nita and I drove to Meena's parent's home. They were away but we met two of her brothers and one showed us his prize-winning rose. His wife served us tea. The other brother spoke with us about education. He planned to go to California to study mechanical engineering. He drove us around the backyard in his 1937 Singer Red car. We spoke continuously as we drove.

In Baramati, we passed the house where Billy Rapp had lived when he was in the Peace Corps and worked for Pawar. He was the source of the two Poona addresses to visit.

Shiela, Pawar's 14-year-old daughter, spoke comfortable English. She served us dinner. Momma watched us eat and commented on how we ate all of it.

"Not too hot?"

It seemed Billy found the food too hot to eat. So Mom brought out her lemon pickles and chutney and gave us a taste of everything. We passed the test and licked our plates clean.

We met another Shiela, who spoke excellent English. She was a neighbor. She took us into her home next door. She sat with us and told us she had studied political economy in school, but her father would not permit her to go to work. She had to marry instead.

We drove on to the farm with Momma, Meena and Ajit in the car.

At the farm we took a walk through the fields and Momma showed us the homes of the workers. The people in the sugar cane fields sang as they cut the cane. We walked through the grape arbors, heavily laden; the fruit would ripen in two more months.

We sat in the back yard and relaxed before visiting the sugar factory. We had the grand tour. The sugarcane was washed and crushed and the juices put back in and crushed some more. The fiber was dried and used as fuel to create steam for all the machines. The juice was heated, evaporated and made into crystals at different temperatures. All of the sugar we'd seen so far was brown.

In the month of January only brown sugar was made and sent to the United States. Refined sugar was made later by adding sulfur and lime.

After the tour we were taken into the office and introduced to the board of directors. The government regulated much of what was done.

We were served sugar cane juice. When Billy Rapp drank it he had landed in the hospital for four weeks. We drank it and liked it. I liked it with lemon and ginger flavor.

Under British rule the workers in the field used to get a rupee or two a day and worked every day. Now their salary was raised and they got higher wages, but, by their own choice, they worked only a couple of days a week. This was a great inconvenience to get the cane cut. They let their children work for a rupee when the children should have been in school and the adults could have earned that money if they had worked another day. They lived in cane huts with fireplaces in front of each for cooking.

The whole family ate together. Then it was off to bed. Nine of us bedded down on mattresses on the floor. Nita got hysterical laughing because we were supposed to share a blanket. I tucked in and she didn't. She put the blanket sideways and my feet stuck out. The girls finally gave us each a separate blanket.

Birds came into the house through open windows and ate the crumbs they found. There were no flies, mosquitoes or flying insects and no screens.

Friday, December 13

We were given a breakfast of tea and sweets.

Shiela Pawar and Momma gave Nita a new brown sari, and some bangle bracelets. She broke six trying to get them on to her wrist. Our hands were hard, not as flexible as our friends' hands. Shiela invited us to stay or return soon.

We drove off to Baramati with Momma, Meela and Ajit.

We drove to town because Momma wanted to buy her grandson a birthday present. We met friends of the Pawars, who were married at 13 and 15. All three of the pairs went to a movie on their wedding night and one girl kept bouncing up and down on the seat. It was her first time in a movie theater. She had twins when she was 15 years old. Now she had five children and she was still petite and young looking.

Yesterday when Pawar left us for a while he met a possible husband for Neela. She would be married when they found someone for her. Her mate had to be educated and the same Hindu religion. He had to be a member of as high a caste as Neela's.

Mother and Pawar discussed all family matters together and shared opinions and decisions until late at night — Neela's marriage, the sugar factory, farms. There were two farms of 50 acres each. They were divided into 18 acres for each family, according to law. The law also said to rotate planting of sugar cane every three years.

In order to enlarge the factory, the family borrowed money from other family members. When the brother ran for assembly, each family contributed to his campaign. Pawar sold his flat to obtain money. Joint families made sense.

Our discussions were ceaseless. We had solved India's problem. I hoped we had gained a little more insight into this way of life. I agreed that the joint family system made more sense than our way, when I saw how members could share work, farm, land and wealth. It was a close family.

There were 14 children in Pawar's family, all with arranged marriages.

\\\\\\Momma was a strong, vibrant woman at 60. She used a cane because a bull nearly killed her 10 years ago. She was still active in running her farm and advising her children. The factory was a farmer's cooperative. She spent days there to be sure they kept up a high standard of production.

Electrification and dams had been used in farms since independence. Electricity and water had reached the farm. Britain was an exploiter and held the people back. Untouchables were now being educated and many held high positions, such as teachers and doctors. Britain used to divide and conquer and used religious differences to keep people apart instead of united.

Momma and Pawar agreed on big changes and a higher standard of living and more education for the Indian people.

India's unemployment was unnecessary. There was enough work for all. They could build more schools, especially colleges, to prepare for the great influx due to come soon. WPA, CCC type work for all the unemployed would have been desirable, 5 to 8 hours of work a day to improve India. They should not have fought automation and machines; it was better to use tractors. There were 300 on local farms. One brother without government help made local Baramati labor build water tanks to irrigate the fields. It made a big improvement in the crops and got good publicity for him. They should have cut sugar cane with machines, not human labor. We spoke of the laxity of workers, especially government workers. We spoke of the problem of the government elected; they were too concerned with being liked and getting re-elected.

Gandhi might be a God in India because his non-violent attitude helped the Indians attain independence. But now there was a necessity for more modern methods. He encouraged using hands to do the work; he did not want to resort to machines of any kind.

A traveling circus came to town. We saw a traveling drama troupe enact a play. It was another way for the people to earn money.

We rested while Meena attended her sewing class.

In the evening we rode to a sister's home. Her husband built his house by himself. She had a beautiful garden with fruit, vegetables and flowers and she did all the work in it plus caring for her five children.

One family grew prize roses. Beauties. We wore roses in our hair now.

It was a great day. I finally mailed my package with Diary #2.

Saturday, December 14

Nita and I rode a bus to shop in Poona. We bought bedspreads for Meena.

We, Meena, and her aunt went to the Educational Center. It was a home extension course held in a school auditorium. It was Meena's final exhibition of her sewing class. They spoke Marathi. Beautiful handiwork was exhibited.

Women presented their recipes as they cooked "sweets" (candy). The candy had sesame seed, cumin and coriander flavorings and coconut in some of it. Delicious.

When Mrs. Pawar and Meena walked out after seeing the sewing and the prize winners, they both complained. "They were friends of the judges," and "The length exceeded regulations."

A brother questioned me. What had I learned? What would I teach when I returned to the classroom? How would my teaching differ now that I was a world traveler?

We were asked, "What do you eat at the end of the meal if you don't have pan?"

Nita made a spaghetti dinner. Cooking with six children underfoot is rough. Meena appreciated having less to do.

Kasha's ear bothered him. Pawar had taken him to two doctors and they put an ointment in his ear. He grabbed the bandage and wanted to pull it off.

Kasha lighted incense and played with fire. I hadn't spoken about it, but it bothered me.

He hit the male servant this day with a stick. Pawar said Subash had been told to take the stick away from him. Subash had a rough time because obviously Kasha got his own way most of the time. How could he override him?

There was a characteristic toss of the head. Rohini always did it, now I noticed many people doing it. It meant "Yes." A sideways nod was "No." Rohini taught us the gestures for beginning and ending a lesson; the hands in prayer formation and bow is "hello" and can be "goodbye" also. The gesture shows respect.

Sunday, December 15

Pratap came home last night.

Nita was angry with him because he did not wake her at 6:00 when he went to play badminton in the morning.

The entire family took baths and washed their hair. We sat in the sun to dry it. Meena brushed mine.

In the afternoon 10 of us piled into the car and drove to Fort Lion on top of a mountain. Here the tired soldiers fought the Moguls and won. This helped Hindu India against Moslem India. We climbed and admired the view, the flowers and the sunset.

Monday, December 16

We dressed up and drove off in rickshaw taxis to Meena's sister's home for a "Naming Day" ceremony for a month-old baby.

An elderly woman made friendly overtures as I entered. She was Meena's mother. Smiles take you far.

What a picturesque ceremony. Flowers garlanded everywhere, in hair and over the hanging cradle. Momma sat with the infant on her lap as each guest presented the baby with gifts in a ritual manner. There were the rituals of the powders — orange and red powder on the forehead of both mother and child and on gifts and presents.

Lullabies were sung.

I counted 35 women and about 25 children in one room at a time. We were invited into the dining room for refreshments. We were given nuts, potato chips and a sweet cake.

We drove home and helped make dinner.

All evening both brothers figured out the best way for us to travel.

All the talk signified reluctance at our leave-taking. I felt that I hadn't made enough of a contribution nor made Meena's life any easier by our visit. We spoke and she didn't seem to resent our intrusion on her life. I wish I could have done more for her. I knew Pawar enjoyed discussions with us.

Meena and I spoke of superstitions for good health. Kasha was a caesarian child and Shema was a forceps baby. Children needed more to keep them busy.

Parwar said Kasha didn't like toys, but he needed construction toys to keep him busy and happier. What about tinker toys? Or some plastic block-building sets? Shema also could enjoy activities. There was the same complaint for Rajar and Profullata, though they wandered around quietly and did not cause trouble or mischief. Neema alone found things to do by herself and kept happy. She wrote and did sums. I figured out gifts for the family. I hoped I could manage to send them.

Tuesday, December 17

We gave Pawar a Kennedy coin. We had nothing else to give.

Nita and I decided to shoot up to Delhi.

I loved Nita and enjoyed her very much. But I was sick and tired of her attitude toward me. She had gained strength since those first days in Spain. She could meet and handle people on her own. Let her do it now.

We needed a vacation from each other. Nita was now caretaker of her own passport and Nepal visa application, pictures and 200 rupees. I thought: I must give her more travelers' checks. She demanded half, and she snatched my address book. In each of these areas I was still "Mommy" and took care of my daughter. Now the independence was established. I'm sure the blow was harder on me. I gave up a great deal of pleasure when we separated.

Meena and Pawar accompanied us to the station. Then we got on our "Ladies" compartment. Better it should be called a children's ward. There were crying children the whole way to Bombay. It was a shock as we entered, but a man came through and swept the filthy floor and that helped. The noise and confusion and profusion of junk disturbed both of us. The mothers breast-fed children. Children were fed rice, chapati and bananas. At major stops men came through and sold nuts and candy. I wrote most of the trip, so there was no time for socializing.

A woman opposite me wore two nose pins and another had six earrings in her ears. The girl next to me had straggly uncombed hair, rags for sari, and a sleeping baby. She decided to wake it to change the dress, then had to breast- feed it to keep it quiet. She appeared to be a very young girl.

Ruth writes:

Dear Mom,

The Pawar family has been our host for a week now. I feel like the man who came to dinner. How can I repay them? You can.

His brother is an architect and town-planning Engineer. Would you send his name and address to Walter Scheiber and also the relative of Walter Goodman who won the town-planning award? Tell them Pawar plans to come to the U.S. and let each write a letter and offer him assistance and support. Please.

Love, Ruth

Nita writes:

Dear Grandma,

We rode third class on hard wooden seats, with no berth, for 24 hours from Bombay to Delhi. It only cost $4 for both of us, but it was a dirty train and crowded and slow. It even had cracks in the window letting in cold air. We froze. Now we learned why Indians carry bedrolls with them.

I bought a Punjab dress with pants, Indian style.

We are sitting on the lawn of Nepal Embassy. It looks like the White House.

We have cards for Christmas for you, but you'll receive them in months from now.

Love to you, Nita

Dear Wendi,

Well, I'm on a train heading from Poona to Delhi. My plan is to get a Nepal visa in Delhi and stay for a couple of weeks in Katmandu. After that, who knows? My mother is giving me a couple of hundred dollars in traveler's checks for the remaining five months of my journey. I doubt if it will last me, so I'll probably have to get a job somewhere. I'm in kind of a depressed state at the moment, since it's scary to depend completely on my own resources for everything. It gives me a very insecure feeling.

Michael Dunn invited me to stay at his house, so I think I'll work my way down to Australia via Africa. Kazumi, the Japanese boy on the other bus, invited me to his house, too.

I'm in the third class Ladies compartment of the train again. Screaming babies are all over me. All the young girls are combing their silky, black, waist long hair. It's so crowded that people are sitting on the luggage rack and the seats are so hard that my rear will never survive the five hours to Bombay.

I have a wide-open window next to me and the sky is bluer than it has been for weeks (usually it is white because of the heat) and the trees are bright green, so my melancholy will go away soon. This year will certainly be a new experience.

This train is too much. One of the babies just urinated all over the floor where I put my feet.

Pratap is 25-year-old civil engineer who was very shy, but once he got used to us he was nice. Every morning at 6 he would take me to a badminton club. He was professional at the game.

At Pawar's we learned to be Indian. We eat everything, including curries, with only our right hand, no matter how hot a food is it doesn't phase me.

We wore saris exclusively; no longer use toilet paper, only wash with water, take only "running water from a bucket" baths; and use coconut oil to make my hair beautiful. (It really does – you should try it – use only a tiny dab at the roots and work it down with your fingers. Also never use a brush). I sometimes helped Meena in the kitchen where there is no refrigerator or oven. I greet and say goodbye to people putting both hands to forehead in prayer position, introduce myself as "Tai" oldest sister and my mother as "Ai" mother, and I wear a tikka – a red dot on my forehead for good luck.

Buying you a present is a hopeless cause. It is difficult to mail anything in India. It must pass through customs, be sewed with special material, and have no notes inside.

I am in Bombay waiting for a student concession for the train ticket. My train to Delhi left five minutes ago, so I'll probably end up sleeping in the station waiting room again. Aside from a crying baby, it wasn't too bad; we've gotten used to wooden benches for beds by now.

I'm not wearing my sari today because I have to change money. Men come to a tourist and ask if they want to change money, but probably they won't today because I need it.

India is having a lot of trouble with Naxalite (Maoist) supporters. Riots have been going on near the Chinese border and in other places also. India's scared and has begun red baiting.

The sky has turned white again. Bombay is hot!

Love, Nita

Friends Mentioned in Chapter 26

Rohani Bhate. She was the principal of a dancing school in Bombay and Poona.

Tai. She was Rohini's sister and a principal of a secondary school

Pawar and wife Meena. They were our hosts for a week.

Sheena and Kasha, 4. His brother Pratap played badminton with Nita.

HENRY AND HIS GANG

BARBER GIVING A HAIRCUT IN THE STREET

TWENTY- SEVEN

INDIA

Wednesday, December 18

We arrived at 4:00 p.m. The reservation office closed at 4:30. I didn't make it.

I couldn't even attempt to describe the grand run-around for tickets.

"I am not selling any," I was told over and over. I was sent from one building where third class was sold to another. I tried for second class deluxe. There wasn't any. All I could learn was: "Be back at 8:00 a.m. and get tickets and reservations then."

We put luggage in layaway and walked. We considered a couple of Indian hotels. No luck.

At nine in the evening, we tried using a retiring room in the station. They were all filled. A kind stationmaster gave us permission to use the first class room because that room was empty. They locked the doors to shut out the noise. We remained alone. Nita turned out the light. It was a great sleep.

6:00 a.m. Lights on. Doors opened. Train and station noises reminded me where we were. We thought the passenger superintendent might help us to take advantage of cancellations. I stood in line for thirty minutes. Nita was on the cancellation line. She got two seats on deluxe. We went to the third class window and now the concession read "Calcutta." The official wanted to sell us a ticket to Calcutta. We told him we did not want to go to Calcutta.

I crossed out the form he gave us. "Can't do that," he yelled at me. He snatched both forms. 9:15 a.m. and more waiting. At this point Nita yipped, "Can't you do anything right?"

Friday, December 20

American Express had two letters from my mother and one from Aunt Minnie.

I walked to GPO and picked up a letter from Adam, a good, interesting one. It lifted my spirits a bit.

We took a taxi and picked up our passports.

In the afternoon, we sat on the Nepal Embassy lawn reading and writing.

Mohinder Pal, a taxi tour guide, came by and made a date for 6:00 p.m. He said he would drive us anywhere.

Saturday, December 21

I bought a shirt with beads for Jack and a Punjab dress. I wound up in the government tourist office and watched films of Indian dances.

We moved into Dr. Harry's apartment for the night. Dr. Harry was on night duty and slept in the casualty room. Nita and I settled comfortably in the beds.

Sunday, December 22

Dr. Harry returned to his room. We drank milk and fell asleep again until 9:00 a.m.

Dr. Harry shared a mutton curry lunch with us.

Ruth and Rodney Smith took us to the American Embassy Christmas party. We met the diplomat, Chester Bowles, and his wife.

We wondered what kind of a party it was without food or drink. We talked a bit and left.

They had an auction at the British Embassy and we enjoyed that.

We bought some fruit and went home.

We met Mohinder in the building and we introduced him to Dr. Harry. Dr. Harry was lonely when we deserted him.

We drove to the bazaar and returned the sari we had bought the previous day. Nita was ready for a dramatic scene. It was not necessary. Our 10 rupees were returned without comment.

Nita, Mohinder and I had a conversation regarding Mohinder's trip to Agra and the possibility of me joining him. It was agreed among us that I would go.

Harry said he couldn't sleep with the electricity of two women in his room. Neither could I, so we talked until after one. He gave me cough medicine for the tickle in my throat. We talked more. He put his arms around me and it relaxed me. He finally fell asleep for the rest of the night in his own bed. Nita and I slept comfortably on the mattresses on the floor.

Monday, December 23

At the YMCA Tourist Hostel I met my fellow passengers Harihal and Diane. We talked all the way to Agra. He was from India and a teacher at Lovell University in Massachusetts. They had met while she was doing research there. They had a two-year courtship.

Mohinder arranged an 80-rupee hotel for them.

Mohinder and I settled for a government rest house for the night, after several hotels refused us. Mohinder explained they would not aid him in his sin of staying with a foreign woman.

Harihal and Diane ate mutton in a good restaurant. Mohinder, always anxious to please, bought our food at a wayside eatery (called dhabas) and we devoured it in the car.

The night was interesting. Mohinder used his own blanket roll on one bed. My bed was made to perfection with mattress and clean, ironed sheets that were beautiful, only cold. Mohinder's bed was warmed with a quilt.

I asked him to shave and reluctantly he did. Lucky I asked, because the next day was Tuesday, and he did not shave nor eat meat on Tuesdays.

Tuesday, December 24

Before 7:00 a.m. a man woke us and brought us tea. Those Indians! Don't they know sleep is more important than tea?

Now we bathed in hot water again. We gassed up the car and ate a breakfast of hot milk and sweet pudding.

I thought love oozed from Mohinder when he fed me. He couldn't buy enough, nor do enough for me at mealtime. It reminded me of my Jewish mother-in-law. No kissing. No outward demonstrations of love at all. Only "eat, eat." So I complied.

We picked up the Harihals and I decided to show Diane where we stayed for the night.

I explained that Nita and I had been rooming with men for two months in the bus and I had no qualms about the two of us sharing a room for 10 rupees.

She praised the size of the room and its cleanliness. She explained that because of her girdle and stockings she needed Western toilets, not squat toilets. But this government rest house had a Western toilet.

On to Agra Fort. We obtained a guide. The heat on November 22, the last time I had been there, was oppressive. This time I learned all about the fort.

At Fatehpuhr Sikri we also learned more than the first time we visited the area with our Indiaman tour group.

The city was built well; it was 400 years old and still standing. The story behind its creation started with a Sufi saint, Sheikh Salim Chishti. Akbar asked his blessing for a male heir. Three sons were born to his queen. The first son was born in 1569 and he built Jami Masjid, near the saint's dwelling. The second son was born in 1571. The grateful emperor built this imperial city. It was bigger and better than London. The name Fatehpuhr means the "city of Victory.'"

The houses of nobles, bazaars, schools and stables sat below the palaces. The city held 5,000 elephants, more than 1,000 cheetahs and 30,000 horses. The library had 24,000 manuscripts. The court in those days was a creative center for artisans.

We had lunch on the lawn of the Dak bungalow at Fatehpuhr Sikri. We shared the box lunch and Diane tasted guava and Chinese gooseberry for the first time. We also ate papaya and bananas.

We browsed in the sari store, handling the delicate silks for a long time. We admired the pure golden shawls.

Patient Mohinder bought tangerines for our lunch. It was thoughtful of him. We ate lunch in a magnificent setting. Harihal and Diane were an intelligent couple and their conversation continued to be stimulating.

Ruth writes:

Dear Adam,

Your letter became a bright spot in our day. I had a hike to American Express, but when I held your letter it was worth it. Thanks over and over for being you.

We moved into the doctor's residence into Dr. Rajendra Harry's room. He is Mauretian, young, well educated and enlightened.

We obtained our Nepal visas and we were sitting on their embassy lawn, a beautiful serene place. Mohinder, a taxi-touring driver, introduced himself.

He receives no money from me, but I ate meals and had free rides. When he took a couple on a tour, Harihal and his American wife, Diane, he invited me to join him. I decided to accompany them to Agra and Jaipur.

Nita agreed to stay with Dr. Harry and he said he would give her a key to the room, so she would not have any more uninvited guests.

Christmas? It certainly doesn't look or feel like it in Hindu India.

In Agra, we saw the Taj yesterday. Then on to the Red Fort where the son kept his father captive the last eight years of his life. From there to the ancient city of Fatehpuhr Sikri, this time seen with a guide.

The man who is paying for this tour is an Indian, who is a Ph.D. nuclear scientist. He rose as high as he could in his job in India. Now he is working at Lowell, Massachusetts. He married Diane there. He came back to India to introduce Diane to his family. They were an intelligent couple and we enjoyed being together.

Two farm women came up to me and invited me to have milk in their home.

I said, "yes," as usual, but the others wanted to get going to Jaipur. I won out.

We all visited the farm. Mohinder and Harihal spoke Hindi to the people. I drank three huge glasses of fresh milk and ate sugar cane and held their baby and admired the nose to ear jewelry.

All these women were in Purdah and their faces were hidden. They wanted us to sleep there. I would have, but our American Diane said, " No."

This is the real India, they displayed many bracelets and silver jewelry, but they wore ragged clothing.

The woman pointed to her dress and mine, so I changed from Western dress back into my ragged sari. It was a hospitable farm family.

In Jaipur by 9 p.m. The Harihal's room cost 60 rupees including three meals. Mohinder and I got our room in the same hotel for 10 rupees.

We took a hot bath in a clean tub. This is the first time since the Iran border. So I took a bath at night and again in the morning. What luxury.

Driving is rugged in India. Trucks drive straight at you and you have to pull off to the side of the road for them. We passed several cars that had accidents. Many times it is because of the animals in the road. No wonder Mohinder gets tired from driving all day long.

Mohinder enjoys feeding me, like a "momma," this is one way he shows his affection for me. He plans all sorts of foods he will buy. Last night, he bought meat for me. But not for him on Tuesdays. It was succulent food, from a wayside stand. Tea and food is often brought to the car in India.

Diary number three is nearly finished and I will mail it to you soon.

My darling, I still love you best of all the men I have met so far.

Love, Ruth

Nita writes:

Dear Aunt Minnie,

We appreciate your faithful letters. We write every opportunity we can.

We have been in Delhi for a few days now, staying of all places, at the doctor's room in a hospital. Our friend, Dr. Harry, is really nice. Mommy and I are sharing a bed, so it's crowded, but at least it is free.

Yesterday we went to a Christmas party at the American Embassy that was filled with crowds of people. But there were no refreshments, so it was a drag and we left.

Tonight I am going to a very exclusive club to play chess. I'll dress up in my best sari, and it should be fun.

I have been spending a lot of time with a Maori girl from New Zealand named Maria. She has been living in the orient for a couple of years now.

Most Indian intellectuals I have met feel that India is going to the dogs. Strikes are everywhere. The economy is low, poverty is everywhere. They feel the best thing is either communism, (not the Russian kind, the Mao-type) or dictatorship. This seems like a very wide "or." But they think that a strong dictator would be able to organize and control the country and that this could eventually transfer into communism.

They feel the United States type politics is a luxury that only a rich and educated country can afford. Education is held in such high esteem that it is almost thought sacred, but still the graduates cannot earn a living wage. Indians are extremely proud of their country, and whenever we meet new people they always reel off names of places that we absolutely cannot miss. They are pleased to see us in Indian dress and eating Indian food. We have made many lifelong friends because of our natural adjustment to Indian ways. Nita was a very popular Indian name.

Delhi is a very complicated city. Connaught Circus, the center of New Delhi, is a street full of concentric circles with other streets radiating from it. I still get lost occasionally. My mother has had a beautiful, intricately embroidered Punjab dress made for her. It is tight on the bottom and baggy on top. Pants go with it. She looks stunning in it.

Happy Hanukkah and I miss you.

Love, Nita.

Friday, December 27

I met Mrs. Nanda Swaranji and Miss Verma Kamklashji, who were Hindi teachers and started me on my Hindi course. Mrs. Nanda had three children, 6, 3 and 4 months. We socialized for a while and then I met Rameshji Verma, the brother, 23.

I would have liked to meet a person close to my age who would accompany me to the cultural activities in Delhi — the theater, exhibits, meetings, places of educational interest, intellectually stimulating places.

Dr. Harry played cards all night and never came back to the room. Nita and I slept on the floor and the two beds in the room were left empty because we were expecting him.

Guests were arriving so we had to evacuate this room.

We carted our luggage over to 2 Hailey Road.

We smoked joints with Marie, Gordon and Rodney Smith at the Gaylord restaurant.

We devoured delicious cheese and chicken rolls. Music at Gaylord's was slow and old fashioned and made me sleepy.

Then we moved on. At The Cellar restaurant I woke up when they played modern records.

I had my first pot cigarette with Mohinder on the trip — one each night. I did not notice any effect. I smoked Saturday night and it should have given me a real high. I know I had all my faculties.

Sunday, December 29

Gordon and Rod walked with me to change money. We met Mohinder and we joined him on a tour of Old Delhi and Red Fort. His customers were a German couple, dull people, and unfriendly. They made no attempt to explain anything to the youngster they had with them.

We went in for espresso and fried cake and a sweet pudding with nuts and soft ice cream, and of course, pan.

We had a crazy time from 4:30 to 10: 00 p.m. We ate, drank and smoked. We Picked up Nita. Jahon took us to his home.

Jahon's younger, educated brother is delightful and we talked for more than an hour. He agreed in politics with Pawer, except that he liked Gandhi. He left his comfortable bed and gave it to me. It was a crazy night because each of us was concerned with the comfort and happiness of the others.

Orin came to our room. Should I go to Nepal or wait for Anand? I was told he was engaged to be married and that put a different light on our relationship. He told me Anand would return on January 4 and I should wait. I doubted if I would.

This evening, I lay in bed unhappy. I always got upset at a pile of errands to do.

Then Britt, a friend, related the recent events in her life. Her bus trip from Istanbul canceled out and they gave her no refund. Her partner obtained a car and it burned in a fire. All their clothes and possessions burned. So they went to Katmandu and on the second day her boyfriend got hepatitis. He was in critical condition. Britt sat by his bed in the hospital morning and night. She lost 14 pounds.

She was now separated from him for the first time in a year, and missed him and was lonely. To be philosophical, Britt was lovely, sweet and weathered all those storms. My own troubles were caused only by indecision and loneliness.

On such a note the diary ends. The next day would be December 31.

What would the New Year bring?

Tuesday, December 31

We moved from Hailey Road to the YWCA for 15 rupees for a curtained cubical. There were no locks. I slept well and felt better.

I spent from 9:00 a.m. to 10:00 washing clothes and from 10:00 to 1:00 getting the visa for Kenya. Things were looking up. I had a date for New Year's Eve.

HAPPY NEW YEAR TO US ALL!!!

Wednesday, January 1

Nita writes in her diary:

And here I am at 3:00 a.m. freezing to death in Delhi. New Year's Eve with Arinder was dull. His only thought was how to entice me to "his apartment," and how to get me to cooperate, if I went there. What a bore! Trouble is, he has such an inferiority complex that I don't know how to get rid of him without his committing suicide. He wouldn't be a bad guy if only he had a little more faith in himself.

Saturday, January 4

Nita writes:

If only Rajan Harry wasn't so gentle, so comfortable. If only I didn't like him so much. He still doesn't know how I feel. I could say "c'est la vie," and disappear forever without a qualm. But, because he is Rajan Harry, I know that a part of me will stay in Delhi completely unnoticed.

Friday, January 10

Nita writes:

I spent the night with Harry. We arrived at the room from the Micado Restaurant at about one. We talked about Shakespeare and Queen Elizabeth's lovers for a couple of hours. He was on one bed; I was on the other. We just talked.

It is now 9 a.m. and I am at the Tourist Hostel. At 1:00 p.m. we will leave Delhi. I said "goodbye" to Rajan a few minutes ago. I am depressed.

No kiss, no handshake, just "Goodbye. Good luck."

This sweet, gentle, wonderful man I would never see again. I felt empty.

He said earlier that he would miss me. I said nothing. He tells me how much he likes me. I said nothing. He says he'll write and asks me to also.

Why this needless agony? Can't I open up, be a responsive human being? And now alone, I cry.

Friends Mentioned in Chapter 27

Harihal and his wife Diane. He was a nuclear scientist.

Mohinder Pal. He was a tour driver and included me in with his paid clientele.

Dr. Rajendra Harry. He let us use his room in the hospital. He was a love in Nita's life.

Mrs. Nanda Swaranji and Miss Verna Kamklushji. They were two Hindi teachers who taught me.

ON BACK OF ELEPHANT, HARIHAR AND DIANE AND RUTH IN AMBER CITY, FATEHPUHR SIKRI

WOMEN CARRYING WATER IN POTS ON THEIR HEAD

INDIAN CHILDREN EATING ORANGE PEEL

TWENTY-EIGHT

NEPAL

January 10, 1969

Nita writes:

Dear Family,

We decided to leave Delhi and go to Nepal. I've been having a panic here. We've been staying for the past week and a half at a Doctor's Mess Hall with Dr. Harry from Mauritius, who is absolutely brilliant. You'd really like him, Daddy. Science, pure math and wit fascinate him. Unfortunately, he has too many friends; many come to stay in his room. So there was not room for us and we moved out two days ago, back into Singh's guesthouse.

This is where we stayed when we first arrived in Delhi two months ago, and when we first came back two weeks ago. Neither Mom nor I like the place because Singh, the owner, is an absolute crook. We stayed there as a last resort.

When we arrived there this time Singh was a nervous wreck and the place was in chaos. A friend who had been staying there for four months, Gordon, had his rucksack stolen. He called in the police who have been dying to get hold of Singh because of his numerous crooked activities. Singh was forced to close the guesthouse immediately.

One thing about the name Singh: over half of Delhi is named Singh. This is true. Every man of the Sikh religion is named Singh and every woman is named Kar. The Sikhs also distinguish themselves by wearing turbans, under the turban is a huge knot of head hair and beard hair. They never cut either. This, they say, is because they are great warriors and must always be ready for battle. Trouble is, it is difficult to distinguish the sex of Sikh children. Boys and girls have lovely braids tied with bright ribbons wrapped around their heads. To make it harder, they wear nail polish, eye make-up and bracelets.

Western food is so bland compared to Indian food. I particularly adore gee (boiled buffalo butter) with chapattis, oriental style bread which is pancake shaped and very crisp when hot, and Bhal, a snack with crisp noodles, banana coins, nuts, raisins and, of course, good ol' faithful chili sauce.

When I get back to the states, I am going to wear saris, and also " mini saris," the latest innovation.

Love to you all, Nita

January 15, 1969
Dear Family,

We finally arrived in Katmandu! It's about time, but how we got here is a long story. A two-day train ride, sitting up with four middle of the night and early morning changes. Without a break, a nine-hour bus ride from the Nepalese border to Katmandu, absolutely scrunched in seats that I'm sure were made for five-year-old children.

Nepal is different from India. The people are Tibetan. They live in thatched huts or houses on stilts, wear a bundled looking multi-piece sari, drink really polluted water, and have a different language and set of numbers. (7=1,2=2,8=4 etc.) They serve a delicious noodle dish called chow-chow, eat buffalo and yak meat, and have nary a toilet or outhouse, except in the city. The streets become the sewers.

The huge Himalayan mountains surround the area. The terrain looks like a cross between Thailand and Tibet as we come by bus, with patches of jungle-like underbrush with heavily-vined trees and then areas of green stepped-mountains going high into the clouds.

We have just spent our second and last day in Katmandu. This place is dreamland! Golden dragon pagodas, windy dark mud streets, wrinkly women with huge bundles on their bent backs carried by a rope around the forehead, men with that long, scale-type pole on their shoulders. They display the loveliest silver and stone jewelry, clothing styles dating back to the early 1100s or older, and they are the most beautiful people in the world.

Quick, bright black eyes, smooth bronze skin, a proud silent regal look in even the poorest farmer.

I am happy here, oh so happy. Life is peaceful, life is good. Everybody who passes by smiles and nods. Language is unimportant because a huge warm smile and "Namastra" says everything. I wish, I wish so much I could stay here for a long, long time, but the tragedy of our visit is that we are bound for a ship to Mombasa on the 18th of January. Nuts!

Although we have been here for such a short time, we have made good friends. Tonight we ate supper with our hotel owner who wanted us to eat "real Nepalese food."

We met a different hotel owner this afternoon while walking to a Buddhist temple high in the mountains. He drove us all the way up there, took us around the immense buildings. He brought us to a festival in the valley, a couple of miles below.

This evening, he took us to a nearby village, Patan, to see some old gorgeous shrines and temples and then to his home.

We met his other brother who worked at the Nepalese museum. He was an educated Tibetan. He said that Tibetan culture was rapidly becoming extinct.

Nowadays it was very difficult to get authentic Tibetan crafts. I did manage to obtain a turquoise and silver ring that I'll be sending home in the next package.

Mommy, in the first fit of extravagance all trip, fell in love with two beautifully carved rhinoceros-bone and stone pendants and decided that she had to have them.

We are freezing to death among snow-covered Annapurna and Mount Everest, but if the Nepalese can stand it with only a slight shawl and no shoes, we can stand it in our heaviest clothing.

Love, Nita

Mother is difficult. I understand and try to put up with her because the rewards are great. We meet many wonderful people, usually she makes the contacts and I continue the relationship while we're with the person.

She writes after we leave. We do things that other tourists and visitors don't, such as going to festivals, visiting people in their home, and getting to see thrilling places as Katmandu.

We often split up when we get to the cities. But, in all justice, she would be a good traveling companion for someone with a different personality from mine.

She doesn't like my, "Let come what may," attitude. My financial dependence on her makes my position very tricky.

The fact is, I don't want to go home. I love traveling and want to finish out the year. We have decided definitely to go to Japan instead of Australia. But I don't want to give up my asserted independence. Usually we leave each other alone; we are both happy and have really good times.

I guess that in seven months of constant companionship friction is bound to happen. I get a kick out of her outbursts because she is really very funny. I think my attitude towards her helps me tolerate her better.

However, normally I am wonderfully happy. I feel free and like a totally different person. Traveling is so marvelous. I may never settle down again.

Love, Nita

A NEPALESE
WOMAN
WINNOWING RICE

WOMAN KATMANDU

TWENTY -NINE

BOMBAY and 6 DAYS on the SHIP

Saturday, January 11

"A young man of strong body, weakened by hunger, sat on the walker's portion of the street stretching his hand toward all who passed, begging and repeating the sad song of his defeat in life, while suffering from hunger and from humiliation."

Kahil Gibran from *Tears and Laughter*.

Begging. Everywhere we went, we heard the beggar's mournful song. Everywhere the ragged, big-eyed children; the bony, shriveled hags, crying, "Memsab, oh, Memsab."

Brushing our arms, spearing our conscience: "Look at me. I am a child of the starving earth. What crime did I do to deserve such misery? All I ask is a couple of paises. What is a paise to you in your rich abundance? A paise could keep me from starving."

I say "Bhag Jaw," get lost – stop bothering me. Why should I feel the burden of your troubles? Leave me alone. "Bhag Jaw!"

But they patiently keep standing. Expectantly, hopefully watching until I go away.

We left Bombay and entered the ship that would take us to Africa.

Sunday, January 20

Once aboard we encountered Zubeida, a beautiful, charming South AfricanIndian 16-year-old girl. Although young, she felt her life had been ruined; in her world, it had. This sweet child was reduced to skin and bone and tears only because of the ridiculous customs and traditions.

She was a Muslim, and last August she got married. It was an arranged marriage (called force-marriage) and she begged and pleaded to be allowed to remain single, but her father insisted on the marriage and, because the groom was willing, it had to be.

The marriage was a disaster. Less than a week after the wedding Zubeida found her husband in bed with another woman. When she tried to ask him why, since he had insisted on the marriage in the first place, he told her to shut up and not speak of it again.

The divorce ended the marriage in September.

Zubeida obviously had done nothing wrong; she was the innocent victim. But now, according to her religion, she was a tainted woman. No self-respecting man knowing her background would dare have her as a wife. She was no longer a virgin, and therefore she was an outcast of society.

This child, a tainted outcast? It was too pitiful.

As an observer, I could despise society's stupidity, and then go on with my life, but Zubeida was tied down and locked in, and could only cry and hope.

Now she kept looking for a love-marriage that would make her as happy as her 17-year-old sister's. It had been a double wedding. Or her cousin's, who in order to marry her loved one, had to get pregnant by him first.

After such a mistake, Mr. Parker, her father, has given Zubeida more freedom so she was able to enjoy herself a little now.

Tuesday, January 22

South African apartheid was ludicrous. It would be funny if it weren't real.

I was now the Parker family's friend. They lived in Capetown, and I had an open invitation to stay with them. However, if I went to South Africa, I would not even be allowed to see them! I could not go to their house, nor walk with them down the street, nor even drive with them in a car, much less go to a movie or other a social gathering. The laws were against them, they said. Most of the Europeans were nice, but the laws were against them.

And the Boars at my table on the ship said how necessary Apartheid was.

"After all, the cultural difference between Europeans and the 'colored' is shocking.

"A person can't be safe in the same city with them, because the second you turn your back a knife goes into it.

"And naturally not all coloreds are bad. There are a few who are servants and are decent people. But the good have to suffer for the bad. Yep, that's life."

That was the point of view of the Boars who sat with me at each meal.

Maxie, Doris and Nande. These Boars weren't good enough to lick Mr. Parker's boots.

Wednesday, January 23

Nita writes in her diary:

This is the last of our six-day voyage from Bombay, India to Mombasa, Africa. I will probably never see Zubeida and her family again. I hope I can cry tomorrow when I have to say "goodbye." I'll miss Zubeida terribly.

At first I had to force myself to be her friend. I wanted to be alone and read and relax and have no responsibility or conversation. But I was seeking her. I enjoyed her company. It brought me back to an adolescence which I never really had, a "Do you know the latest dance?" and "Who's your favorite singer?" and "Oh, look at that boy over there. Isn't he cute? " type of teen-ager. I can't be whole-hearted with her because I'm aware it is an entirely new role at which I'm not very good, but at least I try. And I will miss Zubeida.

Monday, January 29

Nita writes in her diary:

I got complete financial independence today. Mommy gave me $400 worth of traveler's checks for the rest of the trip. Quite sufficient for me. Now all I have to do is leave. It's difficult to be independent.

Friends Mentioned in Chapter 29

Zubeida Parker. She was a girl who had an unsuccessful arranged marriage.

THIRTY

MOMBASA AND NAIROBI

Thursday, January 24

We arrived in Africa.

There was a letter from Elizabeth Bay, who had been in our Russian language seminar.

Dear Ruth and Nita,

Your letter just arrived and I was very glad to get it.

It was high time I came home that eighth of September. My daughter is causing problems. She finished her internship in autumn last year. She hasn't finished her medical training. On account of the baby, she stayed home and felt dissatisfied. She asked us would we, or rather I, agree to take care of the baby while she works during the daytime till five? She would like to specialize in diseases of the skin at the university clinic and that course takes three years.

My husband thought it cheeky, because after all, he is 60 and I am going to be 60 next year.

Her argument was when she feels frustrated and unsatisfied it would not be good for her child nor her husband either.

If she had finished that special training, it will be possible for her to work half time, whereas with general medicine this is not possible here in hospitals. So you see, I shall have to be baby-sitting for some time to come. No traveling for me the way you suggest. You and Nita can do it, and your report sounds very interesting, and if you both were not such nice people I should envy you.

The money you borrowed arrived. Thank you.

I liked your account on India. You must have been very lucky for the people you met there. I hope Kenya proves as friendly. Wonderful that you are in sunny and warm countries all that time while we had a nasty winter. Unfortunately, that awful winter gave me another little fit of depression, but now it is over, thank God.

I met some women who do social work in municipal barracks at the fringes of a poor suburb here. They rented a room and every afternoon help the school children with their homework and play games with them. Then they take them for an outing on weekends. In some cases, the fathers drink, or the mothers don't pay attention, or they are just desperately poor. So I helped a little there, of late. But I shall have to give it up or limit my efforts to money gifts, after I take over the baby on the first of March.

Before that I shall go to our little house in Switzerland and see that some workmen do some repairs there.

At Easter I shall go there with my husband and meet our sons there who come from Munchen on their holidays. They are very busy with work for exams, all three of them. My daughter will have to take some days off from her vacation to take over her son for that time. The little boy is O.K., walks now and collects keys from all the cupboards, so that we had to hide them. Telephone, lamps are put out of his way. Little boys of that age need a lot of looking after and girls as well.

I've received letters from the members of our Russian language seminar. Joel wrote cheerfully. Inga, with the curly hair, wrote to me twice. Boris wrote a very friendly letter telling me to come to Russia again. He did not seem to have minded our quarrels we had with him. Maybe some of what we all said even helped him a bit. He is still young, has not seen the world at all.

I am wondering how you and Nita will feel when you get back. Maybe, through all that you have seen and heard you will feel yourselves to be very different from most other people in your minds and views. Maybe you sometimes have to feign a little bit stupid to make the others feel at ease.

Dear Nita, here is a little present for you. ($5.00) Maybe you want to buy yourself something to remind you of a particularly nice place you visit. Please do not mind accepting it. I like you, you are a good sport.

I hope David is doing well at home and in school, and the rest of the family back home is well. Maybe David was too young for the enterprise.

Much good luck!

Love, Elizabeth Bay

Wednesday, January 30

We had a letter from Poona. It was from Rohini, the director of dancing schools.

Dear Ruth and Nita,

I have received letters from you both.

Sorry I could not have been in Bombay to see you, but I kept the photographs for you. Please let me know the best address where I could mail them to you.

Whenever I receive a letter from you I don't know whether to envy you or pity you. You have a tremendous opportunity to visit all those wonderful places, but still you do not have the beauty of your home to dwell in.

Through your eyes I am getting one benefit of seeing a fully illustrated travelogue and I thank you both for it.

There is news at our end too. A Kathatk dance seminar is going to take place in Jaipur, Rajastan from the 8th to the 11th of this month. We are going to attend it. Actually I am going to read a paper there and my students will demonstrate it. I am supposed to perform too. Do you remember Sharad and Shama, from Poona? They are accompanying me.

We are looking forward to this eagerly, as this is the first seminar of its kind. We will meet all the veterans and up and coming dancers. Oh yes, I am going to read interviews of people, too.

Nita, your letter is like a news weekly and I am glad your impressions about Nepal are so refreshing, that I have decided to find time to make a trip some day.

I am glad to know that you are still practicing your lessons in dancing. It's a shame that you could not learn more, enough to give a short demonstration before a small audience.

Tai has been busy with the Golden Jubilee Celebration at her school. It was very successful and she regretted your absence, Ruth. You could have seen her working in full swing with an exhibition of all the new projects.

You are meeting new friends every day and I don't know really how you cope with the magnitude of your correspondence. You have tremendous zest for life and energy and I admire you for it. It has taken me too long to reply to your letter, Ruth.

I received Nita's letter today.

Rohini

Nita writes home:

In Mombasa, we lived with Ratna, who was one of my roommates on the ship. She was from Bombay, but had been living in Mombasa for more than seven years. She and her fellow nurse-friend Ammini brought Mother and me to stay in the nurses' quarters so we had a lovely room to ourselves.

In the mornings, we often went into town, but in the afternoon everything closes down, because the heat is unbearable, we usually read, chatted and relaxed.

In the evenings, usually Ratna and her friends planned activities. We would go for a drive, go to the "lighthouse," Mombasa's favorite "talking place;" see a Hindi drive-in movie; attend a music party with musicians and dancers imported from India. Or we would converse, which was nice because Ratna and Ammini enjoy the social life.

One evening, Mommy was introduced to Mr. And Mrs. Shah, who took a great liking to her and invited us to live in their house since they had an extra room. We were happy where we stayed, but didn't want to hurt their feelings and accepted. Both Mr. and Mrs. Shah were from small villages in the Indian State of Gujrate, and neither of them knew much English. They had two young adorable girls who insisted on waking us up at six, at that hour I didn't find them too loveable.

Mrs. Shah was a cleaning maniac and a glutton for punishment. Every single day she scrubbed the house till it literally shone. We spent about three days there and although they were pleasant people, I was glad for the peace and quiet of the hospital room again.

We left some of our luggage at the hospital after a couple of more days, and decided to hitch to the youth hostel at Kanamai. No sooner had we put our luggage down on the main road, than who should drive up? Mr. James from the hospital.

Mr. James was our good friend from the first day, he drove us all around, arranged for our stay at the hospital, and here he was driving to his home. Coincidence! He drove us the eight miles to the youth hostel and we've been resting happily ever since.

Love and many kisses, Nita

Kanamai Youth Hostel was in the middle of an African settlement. It was gorgeous — rustling palm trees, the lapping blue sea, a gentle sky and soft clouds. The hostel was a tin green shack with two rooms for dormitories. We lived under a thatched palm-leaf roof.

One night we had seven boys and six girls sleeping there. We sat around in the large room and read by kerosene lamps and shared our travel experiences.

Our food was cooked in rotation over a one-ring, paraffin stove.

Nobody else was there because the place was under repair. Nita and I had our own boudoir for several nights. Nicholas, an art student from Belgium, arrived and Nita spent a week with him at Kanami Hostel. When he wasn't out on the reef scrounging for seashells, we socialized.

Sunday, February 3

Nita writes:

Dear Grandma,

I am sitting at the seaside near a settlement called Kanamai. The coconut palms are making a lovely rustling sound in the wind, and the sand at my feet is much whiter and finer than sugar. Far, far out I can see the white waves of the turf, and I hear its loud roar. The water nearby is calm, shallow and very blue, with faint ripples breaking its surface.

I have been collecting seashells and coral pieces. One of the shells is a common shape, like a circle with the ends rolled together and then pie-wheeled, and it is white on the outside edges with a deep purple oval in the center. Another shaped like a clamshell but small, has the most delicate orange and peach coloring you can imagine.

The tide just this second came in. Before — just sand, now slightly muddy water. With it came a huge flock of long-legged birds to catch the incoming fish.

There were many African huts scattered around, but because of the heavy jungle foliage and high grasses they were difficult to see. None of the people there spoke any English, but Mommy made friends with Shalima, a delightful African grandmother. Mommy spent many hours in her home and played with the newborn grandson and

211

ate dinner there. The language barrier didn't daunt Shalima at all. She talked non-stop in both Swahili and her tribal language. Mommy would smile and occasionally say "Mzuri" when Shalima stopped for breath.

Kanamai was an absolute paradise with one tiny fault — insects. The mosquitoes were ferocious. All night long the sharp buzzing and stinging relieved us of any thought of sleep. After the second day I was so swollen from all the bites that were covering a mean-looking rash, which had mysteriously arisen the first Kanamai day that I couldn't dare go into public. Luckily I had no mirror, but I could feel the awful puffiness.

The ants were the other marvelous feature. Every once in a short while as we walked along the narrow footpaths we'd come into a "ribbon of ants."

Each ribbon was approximately two feet long by four inches wide and they consisted of millions of huge monstrous ants. They had long claws, which loved to grab onto flesh, especially if it was human! The first time I saw them I was wearing open sandals, bare legs and a short skirt. I was fascinated and stood for a second to look at them. Immediately my legs were covered with those stinging ants. The pain was so acute that I went mad and started running wildly and trying to brush them off. It took me more than ten minutes to get them off. They cling so tightly. I learned, though, never to go near another ant ribbon. When I see these army ants I run away fast.

Love, Nita

Sunday, February 4

Nita writes in her diary:

I am in Africa. My dream. But inside I am in apathy.

Yes, the scenery is magnificent — lovely blue ocean, whispering coconut palms, long green grass, delicate, almost nebulous pines, loud broad, dark, dark leaves, brilliant flowers, a calmness that comes from an untamed, free country.

Yes, the people were delightful. Shalima begged us to come for dinner, scolded us for not visiting sooner, wrinkled face and bright eyes, talked ceaselessly, regardless of language difference.

Alex and Jim made our fires, turned our meat, and cracked our cashew nuts. Always ready to give us a hand. Daniel, delighted with my matches, overjoyed when they became his. The many people we pass each day had a never-failing, "Jambo" and huge smile.

But somehow, the realization that I am but another tourist, gawking at "the primitive in his native surroundings," rich enough to be there doing nothing, while they sweat for little pay. The purposelessness of my existence makes me apathetic

Friends Mentioned in Chapter 30

Shalima and her grandchild.

Nicholas Top. He cooked Belgium waffles at the Youth Hostel. He returned the money I loaned him.

Fred, New Zealand; Pat, Australian; Ole, Denmark; Jock, Albert Finney's brother. We met them at the youth hostel.

Alex, Jim, Daniel and Kanamai. They were residents there.

Nurse Ratna and Nurse Ammini. They gave us beds in the hospital room.

Mr & Mrs Shah. They invited me to stay in their home.

Mr. James. He was a friend who gave us a lift in his car.

THIRTY-ONE

MALINDI and NAIROBI

While Nita was confined to the youth hostel, I ventured out into the world beyond Mombasa. I wandered along the coast.

Vinoo picked me up in his VW van. He was selling soap powders and other items to the dukas along the way. While he conducted his business, I visited schools.

Ruth writes:

Principal
The Air Force School
New Delhi

Dear Mrs. Baxi,
The experience of being with you and our enlightening talks are not forgotten. Much has happened to us since our visit with you in January.

We arrived in Mombasa on January 24th and stayed a week there. I visited schools.

A Catholic mission school was the first one and I left upset. I found only rote and copy work going on. The very poorest teaching imaginable. The book rooms were disorganized and even though they had some good materials, cartons of books sent from California, they weren't organized.

I asked them to give me the top class and we had a free for all question and answer session. I spoke about a few highlights of our trip. I told them mostly "David" stories so they could relate to them.

The teachers seemed so concerned with A-B–C levels of intelligence and the kids knew exactly how "dumb" they were.

Isn't it bad enough those CPA exams force kids out of school around the age of 14 just because they flunk one examination? Excuse? "We haven't enough secondary schools to house all the children."

So, make technical schools, or arts and crafts programs or community service work, but do something with these kids. Nita and I wonder why they don't have more juvenile delinquents than they do.

Little ones sitting and writing, writing and copying. So young. There was absolutely no play equipment around for the kindergarten level.

Hundreds of these little ones were "playing" outdoors. Just another word for doing nothing. No wonder adults sit and do nothing. It must be their training in school.

The next morning I didn't return. The teacher who took me the day before called for me at noon.

She said I was expected back. They were having a staff meeting and wanted me to attend.

The staff meeting took over three hours of bickering. It was a show of non-cooperation and disunity within the school. What a miserable display I witnessed.

Teachers stood up and declared, "I can't teach science." " I can't teach Swahili."

I wouldn't dare admit I couldn't teach a subject within the elementary curriculum. If I couldn't, I'd take a course and learn it, which is what I have been doing for the past seven years. I saw elements of the very worst administration imaginable. I watched him use democratic procedures when an authoritarian choice was in order. I heard teachers say me, me, me and in three hours the world "child" was never mentioned. It is a school run for the comfort of teachers, obviously. They admitted to a high percentage of failure on those vital examinations. No wonder.

I went home and cried in pity for poor African school children, if this is what the schools are like.

That was only the first school I visited and it was the very worst. After that I saw better administration.

Reverend Law was headmaster of the Secondary Baptist School. It was a new structure built with American Baptist money. But he had the child in mind and was aiming for good education for these children.

Mrs. Pires runs an Agha Khan elementary school for girls. She was a Goan, who took Kenyan citizenship, and is a fine, capable, strong, good administrator. I wandered around and witnessed classes in session. The blackboards and bulletin boards looked like schools where I have taught. Children's work was displayed. Ford Foundation money helped to build this school.

Mostly Muslim Arab teachers comprise the staff. Only more recently more and more Africans are attending. The teachers still wear the black covering over their dresses and their faces are covered outdoors.

When I joined them in the staff room for the half-hour break they asked me some questions relating to my teaching.

I sat with Mrs. Pires and we talked for a while. It was a good experience and a well-run school. I understand all the Agha Khan enterprises — school, nurseries and hospitals — all have money backing them and have high standards of operation.

Up the coast, in Kikambala, I visited a country school. I hiked several miles on a country lane to find it. The headmaster introduced me to all the classes.

One teacher told me he wanted to mail a letter. Would I take over his class while he was away? I agreed. I let the students question me about the United States or sports or whatever they could think of. But these children were inhibited at first, before a stranger, and a foreigner at that. I had no idea that the post office would be so far away and the teacher would leave me with his class such a long time. But we finally relaxed and had good discussions on a variety of subjects.

Here in the middle of African bush country I discovered one of the best teachers I have ever seen. A young man with nearly 50 first graders. He was using various counters for a math lesson on numbers. Then he sang songs with them.

He had drawn a large picture. "Who is it? What is she wearing?"

The pupils talked about their mothers and grandmothers.

"When does your grandmother come to visit you? What's her name? What does she bring you?"

His patience with all the children was unending. He gave each child a chance to answer each question. It was a Swahili lesson in language. The religion part of the curriculum was the singing. He pointed out the "deaf" child to me. He had a spirit and an interest in every child.

The African school day is long. It begins before 8:00 and with the lunch break From the fourth grade up it continues in the afternoon until 4:00. I know that I'm too tired after 2:00 to do a good job of teaching. I don't know how all these teachers last such a long day.

There is a 10-10:30 recess. Children were not supervised, which is a sacred "must" in our schools. It keeps our teachers on constant vigilance.

In Kikambala I sat and shared lunch with the Headmaster, who teaches a few classes, and two teachers. We talked. There is a good standard for education here, though it is a small school.

One class in each grade, the third and fourth classes, have only a dozen children. What a pleasure that would be to teach.

I was aware that if children were left by themselves in the African schools I visited, they would continue their assignments studiously without any nonsense.

In America, my children would jump around as soon as the teacher turned her back. I'm so sick of being a policeman instead of a teacher that I could scream sometimes. Why? Why can't all children have a desire to learn? An inner push, inner drives for an education and not have to drain the teacher to get all their inspiration from her.

Mrs. DeLord had a special school in Mombasa. She was a woman with heart. She had two classes of deaf children and a class of mentally retarded children. There were also children with physical problems, like spastic children. She does wonders with very little material and a lot of patience. I admit I haven't got the stamina to do her job. A gift of a slide projector was given to her. But she has no slides. I want her to exchange it for a film strip. At least filmstrips have educational materials.

If you get an inspiration and want to write to her, her address is: Mrs. DeLord,

Special School, Mombasa, Kenya, East Africa. She's appreciative of anything given to her. She had her children doing magnificent crafts and sewing. She had a type-writer for her children to use.

An interchange with her might be beneficial to your classes and hers.

I hitched up north to Malindi and wandered into several Arabic schools where they teach the Arabic alphabet and the Koran. Children were sitting on the floor and chanting out loud and memorizing by that method. The teacher had a rope switch that she flicked in their direction if their attention wandered.

I enjoyed my school sightseeing even more than some of the usual tourist traps. I wish I could evolve into a job that would send me to countries to report on what is going on in the educational world. I'm tired of the classroom and I'm ashamed to admit it, my patience with children is not improving with age. Observe and report, wonder who would give me that job? This visitation of schools gave purpose to my days and I needed that. I cannot stand the idleness that exists in our tourist, globe-trotting life.

Sincerely yours, Ruth

It was a shock to learn of the millions of Asians in Kenya. I wasn't prepared for it. It took us nearly two weeks before I met and talked to an African.

We hitched the 350 miles from Mombasa. As we passed Tsavo National Park at Voi, I said to Nita, "We have never been in an African National Park. Let's visit it."

Our drivers agreed to carry our luggage to their office in Nairobi. We would pick it up when we arrived there.

Gordon Tweedie, the Game Warden at Tsavo Park, learned that the lodge manager agreed to let us sleep in the lounge after the guests deserted and went to bed. When Gordon found out our plans, he invited us to live at his home in the park instead. It was a lovely wooden house with a huge fieldstone fireplace.

Gordon and his friend Bill Philips spent time with us showing us the famous "Orphans of Tsavo," two rhinos, a couple of elephants, a buffalo and some ostriches. They were very friendly, and, except for the buffalo, loved to be petted. Ever pet a rhinoceros? He feels dry and hard and bumpy.

The next day, Gordon and Bill drove us around the park. There were 8,000 square miles of wild land and wilder animals. We saw a herd of zebra and many elephants, some jackals, gazelles and orynx, and a dik dik, a perfect deer only 10 inches high, about the size of a cat. There were magnificent birds, paradise flycatchers, wild peacocks and lovely turquoise guinea fowl.

When Gordon left for work in the morning he warned us not to venture beyond the house.

He said, "That roaring you hear is from lions. They are wandering around. They are wild beasts. Don't tempt them."

We stayed a couple of days in the Warden's spacious spare room and then we hitched the rest of the way to Nairobi.

Our ride was with four of the richest Asian Kenyans you can imagine. One owned a restaurant, another a chain of movie houses, another a fancy hotel, and all were partners in a nightclub. However, they weren't pleasant old men and I didn't think we would have trouble resisting invitations to their establishments.

We had so many people in Nairobi to look up that we were overwhelmed.

Back in September, David, Nita and I decided to hitch from Germany to London and it took a whole day, a very hot day, to get to the autobahn with our luggage. Nita sat down on the side of the road and refused to budge.

Up ahead we had seen a young couple who had been trying to hitch for a couple of hours.

They told us they were students in Nairobi. Mommy, in her usual manner, went over and made friends. This was September.

I told them, "Oh, we will be in Kenya in February. Give us your addresses and we will see you there."

They said "goodbye" and reminded us to be sure to visit them when we arrived in Nairobi. We did. I assured them I would get them a ride. They had been waiting for two hours with no luck. A few minutes later I got us a ride on the back of a truck.

Philip was of the Kikuyu tribe and in his last year as a math student at Nairobi University. Jedidah, of the same tribe, took a catering course at the Polytechnic Institute.

Nita writes:

The name of a member of parliament was given to Mommy by a friend in Leningrad. Another was a friend I made on the boat to Mombasa, Ratna, and she gave us many names of nurses.

In the face of such an assortment, we promptly did nothing for the first few days but roam around Nairobi. I expected Nairobi to be a large addition of Mombasa, one or two main streets, a lot of small "ducas" and curio shops, and some outside fruit and vegetable stands.

Instead, we found a large, bustling, ultra modern city. It even had a supermarket. Due to recent student demonstrations, the university was closed and most of the students had returned home. So there were fewer young people running around Nairobi than usual.

Kenyatta closed the university because the students invited the opposition party to speak to them.

It really is funny how one friend leads to another friend leads to another friend. Jedidah introduced us to Gitou, the financial advisor to the Kenyan government.

Mommy went to the television studio and there she met Thuku and Amon, two men who were drivers in the famous and difficult East African Safari Motor Race in April.

Thuku took us all around the Gikuyu countryside and introduced us to his moth-

er. Such a wonderful person. She had 13 children. The oldest is 60, but she herself neither looks, nor acts, over 50. She has no wrinkles, her hair is beginning to go grey and she works hard all day running a tea shop and cooking for the police force. What an amazing woman!

Mommy and I made a real hit out in the African bush country because many of the people in that area had never seen a white person before.

We went to the open market places with Thuku and had swarms and swarms of people following us around.

Jedidah and her roommates Irene and Leah were our "afternoon" friends. Whenever we were tired or wanted to sit and chat we would go to their room and spend a peaceful couple of hours.

Every afternoon Nita would go to the university art professor's studio and make clay sculptures. She created a woman in agony. Her three sculptures were each in a different style and the teacher was thrilled with them. He admired her ability to produce one in such a short time. He planned to cast them, so they wouldn't get broken.

He was an up-and-coming artist. I saw his notebook of photographs.

Nita spent time talking to Philip and his roommate Aggrey, and the two boys in the next room, Rabin and Moses. I enjoyed myself so much that I lost track of time. There was no transportation at the late hour, so I chased poor Philip out of his bed and slept there. I've never slept in a boy's dormitory before.

So it went. Each day we met new and interesting people. Each person gave us names and addresses of other people and we enlarged our acquaintances and friendships. Everyone was good to us — well, that is, nearly everyone.

Philip drove us 15 miles away from Nairobi to visit his mother. Here was another delightful person. She was dressed in the normal Gikuyu, old lady fashion with a shaved and oiled head, ears shaped long from heavy earrings, and a kitanga, a piece of brightly patterned material wrapped around the body. She had bare feet.

As she walked the three miles to market, she carried a basket on her back that was attached with a band around her forehead. She was over 60 and had a 40-year-old daughter.

None of the people in the bush spoke much English, but it didn't seem to matter. Phillip's mother was enthralled with Nita's hair. She didn't believe hair could grow so long, or that it could be smooth, and she kept fingering it in wonderment.

We had lunch at the house, a rather large hut. Our meal consisted of a corn and bean mush called irio. No sooner had we eaten one huge bowl than three more bowls appeared. It was the Kikuyu custom that when a guest arrived the head of each household on the "shamba" (farm) had to contribute food. We had eaten Philip's mother's irio, but we still had to eat each of the three sister's food.

Philip's mother trekked a distance to obtain a special drink for us. It was "honey beer."

At the end of the meal we tasted the local "honey beer" which we could barely get down. I was stopped by the smell.

Ruth writes:
Dear Mother,
We lived in the youth hostel in Nairobi 15 miles out of town. It had room for about 13 people with no electricity and little indoor plumbing. The hostel had two rooms for dormitories.
We sat around in the large room and read by kerosene lamps and exchanged our travel experiences.
Nicholas taught Nita how to cook his specialty, Belgian pancakes.
The setting of the place is beautiful. Mountains, and cows grazing in the fields and when you sit in the outhouse with the door wide open you can appreciate the view. Flowers in profusion and palm forests, and broad-leafed trees I have never seen before.
A lot of weird people stayed at the hostel. We had a hodge-podge of characters. Komici was the full-time resident. He was almost 20 years old, a member of a tribe near Katali, Kukuya, and the youngest Kenyan student at the whole University.
Then comes Fred, from New Zealand. He traveled around the world for four years, and was beginning to look forward to going back home.
It is a social atmosphere most of the time though some crumb-bums pass through — like Pat, from Australia, whom I call "Robot." She was without personality, but she worked on computers; maybe that's why.
Ole, from Denmark, was a Tibetan Yoga practitioner. He stayed in Nirvana with a little help from the marijuana he cooked in all his food, but he did give us some brownies that tasted good.
Jock was a wandering English-Canadian whose brother is Albert Finny, the film star, although he doesn't like to admit it. Jock has spent a lot of time living in the lower East Side in New York. He has been traveling around the world trying to "find himself," and spends most of his time getting philosophical about life.
The day after we arrived in the Nairobi hostel who should turn up but Nicholas, the Belgium, from Kanamai. Nicholas is quiet and slow, but very deliberate in everything he does. He is a fastidious cook. It takes him hours to make his specialty, Belgian pancakes.
But he refuses to clean up after himself because that's "woman's work." No need to guess who did it.
He is the Belgian artist who hitched his way to Africa. With only $50 left to his name, he'll be hitching back to Belgium any day.
We received all your letters and it sounds like everything is normal in New York. You have no conception how much your letters mean to us.
Love and kisses, Ruth

Saturday, February 24
Ruth writes:

Dear David,

HAPPY BIRTHDAY!

Nita and I find ourselves talking about you very often these days. Many of our African experiences you would enjoy. Can you imagine that we are going with two drivers from the East African Motor Safari to Uganda? They are going to follow the route and map out where they have to slow down, where the sharp curves are, and they are not permitted to go on any tarmac (hard surface) roads. It should be an interesting journey for us.

Meeting people is no problem in this country and the number of our acquaintances grows daily. The youth hostel is good.

We spent a couple hours at a time in National Park seeing herds of animals. Nita petted a rhinoceros at the "orphans at Tsavo." It was a thrill seeing giraffes, and the beautiful gazelles, wildebeest and baboons roaming around without cages. The baboons jump up on the car.

On Sunday we found a pride of lions. One car was sent out of the park by the game warden because they opened their door and got out. There were five lions, but they sleep 17 out of 24 hours. They were too sleepy to suit us.

Are you still working or was it too much? What happens to your money? Gambling it away? How is the schoolwork coming? Do you tell some of our adventures to people? What are members of the family planning for the summer?

This is like a European city, full of white faces and tourists.

We leave Nairobi at the end of the week. When you receive this letter, if you answer it, I will receive it before the end of March when we leave East Africa and return to Bombay.

Considering the wonderful weeks you spent with us, I feel you are not justified in not writing. Now that you are a year older, please do this for us. You can't have forgotten so soon what the looking for mail at the post office means to us.

We miss you very much. Nita goes to chess club every week here in Nairobi.

Love, Mom

Nita writes:

Dear David,

Our days in Nairobi were completely filled with friends. This is due to that wretched hitching day in Berlin. David, you remember when we picked up the two young people from Kenya?

Thuku, a driver in the famous East African Safari car race, drove us all around the Kikuyu country. The Kikuyus are one of the largest tribes in Kenya.

Jomo Kenyatta wrote a book: "Facing Mount Kenya." He is from that tribe.

Philip, the Kenyan boy who we hitchhiked with in Germany, is also Kikuyu, he invited us to meet his mother. Thuku also took us to see his mother. She is over 80, but refuses to quit work. She had 13 children, the oldest is 60 and the youngest is 18. She doesn't look over 50 herself, not a wrinkle on her face.

Two art students gave us a tour all around the gorgeous campus. I remained with the sculpture teacher and worked with clay. He liked the figure I made and decided to cast it.

I went the Nairobi chess club and watched chess for hours. We are having an unbelievably marvelous time.

Love your loving sister, Nita

The Nairobi University was closed when we arrived in Kenya. The students invited a member of the opposition party to give a lecture. It was not a political lecture, but rather on an aspect of sociology. Even so, the Kenyan president, Kenyatta, prohibited the opposition leader from speaking and closed down the university.

This was the second incident like this. The students had petitioned and were rejected. Finally, they organized a rally, which was swiftly broken up by the police, although it was very peaceful. After one more demonstration, the college was closed.

Jomo Kenyatta made a speech condemning all "thieves, lawbreakers, rioting students, prostitutes and student-sympathizing professors" for trying to sabotage Kenya.

The day before he opened the university for a few selected students and teachers, who were all compelled to sign a pledge saying they would uphold the present government and not demonstrate on anything for the next four years, or else go to jail for three years.

Kenya was in a mess at that moment, with each of the 17 tribes against the others. It was like Europeans disliking Africans, Asians disliking Africans, and Africans disliking Europeans and hating Asians.

The non-citizen Asians, of course, had to all leave by July. But still so many Asian-Kenyans were left that there would be trouble. Prejudice and discrimination were not hidden.

To the Kenyan education was important. I had no idea of the political situation before I arrived. I read both Kenyatta books and learned his views. Africanization was taking place. The Asian who was the shopkeeper and businessman in Africa was being displaced. The government was trying to get Africans to take their places.

When the Asians (Indians) arrived to build the railroads, they were promised a future. They built the country up financially, developed it, built homes and continued customs and life as though they were still in India. Their standard of living was superior to that of the African. I met millionaires among the Asians. In Kenya theirs was a higher standard of living than in India. Many households had houseboys and servants. They owned new, imported cars. Highways were being built.

Of course, the Europeans, as the British and Whites were called, had the best standard of living. They were the managers and the "brains" behind most Western industries. Their salaries were high and they owned land.

The Asians were losing out, not getting work permits to stay in Africa. There was mass emigration. However, they had no place to go. These people never lived in India. And India certainly didn't need this additional population. England was tightening up; the country's anti-colored attitude didn't entice either Africans or Indians to move there.

Wednesday, February 28

We had been in Nairobi for three weeks. We never had a dull day. It was 9:20 p.m. and I was sitting in the newsroom of the "Voice of Kenya" with the teletype machines and typewriters clicking out the news.

There was no end to the activity and I loved every minute of it. My day had been spent in the television studio. I heard a director of education speaking over the radio Tuesday, February 25, and I decided I wanted a reprint of his excellent speech.

I visited the day before and located the man in charge. He asked me to write him a letter making my request and telling him how I would use the speech.

I left the studio and got a hitch with a kind man who worked there. His name was Hussan Mazoa. I told him my purpose and he became my production man, who ran around to help me the following day.

I watched the "Mamba Leo" show with my good friend Norbert Okare. He was the Jack Paar of Kenya television.

The president of the Areo Club talked about the air show, which was to be held the following Sunday. We heard interviews with the East African Motor Rally men, who took a dry run of the route and described the impossible routing because of the deep ruts. A magician from Germany was a real showman. It was good program.

I left the studio around 5:00 p.m. I got a hitch. With who? The Areo Club president, who assured me I would enjoy the show.

I said thanks to his guest card to get in.

I spent the early evening with Jedidah, the girl we hitched with on the autobahn in Germany. She lived at the Polytech Institute with Leah and Irene, both friends. We went to the school when we wanted to rest, sleep, talk or get a free meal. I used their typewriter when no one was sleeping. The Institute was a relaxing place and full of "girl talk."

After Norbert was finished with his newscast, he invited me to Chopsticks restaurant and we talked, ate and met some of his friends. I wish I had a better memory of our discussions, because they were enlightening.

Norbert attended Columbia University in New York for two years. We dated in a very sedate manner. We shook hands good night.

Jedidah introduced me to Gitau, a financial advisor to the Kenya government. His father happened to be the longest and best friend of Kenyatta, so he was Treasurer of Kenya. They all lived at the State House.

Gitau drove me home at Jedidah's request. When we arrived, he decided we ought to go to a dance. So I got back into the car and drove the eight miles to town to a dance, after we ate dinner at the Steak House.

Starlight Club is a large hall crowded with dancers. I was self-conscious when I first got on the floor with the African girls. I could hear Nita's criticisms from Delhi, "Don't wiggle your hips, toss your head, etc."

After a while, I relaxed and threw myself around as they did. Several white men were there and only two of us white girls. I danced until 1:00 a.m. Gitau drank all evening and I was afraid he wouldn't drive me home. But he did!

I met Gitau in an emergency at the bank one day. I needed him badly and he appeared like the Genie from Aladdin's lamp. His presence helped me get a paper, which earned me the small sum of $20.

Nita and I went to his flat and while he took an afternoon nap Nita and I took hot baths and washed our hair. That was always a high point in our daily life.

I did a lot for Nicholas, our friend from the youth hostel. I lent him money for his plane trip to Juba, and gave him the Areo Club pass, which I didn't use. He had a great day and was there from 10:00 to 6:30 on Sunday watching airplane showmen.

After our rest and bath in Gitau's home, we spent a few hours in town and met him again at the Norfolk Hotel, where a huge group of men were seated around a table. They included Mr. Rao, who recognized us from Indu Dayal's description. He had found us a place to sleep in town weeks ago. We never got in touch with Dayal. Mr. Rao was the owner of Maida Flour Mills. We met two other men, Africans who owned woolen mills.

We had a drink and then walked to the Voice of Kenya station. We remained in the studio for the next couple of hours. The "Mambia Leo" show was about to begin taping.

Dr. Kaunda, president of Zambia, arrived and was interviewed first. Then Dr. Patel, who spoke about the Gandhi celebration.

The president of the Motor Rally Clubs was presented with money. Some of the drivers told about the rally. The East African Safari is known worldwide. Only Nita and I were ignorant about the rally, which was one of the most dangerous. Hundreds entered it and only a very few finished.

Before the evening was over, we met Amon and Thuku, who were drivers in the rally and decided to take us on their dry run up to Uganda and back. We saw them many more times before that date. The trip was 3,000 miles in three days. No tarmac roads. We would have fun.

When the program was over, I spoke with Norbert Okare, the interviewer. He made a date with me.

That was a Friday, our day with Gitau. Saturday, we met Thuku and Amon and they took us to the National Park.

We saw giraffes, gazelles, hartebeest, wildebeest and a crocodile, and we heard a hippopotamus breathe under water. We gasped at how fast ostriches can run. It was a thrill, especially when the baboon jumped up on to the hood of the car. The boys were enjoyable companions.

Amon and Thuku took us to the Pan Africa Hotel, a huge structure, famous and fancy. We said it cost too much, but they insisted. We ate irio, a green potato, bean, maize mash, layered with a meat stew. This was a typical African meal. Before we left the hotel we became friendly with Mr. Kenneth, the manager, with invitations to return.

We had another date with Amon and Thuku Monday night. They took us to a butcher shop at the end of town. They selected our piece of meat from those that were hanging on a line. It was laid out on a charcoal grill at the back of the store. We wandered around town while it cooked. It was put on the table with no dishes and no silverware except a knife. We cut a piece and ate it with our fingers. This was a distinctly African custom.

Thuku decided as long as we stayed in cities we could never know Africa. So February 25 he drove us out of town. We spent from 9:00 a.m. to 5:00 p.m. in the Kiambu and Riuru areas. He delivered the daily newspaper "Standard" and collected money for it.

We met hundreds of people on whom we practiced our three-word Kikuyu vocabulary. They were such friendly people — duka after duka (store after store). We shopped for pineapples in a market place — a huge green area with the beans, greens and pineapples displayed on the grass. The juicy, sweet pineapples cost just pennies. They were 1/5 of a shilling, which equals about 13 cents.

We drove to the top of a hill where John, a policeman, lived. The view was magnificent. We ate our pineapples and danced to radio music. Later, when John arrived, he insisted we eat meat. He climbed down the hill to kill a steer and brought back fresh beef, which was roasted for us. We dove in with our fingers, as was customary. We were invited back. John promised that if we came on a Monday, Open House for visiting the president of Kenya, who lived nearby, he would take me to meet president Jomo Kenyatta.

Philip Ndehi had accompanied Jedidah in Berlin. He was a math student in his last year at the university. We spent time pestering him. He arranged classes for us to visit. We ate meals with him, and we were invited to the home of the warden of his dorm, Mr. D'Sousa. He was a Goan and an engineering professor, and his wife was British and a district health nurse. They had a rough time making it to marriage because of cultural objections. They met at Manchester College. We had an interesting evening talking to her. Nita played chess with him. Unfortunately, she beat him both games easily. He promised to try to get the best chess player in the college to challenge her the next time she came.

Nita kept track of how long we stayed in Nairobi by the Wednesday night chess club meetings. She had attended four of them and claimed that it was four weeks rather than three that we had been in Nairobi. One week, two good players challenged her a little, but usually she watched. We had been traveling for eight months now and only two people had managed to beat Nita in chess. The best of her opponents was in Tehran. She appreciated those games.

Philip found a friend to drive us to his mother in Kiambu. This was the stronghold of the Kikuyu tribe. His mother lived in a "modern house," which meant the family did not live in the round, thatched homes, but in a rectangle house with several rooms and a tin roof. They liked the tin roof because it caught the rain in drainpipes. They had drums attached to each house that captured 300 gallons of rainwater. This was much safer than the river water and more readily available. I commented that the thatch served as insulation against cold, heat, and rain, the opposite from the tin. Philip claimed that thatch was not as readily available now that land was being used for coffee production.

Only the Europeans were permitted to grow coffee, the cash crop. Some of the impositions of the British were hard to believe. People were forced to live in communities and had to travel to their shambas — farms. The British soldiers could "have fun" with the Africans and bully them for evening entertainment.

We saw three houses and many, many children. We were fed irio from Philip's sister's kitchen. We finished a huge plate of it and his mother sent around three more plates. Philip said all guests were treated this way and had to eat food from the kitchen of each home.

We drank tea and tasted honey beer.

We socialized in the company room and took a trip to market. We decided to carry the baskets with the strap around our head, Kikuyu fashion. Everyone laughed at us. They called out to the sister, "You are making the white girls do the work." It certainly was a switch. We were in a section far from town and from the fervor we caused we realized white people were not usually seen in that vicinity. We had a pleasant day.

The pineapples were huge. We traipsed around the farm and saw maize, cabbages, beans, onions, potatoes, sweet potatoes, sugar cane and coffee growing.

The family wanted us to sleep over, but I couldn't find enough beds in the rooms I investigated. We took photos. Philip's mother expected to put a photo of the family on the wall. The sister was a teacher and she understood English.

We chalked up another good day.

Nita was introduced to the art director by Neema, an architectural student. We spent hours touring her dorm and eating with her. Now Nita had free access to the sculpture studio and each day she went there and sculpted a woman in agony.

So it went. Each day we met new and interesting people. Each person gave us names and addresses of other people and we enlarged our acquaintances and friendships. Everyone had been good to us.

We hitched a ride home, one Saturday night, with a Sikh, Gudial Singh. He was quiet and made a date with Nita for Sunday afternoon. Nita said, "Not without you, Mother."

I hung around and we set off together. He was a quiet chap. He was a contractor and builder.

He couldn't suggest what we should do, so we decided to use him to help us locate Indu Dayal, the nurse. We found Indu's home and met her husband and the 3 and 4-year-old daughters.

Indu suggested we drive out to Kikuyu, where there is a submerged lake. We walked down a steep embankment led by guides, and walked on grass, which gave way with each step. We experienced "walking" on water.

Nita lost her wristwatch that afternoon. One of the guides must have slipped it off her wrist.

The Sikh, Gudial Singh, drove the car to the home of Mr. Dayal, the principal of his school. We spent hours there. My only faux pas was telling the wife how good the "tea" was. It happened to be coffee. Coffee and tea were served with milk already poured into the cup.

We let the Sikh drive us home, still silent and dull, and said goodbye to him, because he contributed nothing to our day.

We still had not visited the arboretum. We spent a day at the museum and Snake Park and found it one of the best museums in the world. Joy Adamson, the author, was also an artist. Her flowers were drawn with skill and beauty. She later did portraits of Africans. They lined the walls of the museum. I wouldn't have minded a collection if each one did not cost 30 shillings. They were done with sympathy, understanding and skill.

The Tuesday night after the Sunday outing, we arrived home about 9:30 after a full day in town. After dinner with Indu, I was tired and ready for a warm bed and sleep.

The Sikh drove into our driveway and said to me, "Send Nita out. I have two tickets to the National Theater."

She had no desire to go out with this boring man.

If we did not feel guilty about the way we had shunted him off on Sunday, we would have thought more carefully. Plays began at 9:00 p.m., or before, not at 10:00 p.m.

He didn't invite mother; that was not nice of him. But we didn't think and Nita got into his car and drove off.

A couple of hours later she returned.

"I never got to the theater. He didn't have tickets," she said and laughed, a bit hysterical. A European couple was with her. After a quick introduction, they made a hasty departure.

Then she told me what had happened.

"Instead of driving along the main road to Nairobi; he took a dirt turn off saying it was a short cut.

"It was through an isolated country road in the middle of a coffee plantation. It was dark outside.

"His arm edged toward my shoulder as he admired my hair.

"'You like me, don't you?' he asked.

"As politely as possible, I denied it. After all, I hardly knew him.

"My suspicions, which had been steadily mounting, suddenly crystallized when he stopped the car.

"He grabbed for me hard and it hurt. I reached for the door. I turned the handle and got it open. I tried sliding out. He grabbed on to my 'beautiful' hair and yelled for me to stay put. I edged over more.

"He grabbed me ferociously, screaming, 'I've got a gun! I've got a gun.'

"I reached for the door handle, and a big struggle ensued, with me sliding towards the now open door and him screaming at me to stay were I was and grabbing my hair.

"Finally, as he reached for his gun in the glove compartment, he loosened his hold on me. I wrenched myself free and jumped out of the car. I raced for the density of the coffee bushes. He gave a couple of fruitless hair-raising screams for me. I tried to quiet my gasping breath. I ran and ran and hid — huddled beneath a coffee bush. My black jacket concealed me with the darkness of the night. He was in close pursuit. I was sure he heard my heart pounding. After a fruitless search on foot he circled the area in the car. I managed to escape the headlights. He gave up and drove away.

"Meanwhile, I trudged through mud, hoping for a sign of life. About a mile later, I saw a house. I was scratched, and tore my clothes trying to get through the barbed-wire fence surrounding the estate. Trudging around the front of the house, I knocked on the door and I ended up in the arms of a motherly European woman. The husband lectured me.

"It was a huge estate. They were rich Europeans, dripping wealth. The man wore a black jacket and black tie and tails; the woman was weighted down with diamonds. A rich man's party was in progress.

"The people finally deciphered my story. My clothes were torn and streaked with dirt and my hair was wild. It wasn't too difficult to see I had had a difficult time.

"I was very impressed with their wealth.

"The dining room had a mahogany table longer than our living room. They offered me an expensive brandy, which I sipped. They decided which one of the five limousines to take. They drove me back to the youth hostel.

"They wanted to call the police, but nothing had happened to me. I let it go. It was a nerve wrenching experience," Nita said, finishing her story.

At 1:00 a.m. the couple drove up to the hostel and saw me standing in the doorway talking with Jacques, a Canadian.

I was wearing a pink nylon nightgown. They took one look and made a hasty departure, probably thinking: "With that kind of mother what can you expect?"

Nita felt a little sorry for her Sikh because he was very frightened, and she was convinced he would never try this again.

We laughed over the "adventure." We had been waiting for this sort of thing to happen since the Middle Eastern countries. We were happy that Nita managed to control the situation. Nita slept that night. I didn't.

Friday night I returned home at midnight after the newsroom night date with Norbert. Then Khamisi, our African University student, who resides at the hostel, took me to the dance across the road at the Kenya Institute of Administration. We danced from 12 until 3. A grand night and fun, except that I was worried because Nita did not come home. Where was she?

The next day, Saturday, March 1, I went to Jedidah looking for Nita and then to River Road looking for Amon. I shopped for vegetables in the market place and started to walk back to Polytech.

I felt the klunk as my head hit the road. As I got up I realized a country bus had knocked me down into a mud puddle. Dazed and with severe head pains I asked a car to drive me to Polytech. Oh, my head pained. I had our car stopped and someone handed me my eyeglasses. The driver seemed "dopey" and he got me to Jedidah and promised to take me to the hospital, but disappeared when I came back out. I was upset about that. Later I learned he did go to police station and made a report of the accident, the only person who did it. The bus driver did not.

Jedidah introduced me to her mother. I dropped my muddy coat on the floor and asked them to take care of it. I was teary and upset and very shaken. Out of all those people at the scene of the accident, no one stepped forward to help me get up, or to call an ambulance to take me to Kenyatta Hospital, which is the government hospital where the police report would be taken, I was told. It was not.

The ambulance drove me to the hospital, but I felt so alone and dazed and shaken and upset. My head was splitting with pain, where was Nita? What had happened to her kept bothering me. If only I knew where she was.

At the hospital, I got a shot of tetanus, penicillin, bruises rewashed and bandaged and then came the dreaded part.

I walked to another section for X-rays and waited more than an hour for them to be taken. I saw one man shaking, his foot bloody and swollen and another with glazed eyes and a deep gash in his head and blood dripping down his face. The dirt still not washed away from his head and face. I got up and begged someone to take care of these two bloody people soon.

Only two girls were taking X-rays and no aides around at all. A blind man helped carry the foot sore guy into the X-ray room. This place was torture for me. After the head X-rays were taken, I was told to wait around for another hour until they were developed. Not me.

I took my records with me and left the hospital. The next hour was an unbelievable nightmare. I took a bus back to town and a nurse befriended me. I would have fared better without her. She took me to her friend's house, walked me blocks and blocks. All I wanted to do was lie down and rest. No place or chance for that. And I met her friend's family, who were no help at all. Finally, I hitched my own ride to Parklands to Indu's house, because I knew they would be home with a car at my disposal. They were helpful people and since she was a nurse she could help me.

The man who drove me there told me he had a movie ticket and couldn't help me further. Indu gave me tea and Mr. drove me back for the X-rays after leaving a note for Nita at Jedidah's house. Then I went home to Lower Kabets to rest.

The nurse in the hospital looked at the four X-rays and said, "No cracks are visible. Go home." So I went. She refused to write me a letter for the insurance company. Nice person!!

Nita found the note about getting X-rays and rushed to the phone. There was no number in the book for the hospital and she hitched home fast as she could —worried.

"James James Morrison's Morrison
Weatherbe George Dupree
Took great care of his mother,
Though he was only three.
Mother you must never go down
To the end of town
Without consulting me."

Nita said, "One day I leave you on your own and look what happens!"

I rested the remainder of Saturday. New people came to the hostel and Cynthia was pleasant. Nita confined me to the hostel on Sunday, and I kept hoping someone would come to visit us. That morning I washed clothes, everything I owned, and the sun and wind dried my sheet and dresses without the mildew odor that sickened me. It was the first day of radiant sun in weeks. It was the rainy season in East Africa now.

As the day progressed, my aches and bruises began to develop and I figured out the bump on my right hip was where the bus hit me. My dress was torn through my raincoat. I must have slid on the road. I was unconscious. No idea what happened at all.

I was alive! My eyeglasses and watch did not break. Thank goodness. I was healing and now I has something to talk about, the day a bus hit me and I lived.

Two days later, I went to the police station, two of them, to tell my tale and try to get written reports, which I was sure Al Preller, my insurance man, would demand. Ha, he should try. I couldn't get them.

Nita and I decided to leave Nairobi. We hitched to Lake Naivasha to the youth hostel there. We saw Jomo Kenyatta along the way, driving in the biggest car I had ever seen in my life. We passed colorful African dancers, but our driver did not stop. School children lined the road for hours waiting for their president to pass.

This hostel was beautiful. We saw swamp instead of a lake, with herons and ducks and hundreds of birds in the water and in the trees. We lounged around all day in solitude. No one else was there.

I was reading Jomo Kenyatta's two books, "Facing Mount Kenya," an anthropological study of the Kikuyu people written in 1938, and "Suffering without Bitterness," written in the 1960s about his political trouble and imprisonment and rise to power and leadership.

The neighborhood was full of things to do. We could go boating on the lake, seeing the bird sanctuary. We learned about the other places to go and decided to set out the next day.

We were told Hells Gate was warm springs. A couple of people gave us rides along that road, but we never arrived at our destination.

We met a couple who took the plane from the U.K. to Nairobi, got the Pollman tour VW bus, and along with Mr. Damson, the driver, would spend 14 days riding around searching for birds. We saw how it worked. The driver drove into a gorge, wild looking cliffs, and they saw their beloved rare vulture, which only can be seen in this area in the Rift Valley. How excited and pleased they were. The man, Dave, was an engineering lecturer at Cambridge. He sat for two hours by the cliff with telescope, telescopic lens on his camera and binoculars and studied birds.

Nita and I missed another ride, which passed through. Finally, we hitched back to the hostel. We never got to Hells Gate, but had seen some wild animals on this trek and learned how other people find purpose in traveling to East Africa.

They knew their birds, but what a pity to be so narrow in your environment. They would never meet an African or Asian except the African driver, Mr. Damson.

We hitched to Lake Naivasha Town and ate lunch in an African restaurant.

Then we had another hitch with Abdul Manji who was driving to Eldoret. We had made our plans to stop in Nakuru to see the Menengai crater and then to see the bird sanctuary, where there are thousands of flamingoes. But hitching can render you as helpless as a tour. We passed through Nakuru with a short stop for a bite to eat in an Indian duka. Good sweets.

We stopped in Eldoret, at New Wagon Wheels Hotel, a beautiful place. We were the guests of the owner, Mr. Manji. Our room was beautiful and we both immediately plunged into a hot water bath, such a pleasure after hostel living.

Come to think of it, we had only had four days in a hotel in about four months. Noori, the 23-year-old daughter, immediately befriended Nita, who enjoyed talking with her.

Noori had attended Friends College near our home in New York.

They shared experiences, admiring saris and other clothes and jewelry. Noori had a sister who was a talented artist and expressed it in beautiful embroidery. It was a thrill to know people who could do beautiful handwork. We ate and saw a silly Italian-Spanish dubbed English film. We came back to more food and and three people named Patel, a doctor and two teachers. We talked until late at night.

Thursday, March 6

I joined Noori for a morning at her typewriter. I spent nearly four hours typing, when suddenly I remembered Mr. Manji wanted to take us to the dairy.

I was supposed to meet Miss Barnes, an American in charge of schools.

I forgot everything, wrote and relaxed with Noori, who was not pressured because her two bosses were on safari.

These good people invited us to stay and be with them longer. The Patels invited us to be their guests in Kitale.

Nita said, "Mommy, the days are fleeing by and we must get to Jinja and Kampala in Uganda."

Nita's two ship roommates lived there and we wanted to see Stella, the schoolteacher. We had loads of names and addresses to visit before Saturday.

Saturday we had to be at the Apollo Hotel and to leave a note for Amon and Thuku, who expected to arrive during the day to pick us up and take us to the National Parks and Murchison Falls.

It was Thursday at noon and all we had was less than one day and two half-days. Yet we had so much to see and so many people to meet.

We felt rushed and never wanted to leave our friends where we were.

Nita made fun of my "having experiences" to relate.

Nita met people on a different level. When she was with a person she drew their lives from them instead of inflicting ours upon them as I did.

In this way, she established her relationships, which was especially effective with the young people she met.

When Nita wrote, it was not the "experiences" of daily living, the we did this and then we did this," which I wrote. Her writing was far more descriptive. She used her creative writing techniques and described the way people dressed and looked and she gave picture words of the scenes more effectively than I did. I relied more on the photographs I was taking and hoped that they would demonstrate what my lack of descriptive writing failed to.

However, my African experience was still a jumble and it would take me a long time before I could sort out my feelings and think through the politics and the lifestyle of the various people who lived in Africa.

Nairobi is a big city. It is modern, with wide highways and beautiful modern architecture and gigantic expensive Western-type hotels. It was the first place we had seen supermarkets with foods from all over the world. It offered modern cinemas, drive-in movie theaters and expensive boutique shops with modern London-Paris styles. This was the tourist section and we saw mostly Whites walking the streets.

Then there was River Road. The beginning of this road, which was not even mentioned on the tourist maps, had Indian dukas and Nita and I learned to do all our shopping along this street.

The food market displayed fruits and vegetables on Market Street. Pineapples cost a shilling here. If you walked to the other end of River Road, the African Retail market charged one shilling for several pineapples, mangoes and carrots. Beautiful fruits and vegetables fresh from farms were available at less than half the price of the tourist market.

In Nairobi, and this was especially apparent at the university, the separation of Europeans, Asians and Africans was clear-cut. No one ventured to befriend a person in the other group.

Philip told me this stymied the usual college-type social life. What a shame, such a damper in a place where education should break down these barriers instead of continuing them.

One of the major areas I had to straighten out in my own mind was the "justification" for each point of view. Europeans felt they had "done so much to help develop Africa."

Africans denied this and when the British mentioned schools and hospitals the Africans claimed the mission schools fought against the African culture and society and broke down their way of life. An example was that the schools were against polygamy, an essential to the structure of the society and its growth.

Cliterotemy was performed as part of the initiation ceremony for girls. At this time the girls were given their sex education, organized into essential age groups and began relationships with boys.

Friday, March 7

Ruth writes:

Dear Jack,

Your mention and concern about our time in East Africa somehow gave us both the feeling that we would receive mail, at least a birthday letter.

We had a unique experience in East Africa. No tourist could possibly have the varied experiences with the variety of Asians and Africans which we have been having. Our contact with "Europeans," as all Whites are called, was limited. It was mostly the people we met in the youth hostels.

I have managed to sit at typewriters a couple of times and I shall send Olga our epistles, which you must realize is only an essence of things that we do. Each day holds so much and we meet so many people it is impossible for me to recall it all in type. Perhaps if you spend some time at her home, she will share her letters with you.

Ruth

Nita writes:

Dear Family,

Somehow in the past few weeks we have had our "calamities" but with each one there is always humor and relief that in actuality the end result was not calamity at all, only another experience to add to our long roster.

Nairobi is so Europeanized that it even has a chess club. It meets every Wednesday and I have gone four times, so far. I always beat the best player at the club.

Kenya is beautiful, and I love it here. But I can't stay because they won't give me citizenship because of my color. They are getting strict because everyone who visits wants to stay.

Have any of our travel friends come to America and contacted you yet? Many people we met and like say they are coming to New York. If they contact you, show them around or give them a meal and a place to sleep. They usually do much more for us.

What has been happening on the American scene? Campus? Civil rights? Politics?

Love again, Nita

Friends Mentioned in Chapter 31

Vinoo. He took me to visit the schools in his VW van.

Mrs. Baxi. She was the principal of the Air Force School.

Mrs. Pires. She was the head of the Aghan Khan school for girls.

Mrs. Delord. She was director of the Special School, with physically and mentally challenged pupils.

Philip Ndelu. He was a student at Nairobi University and drove us to his home.

Agreey Zubuliwo. He studied science and we spent time in his home in Uganda.

Jedidah Karanja. She studied catering and was a good friend to us. Her room became a home for us.

Gitau Gichuru. He was a bank executive. He helped me with bank papers and took us to restaurants and a dance.

Norbert Okare. He was the "Voice of Kenya" on television. He dined me.

Mr. Rao. He found us a place to sleep.

Thuku. He delivered papers in the country. He invited us to drive with him. We were introduced to his Kikuyu family. He drove in the East Africa Safari races.

Nandi. He was an architect who held our luggage and took us to the Nairobi Game Park.

Gordon Tweedie. He was a Tsavo game warden, who invited us to stay in his home.

Bill Phillips. He was a railroad trouble shooter. He lived on the Tsavo game preserve.

Sikh Gadial Singh. He was a villain.

Abdul Manji. He was the owner of Wagon Wheels hotel. He gave us room and board.

Noori. She was Mr. Manji's daughter. She attended Friends College in New York. Nita and Noori enjoyed being friends.

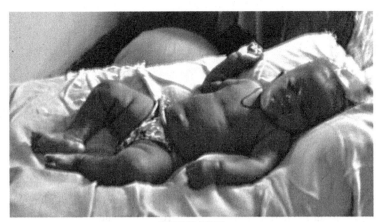

CRY BABY

THIRTY-TWO

UGANDA

We hitched again, but we noticed the driver picked up several people and they paid him money when they got out of the van. Our driver did not speak our language. We now learned about the taxi system along this road. We paid him two shillings, less than 25 cents, for our 10 mile ride and then got out.

Hussein Ismali picked us up and drove us all the way to Kampala. He took eight hours to make the three or four-hour trip. He drank three bottles of beer along the way, stopped for a thunderstorm and stopped to rest. We got into Kampala at one in the morning.

At that hour Hussein was stuck with us and had to find a place for us to stay for the rest of the night. He dropped Nita off in his own home and found a guesthouse for me the first night.

The next night he found a friend's house for Nita, and he slept on a couch in the same room with her. He liked her in a very possessive, jealous fashion.

He found an African Hotel for me. I liked it. It was clean, and I was alone and peaceful after hectic feelings of Nita and I being separated in Kampala.

But he brought an Indian lass, Shalom, 25, with her 3-year-old daughter into my room. So I had to listen to her sad tale of woe. She had an unhappy marriage, husband was "married" to his mother, not her, and she had in-law trouble. This was common among Indians. We could relate worse tales than this one.

Her husband would not return her college certificates to her. She needed them to prove she was qualified to teach her French class. For three months she had held the job. Now she was fired. In Africa they do things like this. She was destitute.

So she stole 250 shillings ($35 dollars) from me. I confronted her with it, but she denied it. I was powerless. Cash stolen is gone. Threat of police did not phase her. How could I prove it?

So we added, to the near rape and the bus knocking me down, stolen money. What else could possibly happen to us?

Don't worry, it did.

I met Ole at the dance and he became infatuated with me and we had a grand time dancing together.

The next day, Saturday, I arranged a picnic for us, and we ate matoke (plantain) and meat in the park. Then Ole disappeared to help some guy in trouble. On the way,

236

Ole's car ran into an African cyclist. (They are prolific in the streets of Uganda and hitting them is easy to do.) He landed in jail, his car was detained, and there were all kinds of accusations about lousy Asians trying to wipe out Africans. He happened to be Portuguese, not Asian, but only black-skinned Africans counted. All people with lighter skin were hated.

So my picnic came to an abrupt end and I waited all afternoon. I returned to the nightclub in the evening, waiting for my friend Ole to return. It was a long wait and meanwhile I used the typewriter at the club.

Nita was with me this night. (The night before Hussein took her to a different nightclub.) She had a good time. She spent the afternoon with Amyn, whom I had met the day before, and made the date, because he played chess better than most people.

Ole arrived, we sang songs and I perked up again.

Then Patrick danced with me. What a delightful guy. He invited us to Murchison Falls National Park where he said he was the game warden and we would be his guests.

O.K. with Nita and me. We were thrilled that this could happen to us twice. Remember, we had been the guests of Gordon Tweedie at Tsavo Park, and we slept in his home for two nights. We were fed by him and taken on safaris with him and Bill Phillips, our train trouble-shooter.

Friday, March 8

Nita writes:

From very highest high to deep, deep low in swoosh, a few seconds. I was at La Quinta nightclub having such a good time. Dancing with Amyn, talking, laughing, beautiful, popular, witty. I was flying. No doubts, no cares (except Hussein, hovering over me, sullen, treacherous, jealous.) But why should I care? I had a place to stay, an apartment with just Mommy and me. I didn't have to worry about Hussien's "separate rooms." Tonight I was free and happy.

Then, at 3:00, the apartment owner decided to go home. Immediately. No time for anything. A rush goodbye to Amyn, not even a future meeting place.

Hustled out and taken not far away to a lovely apartment. Settled down, the two of us nice and peaceful.

A phone call at 4:15 a.m. His wife complained that the water pipes broke on his shamba, where she was staying. She was arriving in half an hour. Instead of letting us stay in his apartment, in comes the owner and says, "I'm very sorry you'll have to leave. My wife is coming home."

Homeless. What to do? Where to go? Mommy immediately gets Hussein. No, no I can't go through that. I won't go back to him. He comes, with the owner of La Quinta. Mommy in one room, me in another.

I won't. I wont. I'll sleep out in the streets. La Quinta man offers me his club until 7 in the morning. I seize the opportunity. Mommy goes off – dazed, almost crying, blaming everything on everyone else. No meeting place, me without a cent.

As we approached the club the La Quinta owner sternly lectures me on my "atrocious behavior" during the evening. Why did I go with the apartment man in the first place? The fault is mine. I should have used Hussein. I can only use the club on condition I don't "fool around" with any of the men. I was with a bad bunch anyway and he tried to warn me, but did I heed him? I deserve whatever I got.

So here I am. In the gambling room with a curtain separator. No home. No friends. Amyn gone. All I can think about is let me get back to Nairobi. Let me get away from this place of liars, deceivers, and people whose characters and motives I can't decipher. Who to trust? Who is telling the truth? Each one says the other is evil. Is there a truth? All I want is a place to go to. A floor anywhere to rest my head in peace, without being dependent or indebted to anyone. I am homeless here. I am miserable.

Saturday, March 9

I had a few minutes rest on three chairs put together at La Quinta. The next thing I know all is silent. The owner, Mr. Lecture man, comes over and says that everyone is gone, but that if I want I can rest here for a few more minutes. I'm so tired. This is my fifth night with almost no sleep

Despite my refusals he goes about getting rid of the three chairs and puts down a large blanket on the floor instead. It was soon obvious that he planned to get on it too, but he kept reassuring me not to worry. I flopped down on the blanket so tired that I couldn't see straight, and then he flopped down next to me. In a matter of seconds it was quite obvious that I should worry.

I tried to talk. He got angry and rough. I, about to break, started screaming. He chased me out, telling me that if I chose to go outdoors at that hour alone, instead of having him, I was sure to have everything stolen and myself raped and maybe murdered by the Africans. Pleasant guy!

I decided to chance the Africans any day. I walked the mile to the police station and here I am, wondering if I should risk going to Nairobi alone, or try Makrere University, or wait around the Apollo Hotel and hope that Amon and Thuku will show up. How can I get in touch with my mother? Where is she?

I'm so despondent. If I didn't have complexes before I'm sure to have them now. I could go psychotic from such experiences. I think I must have to keep a sense of humor and a sense of detachment. Otherwise I'm sure to crack.

The only thing I wish right now is that I had arranged a meeting place with Amyn. I miss him. I must be a fool.

I deliberately signed myself into the police station for the rest of the night. It is now 7:05 a.m. I am sitting on a hard wooden bench in the police station in Kampala, trying very hard not to cry. I don't think I'm succeeding.

Hussein finally connected me with my mother and we both were anxious to move on.

Sunday, March 10

We thought Patrick's invitation delightful and we left for the Park 170 miles away. We were picked up by a Land Rover and sat in the uncomfortable back seat. The sides were open, so sun and dust covered us. But sleepily we were both transported – we were exhausted.

At the park entrance we handed them our letter explaining we were guests of the warden. It got us in without paying an entrance fee.

A tractor gave us a lift into the park. We sat in the wagon behind the tractor with three African women who were nursing babies. I sang and one woman imitated me with "Dee dee." I referred to her as the "Dee Dee" woman from then on. We enjoyed singing together as we traveled along the bumpy road.

Nita had no sleep the night before. Our wagon ride was 10 miles. Dust covered us and we were exhausted.

We located the game warden's home, met his young blond wife and our "hearts and flower" story was lost on her. "There are only three Europeans in this park and Patrick is not one of them," she informed us.

We went to the lodge to ask around there as Patrick had commanded, but the bar man and the manager both told us, "There is no Patrick in this park."

Again the lodge manager offered nothing except, "Two girls hitching in Africa? You're mad."

Back to John Zeigler, game warden, who proved as heartless as the others were. He dropped us at the Rondoval camping spot for the night.

Nita fell asleep, exhausted. She had gone five days with practically no sleep.

The Dee Dee woman arrived at our entrance with her lantern and led me to her rondeval home. Three men and two women sat outside in a circle. She cooked stew meat over an open fire. She brought me a chair to sit on. A cup was passed around, each person taking a drink of the local banana beer. I faked most of my drinking after the first taste. Then she brought out a flute and a man played lovely tunes. Dee Dee and I sang and danced. Then she brought a pot with meat and jellaby, an Indian sweet, and we all ate the sweet. The meat needed more cooking. The only light was from a wick lantern and the flickering light from the fire.

It was a delightful evening and I reluctantly left because I couldn't hold my head up any longer.

They spoke not one single word of English. I used every Swahili word I knew during the evening.

The next morning Warden John woke us at 7:30 and asked us our plans. He let us know in no uncertain terms that if we stayed we had to pay 40 shillings.

I asked, "Why can't we be your guests?"

I got a sharp pinch from Nita for that one.

He replied, "I think I have done quite enough for you. It should have cost you 30 shillings to sleep in that bed last night."

He dropped us off at the lodge.

I asked those British and American tourists who came to breakfast to give us a ride out of the park. They all said, "No."

I went back to sit in the foyer, undaunted.

An African waiter offered us coffee and a piece of pineapple, nearly the only food Nita had for two days. She had eaten a cucumber, avocado and a small apple the day before.

Finally, three Asians, two men and a woman, passed by.

"There's our ride," I told Nita.

Of course it was.

They made a stop and entered a house. We were curious and followed. They left a token offering of fruit. Their explanation when they returned was that one day footprints suddenly appeared in this room. It was unknown to the occupants how they got there. Since then this had become a sacred visit.

Friends Mentioned in Chapter 32

Hussein Ismail. He was deceitful and a villain to us.

Shalom She was 25. She stole $35 from me.

Ole. I met him at a dance.

Patrick. He sent us to Murchison Falls as a joke.

The Dee Dee woman. We sang together.

John. He was the warden at the park.

Three Asians. They drove us out of Murchison Falls to Iganga.

THIRTY-THREE

IGANGA

We were dropped at Tororo, Uganda-Kenya border, headed for Uganga. Philip's had a roommate named Aggrey whose family lived here.

The hitch we got was with an educational director, and when we showed him the address and name he said, "I taught Aggrey. His father got me my job."

We were lucky Aggrey had written to expect us. I was glad we came back. We could easily have become disgusted with Uganda and returned directly to Nairobi.

How can you describe "Home?" After an upsetting weekend in Kampala where we never had a home to return to, or a place to keep our rucksacks, we now were accepted as part of this family. We were contented once again.

The mother and I prepared food. We sang our songs. I sang nursery rhymes.

Mr. Zabuliwe was married to his first wife for 20 years. She liked the idea of his marriage to a second, younger woman to help with the household chores. They worked well together.

We'd bought saris and lived as Indians with Indian families in India and Africa. Now we owned a conga. We were living with African families again. Sylvia and the two young children took walks with us and we met neighbors. They questioned me about growing tomatoes.

One beautiful woman gave us a pineapple as a gift. We sat and talked with various people. It felt so good.

We loved every member of this family and they made us feel happy in their midst.

What did we come to Africa for? We came to Africa to meet Africans and live with them and learn their attitudes and try to understand their politics and have discussions to find out what was on their minds. To know them was to love them.

My relationship with Nita would take years to sort out. It was unique.

I took down addresses of places to go and steered us into situations that enlightened or entertained us. There is no doubt that I embarrassed Nita many times. We had completely different attitudes as we traveled.

For instance, the day before we sat for the entire day in the Apollo Hotel. We never heard from Thuko and Amon, our safari drivers, who were going to pick us up and drive us around Uganda. Back in Nairobi we would contact them and find out what happened.

241

When I sat in Noori's office typing I met her boss, who gave us the address and a letter to the Chief Justice of Goa. How could we fail to stop off there and meet him with this letter of introduction?

Our adventures were getting ludicrous because they were so incredible. For instance, the day of my bus accident I was quite concerned because I did not know where Nita was. Nita slept in the men's dorm at the university. The two boys slept in one bed and gave Nita the other bed. Only to Nita could make this happen.

Tuesday, March 12

Nita writes in her diary:

My spirits have somewhat revived.

I am at the home of Mr. Zabuliwo, Aggrey's father. A home! This was our purpose in coming to Uganda in the first place. After the misery of the past Kampala days and the Murchison Park fiasco, I am at peace. I caught up on my lack of sleep, I am eating regularly and I have friendly loving people around me. Yes, my spirits have somewhat revived.

Friends in chapter 33

The Zabuliwo family. They were Aggrey's family.

THE ZABULIWO
FAMILY 106
AKHI MAN

THIRTY-FOUR

TO NAKURU

Wednesday, March 13

We hitched the way back to Nairobi, but we had a two-hour wait at the Uganda immigration center on the border. Only two cars passed in two hours, and that was the main road between the capital of Uganda, Kampala, and the capital of Kenya, Nairobi.

George, an African personnel manager of meat packers, gave us the 200-mile hitch in his new Citroen. We rode in style, in bliss, and had an intelligent, smiley, good-looking driver and companion.

But I'm one for sightseeing. I didn't want to miss anything and I suddenly panicked and realized I was leaving the country and what had I seen?

So I rode back to Nakuru.

A young Dutchman drove me up to the crater, one of the largest in Africa. It was 25 miles across. The scene was beautiful and lonely and the Dutchman enjoyed nature. He was a manager in a fertilizer plant. They sent men out into the bush country to explain about growing green vegetables and using fertilizer.

He drove me back to the highway and I left Nakuru again without seeing the park.

CARVING A MASK

THIRTY–FIVE

LEONARD IN NAKURU

Leonard Allen drove toward me, saw me and turned his car around to pick me up. He drove to Lake Naivasha on the back roads. It was a desolate place and we bought our petrol before starting out.

Leonard took me to a British club and rented a motorboat for us. We drifted in the evening sunset. Just what I wanted. I was so happy that day.

Leonard was the manager of Proctor and Allen, part of the Unga Flour Mills unit. They made porridge oats, custard powder and dog biscuits (which birds eat while they are drying on the screens). He had been working in this East African plant for 18 years. Before that he worked as baker for Peak and Freen, the English biscuit makers.

He was not yet 60. His divorce became final the day I was with him. It was a good way to celebrate. His wife was not happy in Africa. She was a small-town person and wanted to "stay put." He had a 23-year-old son, but saw him infrequently.

We spent a delightful Sunday and I was so glad I had ventured out again. He drove me home to the youth hostel where we picked up Nita and brought her into Nairobi to the Rendezvous Restaurant for a steak dinner.

I thought: Nita is lucky she knows me. She didn't appreciate one iota of it, believe me. Most of her steak dinners had been as a guest of my friends.

Leonard had to drive 100 miles at 12:30 at night. I was too stimulated to sleep and sat in the miserable light of the gas lantern and read until 12:30, when I knew he'd arrive home.

On Monday we had errands again. I had gotten to despise the word "errands." They haunted me. But during the day we discovered our "money man" finally landed in jail and I would have to cash money in the bank.

Then I picked up a roll of film I had made into slides and saw our pictures of Uganda. Only my little Justine wasn't there. Adorable, impish, dimpled face of our 2-year-old. The printers used a hard glove and scratched through my roll while waiting for it to dry. Some people!

At Pop-In we located "Joe," a Polynesian, who never let you forget it. He was someone who knew the underworld of Nairobi.

He introduced me to Balu, an Asian, who drove me around. I returned books

244

to three different people and then he took me to a steak luncheon. He offered me nightclub life if I showed up in the evening. Only I was bored with him.

I had to face seeing my friends and saying goodbye and I couldn't do it. I just couldn't. I was restless and irritable and Nita knew it.

Finally, she said, "Why don't you go back to Nakuru to see Leonard?" It was the best idea yet.

At 2:00 I telephoned Leonard's plant and left a message for him to meet me at 6:00. I phoned from the gambling pin-ball machine room of Pop-In and I couldn't hear anything on the phone. So I felt I was taking a chance in setting out on my journey.

I hitched my ride and it turned out to be Willie Thom, British East African man, who had sat in Pop-In with us. He offered me dates to take me anywhere, do anything.

If I remained in the area he would take me mineral hunting. Why did I have to leave East Africa now? But meantime Willie drove me to Westlands. It was a few miles out of town on the main highway to Nakuru.

He drove at 80 miles an hour and I shut my eyes tight rather than know it. We got there early and when I asked for a ladies room in Midlands Hotel the manager opened a guest room for me. In a few minutes I took a bath and refreshed myself. (Please don't ask how these things work for me; I didn't ask him for it.)

Leonard arrived on time. It was good to see him. He had been posting a letter to me and that was the reason he wasn't there when I called.

Leonard was a British gentleman like Bill Phillips and Gordon Tweedie at Tzavo National Park. He offered me his guestroom and he took the room that was not furnished.

While he was at work I relaxed, listening to his high-fi piano concertos. I enjoyed good food and a sofa to lie down on while looking out into his garden.

After Leonard quit work we drove through Nakuru National Park, the bird sanctuary. We finally saw those thousands of flamingoes, lesser and greater the two species are called. The swoosh of their flight sounds like an ocean wave. We saw pelicans, malibous, ibis and storks. We saw birds flying and landing on the lake and saw herds of leaping gazelles. We drove on the wilderness roads that led nowhere. We had an enjoyable outing.

Unless you travel as we did you cannot appreciate the interior of a European home. The comfort of a Western-type hotel is sterile despite the modern plumbing. But a home with a rug on the floor, pictures on the wall, a cloth sofa to stretch out on in comfort with feet raised, is the height of luxury. Clean shave, hot bath, hair wash, and easy living to the tunes of Chopin's Polonaise and Hungarian Rhapsody.

Leonard was a challenge and he was such a good man in every single sense that I so desired to "give of myself" in any way to make him happy and give him memories to cherish when I had gone.

Friends Mentioned in Chapter 35

Leonard Price Allen. I was a guest in his home.

Joe. I met him at Pop-In. He was a Polynesian introduced me to Balu.

Willie Thom. I got a hitch with this British East African.

**LEONARD PRICE ALLEN,
A PROFESSIONAL BAKER AND ACTOR**

THIRTY-SIX

NAKURU TO MOMBASA

Wednesday, March 19

I hitched the 100 miles to town, but had to walk from Kabete to Lower Kabete and dreaded Nita's wrath at my late (9:30) arrival.

Only my bedding was in the hostel. She had left it for me in case I arrived Tuesday night. She spent the night again in the University dorm with Philip and Aggrey. It was their decision to sleep in discomfort as they gave her their room and bed.

Nita writes in her diary:

It is now about 9:00 a.m. I am in Jedidah's room, and have finished packing. Mommy is not here. We have a boat to catch in Mombasa, 350 miles away, at 7:00 a.m.

Mommy has the tickets. Mommy is not here yet. We were supposed to get an early start this morning. It was pre-arranged when she went to Nakuru yesterday. Hitching. Alone. She should be here! If something happened to her, I wonder what to do. If something didn't happen I'll just be very angry but what if??

I'll try to call Leonard Allen in Nakuru first because she went to see him. Then the hospital. Then the police. She has the tickets. What am I supposed to do, wait around for her or leave for Mombasa (with all that luggage? Who am I kidding?) What an unreliable Mother I have!

When I got to Nita at 10:00 she was in the process of calling Nakuru for me. She was in some mood all day. We each had traveled 300 miles that day. It took us 8 hours. I tacked on 100 miles at the beginning of the day and she at the end.

Our second hitch took us 100 miles in the back of a Land Rover, but our own gear became our pillows and the ride was more comfortable than the dusty Land Rover ride from Kampala.

The two Africans drove to a broken-down double petrol truck. Their job was to fix it.

But first they hailed another passing petrol truck and put our gear in. We sat on a foam cushion behind the seats. It was comfortable and pleasant. Our driver owned two trucks and knew everyone on the road. He often stopped to say hello.

We were dropped off at Voi-Tzavo National Park.

Bill Phillips was in Mombasa. We asked a policeman to drive us to Gordon Tweedie, the Game Warden's home.

We found him and he gave petrol to the "jerks," who were about to drive away with an empty tank.

Gordon was having a malarial attack, had a high fever and felt sick. The pile of books we brought for him suddenly seemed an empty gesture. There is so much more I would have liked to bring him — material for curtains, silverware, new crockery and better books.

We talked for three hours before he retired with his warm Ovaltine at 9 p.m.

This hot, miserable day would go down in infamy. I stood at the wrong spot to hitch and sat for hours in the broiling sun. There were no shade trees and practically no cars in my direction for two hours. Then only four cars, all with Europeans, sped by me. Cussing was too good for them.

I got the next car that passed. It contained East African, white youngsters, who said they were professional hunters and beach comers. The young girl had a story that was hard to believe.

Her mother was French. She was picked up as a slave girl and landed in an Arabian harem in Libya. Her father struck oil and her mother became the favorite wife, so she had money and the Citroen we drove in is hers. She kept the driver as her general man for chauffeuring, running errands and lover. She couldn't have been more than 20 years old.

THIRTY-SEVEN

THE STATE OF HARYANA

Friday, March 21

Early in the morning I hitched to the dock and met Aloo, who told me he knew the Haryana purser. We watched the ship dock. Aloo said he was a manager in the documentation office on docks.

Aloo drove me back to the hotel. I picked up my bathing suit and, in the afternoon, after work, we went swimming on Nyali beach. I wanted Nita to join us.

I had written to Vinoo that I was returning to Mombasa. He had booked a hotel room for Nita and me, and he sent a telegram informing us which hotel. Unfortunately, Nita never went to pick up our mail when I was in Nakuru. So we didn't know.

While I wandered around the streets of Mombasa that Friday morning doing errands, Vinoo located Nita and started a systematic search for me. After an hour he found me. I was swept up into a tornado for the rest of the day.

Vinoo had his truck. I was whisked into the shoemaker shop to get a new zipper for my handbag.

We visited Ammini and Ratna, our nurse friends at the hospital.

Later Aloo arrived. We went for a refreshing dip at the beach. I was back to my hotel by 6:00 p.m., waiting for Vinoo and his friend, who promised to take us to the drive-in movie, "The Moon is Blue." I had seen it years ago and loved Maggie McNarmara. Nita agreed to join us.

Steak dinner, of course, before going.

The friend had a car that replaced the VW truck. Nita and I enjoyed the movie, but the men were bored stiff.

The next morning Vinoo arrived at 7:00 a.m. and drove our baggage and us to the docks.

It was Saturday, his day reserved for his family. He was a great family man. Vinoo kept a happy marriage going, despite his erotic exploits.

So Nita and I settled into the business of embarkation. This takes place in Mombasa, not at the docks.

We had no idea what to expect. Our optimism, now that we look back, was appalling. We were told to be at the docks at 7:00 a.m. The customs and passport business was finished in only three hours, record time.

In town we did last minute shopping. We had no idea what time the boat was leaving. The newspaper said 9:00 a.m., but it was already after 10:00 a.m. The customs officer said 12:00, the passport officer said 3:00 p.m. In fact everyone had different "inside information."

We hitched a ride to the Haryana ship, and waited two hours to board it, in the blazing heat, among screaming babies.

We waited from 7:00 a.m. to 10:00. We asked what to do, where to go, always getting misinformation.

On deck we endured passport inspection and health certification. The inspectors kept our papers, both passports and health certificates. This caused trouble for us later on.

Finally, we were permitted to board the ship.

We ensconced ourselves in the luxurious first class lounge and sat there for hours before facing the reality ahead. What was Bunk class like?

Fredrick became our friend. He was the chief policeman and in charge of all the policemen regulating ship lines, activities and stowaways. Naturally, he became infatuated with Nita.

He bought us a sack of oranges. There had to be more than 100 in that heavy bag, so we ate oranges in place of meals.

The State of Haryana is a cargo ship of the India Line. It was carrying us back to Bombay.

Finally, we had to face reality.

The amount and weight of the luggage Indians travel with must be seen to be appreciated. Tara Mehta, who roomed with Nita last trip, had 14 trunks. They were heavy steel, with large locks and rope, and many other bulky packages. All luggage got hauled on to the ship in those huge nets, then carried into one of the three holds. People had to find their own luggage and claim it themselves.

Panic nearly struck when I realized Nita's chess set had become separated from our luggage. She lost a precious slipper en route from baggage room to hold. Her shoes and clackies both gave her blisters, and slippers were the only footwear that didn't.

We had two damaged suitcases. Nita's zipper was more broken than mine. We also had two rucksacks with books and blankets.

The next step was to have a porter carry the luggage into the hold where we slept. We staggered down, down, down precarious steps and we faced reality. This was bunk class.

The double-decker bunks were placed so as to provide a minimum space to walk between them. People were sprawled on those dusty metal bunks with mattresses and bedrolls. We had only one blanket each to use as a mattress and one sleeping sack as a sheet.

The single fan threw little breeze. The first night Nita kept changing from top bunk to bottom bunk to top bunk, because either the hot glare of the ever-present and necessary light burned her, or the lack of air circulation in the bottom bunk made it hard to breathe.

The congestion and the crying children and the noise level were another part of the nightmare.

These people were delegated to the area for the entire voyage. A very small area has some sunlight they could sit in, but it was still in the hold. Children exercised on ropes in the gym/play area.

We had somehow found our way through the maze of corridors and decks to our "home" for ten days in bunks 416 and 417. Help!

Nita writes:

Dear Wendi,

This trip is wild, fantastic, and extraordinary. We left Mombasa for Bombay on the Haryana ship on March 22. We had a bunk class ticket for the simple reason that it cost $66 each, rather than $140 each, which is the cost of the lowest class cabin.

We had originally wanted the Karanja or Kampala ships of the British line, but our race and sex worked against us. No female 'Europeans' were allowed to travel bunk class on any ship but the Haryana, an Indian line.

Wendi, it was really unbelievable. The atmosphere was gummy and sickly, and I was sure I was going to vomit. 400 people packed together without one foot of space apart, and breathing the same polluted air without a change. Everybody stank from the heat, including us, and if you tried to flop down on your bed for relief you would get a concussion and a broken rib, and an earache from the clunk of your body against the bare metal. The little baby, two beds away, relieved himself all over the floor, but that was duly ignored. It would dry up in a few minutes, anyway.

In order to get to our bed we had to pass through the kitchen, because the pathway was the kitchen.

The men sit in the corridors with mounds of dough and roll out chapatis on the floor. We have to carefully step over the food as we make our way up the deck, but the children running through don't bother. So the bread gets additional flattening.

There are over 400 fourth-class people with another 100 people sleeping on the outside decks. It was a nightmare. Those ancient Roman galleys or the Negro slave ships had nothing over us. Hundreds of sweaty, smelling bodies stuffed together. No room to move, no air to breathe. Hot lights glaring overhead. Screaming babies, big voiced men, shrill mothers. Get me out of here!

A dusty metal slab for a bed, everybody staring; no air, no air. They don't actually expect me to sleep here, do they?

More later,

Love, Nita

Sunday, March 23

People, people everywhere. I couldn't get away from the milling crowds. Oh, for a minute alone. I thought: I must have personality this trip — can't afford to be anti-social — must befriend the officers to get away from that hellhole below. Which was worse: that mad dungeon or the put-on pleasantness? Schylla or Chrybdis. Was there no in between?

I was reading Montserrat's "Nylon Pirates" and it dealt with a sea voyage. It was the first time I had read a book apropos of my immediate situation.

We both made up sleep in the afternoon in the first class lounge.

I decided that I could not live for 10 days in that dungeon.

It really looked like one. There were even cage bars surrounding the vegetarian restaurant where we ate because the food was edible.

There were less than 10 vegetarian tables and 5 non-vegetarian tables on which to feed all these people. Therefore, every mealtime there was a mad rush to the tables — eat or be eaten.

The air was death-still and steamed with perspiration. We finally grabbed a seat. Wait. Wait. A dark glistening Indian came by with a dirty rag and wiped the table refuse to the floor. The plates and spoons were hurriedly passed around. The "food" got slopped on the plate tray, curry mixed with puree, mixed with sag (a vegetable like spinach).

In a real state of hunger, one eats. The food, under other conditions, would be considered tasty. We tried the meals with meat at first, but they were inedible and unappetizing. The vegetarian meals were not as repulsive.

We never did get used to the emptying of water glasses by tossing them on the floor right next to us, nor the way the food was slopped into our cubicles on our tray. Animals are fed with more decorum.

A glass of tepid water splashed in front of me. The glass was full of caked-on curry. I look at it; the man across from me looked at it. We burst out laughing. No, no, no. It can't be true. This is ludicrous. We must laugh and maybe we'll wake up from this nightmare.

The first night as I delayed my return to the "dungeon," I sat on top deck and spoke to people. Finally, past midnight, I received an offer to sleep in the empty bed in Adatia's first-class room. Who could refuse?

So it went according to plan. Nita would sweat out our choice of passage, and I would "manage to get us out of it."

What is the best way to get out of the dungeon? Easy! Make friends with the crew. Become a personality.

We sat in the first class lounge, the only lounge, and waited for something to happen. It did. Vilos appeared and we started talking. He was the first mate. Doc, the second mate, arrived and joined us.

The second day on board, I paid a visit to the captain. A party was about to take place as we spoke. The officers celebrated the Parsee New Year. I brought Nita into it. Doc brought out his guitar. I again drew Nita into the melee and we sang along with the men.

As usual I played an aggressive role. Nita became the "darling" of the three top officers, Captain, Doc and Vilos. The whole venture paid off when a cabin was arranged for us with comfortable berths and privacy. Hooray!

However, after one venture into the dining hall, we were told to continue bunk class meals. Most of the time we skipped the first two meals of the day and dove into the bag of oranges Fredrick had brought us. Thank goodness!

The beautiful Nita was invited up to the bridge each evening, and I joined her to spend pleasant hours with the captain in his cabin. She conversed and played chess. We played cards and danced to good music. The captain was an exceptional person, capable in all of his undertakings and personable and attractive. We both admired him. We stayed with the captain from nine in the evening to one in the morning.

We finished off Doc's midnight to 4:00 a.m. watch discussing astronomy and navigation.

We spent time investigating the various instruments from the bridge. We watched the three top officers use weights on a ship layout to see if it was properly balanced for speed. If it was a little off, the baggage and cargo had to be shifted around.

The barometer was a wet and dry thermometer. We could listen to the weather reports from the radio room. There was a storm at sea, but fortunately it missed our area. The log had to be written in five different places, and it kept the navigation officers, our Doc, and second officer busy all four hours of their watch.

We both looked forward to our nights more than any other part of our trip. We slept and read away our day. Nita pieced and basted the dress she designed as "busy work."

At about 4:30 a.m. I wended my way to bed. In the dungeon people were awake and chirping. With all the roar, it was impossible to sleep. I waited until 5:30, when the water came on, to take a shower, get refreshed and read. At 9:00 a.m. I visit Vilos' cabin for breakfast. I sleep for the rest of the day.

Now that I had my own cabin, this procedure was simplified and I slept more hours during the day.

Nita writes:
Just had a fabulous evening. It is now about 5:00 a.m. our time, and I reached my bed in the dungeon.

At about 7:00 this evening I was talking to Terry, an Englishman, fresh out of South Africa and Rhodesia. He's not really bad, he wanted to see the situation for himself. When Mommy pulled me with her with the news that we were going to crash the captain's party up-deck.

I was hustled up. I saw Vilos, the chief officer who had befriended me yesterday.

We entered into a lively discussion, which ended with existentialism. Meanwhile Vilos disappeared

There was a man next to us, alone and in the dark, who sometimes added a crack, but who was otherwise ignored.

He turned out to be the captain. I started getting into a conversation with him. Mommy pulled me away to join in this Parsee Party and to help her sing a song with a group of crew members. Doc, the second mate, who we also befriended yesterday, was in the middle, playing his guitar.

It was fun. Things livened up considerably when we got there, and the songs became more and more rowdy as the men became more drunk. Finally, there was a Swahili song that, from the sound of the men, I'm glad I didn't understand.

I was the center of attraction. I'm getting quite used to it, and the ship's doctor, an older man, sung songs of love to me.

Mommy picked up an adorable, but drunk, young officer and danced with him. I even compromised enough to swing my hips at the more rhythmic numbers.

After a couple of hours the men were too drunk to hold a tune, Doc became hoarse, so we quit. I went to starboard, peered into the sky and all by myself located the Southern Cross. What a thrill!

The officers walked to the mess hall to eat, and although I was invited, I didn't join them. The first class lounge had become my home, where the lights were bright enough to read.

Doc traced me and upon my telling him that I wasn't hungry, he brought me to his room for potato chips and to listen to records. I had been beefing for a dance on board. Doc danced with me to the tune of Jack Jones. I can't say danced, actually, it was really close swaying, but very proper, and we both felt good. Doc was called away and the record went off.

Vilos came in. We chatted for a while and he invited me to breakfast tomorrow morning.

Then Captain Keith arrived, noticed the Jack Jones records and invited me up to his room to hear some good music. Doc and Vilos showed no sign of coming back, so I went. He had a nice collection of records and a beautiful Hi-Fi set. We listened for awhile and then danced. He was a marvelous dancer. The conversation evolved and we floated.

I told him about my life — home, Puerto Rico, summers, the trip. He told me about his various adventures. He was going to marry a German girl, but a barrier of distance, customs, and his job, stopped him.

The dancing got closer, and I had coffee and crème de menthe liqueur and it got to be 3:30 a.m.

I finally left and instead of going to bed, I was stimulated rather than tired, I went up to the navigation bridge to see Doc, who was on duty. We spent a half-hour watching the stars and sea.

Down to more music, but I refused to stay more than twenty minutes. I'll see him tomorrow evening, too. I like Doc, Vilos, and the captain, but trouble may arise from the trio. After all, this is only the second day.

Guess what happened next. It is now the fifth day of the "cruise." Mommy and I have our own cabin.

We still eat in the hole but if we wanted we could eat in first class. It's European food, more tasteless than the Indian meals.

I spent the first two nights sleeping (sleeping?) down in the dungeon. Then we were moved to a comfortable cabin.

Since the party, I have spent every evening till 2:30 a.m. or 3:00 a.m. in the captain's cabin listening to records, dancing and talking. He's a really good guy and loves to talk. He has been around the world; graduated from high school at age 16, was engaged to a German girl for two years, but broke it off because he thought the cultural and mileage barriers combined with his "away-from-home" job would make a difficult marriage.

His father, an Anglican minister in Bombay, died three weeks ago and his wife and two children lived in Poona. Captain would never live anywhere but India, because he "belongs" there.

As soon as I left the captain I go up to the Navigation Bridge to keep Doc company. He had watch from midnight to 4 a.m. every night. He taught me navigation and star constellations. Last night, we saw the Southern Cross and Polaris in the same sky at the same time. Scorpio and Jupiter were very conspicuous around here.

To keep busy I am hand-sewing a dress. Enclosed is a sample of the material. It should disclose to you the state of my mind. I am making up my own pattern. Hopefully it will look like this: It has puffed sleeves, a low neckline and Empire line waist and A-line skirt.

Our cabin isn't good enough for my mother. Now she wants a cabin with a porthole! If we asked the captain we would get it, but I think it is ridiculous.

Last night Mommy and I were in the captain's room playing cards until almost 4 a.m. We played three-handed bridge for a while, and then played flash, three-card poker, and pantoon (twenty-one) for matchsticks. I wiped everybody out both games.

It's a very depressing thought that I only have four more months of traveling left.

Many of the Indian women on the ship are dying to be friends with me, but they are boring! The male Indian passengers on the ship aren't much better. I think they have nothing to say. An exception would be Vilos, very intelligent and a good conversationalist.

Write to Ceylon,
Love, Nita

Friday, March 28

Ruth writes:

Dear family,

The days are fleeting now. Even as I read this it reads dull and lifeless. One must envision the two of us completely vibrant and aware each moment of our release from our bunk class.

We relaxed in the most comfortable living quarters on the entire ship from 9 p.m. to 4 in the morning. It had the best light available for reading, dancing with the smoothest dancer, our captain, and drinking. I'm advancing to brandy now in addition to the bottle of Creme de Menthe, which Nita and I have "killed" during this week.

We can look at one another and laugh. Look at us. We were bunk class; we now have a private cabin to ourselves. That isn't enough? We relax in captain's quarters all night until dawn. Most recently, we partake our evening meal there. The best food on the ship, of course. Dinner last night was a mincemeat dish and omelet cut up with sauces and rice. Today I fast and eat none of those meals below. That way I can really enjoy our dinner tonight.

But keep in mind one important fact. When I took 4th class, we knew I would get out of it, regardless of with whom I had to do what. But Nita?

But this is better than anything we could have dreamed possible. We reverse day and night. Captain doesn't want me to "Sir" him. We told him to stop "Ma'am'ing me. We are now on a Keith and Ruth basis.

Captain Keith was tall, good looking and 32 years old. He talked to me of his delight and his enjoyment of Nita. Their discussions were sometimes serious and sometimes just to get to know her better in this platonic relationship. He kept finding items to give her, Kitenga shirts, soap and already he had her birthday gifts lined up.

We begged him to stop loading us up, because our luggage was already too heavy and a problem. What can we do? His joy, as ours, spills over and none of us wanted the evenings to end.

I ran in and out from 1:00 a.m. to 4:00 a.m., keeping Doc company while he was on watch. It used to be Nita's role, but each night the hour she left captain approached closer to dawn.

Nita tried to sleep her days away. She bought material and designed a dress for herself. We both read.

I set myself a book for every two days. I finished Belfrage's, "A Room in Moscow," which brought back so many memories of our days in Russia. Her book was great because her descriptions were so accurate from my own feelings about the country. Her personal relationships were the only varying factor.

I read Carrighar's, "Moonlight in Midsummer." It is about Alaska and her re-

lationships and knowledge of Eskimos while she was learning about arctic animal life.

Today I should finish "Illustrated Man," by Ray Bradbury.

Montserrat's "Nylon Pirates" deals with a sea voyage. I consider my shake-down of the husband who took separate cabins from his wife, and had been on my tail all trip.

Nita hoped I wouldn't find this book during the voyage. I'm so susceptible to corruption.

To salve my conscience for all I'm taking from the crew, I begged for work. At last, I was given stencils to cut for the ship's list. Good busy work for me during the day, because I'm up at 7:00 a.m. regardless of the two hours sleep.

Three white males were bunk class also and two couldn't get less than first class; they live in style.

Nita spent some time with them and said they were decent chaps. Bill was study-ing Hindi and wanted to get to know the Indian people. John sat and wrote his diary experiences every day, as I do. He read and stayed to himself. He appreciated the fellow passengers ignoring him, because when he was in Ethiopia people shouted "Foreign Devil," and haunted his life.

Love,

Ruth

It began back in Nairobi nearly a month ago.

"I must get a visa for India. We already have our Japanese visa in our passport."

After searching, I located the High Commission of India and walked into the of-fice ready to buy another visa. We obtained our first one in London, which lasted for two months. In Delhi, we extended it for another month. Now we were re-entering India via a ship. The gentleman in Nairobi, in his Indian accent, told me I had 72 hours, free with no visa necessary, as we pursued our journey.

He told me I could get a transit visit at the port and he refused to give me any visa, or any papers to sign.

But I knew better.

So I asked, "Will you kindly write me a letter to this effect? I can give it to the immigration office in India."

"Oh, that isn't necessary. Here is the tourist pamphlet. It says right here that you do not need one."

So I tore out that special section and pasted it into my passport, ready to face immigration.

At last the 10-day trip was over.

Nita and I were on the bridge and watched the boat docking. The second officer disappeared to oversee the anchor dropping and the third officer moved the speed level — dead slow-slow to slow us down to a stop.

He used binoculars to watch the many fishing vessels in the harbor. We anchored about a mile and a half off shore and a tug guided us into the Bombay dock.

As we approached shore there was constant radar watch to see how close we were to the small boats and shore. There were two sounding machines. We watched the gauge as the fathoms decreased from the hundreds to the twenties. We dropped anchor at about eleven fathoms.

Our ship pulled into port around 4:00 p.m. We searched the docks for our friend Henry. He managed to locate us. He had arrived at 10:00 a.m. to meet us because yesterday's paper announced that time for arrival.

He never saw today's paper, which listed arrival at 2:00 p.m. Henry and Alwyn's brother, Reggie, waited all day long at the docks in steaming Bombay sun. He also paid the three rupees to board ship, another Indian custom. We were glad to see Henry. He always carried our luggage and helped us find lodging. His capable manner and pleasantries boosted our morale. He hung around with us until 7:00 p.m.

A woman came on board asking for Kaufman. Ratna had written to her mother all about us and she came to see us. Only she couldn't speak our language and everything we wanted to say to her Ratna had already told her. We went to get the radio and wristwatch for her to take. They were Ratna's presents to her family.But she couldn't take them off the ship. We had to take them through customs for her. At 7:00 p.m. she left and said she'd return tomorrow because she worked nearby and it would be no trouble. She turned out to be a police constable.

We tried lining up for immigration clearance several times as they thinned out the salon and cabin passenger first. Remember, we were fourth class. Eventually, we moved to the front of the line.

"Where is your entry visa?" the officer demanded.

"What entry visa?"

I show him the clipping from the tourist manual. I was unable to understand his explanation, but he told us to go away and come back later. We did that. They cleared out every passenger before us. All the passengers departed. Now us!

"I can give you a seven-day visa."

"The manual said there was a 15 day visa we could have."

"I cannot give you that today. I can give you seven days, but today is counted as one of the seven."

Nita said, "Let's take it. Seven days is long enough for me!"

"No it isn't. Three days in Bombay, Poona, Goa and then the train trip through South India to Ceylon. It must take more than six days." I insist. "No."

Well, that took time and different men became involved. New ones came on the ship to handle us. The kept yelling at me angrily to go to the immigration men.

Result: We could not leave the ship until the next day. They kept our passports and health certificates. They said in the morning they would put the visas in them for us. Meanwhile, our luggage, brought up from our cells, had to go back into our cabins. A steward made arrangements for a meal to be served to us at 7:00 p.m. in the salon dining room. Our status rose.

The purser told us to remain in the same rooms. He didn't offer us a luxury cabin.

Tuesday, April 1
Nita writes:
It is 4:30 p.m. and the Haryana is docked at Bombay. Everybody is milling around apparently not knowing what to do. I went up to Keith's cabin earlier, but he was running around and paid no attention to me at all.

We said goodbye last night.

We had another customary good time. There was less dancing than usual and very personal conversation.

I had a wretched cold and Keith massaged me for hours while Mommy slept in the next room. He got his thrills, although anytime he was carried away I quickly quelled him. I had a luxuriously relaxing time.

If that brief encounter with Keith this afternoon when he gave me back the loaned books is the end of our relationship, then it is very unsatisfactory. I don't even have his last name, and he doesn't have my address for when he comes to New York.

Oh, Bombay is wretchedly hot!

Wednesday, April 2

Nita writes:
Prisoners! That's what we are!

We were ship-bound for an extra day due to a lack of an Indian visa. Naturally we landed back at the captain's cabin all night. He appeared very happy to see me.

He's pounced upon a scheme to get me to write to him; namely, by loaning us money for the trip we would be obliged to pay him back when we reach home. Very ingenious.

At the beginning of the night a friend of his, another captain, was also in the cabin. He maintains that he is a staunch conservative, and talks against individualism, but he is the weirdest individualist himself. His daughter, Niti, was doing honors work at Beaver College in America.

He got good and drunk before he left. My ego needs a bit of bruising. I'm getting to be a spoiled brat. Everything goes my way and everyone I want to like me, likes me. I get so much and give nothing in return, except if I count the other's pleasure in my company. These are Mommy's sentiments word for word.

Keith went to Poona today to be at his new son's baptism. We did not say goodbye, but we have a date for tomorrow evening. Hope it turns out O.K. I do want our relationship to end on a good note.

Poor Henry and Reggie waited around for us in the blazing heat all day yesterday and today. We are fortunate to have such loyal friends.

I hope that when the immigration finally does come that we can get a fifteen-day visa and not have to settle for the seven-day one. That would really be terrible.

April 2
Ludicrous! We have been waiting to get off this ship since 3:00 p.m. yesterday. It is now 6:30 p.m. today. We have just been told to wait until tomorrow morning. We are literally prisoners. Four policemen body-guarded Mommy all yesterday until it became the ship joke.

Mother was becoming more and more upset as the hours passed and the police tailed her every move.

"Why are they doing this?" She kept asking over and over again.

They even woke us up at 10:00 a.m. this morning after we had gotten in at 6:00 a.m.

The police continued following us today. I was missing for an hour since I fell asleep in a first class cabin. During that time the immigration officer was looking for me. A policeman informed me that I was not to go anywhere without first telling him where I was going. This was distressing to us. What had we done that made us criminals pursued by the police? But at least we keep the policemen out of trouble.

Henry said he would return about noon. What a good dependable friend he was. Ratna's mother will return today to visit with us. And the immigration men will return today. The office of Immigration doesn't open until 10:30 a.m.

We relished the dinner specially prepared for us.

When I left the dining room I had a police escort. He watched, and followed me ever since the beginning of the immigration run in. Now as I was approaching my cabin I had four policemen following me towards the locked room. This is ridiculous, as I climbed to the bridge my "favorite" policeman followed me to the captain's cabin.

I complained to the captain that this was harassment and I had done nothing to deserve it.

The captain told the man as long as I was in the captain's cabin he would look out for me. He told my dear policeman to retire to some other place.

Nita had disappeared. She had to be in her usual hideout.

As I approached the door of the captain's cabin I saw the Crème de Menthe bottle on the desk. I guessed that Nita was there.

I was introduced to two other captains who both worked dockside now. Nita had already been in a discussion with one and they had their arguments on religion, individualism, etc. He was 53, vital in looks and personality. His daughter Niti had been offered three jobs, one of them with "Newsweek" magazine. She had honors and was on the dean's list. What a joy to her parents. She had a problem in terms of her non-conformity attitude. She appeared to be a great character and personality from all her father related to us.

Our evening with the two captains was enjoyable as always, talking, relaxing and drinking. It was a brief respite from the tailing police. One captain insisted I should leave with him.

Keith said, "No, they can't leave ship."

Keith told me to join the captain in the other room, which I did and we sat in the "ice box," the only room that had air conditioning, and discussed the "girlie" photos hanging in all the crew's cabins. We talked about geography and his travels.

All evening he claimed what Nita was missing was being taken over Daddy's knees and spanked. I offered him to do the job. He looked at Nita, and then his knees, and decided his knees could not take her weight.

He took a couple of verbal whacks at me, claiming I was ruining my life with too much involvement and affection for my family, and letting myself be hurt by my own children, by being a softie. His remedy and prescription for me was "Live life and enjoy yourself and consider your own happiness, because if you don't, no one else will."

Nita kept trying to assure him that this was exactly what I was doing and I was enjoying myself this year.

We spoke of Yoga, not for women over 40 without a master in charge. But it would do Nita good, he said. He used a Yoga master to cure his cracked shoulder last year. He had fallen 30 feet off a gangplank and lived. The broken shoulder would not heal for any of the various doctors he tried.

Fascinating character. He wanted to take me to the horse races on Sunday, but today was Wednesday and we wouldn't (we hoped) be around by then.

I walked the Captain to the gangplank.

I said, "I'll walk you down."

He walked the gangplank backwards to show me the safe footing. We had no sooner gotten to the bottom than a policeman walked up behind him and with his nightstick blocked me.

The policeman said, "You must not break the rules. You are restricted to the ship. You cannot leave it. Move along now."

New experience? Know what it was to be a real prisoner by a policeman? The captain, drunk as all get out, got into a semantic argument with the policeman, as I slowly backed up the gangplank. Captain claimed the gangplank was part of the ship and I never left the ship. I disappeared as they continued their argument.

During our two extra days on board I was taken to the engine room. The engine broke down three times en route to Mombasa, and two times while we were on the ship from Mombasa to Bombay. One afternoon we were aware the ship had stopped. My engineer companion explained that every single engineer on board worked steadily for 22 hours to fix the engine.

The ship was 19 years old and ships last about 20 years, according to the captain.

There were two lifeboat station drills for the crew during our 10 days at sea. But yesterday there was one boat station drill that lasted more than two hours. It included dropping the lifeboats and getting the crew into them. I took pictures and enjoyed watching the crew struggle up and down the shaky rope ladders. I kept trying to picture the ship in an emergency. Did people have to go down those rope ladders? Just looking at them scared me.

Then one lifeboat dropped, swung shakily and slam-banged into the lifeboat underneath it, smashing into that one also. The huge arm made of iron dropped a bolt and broke. It in turn dropped the lifeboat, a real life ship emergency.

I took pictures of that sad boat.

As a result of that incident Captain Keith couldn't return to Poona to see his family. Many other sailors got on the phone and were apologizing like crazy, "But Dear... I can't get away now."

Keith continued drinking. He was no way near ready for bed. Finally, at 2:00 a.m., I fell asleep.

Nita woke me at 4:00 a.m., their usual parting hour. Keith claimed in another hour or so they had to move the ship. No sense in going to sleep, but I returned to bed and slept until Nita woke me up for a "cuppa" coffee.

We had both taken baths in his bathtub and refreshed ourselves. Finally, close to 6:00 a.m., I staggered sleepily back to our cabin.

In the morning my four policemen opened the door and insisted that I get up. The lady who slept in a sari on the bench last night was with them. She followed me around. They told me immigration came. But it didn't.

Ratna's mother came for her radio.

I awoke to the pounding on the door, slipped on a dress and opened it. The four policemen and two ladies were standing there. Annoyed as all hell, I brushed them aside and looked for the nearest toilet. I entered the one in our sector. They followed me in. The doors were locked. They followed me out. I went to the next ladies W. C. and they followed me. Again it was locked. I was getting desperate and raced up to the crew's lavatory and finally ditched the policemen temporarily.

Mr. Mehta, director of the Shipping Company of India, finally came to escort us off the ship. No Henry. We reached the customs officer and Mehta drove off in his car, deserting us.

Customs was funny. I declared the radio for Ratna's mother and had the serial number put into my passport. The paper had to be shown on the way out, I was told. (I didn't even think to open it to find that number.)

The only thing we feared duty on were the toys for Pawar's family. They were in Nita's suitcase, held together by a rope. The custom's official insisted on opening that one, not mine with the easy zip. He pulled out the wrapped packages, laid them out and never asked what was in them. He dug down underneath for something. We don't know what. Then he had to put back the ropes on the valise.

I called Allwyn and he said he would come with Henry. We took a taxi. It was a strange feeling looking back and knowing that the ropes tying us to the ship were loosened and we were free at last.

It felt good. Today, our first day of freedom, happened to be Nita's birthday.

Friday, April 4

Nita's Birthday

I hoped Nita would have a happy birthday. The best present we received was our freedom last night. The realization that the policemen and policewomen were off our tail was a delight and our spirits rose. I hoped it continued to be a Good Friday for us!

The CID (Criminal Investigation, no less), were coming to help us get through customs.

The very first thing I did when I got off the ship was to visit the American Embassy.

"Why were those two American women kept prisoners on the Haryana ship for two days?" I inquired.

"Immigration believed that you were importing gold bars from Africa to India."

So our being prisoners had nothing to do with the fact that I did not have a visa to enter India. Have you any idea the size and weight of gold bars? They were digging around in our suitcases looking for them. Neither Nita nor I were strong enough to have carried even one of them. What a shocker!!

There were several errands to do before Nita left for Poona.

Friends Mentioned in Chapter 37

Fredrick. He was a police chief who gave us a bag of oranges.

Officers Captain Keith, Doc, Vilos. They located a cabin for us.

Henry and Reggie. They ran a gang.

Fredrick's Chinese Restaurant. We were fed when we only had 2 rupees.

THIRTY-EIGHT

BOMBAY AGAIN

Our lodging deserves description. The hall was picturesque. In the dark, it was difficult to avoid the sleeping bodies. A mother nursed her baby when she wasn't sleeping. The steps were wide, filthy, smelly, and there were holes in the walls for rats.

But as we stepped inside the door of Woods guesthouse, it was not so bad.

The room had five beds. In our five nights there we only had men sharing it with us the first night. When they left, we spread out our junk on the empty beds. There was poor light from one bare bulb, but you could read. A fan was too high, but it worked. An open porch next to my bed provided light and fresh air.

The toilet was odorous, but the shower worked. It only had hot water, but we took several showers a day.

That night I took a shower with bra and panties on, and returned to my bunk, sopping wet. I lay with the strong fan playing on me. Only then could I fall asleep. It was 5:30 in the morning. Such is the heat of Bombay.

We received mail from friends we made earlier in our trip.

Dear Ruth and Nita,

We're home and spending a good part of our time looking back at our friends and adventures of the past three months. I think you influenced how we spent the remaining three weeks of our trip.

We did go to Nerja caves in Spain. The happiest of our whole time. Mr. Adrian remembered you both well, and we stayed in "your" room.

The Indian cookbook that I found useful is "Mrs. Balber Singh's Indian Cookery," Mills and Boon Ltd. London 1961.

Love to you both,

Cynthia Aguilar

Ruth writes:

Shipping Corporation of India Ltd.
Steelcrete House 4th floor
Dinshaw Wacha Road, Bombay 1

Dear Sir,

Becoming Ruth

We would like to take this opportunity to thank Mr. Karnik and the other men in your organization that were involved in obtaining an entry visa for my daughter and myself.

I still have no idea what all the complication was that detained us on board for two extra days.

At this point, I know that the American Consulate and the CID were both involved. Why it was necessary we still do not understand.

On Saturday, March 1, 1969, I went into the High Commission of India on Harabee Street in Nairobi and handed them our passports to get our visa. The gentleman there told me I had 72 hours in India and didn't need one. I asked him to put it in writing and he handed me the tourist pamphlet. I tried.

Again, I am sorry to have put your company to so much trouble. The men I met told me they spent days doing paper work to get us released.

While we were kept prisoners on the State Of Haryana the crew did all in their power to attend to our needs. Of course, your Captain Venkataramiah was one of the finest people we have met in our nine months of travel. He did everything in his power to make us comfortable. Regardless of the crisis in his domain, he still managed to make us laugh and keep up our morale. He is an admirable man and as a professional educator I can appreciate his administrative ability and his rapport with his staff and his passengers.

The other officers offered small services whenever possible. The steward provided meals. We appreciated everything that was done for us during those two miserable days.

It wasn't easy having four male policemen and two female policemen waking us up early in the morning and trailing us everywhere for two days. We were very happy to see them leave the ship last night. Then our spirits rose.

Thank you again, and please know we appreciated everything you have done for us.

Sincerely yours,
Ruth Kaufman

When we finally passed through customs they returned our passports.

Henry had come down to the ship to meet us, but they wouldn't let him come aboard and they said we were coming out.

They told him it would make no sense to have him come aboard. Of course it made sense; we needed him to help us with the luggage.

We decided to get rid of the radio and watch the first thing. We delivered it to Ratna's uncle at his home. Since he was a police constable I asked him to write a letter that the radio had been lost or stolen so I could pass through customs.

He wouldn't do it. Ratna's uncle and mother did absolutely nothing to make life easier for us. They were not our favorite people. They fed us fruit, Indian sweets, and tea and we left their home.

We were under the impression that we were kept on the ship because of visa trouble. That wasn't it at all.

The American Embassy explained they were worried we had GOLD CONTRABAND.

That was the reason for the police escorts who were confining us. We wondered why no explanation was given to us regarding the reason we were prisoners on the ship.

We left the American Embassy and we returned to Woods' guesthouse to shower and relax.

Henry arrived later that night. We fasted all-day and went to church at night. After dinner we were taken to Blow Up, a discotheque. Henry danced with Nita all night long.

The two go-go girls were fun to watch. They were Ceylonese, and one had amazing rhythm that oozed from her. The crowded dance floor didn't entice me to dance.

Movies flashed on the walls, lights shone with effective brilliance. At 1 a.m. we went home to bed. That was the end of Nita's birthday.

I bought her another change purse.

Saturday, April 5

I mailed 30 rupees worth of letters, then met Reggie at "Gone with the Wind." Henry was late again.

Nita and I became annoyed. Henry owed me money. I paid for the tickets.

I should have bought them when we arrived, to ensure better seats.

Henry missed his court trial because of his fighting. Instead, he sat in the movie with us.

Henry spent Saturday night and Roman Catholic Easter Sunday in jail. Reggie reported to us. Henry needed new clothes, and he hated the food in jail. His trial was set for Monday.

Sunday, April 6

Reggie said he'd try to get a car about 3:00 p.m. to take us to the beach.

Nita discovered the Sea Lounge of the Taj Hotel and we sat in the air-conditioned room comfortably all afternoon.

On the first day we arrived, Babu took me in his taxi on an errand. He owned a factory for rubies, sapphires and emeralds, and he sold them worldwide.

He had a hand tick, not the greatest guy we'd met, and tapped me on the shoulder several times during the night. His bed was situated next to mine. I chased him away without being too nasty and learned a lesson: Never sleep next to a man who is reading Kama Sutra before he falls asleep.

Thank goodness Babu left for Germany the next morning.

I had Mark's and Dillip's telephone numbers. I debated between these two and my movie director and gambled on the new guys.

Mark called for me at 2:30 p.m. I got home that night around 9:00 p.m. He was 22, intelligent, good looking and in a finance business with his father. He passed the exams and was about to become a student at MIT, but the family needed him and would miss him.

We relaxed at his beach house, drank Indian beer and frolicked in the water.

We ended our day consuming a Chinese meal, then home to read and bed.

Monday, April 7

It was another Crazy Day.

Nita tried to sell my suitcase to no avail. The broken nylon zipper hadn't been repaired, so I would travel with the defective case.

Nita's suitcase has been repaired for $4.00.

At Ceylon house I was told no visa was necessary.

At Air Ceylon we learned the time of the plane departure. An airport bus could take us there. My flight was Air France that left Wednesdays. Pan Am would take care of us.

Suddenly it occurred to me that my health papers were missing. Customs never gave them back to me when they returned our passports

Mr. Karnick, the manager of the shipping line, suggested we go to the hospital and get the cholera and small pox shots again, because the papers could not arrive in time. The Haryana ship was at sea and would arrive in Seychelles on April 12.

Nita got excited. "Mom, don't you recall the painful reactions we had from those shots? No way will I take them again because of the ship's mistake."

I proceeded to the Indonesia council for visas. I dropped off two more of our passport photos. India took three more for this visa. It costs $10.00 for visas to go to Bali Island, Java and Djakarta. I looked forward to those places. I started out with 32 photos and this was the end of them.

Finally, I took a bus home in time for a rest and shower before our 2:00 lunch date with Mark. We met at Frederick's Chinese restaurant. We met Dillip and Raj, a movie actor we met the day before. Nita approved of them. We were set for a date at 6:30 p.m.

Pan Am fixed our ticket and told us if we found other means of island hopping we could stretch our plane ticket from San Francisco to New York.

A man there agreed it was outrageous to ask us to retake the shots we took only three months ago. Nita recalled the violent reaction to the cholera booster in Delhi. We couldn't raise our arm and it was painful to sleep on our side.

He said the ship confirmed that they had our health papers. Ceylon would accept the passports until the ship sent us our forms.

Not satisfied, Pam Am called the tourist director and ascertained she was in.

So we headed for the tourist office. Mrs. J. was strong, quiet and capable. Yes, they had already cabled the ship. So the Pan Am man worked wonders for us. We were very impressed with our Mrs. J. and told her we would return the next day.

Back home, after some sleep from 5:00 to 6:00 p.m. and a shower, we were ready for our date with the boys by 6:30.

I was refreshed and in a spirited, devilish mood, ready for anything. Dillip picked up Mark and drove all of us to Juhu Beach House, where we changed into "bathing costumes," and drank Indian beer mixed with lemon soda.

Swimming in the dark was fun. I swam all slippery like a fish. The boys were worrying about us. "Don't get into deep water. Stay together."

Nita and Dillip danced under the stars on the roof terrace to Sinatra's voice on a tape recorder.

Nita discussed politics with Dillip. They liked and respected one another. All of us felt the way Mark expressed it. "It's beautiful."

At midnight, we requested the boys feed us. Their choice was an expensive hotel. The meal consisted of tandoori chicken, peas and carrots and a Russian salad. It was similar to those salads we had in Russia, Nita exclaimed. We laughed as we realized a year ago we couldn't have made that statement.

The tomato cocktail was not juice, but cut up tomato in a sauce. For dessert we ordered cassata and peach melba. The boys watched us eat and for the first time in their life, they wrapped up food and we took the left-over chicken with us.

Still sprightly and in good moods, we drove home about 1:30 a.m. They both had work the next day. Mark bowed out of future dates with us. He explained he would be in Delhi on business for his father.

Dillip would see Nita the next day, if he could arrange it.

Tuesday, April 8

Nita spent the day at the Taj Hotel and relaxed there in comfort until she heard from me.

I went by bus to Bakelite. The secretary, Joan Fernandes, brought me to her office where they made metal parts for Norwegian ships. I typed eight pages on her typewriter.

Joan and her friend joined us for a Chinese meal. They were enchanting women, though they encouraged me to monopolize the conversation with tales of our journey.

Mr. Fernandes was in the office when I returned. He was in my age range and very formal. He had studied at Brooklyn Polytech in New York, was quiet, a very shy man. He said he is taking Joan and me out to dinner.

He arranged to pick me up at the Taj around 7:30.

Wednesday, April 9

Nita was going to Poona with the gifts we bought in Africa for Pawar's family.

She arrived at Victoria station by 6:30. They gave Nita a 25 percent student discount, 266 R, or $35.00. It was worth all the trouble.

I drank coffee in the shipping office with Mr. Saggi and received the cabled confirmation that our health papers were on the ship

We had another day at the Taj Hotel in the air-conditioned lounge looking out on the ocean and ships at Gate of India. Nita had a new boy friend, artist Nailsun, with beautiful, long curly hair.

Nita writes:

I want to go to Goa since I've met Nailsun. He lived on his own island in Goa, in Indian Hippie style. But someone must visit our Poona friends. I'll try to join Mommy and him in Goa in a few days.

We wasted time on errands in Bombay. With only four months left, time becomes precious.

Nita was on the 7 a.m. train to Poona.

I was in a plane to Goa. My contact was the chief justice, no less. I splurged on a plane for $15.00 because Tristino Line (the ship we took from Bombay to Mombasa) came through with a student discount of $35.00 or 266 rupees for Nita, but not for me. No one in India studied at my age.

So I took the plane instead of the 24-hour train ride to Goa.

Friends Mentioned in Chapter 38

Joe Ferandes. He studied at Brooklyn Polytech in New York.

Joan. She was his secretary.

Mark. He had a beach house.

Dillip. He was a friend of Nita's.

THIRTY-NINE

ON TRAIN TO POONA

Wednesday, April 9

Nita writes:

Dear Daddy,

I am writing to wish you a Happy Birthday.

At the moment, I am on another third class train going from Bombay to Poona. It feels like I've gone in circles. This is exactly what I was doing at the beginning of last December. The big difference is that now I am visiting friends, Pawar's family and Rohini, not just going to names on paper. It is now 7:00 a.m.

Mommy is catching a plane later this morning to Goa.

Yesterday, I was befriended by Nailsun, an up and coming artist from Goa. He is a fascinating character and will probably be coming to America on scholarship in six months.

Henry, our best Bombay friend, was put in jail on Easter Sunday. He was taking us to "Gone with the Wind" when he should have been at his court trial. The jerk!

I'm exhausted. We danced till 2:00 a.m. last night at the Blue Nile nightclub with Nailsun and two bosses of a company and their lovely secretary, Joan, who looked part Indian and part Chinese. The two men were boring, but we ate a sumptuous meal. I saw my first strip tease dancer, she was neither aesthetic nor graceful.

Our time on the Haryana ship was madly marvelous because of my friendship with Captain Keith. On my birthday I went to Bombay's first discotheque, "Blow Up," with Henry. I'm beginning to dance.

While I'm writing we've passed through the worst of Bombay suburb poverty. The worst part of the poverty were the babies with beautiful bright eyes; lovely soft brown skin, caked with grime, pot bellies and skinny limbs, and greasy matted hair

Poverty means a bunch of bare rear ends scattered around the ground relieving themselves and a mass of dirt hovels held together with clotheslines. Rags on the lines.

This trip has been too rich, too wonderful to contemplate. While it was happening we enjoyed it for the things we saw and did, for the people we met, but it was too overwhelming if we try to appreciate everything. In retrospect it will be easier.

I think I'm a changed, but a better person. The changes have been gradual and subtle that, living with myself, all the time I cannot analyze them.

I'll probably be coming home in August from San Francisco. I'm going to hate to end this trip. College, even Marlboro, will seem so tame.

What has happened with Wendi and college?

What about Lori? Does she still like school? What about her dancing?

Is David still holding all those jobs?

Say Hello to them all for me. We never get any news of your activities and we get to wonder what's been happening.

Our friend Dillip says that if a Hindu runs over a man, then he is attacked from the outside by the law, but if he runs over a cow then his spirit attacks him from the inside.

Happy Birthday,

Love, Nita

P.S. The most exciting group of people just sat down next to me. They look like Arabians, out of Purdah, but I'm pretty sure they were gypsies, two beautiful young women, one older woman and two children. The woman's hair was short and curling in the front, and thick and long in the back. The eyes were slanted and glistening and the skin over the high cheekbones was taut and smooth bronze.

The older young woman was brilliantly dressed. She wore a bright turquoise mirror sleek dress extending to the middle of her thighs. Under that was a long very full flowing flowered skirt with a large red and yellow border. They all had full ankle length skirts and the old woman's hair was brown rather than black. She spoke to me in a weird sounding language, definitely not Hindi.

The little girl was a gem, short, straight dark brown hair and solemn almond eyes staring up at me. They entered our compartment like a circus, after one stop whizzed out with a whirl. So beautiful they were.

The old woman behind me is still muttering, "Gypsies..Gypsies..."

Love, Nita

FORTY

GOA

March 1969

Dear Ruth and Nita,

I just received your manuscript. After re-reading it, I realize how magnificent this trip of yours has been. Even with all the hardships you both had, your enjoyment of the places and people is infectious. You are so right nobody, but nobody, could have the experiences you did in the ordinary way of travel.

The unusual people you meet, getting to know the Africans and Indians the way you did, finding your way around, has been a unique experience. It is as you say, hard to believe.

Well, you certainly have had a multiple of experiences and adventures. That must have been a pretty frightening experience for Nita with that Sikh. I do hope you are over whatever you suffered from the accident when the bus knocked you down in Nairobi. I hope the clunk on your head and the rest of the pain from your accident left no ill effects.

My days are calm, in spite of the rapidly changing times around me. I read interesting books. I am now reading the "Life of Madam de Stael." Although it is supposed to be a novel, it is really a close look at the history of the French during the revolution. So I am meeting very important people who made the revolution.

I'll go out with Cele, to a movie, art museums and the flower show.

Wendi and her friend, Eloisa, went to a dance recital at Julliard on Saturday. They met in my home. She looks fine and is enjoying her Saturday morning course at Cooper Union, where she works in paint and clay.

She related only good things about Lori and David. I haven't seen them for a long time, but I talked to David on the phone. Lori is very busy and I hardly hear from her. I spoke to Jack, who seems to feel they get very little mail from you. Do you get his letters?

It's interesting that Nita has been able to make contact with so many people who play chess. How fortunate that the art teacher gave her the freedom of his ceramic studio to make her sculptures.

I enjoy your letters. I feel as though I am traveling with you.

My love to both of you,

Mom and Grandma

Wednesday, April 9

I arrived in Goa at 2:30. I spoke to a man seated next to me, Mr. Dillbugh, who was going to Panjim, and he paid the 5 rupees for the taxi for me. I promised to leave a note for him on Saturday at Tourist Hotel.

Tourist Hotel sent me to Imperial Hotel for six rupees a room. My room opened on to a porch overlooking the water. I was alone in a room with three beds. What luxury — spacious, two tables, dressing table and mirror, clean sheets, clean tiled floor. I thought: I could be happy in this room, IF I had a fan.

Until 9:00 I walked around town. I located Central Market Place and both theaters. Goa was different, as promised, with wide, clean streets. It was not smelly like other towns in India.

I purposefully ate dinner in Tourist Hotel to meet someone. Four men sat alone at tables and not one of them made overtures to me. Was I slipping?

I realized I was tired and went home. I couldn't keep my eyes open to read. I must have needed sleep.

Thursday, April 10

Met Tito de Menezes, chief justice of Goa, a busy man. He had court sessions all day long. His wife was a doctor, pregnant, lying in bed, vomiting and hemorrhaging. I would not be a guest there. Hizzoner went home early to attend to her needs. He lived in an area with no facilities, no phone, no car and he lived six miles from his office.

He introduced me to a young man, Anthony, who took me to the bus. Tomorrow he would take me home with him to Margoa and the Colva Beach area, and show me around on Saturday.

The convent was next on my tour. A young girl guided me through the library, lecture room, sitting room, chapel and refectory. Later, I learned 200 sisters from all the Catholic sisterhoods came here for higher spiritual religious study. They already were nurses and teachers and social workers. Community development courses were important for their service to humanity.

A woman from San Diego who was hard of hearing sat next to me at lunch. She was studying philosophy and religion in India and was not talkative. I wanted to ask her many questions, but she requested, "Don't squeeze me like a lemon."

I had soup, a buttered roll, meat and potato in tiny chips, and rice with a tasty curry sauce. I had two pieces of papaya and some mango and a Chinese gooseberry. I tasted a purple fruit that looked like an olive.

I showered, cool and refreshed. I left the monastery combed and powdered. A nurse Sister explained the heavy menstrual flow I was experiencing was the change of climate. She told me it happens to them also.

Back home, I rested, wrote in my diary and then went off to meet Egas Aleixo Leobo. First I took a ferryboat then a taxi to his home. I met his father, a doctor, and a couple of his brothers. I sat around with the father, who had to learn his medical studies in French, because there were no Portuguese books in his medical field.

Friday, April 11

I anticipated a good night's sleep with the cool breezes. It rained hard and I slept from 10:00 p.m. to 5:00 a.m. and did not hear it.

Anthony arrived at 8:30 a.m. and spent an hour talking with me.

Still a heavy flow, so I took it easy. I left a letter for Nita at the General Post Office. I left a letter to Dilbagh at the hostel.

I located Nailsun, the artist Nita meant to meet in Goa.

Nailsun and I went to Mapuca, a big city. Nailsun's birth record, submitted by his Godfather, was wrong. It said he was baptized before he was born. In order to get a corrected copy he had to pay 75 rupees or $10.00 and write letters. It would take weeks. He saw the man responsible and asked him for help.

We took a ferry across the river. Anthony was still at work. At 6:15 we took a bus to the ferry and another bus to Margo.

We walked in the dark to the house. It was a large house, well constructed. It had high, high ceilings and six rooms, a large living room, dining room, kitchen and three bedrooms. There was no bath or toilet. There was a large porch with built-in cement benches. The floor, hard as cement, was made of cow dung mixed with water.

As honored guests, we conversed while the meal was prepared from 8:00 to 10:00 p.m. Only the guests ate the meal of stewed fish, smoked fish, rice and mango in curry sauce, mango pickle sausage and potato and onion. It was a filling meal.

They fed honored guests first and the family afterward, though the huge table was capable of seating all of us: Anthony 23, Petunia 18, Rosalind 16, and Agmut, a boy of 12.

The mother had no contact with us after she asked a few questions. She invited us to stay longer. Petunia married at 17 and had a 9-month-old son. She was a very pretty girl with long, shiny black hair. Rosalind was shy and spoke English, but she didn't respond to many of my questions. Anthony was in high spirits.

They gave me the huge bed, but no mattress, so it was as hard as the floor mat would have been. Rosalind showed me the beautiful new bedspread her father bought them. It became the sheet on my bed.

Rosalind fell asleep on the mat on the floor next to me and slept 11:00 to 5:00.

During the night Agmut had a high fever. I searched through my suitcase and all I found were diarrhea pills, entrosulfa and Dramamine for nausea and ear oil. No aspirin.

Anthony was cupping his brother when I went in. The candle caused a vacuum and six or seven glass cups were placed on his back and raised welts. But I did not see what other good they did. His fever was high. I used my wash and dry pads to cool him off. He needed an alcohol rub and I remembered the strong drink I tasted earlier. I used that as an alcohol rub on his back and neck and he fell asleep.

Anthony shut the front door and went to his mat on the porch with Nailsun.

I slept for a few hours. Then the baby cried. Mother gave the baby milk in a bottle shaped like a crescent.

Saturday, April 12

At 5:00 a.m. the mother of the three young children woke Rosalind and told her she wanted a bath. Rosalind put away her mat. She drew water from the well and filled a tub.

I went to the outhouse. The hole in cement had a slanty floor. As I urinated a pig stuck his nose under me and snuffled it up. He did the same as I defecated. It inhibited me.

Then I was taken to see a fresh, butchered pig. Bones were cleaned well. Intestines and bladder were separated to make sausage. The insides, head and lungs, were separated. Fat was cut away from the meat. The animals roamed freely and rooted around for food as chickens do.

Anthony had to go back to Panjim, a two-hour trip, because a dog bit him last week and he was taking rabies shots.

It was Saturday, and Rosalind had to go to school all morning to take an arithmetic test. Brother Agmut was up and around, feeling and looking better. He was playing with the babies on the porch.

The mother was sick. She had a fever and had not risen from her mat in the dining room. She claimed the aspirin she took did not help.

I sat on the porch all morning, read my book and observed activities. Women and children trekked back and forth to the well for water. They had bright, red flowers in their hair. A man climbed coconut trees. A woman scrubed clothes on rocks.

Women were busy sweeping the house, making food. I was content sitting and watching. Young girls came up on to the porch and said a few words to me. Goa had more nude children than elsewhere.

Nailsun returned, restless from his morning bike ride. Colva Beach was empty. He wanted to go to Colanthe Beach. I did not think it was right for me to run off until Anthony returned.

Nita writes:

Panjim Goa

I am now on a bus, which in five minutes will be heading towards Panjim. I just walked here from the Margoa train station. I was supposed to get off in Marmagoa, but the man in my compartment assumed I was getting off here and he invited me to his home for a meal. In the shuffle of getting out I lost him, though I think he thought that I had forgotten his invitation.

Mommy was supposed to leave me a message at the Goa GPO, but the problem was Goa didn't seem to have a main GPO.

Standing in that train station platform I felt so alone, so lost. I had one thought — Panjim, Panjim. For God's sake, I didn't even know where Panjim was.

Miracles, Miracles! I was on my way to Mr. Demelli, who was Nailsun's uncle at the deputy collector's office, when a man came up to me and asked, "Are you Nita Kaufman?"

Anthony arrived with Nita. He noticed her in a rickshaw and recognized her from the passport photo I showed around last night. It amazed both of us that we located one another so easily.

Eventually, we went to Colva Beach. Nailsun made artistic sand paintings and we swam, then it was home and back again to Margoa.

Finally, at 7:00 p.m., we left on the bus for Panjim.

Anthony was indefatigable, his energy, go-power and spirit. He was an admirable person, responsible and spontaneous. He wanted to travel like his father, who was a laundry man on a ship. Nailsun suggested he join the Portuguese Navy, a two to three-year stint and a good deal. I wished him the best. Anthony was the friendliest person we met in Goa.

Rosalind took a quiet role of responsibility in the household. I gave her my polka dot dress that we had bought in Florence, Italy, and my yellow dress. That left me two dresses. I was glad to give her something. She was very sweet, despite her inability to hold a conversation.

Nita's hotel was much crummier than mine. It had bugs and the sheets were not as nice. I did not see even an ant at the Imperial. But there was a fan in Nita's room.

Monday, April 14

We took the ferry to Betim and left our suitcases at a home there. No bus was available, so we would take a ship to Bombay on Monday morning.

We arrived at Lobo's home and saw Mathias, who we met when we left the chief justice's home. We received a colder reception than our previous one. By 4:20 the family had to be at mass and they would do nothing for us. There was no car to drive us, no place to stay. They were a family of devout Christians. They bragged about donating huge sums of money to the poor house, which was a ladder to heaven for poor people.

I thought: The richer people are, the less they give. It was another universal I could chalk up.

We walked to the beach and I found Royal Hotel with a 10-rupee room for us. Boys were charged only 6 R. Nita ate some chips and pudding and didn't pay for it to make up for our overcharge.

The swimming was good. Nature took control of our lives. The waves were the highest we ever had. They pushed us downstream and tossed us about and tired me out.

Many Americans and European hippy types in bright garb were sitting alone and stringing beads. We noticed, however, that their reading included authors like Andre Gide and Julian Huxley. These hippies were intelligent humans.

Which brings me to Nailsun. Nita wanted to leave him because he was becoming too familiar with her. She did not like to be touched. She was bored with him. Me, too. He did not read and did not find need for further study. I suppose it is good to be that self-confident. But I find intellectual curiosity and enlightenment that is a result of reading makes for the more interesting companion.

That night I bedded down on the porch outside the room after another swim. This time there were tamer waves, but an itching insect in the water drove us both nuts.

During the night I woke to see two men standing by me, lighting match after match and looking at me. One knelt down beside me and I told him to go away and he did. I started to fall back to sleep again and the sound of a pail jarred me awake. A man crouched close to me. I grabbed Nailsun's feet and called his name.

He yelled "bastard" and the man flew over the wall and away. It was frightening.

A whole bunch of people came by. They were all sleeping around the corner and said, "There were three men."

Monday, April 14

We took the bus to Betim and picked up our luggage. We said goodbye to Nailsun.

There was no organization and no lines to disembark and embark on the ship. We spent two hours in the hot, punishing sun. Nita's head was jammed with a steel trunk.

Our tickets read lower decks, but we stayed on the upper benches. The boat didn't leave until 11:30 a.m. We had a 20-hour trip ahead of us.

Eating was the occupation. We made our way through nearly two dozen bananas, a box of Chiba nut candy and cold drinks. I bought a 1.50 R, or 20 cent, meal ticket for lunch.

A man asked us if we were allergic to bedbugs. He said the ship had them now, but it didn't used to. So far we had had nine months of travel and never encountered bed bugs.

I was very happy I had been to India before East Africa. I had more tolerance for it. We wandered around ship and discovered cabin class and the showers. They only had hot water, but it felt good to get the remainder of sand off our neck and back.

We stopped twice to pick up boatloads of passengers from large rowboats. They used tiny shovels at the end of a pole. Why not wider oars?

And what do I teach about India now that I have seen it, I wondered. What is most important about these people? Their ability to survive? This rested in the hands of women. Every man told me it was the woman's responsibility to make or prevent children, not his. But women were still submerged beasts of burden.

Romance was dangled before them more than in America. They worked hard and all day long with no rewards that I could see. Men went out with other men and left the women home alone.

The men told me the women were happy. I didn't know. Did I only see it through my eyes and not appreciate the fact that they were fulfilling their accepted roles?

They said, "Crawl into the skin of a snake and think like him. See the world from his eyes." And I tried. But the other snakes cried out, "Fraud."

My thinking was American and no matter how much I wore the clothing, and ate the food, and slept in the bed of the uneducated native of any country, I remained an educated American woman of 45 years, who had four children and left her husband at home. This latter could not be understood. How could you leave your husband behind?

Friends Mentioned in Chapter 40

Anthony 23, Petunia 18, Rosalind 16, Qgmut 12. I was a guest in their home. Nailsun. He was an artist.

GOA MAN

WOMEN STREET WORKERS

FORTY-ONE

BOMBAY BEFORE CEYLON

Tuesday, April 15

Rohini arrived in port for us around 9:00.

We were at Woods Guest House again. This time a messy-haired, bearded Frenchman and monkey were our roommates. The monkey was an adorable loving creature, but he cried when left by himself. He gave me a second thought about owning a monkey. He was capable of getting into all sorts of mischief and needed toilet training like a child.

Henry and Reggie arrived. Henry claimed he had just gotten of jail the day before. His new court case would be April 28. They took us to a friend's apartment over the causeway. It was one room with two beds. Four people slept and also cooked in that room. The fan was over the partition so only one bed got the benefit of the moving air. The lucky person near the window got rats coming in and out of the window. Bombay heat made one lethargic.

The lady served us Bournita made on a paraffin ring. She told us she had a big flat, but her guarantor had left for the U.K. They invited Nita to a party where Nita could get 200 rupees by being "nice" to a rich Parsee man whose birthday it was. Nita declined the offer.

Finally I got hungry. We had had no meal all day so we went to Fredrick's. I showed him the two rupees I had left and asked for the free meal offer he had made last week. He smiled and in his inimitable, pleasant fashion brought Nita her "water" lemonade, and fixed prawns and a noodle dish, all excellently prepared. We enjoyed the music too. We liked Fredrick's Chinese restaurant.

Back at home we talked to an old gentleman and learned he was a writer who had a published novel and another book that included 6,000 years of Indian history. He was 73, looked older and had lived in India 39 years. He came from France and his accent was still thick French. We only saw him read. He got four books from a library every week. I would have loved to hear his wisdom, but he was getting senile. He asked the same question over and over, "You don't smoke, do you?"

Henry arrived at 11:30 and we said, "Thanks for being such a good friend to us. Goodnight and goodbye."

Wednesday, April 16

I was as excited as always before an airplane trip and the prospects of being in a new country. An Indian Airlines taxi drove us to the airport.

At the Air Ceylon office I discovered 30 rupees in a ticket envelope and rushed out to spend it. Then I suddenly recalled it was the airport tax money I had purposefully saved.

At the airport we went through the first custom's man smoothly, but the second saw our radio endorsement and wanted us to show the radio. I was glad Nita had gotten "stolen" recorded on the declarations form.

No one looked or cared about the money I cashed in India. It would cost 75 cents to cash $30.00 more so I didn't do it.

Nita was sore about the 4 rupees or so we still had at the airport. I forgot to mail film or that would have used the rupees up.

Air Ceylon was the smallest plane we'd been in so far. It was a smooth trip though, and the food was filling and good. It was hot chicken and rice, peas and carrots, rolls and custard.

I learned that we had missed the big festival and Elephant Round-Up in Kerala. Too bad.

FORTY-TWO

CEYLON

Wednesday, April 16

On the plane Clarence Watigatunga came over and sat next to me. He asked a few questions, such as "Where are you going to stay in Ceylon?"

"Youth hostels," I replied.

"Don't make a move. I'm the executive director of youth hostels and I will take care of you. I am returning from a meeting in Morocco of the International Youth Hostels."

Karma. That's it.

So he said, "No more worries. I'll take care of you."

And he did. We were entering the country without our health certificate, which they considered more important than the visa.

Clarence's family met the plane and took us for a ride in his car with his wife, 17-year-old son Manuela, and daughter Bhudeni, age 8.

We drove to the youth hostel. Nita thought the place luxurious, but Clarence felt it was not good enough for us. He drove on to his home and settled us in a room for ourselves in his own home.

It was the most beautiful house of our trip. Clarence has traveled extensively and bought many items. It was a spacious, comfortable home, and everyone in it put us at ease.

In the evening Clarence's brother Jim and his wife visited with us.

Thursday, April 17

We sat at breakfast table and planned our trip.

"How long do you plan to stay in Ceylon?" Clarence asked.

"April 17 to April 28, two weeks."

"Not enough time!"

Ruth writes:
Thursday, April 17
Dearest Mother,
We arrived in the capitol of Ceylon, Colombo, yesterday.

This morning we picked up four letters from you, one from Aunt Minnie and two from my British friend in Nakuru, Kenya and one from Mr. Long. I shall answer your letters.

My beautiful black and blue hip mark from the bus accident has faded and all I have left is talking about it. I am fully recovered. The same for Nita's experiences. We laugh over that one, even that night.

Most of our lengthy relationships speak English, only a few contacts didn't, like Shulini in Kikumbala and the adults, except for Sylvia in the Uganda household.

Our itinerary is Ceylon, Djakarta and Bali in Indonesia, then Singapore, Bangkok, Hong Kong, Taiwan and Japan. You can continue the same way, writing to GPO addresses in those places.

We look forward to sitting with you and Aunt Minnie and telling you about our experiences and showing you slides for hours and hours. I've taken 21 rolls of film with 36 slides in each.

Karma is the word for FATE – our luck.

Love, Ruth

April 5
Dear Ruth,

Jack visited me yesterday it was an Eisenhower holiday. He stayed two hours and I could have cried my eyes out after he left.

I know you don't want to hear any bad news, but as a mother, I am taking the liberty of asking you to come home as soon as possible.

Your children are miserable. David resents very much having been sent home and Lori feels totally rejected. Wendi has to be helped to apply for college. She is interested in going to Marlboro just now and the whole scene according to Jack is pretty awful.

Please take this advice for your own sake. I feel you may still be able to save your family from cracking up completely.

Please forgive me, if you feel this is not my business. You have enjoyed adventure and to give up only four months is not too great a sacrifice.

My love to you both,
Mother

Dearest Mother,

We received your "STOP THE WORLD, IT'S TIME TO GET OFF" letter. We have a lot of thinking to do regarding it.

For years I ran the household while Jack worked out of town. For one year I put the family in his hands. At the time they related better to him on most levels than to me.

We have begged, cajoled, pleaded in every way we know how that they should correspond and let us know what is going on at home and in their lives. They should avail themselves of the opportunity to confide in us now, even at this distance, for help, for suggestions from either of us. All our pleas have been ignored.

If they feel, all of them, that they can ignore the hurt they have done to us by not writing, by cutting us off from the family, then what can our rushing back to them do for them now?

I'd like a tape recording of Jack's talk with you. What did he say? What did you say? Did you tell him to write and tell me these things?

Did you tell him I blame him for the family not writing because I feel as a father he could have insisted? He could have done it in terms of round robins and made it family fun time.

You say David has resentments. He had his chance, but he proved too immature. He is young enough to profit by his experiences. I definitely would like to send him back out into the world as soon as he grows up.

Lori has had problems for a long time. Is she getting psychological help now? She didn't want to go with us. My planning included her on this trip. What rejection does she feel? Within the family or from us?

Regarding Wendi and her application to college, we keep asking about it and no one tells us anything. Her school advisor helps her. It is too late for me to do very much even if I were to rush home.

Applications are decided and returned at this point in her senior year.

O.K. Mom, item by item. What does "family cracking up completely" mean? Nita and I are upset, naturally, by your letter. We want to know further details.

Exactly what is what and exactly what would my presence home do for each individual family member?

We both want you to tell us more. You are their grandmother, and we both agree that it is your business.

I only wish you were more involved, had their confidences, and could substitute for me.

We leave Ceylon on April 20. We wrote nearly 50 letters to you and Minnie and about 40 to the family.

You say, "Jack seems to feel they get very little mail from you." It is difficult to write to a vacuum and "Did you get Jack's letters?" you ask me. No, not since November did we get any letters from the family at all. None for my birthday in January. None for Nita's birthday in April.

Love, Ruth

Nita writes:

Thursday, April 17

Dear Daddy, Wendi, Lori, and David,

Colombo for the day,

We reached Colombo yesterday. We are staying with the family of the man who is head of Ceylon Youth Hostels and today we went to get mail.

Once again nothing from any of you. Once again a pile of letters from Grandma and Aunt Minnie and friends from both home and our travels.

To tell the truth I still don't understand your undisturbed silence. Are you not getting our letters? By now the count is over 40. We keep track of each one we mail.

Are you not getting the packages? The last word from you, Daddy, was at the beginning of November.

Every mail stop we say, "There must be something from the family now," but there never is.

We just received a very disturbing letter, which informed us that everything is not so hunky-dory at home.

David it seems is still angry at being sent home. We were not aware that he was angry at all. Lori feels rejected and Wendi feels dejected. The source suggests that we rush right back to New York to try to save the situation.

What are your attitudes toward this? What has been happening? If only you would let us know where we stand and where you stand then we would know if we really should do something. Would our coming home be welcome at this time? Say something.

This was our first whiff that things were not all well. Although we have been feeling perplexity and resentment that no one will write, we have been wondering what everyone has been doing and what they're feeling.

I particularly have wondered about Wendi and her college applications. It was such a hellish job. Did she apply to Marlboro? I would love it if she went there. We'd both be freshmen students.

Ceylon is an absolute Eden. I have never seen a happier more contented people. They know their world is best. The pace is relaxed, the scenery is magnificent. Nobody is actually poor. Everything is clean, even the seaside of Colombo, a large modern city, is striking blue. Everything is in total contrast to the rat race in India. I love it here.

Please, please, please, communicate. Tell us what is going on. Tell us.
Love, Nita.
Thursday, April 17, 1969
Dear Ruth,
Your comings and goings, the people you meet, it is fascinating and utterly confusing.

In each place its like a lifetime concentrated into a short period of time, with the friendships, some casual, some deep, some disappointments, some unexpected happy surprises.

I am always eager to open your letters when they come in; drop what I'm doing. You must be exhausted. I have been making copies of your letters for myself and sending the originals to Olga. I speak to her whenever the letters come in. Now she is concerned about when you will come back, because the girls will have to be gotten ready for school.

My sweet little mother died about a month ago. She was trying so hard to live, mostly to please us, her kids. So patient, so considerate. All the good things in her personality intensified as she got weaker. I am left with the most marvelous memories now of her. A rare person.

When are you planning on coming back? Can you possibly hang on with the money you have for another five months? That would be at the end of August, wouldn't it?

Love, Gladys

Ruth writes:

April 25,

Dearest Gladys,

Your letter to Ceylon did reach me. This period must have been some emotional strain on you. Now the tourist season rises and the vivid memory of your office assures me that you will be immersed in activity for the next few months.

I'm quite disappointed to learn that my writing is poor and as confusing as my correspondents admit.

Everyone says, "But you must write book."

Too much waiting? Maybe true but the heat is no incentive to activity. We talk, read, write, relax in all waiting periods and seldom mind them.

We met Clarence Watigatunga, the executive director of youth hostels, on the plane.

He was returning from the International Youth Hostel conference. We became guests in his home and fed by Manelle, excellent cook, and intelligent, friendly wonderful wife. Guided through the zoo by Bhudeni, 8-year-old mature daughter, escorted and chauffeured by 17-year-old Jayantha, son, and lectured by Clarence himself. Unbelievable.

We joined a party from India to do some sightseeing. Clarence guaranteed, "These are aged people, cranky miserable."

"We don't care," Nita and I proclaimed.

We befriended Parsees this time and we discussed Zoroaster for a change. Only Nita and I and Jay brought swimsuits. The whole busload went swimming in frocks and saris. The underwater world was worth the hours we traveled in the bus.

We walked to the Buddhist temple with Clarence. We learned about Buddhism inside the spectacular temple. Suddenly it all makes sense and I can respond sympathetically experiencing each routine, not as tourist onlooker.

Gladys, my inward appreciation of what we perceived, and what we draw from our relationship with people is conscious. And this awareness swells my eyes with tears of gratitude to the guiding spirit.

I know that other Americans are richer in money, more intelligent, cannot experience the wonder and the living experience in each country as we are doing.

In decades hence Nita and I will value the fact of our personal relationship, which each one of us brings into each contact we make. Singly neither of us would have what we have.

Clarence, though we are his guests and his responsibility, is unhappy about our staying only twelve days in Ceylon. The decision is to stay longer or see another country.

Dr. Harry misses us. He was a "true love," in Nita's" life. Mauretian, intelligent, full of integrity, friendly and he has Mauretian presents to send to us.

I joined Nita and the Indian party in Kandy.

Clarence suggested instead of the direct flight to Djakarta we let Pan Am hotel us overnight in Singapore on April 28.

Oh, we have so much to learn, and we are very much aware of our ignorance despite our developing knowledge.

We don't see the extremes of wealth and poverty here. The flow of thought goes on. It is the paper that ends.

Love, Ruth

Friday, April 18

We were on the train at 2:00 p.m. to 6:00 p.m. Clarence was doing everything for us.

He got us tourist discounts on the railroad and was running us around everywhere.

"Slow down, Ruth. There is no rush." He teased us constantly.

He complained about rich crotchety Americans.

He made fun of the women who bought jewels in the expensive shopping counters in the luxurious hotels. They say if one is good, two are better.

Rightfully upset that his beautiful Ceylon was going to be spoiled, made noisy, garish, in order to attract American tourists. We all agreed, build air-conditioned hotels for tourists and make it easy for them to travel, but don't change the scenery or the people for tourists. They come to see the country as it exists.

He told us about free health services and free education that this country offered. After we received and shared my mother's letter, Manelle remarked, "What if you died? You are doing them a service by forcing independence on them. No. Don't go home!"

I never had confidence in Jack to run the house and involve himself with all the children. But I did have confidence and faith that each child was self sufficient enough to manage his and her own life within the routines and framework already set by the many years past.

I couldn't forgive Jack for not writing and keeping us in closer touch with the family all year. He planned alienation and then systematically carried it out!

Since Wendi wrote such diary–like letters, we could have regained a relationship by her confidences revealed, instead of experiencing deprivation. A big mistake, which still could be remedied in the next four months.

Ceylon was not India. It was a clean country. The garbage and urine smell was not apparent. The people wore clothing, not rags. There was quiet even in the big city. It was beautiful; coconut palms dominated the island. Water edged the city and rice paddies illustrated the window view from the train. Water buffalo in the fields were either working or eating.

The houses were spaced and built in shaded groves of king coconuts, mangoes, jackfruit and bananas. It was relaxed living, people did not rush about. Everything was at a slower pace. They rested at midday. Jobs could wait. There were more conveniences — refrigerator, gas stove, washing machines in Ceylon.

We arrived in Anuradhapura and with Clarence's letter in hand we found Mr. Paiva. He was a cheerful chap, enjoyed socializing. He was most anxious to please. He gave us the room with the most windows, clean-ironed sheets, ice water, and a bowl to wash fingers after eating papaya.

We fell asleep fast, but woke up to a horrible body itch. I had, Nita also, what she had at Kamanmai youth hostel near Mombasa. Spots all over feet and belly, plus the poison ivy rash on a couple of fingers. It was prickly heat on the thighs. It itched and the heat was bad.

Saturday, April 19

It took until 10 to get on our way. We breakfasted, had bikes lowered to fit us, and found two boy guides to show us the area. We rode from 10:00 until 2:00, four hours. We saw Buddha temples, statues, museums and an ancient palace with only columns left.

We walked up steps to see the view of an artificial lake. Beautiful views.

People were bathing in rivers and we heard the flapping sound of beating clothes against rocks.

I took pictures of fish sellers, women selling pan and people planting rice.

Finally we rode home through New Town. We bought curd and fruit salad.

We brought curd home for Mr. Paiva and Mr. Paiva had bought some for us.

We rode on our bike in a bathing suit that made townspeople laugh. We rode to a stream where I joined ten boys swimming.

Then it was back home to the hostel for sleep, with sweat pouring off me.

Mr. Paiva had four boys, no girls. He was glad he had no girls.

"Too many schoolgirls are pregnant," he said. "Intelligent boys go to the beach just to sit and watch for sex," he said.

His family lived in Colombo. He did not borrow to buy this youth hostel. He put in what he could afford and nothing more.

Who said, "The night is for sleeping?"

First we borrowed a clock and fell asleep. In an hour the alarm went off and woke us up. The alarm did that several times during the night. The sound of voices and the midnight train whistle also interrupted sleep.

Sunday, April 20

We arose early and took a bus to Minhatale. I started climbing those 1,000 steps.

I lost count. At the top I started to go to Miniavas cave.

"I'm waiting for you here," declared Nita.

I set out alone. First the pilgrims made you take off your shoes. I passed drink sellers and asked, "How far?" They used a one-arm motion — onward.

Down rocks, across pebbles, finally steps and a railing. I got up to the rock. The camera view would show nothing but a vista of trees. The rock had a hole in it, with candle drippings and a flat place and there were the ancient paintings.

Who would be silly enough to trek nearly a mile down here? I braced myself for the ordeal back up hill. Decided to take a picture of the rock (cave?) to go with the story.

People came down. "Don't take pictures of people" was my warning yesterday. These people requested I take their picture.

As I lumbered upwards those sob, sob pilgrims were all coming down chanting. What's this? "Hello Nita." An old woman was holding her hand and escorting Nita down the rocks. The pilgrims insisted she accompany them.

Back at the top she hid, so they wouldn't force her up to the high temple.

We finally swam in that pond, just the two of us. I took off my dress and Nita wet her dress.

We wondered why they were called ruins. We saw hundreds of pilgrims actively praying on those sites.

It was a long wait for the bus, so we played jotto and Guggenheim and attracted a crowd around us.

Back at home we had lunch. Mr. Paiva got us a ride to New Town.

The Kandy Express bus left at 1:00 and we arrived in Kandy at 5:00 p.m.

It made many stops along the way.

At the Kandy railroad station we asked a policeman to take us to the Boy Scout Headquarters. Forty people were scheduled to use the big room.

He opened a room upstairs, and we were considered contraband. We couldn't open the windows and let in fresh air because Scout officials might discover us and it would get him in trouble.

One mattress. How could we fight over it? An hour ago we had none.

We had pineapple and cashews for dinner. The rain stopped, but I was too tired to walk around town. Sleep? Who slept? No air and mosquitoes. Rashes itched. A lousy night.

Monday, April 21

I lay awake for hours and hours and let Nita sleep. Finally I got up, thinking it was noon, but it was only 8:30 a.m. I was lost without a watch. I left it in Colombo to be cleaned.

We were glad to leave the Boy Scout headquarters.

We took a bus to the YWCA. We sat all morning on a shaded porch reading and waited for the warden.

She had exactly two beds and she personally supervised our meals, adding more delicious food to our plate as fast as we as finished it. Stringhopper, curries, not too hot, and fruit salad with custard.

All for 10 rupees a day, room and board.

Nita discovered Tolkien's "Ring of the Fellowship." She spent from 4:00 to 7:00 at the British Council library.

I located bookstores, but hesitated spending 14 rupees for the two books I wanted on "Ceylon" by Fujjik.

In the United States library I enjoyed reading "Women in Asia" until they closed at 6:00 p.m.

I went to the British library and read other books.

"Let's Visit Ceylon" by John Cadwell, was for 8-11 year-olds. I didn't like the tone, though I did learn a lot. Peggy Warner's "Asia is People," covered the same territory we traveled. She had an easy style of writing, personal, but descriptive. Our trip was far more adventurous and detailed.

It rained hard! We got home by 8:00, ate dinner and did more reading in bed.

I slept and woke in two-hour intervals. Why? I broke a slat in the bed immediately and turned gingerly, afraid of breaking more.

Nita realized the windows were shut tight. Why? Thieves came around at night and poked sticks into open windows and stole. We had looked forward to a cool, airy night in Kandy.

Tuesday, April 22

The Botanical Gardens of Kandy were worth a day. We enjoyed all that we saw, orchid house, cactus, African violets, large magnificent almond trees. We ate gauchin fruit and star apple. I didn't care for either one.

After lunch we were off to the railroad. On the way we returned books to the library and then took the train to Colombo. It took three and one half hours.

We were glad to be "home." Clarence was at a square dance. We missed it.

Bhudeni had chicken pox. But we enjoyed being with the family again.

We received a letter from Jack:

Dear Ruth and Nita,

I just received Nita's letter from Ceylon so I rush this letter to reassure you that our problems are not of a nature that you could resolve by taking the next plane home.

The poison pen letter you refer to was, of course, written by Olga. I suppose that I am in part to blame, because I visited her and made the mistake of trying to communicate with her as one human being to another. She described a world all solid red, pink, yellow (in discussing your travels and our family) and I tried to show her that there were gradations, shadings and shadows, and subtleties and nuances. Of course she must have misunderstood and thought I was describing black.

Don't scold her, or be too hard with her, that is the way she is, just know and realize it. I'm sorry that you had to get your news about us from her.

You say you haven't heard from me since November. I'm shattered. I wrote a long, long letter to India and waited and waited, but there was no indication that you received it. So I wrote another long, long one to Kenya recapping the main points of the other and bringing you up to date on goings on at home. These two letters from Nita (received today) are the first direct word we have from you since then. Evidently you never got the second one either. I despair.

The highlights about us — We are all O.K. in health — outside of the usual colds and Dave's spring allergy.

I am working in New York near the battery at the present. I don't expect I'll be there too long, I'd like to keep the summer uncommitted.

Cooper Union has rejected Wendi, a severe disappointment because that was the only place she had a real desire for. She absolutely can't be moved to apply at a school she can't respect, like the local ones, or the State U's. Marlboro she would like, but has no hope for, and I'm trying to push her to apply, but don't know if she will. She has to write an essay for her application. If she does, I offered to take time off to drive her up there for an interview. Don't know if she will.

Lori is dancing (as are Wendi and David) and looks well. She won't let me get too close to her. Goes to therapy Saturday mornings. I don't think she is getting much from it though she won't discuss it with me. I don't think her therapist is sharp enough. She likes him and tolerates him for that reason because she can control him. She could not take a therapist with whom she was not in complete control.

Wendi and I will try to get her interested in LRY, the teen group in Unitarians. I think she might be ready now.

David is just going along — though more moody.

I'm troubled about the summer and haven't decided what we'll do. I'd like for us all to go up to Nova Scotia. They all would like to go, but Wendi can't get along with Lori because Lori won't cooperate in work and activities and David won't go with Wendi because he feels she is too bossy. And because Lori eggs him on against her and I can't send one off somewhere else and go anywhere with the other because they're pretty sensitive now about being shipped off to be out of the way and I don't feel like going anywhere with a bickering bunch. I think Homestead might be good for David for a few weeks.

We received two packages last week. One from India with the doll, which I'm sorry to say was somewhat broken, but might be salvaged, and one from Africa with the beautiful materials. Custom charge and mail charge total $4.00. There was a previous package from India with saris and lots of other stuff. Before that, packages from Russia with films.

Please acknowledge if you receive this. Please.

Love, Jack, Dad.

Wednesday, April 23

Manelle and I sat over lunch and talked. Nita had her clay and sculpted. Then Manelle got the "bug" and made a bust of her mother. She was so happy, so pleased with us for thinking of this creative activity.

We sat, Clarence and I, and discussed Ceylon politics. It was a good country and headed in right (rather left) directions.

He said the government had free health care and free education.

Unfortunately medical schools do not combine the old and the new.

We discussed herbs and old-fashioned medicines. Belly fruit, a plant, boiled got rid of phlegm in the body and was good for coughs.

Clarence's father had two wives, one after the other. Very close family, nevertheless. Brought up as Christian like his mother. He became Buddhist like Manelle when he got married.

We walked to the Buddhist temple with Clarence. We learned about Buddhism inside the spectacular temple, as he placed flowers in front of Buddha, and gave me the feeling of significance for it. The incense was burned as the monk chanted the prayers. Suddenly it all made sense and I could respond sympathetically, experiencing each routine.

No pressure, no rules. No one made you do anything. Everyone could contribute a flower or a bit of food. Buddhism broke down classes.

Thursday, April 24

We visited the coral gardens in Hikkaduwa and the Galle Dutch Fort and lighthouse.

All day in bus with the Indian party. Great happy singing people. Average age was 50 and there were old folks too.

Friday, April 25

In the afternoon we stopped for ice cream. Good day.

Nita went to climb the rock in noon heat to see the ancient paintings. She accompanied the Indian party to Sigirya, the rock fortress of King Kaseyappa that had the frescoes.

On our tour there were many Parsees and we discussed Zoroaster for a change.

Only Nita and I and Jay brought swimsuits. The whole busload went swimming in frocks and saris. The underwater world was worth the hours we traveled in the bus.

We slept in Kandy at Trinity College. Had a great time dancing in the evening. Day disappeared fast!

Saturday, April 26

We met the Indian party at the Miss Tooth Temple in the Botanical Gardens.

It would be our second visit there and we would sightsee with the crows and then on to hill country and cooler temperatures.

We learned that Parsis wear Kasti, a white string and sadru, white shirt.

The Hindus wear Janoi, a black string worn around waist. This is for good luck.

It was cold like they promised.

In the evening we played games, musical chairs using men instead of chairs.

Another game I learned was sweetheart, bitter heart, sour heart. You changed seat with an extra person.

The evening was fun, but Nita had an earache for the first time in Kandy and again today. She was in pain. Poor kid.

Sunday, April 27

In N'Eliya we made two rounds through the tea factory. I tried to learn more.

Buy Broken Orange Pekoe. BOP Fannings is the next best. Only tip and two leaves used in this factory. I was annoyed as were Mannoo and Mani at the lack of labor saving devices. There was so much unnecessary moving of tea instead of connecting tubes and belts or using sheeting.

We took an afternoon walk through town and slept from 4:00 to 6:00.

I spent the rest of time talking to Minoo. He was getting his doctorate in Electrical Engineering in London. He had to marry before leaving. He had a plastic disk in his back and leg.

Friends Mentioned in Chapter 42

Clarence Wanigatuna. He was director of the Youth Hostels. He had a wife named Manelle; son, Jayaantha, 18; and daughter, Bhudini, 8.

Mr. Paiva. He treated us cordially at the Youth Hostel.

Minoo Dahal. He was an electrical engineer, a Parsi from Bombay.

NITA

RUTH IN SARI

OLD MAN

FORTY-THREE

SINGAPORE

Monday April 28
We went to the Malaysia Hotel in Singapore. I had dinner at midnight and a luxurious bath.

Nita writes:
April 29, 1969
Midnight
Dear Daddy, Wendi, Lori, and David,
BOAC was too good to us. They supplied perfumed towels, peanuts, two lamb chops with gourmet gravies and Brussels sprouts, cheese and crackers plus prawns, cake oozing whipped cream, coffee with aroma, free soaps and we perfumed ourselves in their toilet.
In Singapore, a bus, special for us, took us from the airport to our hotel.
I think I have the disease known as "culture shock."
From the plane, Singapore was a glistening necklace of lights — dazzling and breathtaking.
As we rode though the wide city streets, billboards cried out: "Buy Olympia Cameras," "Benson-Hedges for expensive tastes," "Put the flavor where the fun is."
Neon lights jumped out at us, great glass and steel structures towering overhead.
This morning I was basking in the dancing palms and softly lapping sea waves, and now this! I was overwhelmed.
We entered the hotel that the airlines provided, all expenses paid. The Malaysia Hotel, brand new, one of the highest rating in all of tourist-filled Asia.
Luxury seeped through the marbled corners, the golden and crystal chandeliers, the foot-thick carpets, and even the glass bubble telephone booths and the sliding automatic glass doors.
Mommy and I occupied a magnificent suite, two rooms and two more rooms for bathrooms. Furniture décor, lighting all praiseworthy. The huge living room was decorated in olive-green and orange-yellow with colorful Chinese paintings on the

wall. The bedroom was in shades of yellow-gold with two giant beds and a window overlooking the colored fountains.

I sank into the bed, a change from the lumpy coconut-husk mattresses and wooden benches we've been sleeping on. I would have been happy never moving from this room.

They gave us three cards to present at mealtime and we ate our dinner at midnight. We devoured a chicken dinner, gazpacho, salad and French pastries. Did the same at lunch today at 3:00 to 4:00 p.m. and had rare roast beef and salad and hunks of crab, shrimp and lobster.

Our meals at the hotel were another exhilarating experience. We had major decisions to make when we beheld all the varieties of cream pastries, fruit pastries and gooey cakes. We ordered three deserts because we didn't use up our allotment on coffee.

This morning, we left the hotel to get our first glimpse of Singapore in daylight. We left the hotel about 10 a.m. I stepped up to a car and asked the gentleman to take us "anywhere." We never did find out where he was headed.

He whisked us away, escorting us on a three-hour sightseeing tour of Singapore through Chinatown, through the ritzy residential sections. The Tiger Balm Park, situated high on a hill, gave us a view of Singapore, to the harbors and to the hundreds of newly arising ultra modern apartment buildings.

He ended our excursion by treating us to ice cream. He gave us his address and phone number to visit his family, wife and 4-year-old son on our return to Singapore. He dropped us off at shopping area. Our driver, Andrew, gave us a wonderful time.

Don't ask us how we do it. We don't know. But few people could have only one day in a city and do and see as much as we did. We didn't spend a cent at all.

Remember, my watch was stolen in Kenya, the rest of the day I shopped for one. Watches galore. I'd love to arrive home with a white-gold Omega, but I settled for a reliable Swiss watch.

We saw people with poles on shoulders to carry goods and I priced beautiful oriental dresses. We window-shopped. Bought a pair of shoes and some drug items. Cashed $20.

The city is building apartments and slums are disappearing.

Daddy, I was thrilled to hear from you and to learn that you have been writing, even though your letters have not come through to us. It was probably because they were too thick; airmail always arrives.

My letters to you were also quite heavy, at least fifteen pages. Have you received the happy birthday letter yet?

Family life, from your description, sounds normal; we never did have an extraordinarily smooth family life.

Of course Mommy and I did take into consideration the sender of the letter. It was just the suddenness of her ill findings that startled us. And please, don't stop visiting her; just guard your tongue.

We returned to the hotel after locating a cheap hotel to stay in when we return to Singapore. We repacked and left half our luggage in storage at the hotel free so we can travel light for the next two weeks in Indonesia.

We would have been happy to luxuriate in our hotel suite. Unfortunately, a plane JAL, Japanese airlines to Djakarta, awaited us at the airport.

Friends Mentioned in Chapter 43

Andrew. He gave us a tour during our one-day stay.

FORTY-FOUR

INDONESIA

Tuesday, April 29

JAL, Japanese airlines evening plane to Djakarta. Linda, my seatmate on the plane, became my companion. She was part of the Good Will Tour of students. Her aunt, Luz Dayrit, the cultural attaché in the Philippines Embassy, waited for us at the airport. Linda introduced us and Luz took us to the Philippine Embassy for a dance performance. It was the Javanese and Philippine "Rice Bird" dance.

Miss Dayrit invited us to be guests in her home.

Nita writes:

Wednesday, April 30

Dear Family,

At the moment I feel lousy because I am suffering from a terrible ear infection that began two weeks ago in Ceylon. I had a caked-up wax deposit that caused an ear infection. I'm in pain and am deaf in my ear. The doctor has me doped up on eardrops, tetra myiacin, pain pills and vitamins. I feel like I'm floating in another world.

I have definitely arrived in the shopping areas of the world. I was going out of my mind admiring the gorgeous embroidered silk and satin materials, those delicate wall hangings, the lovely jade jewelry, and I've been warned that Hong Kong has more shops.

You should have seen the outfits the Indonesian students were wearing last night. They were relatively well-to-do, so the materials were magnificent. The girls were all slender with small, high busts and diminutive waists. They were exquisite.

The Philippine boys had embroidered, blue silk blouses.

Linda and her aunt invited us to stay in their home.

Love, Nita

Wednesday, April 30

Luz and her housekeeper, Gem, accompanied me to the market and guided me to my errands.

The Golden Tours in the Indonesia Hotel gave us the train schedule to Den Pasar.

Pan Am reorganized our ticket to fly us to New York.

In the evening, we socialized. We learned a little about the Philippines and their three years of Japanese occupation.

All American reparations came too late. America did much more to build up and help Japan "get on its feet" than it did for the Philippines.

We walked through the department store. I discovered a gambling den on the 13th floor. I was chicken. "Sarinah."

Nita writes:

I really think I am maturing to a great extent. In Ceylon, we traveled with an Indian group for four days. The people I was with were in their 20s. It was a summer camp situation. I was constantly around the same group of people on the bus for hours and during the evening activities. And guess what?

I could relate. I could have fun. I could enjoy being with the people. I liked Carmen and Minoo and Mani and Pat and Jayantha.

And you know what? They liked me!

I was able to sustain the people without breaking down. I enjoyed myself without pushing myself to have fun. I danced, sang and played games without shyness. I am more mature.

Thursday, May 1

Ruth writes:

Dear Jack and Family,

Nita brought you up to date for the most part. Our stay in Singapore at the Malaysia Hotel was fabulous and I had mixed feelings about going out and seeing the city at all. I was content to stay in the room and bask in the luxury, enjoy the music, and the lighting, and the décor, and the very comfortable bed with crisp sheets. Air conditioning was a bit too cold, but we adjusted it.

Our sightseeing tour was enjoyable and we always mention politics and religion and education of the country. We saw skinned snakes in Chinatown and will sample them on our return visit.

Nita didn't go much crazier over the shopping than in other towns, only she planned to buy more expensive items here. We only looked on our first visit. It was so commercial.

In Djakarta, we lived in a home again. Nita slept on a rug on the floor and I had a good firm bed. Meals were prepared for us and all we had to do was eat.

We went to market today and shopped with the housekeeper, Gem.

Indonesian money system has no coins, only bills, and I can't get used to it. 400 Rupiah is about $1.00. All of our shopping cost $1.50, our money. It included one *chicken, three small fish, carrots, cucumbers, bean curd, chilies, a large papaya, and rambutans (a local fruit).*

We also bought flowers, golden lilies and deep red gladiolas for our hostess. Cost was 12 cents for flowers. Beat that?

We reorganized our plane ticket and dropped our stop in Honolulu.

We also decided against using the plane to Den Pasar. We will take the train to Bali Island instead. That way we can stop off and see more towns.

We also stretched our trip back across the states to New York, but a word from you and we can rearrange it and have it end at San Francisco, meet you there and get a refund.

I am sitting in an air-conditioned room in the Hotel Indonesia, the newest and most beautiful in Indonesia and I'm using their typewriter. We are beginning to get the hang of how to use the luxury hotel services without spending one cent.

I had the tourist office plan my train trip to Bali for me and they listed the train schedule and the prices. Now we'll know exactly what we are doing.

Our hostess is waiting for lunch for us.

Love to all of you,

Mom

Friday, May 2

I walked to the clinic for a doctor to heal Nita's ear. I walked through the maternity ward, babies swaddled tight, so tiny in huge cribs. A nurse sent us to the General Hospital.

That was another experience. There was a huge, crowded waiting room. Doctors sat in cubbyholes with a few instruments on the table. Did they sterilize them?

They used the flame at the table to sterilize the instruments. I couldn't watch a doctor probe in a Nita's ear and feared for her. She still had her infection and she had to continue medication. It cost 500 rupials for the visit.

The hospital had lovely, gracious rooms with patios on courtyards. It was a peaceful environment for sick people.

We walked back to Jikini through the Indonesia University grounds. Back at the house, we packed and left a note.

We boarded the bus for a long trip, 1:00 to 7:00 p.m., six hours with only one stop. The driver took us into a restaurant and dozens of small dishes were on every table – curries, eggs, omelet, fish, two meats and platters of rice. We took small portions and tasted the sauces and ate with our fingers. This was the famous RIJSTAFFEL.

The scenery past Bogar was magnificent and we should have embarked there. It was a six-hour ride of the most exciting scenery we had seen yet.

The atmosphere as we rode was very different from other countries, despite the banana trees and coconut palms. Water was everywhere. We passed tea plantations and slashed rubber trees. The major crop was rice. The rice paddies were sopping with water. One layer dripped water down to the next layer. Rice was grown in front of houses. No land was wasted.

Houses were a different architectural style and much more sturdy than the mud and wattle huts in other countries. Some had walls with a woven mat finish on the outside.

We passed families sitting on porches and socializing. The father and mother sat in front of the house cuddling babies.

The man seated next to me in the bus spoke English and I expected him to help find us lodging. He deserted us and said the bus driver would find us a place to sleep.

At the bus station in Bandung, we were told to sit. A drink was given to us and we kept expecting help for accommodations. The driver wanted to take us to his house, and we said, "No thanks."

Finally a betjak driver took us to Hotel Savoy Homann. We explained to him we wanted the cheapest hotel. As we drove up we faced one of the swankiest hotels we had seen. It had a large lounge with open portals. I sat in the betjak with the luggage.

Nita explained to the proprietor, "Our being delivered here was a mistake. We asked for an inexpensive hotel."

I sat and watched her. Finally, I saw her writing in the guest book. She called me in.

We met Martin, who sang in the hotel's nightclub. He got on the ball and started organizing a place for us.

"You are my guests and no charge for the room. Leave it to me."

We were introduced to Mr. Jonkers, the assistant manager, and the proprietor, Achmat Kartadibrata, and Raden personally escorted us.

Our room was part of a complex of attached rooms behind the large hotel. It was obviously staff quarters. Hotel rates are 1,600 or about $5.00 for a single room.

We entered our room. It had one bed and table on the porch that was cool and comfortable. That was the only entrance. The second room was large, with wardrobe, towel rack, two beds, sink, table and chairs, and a rack for the valises. A door opened on to the toilet room and bath chamber. It was the same as the one in Luz's home. It had water running into a person-sized receptacle like an upended box. You poured the water over you.

We socialized. Raden asked if we were writing a book and asked to be put into it. We said we would do that. Then he returned and gave us dinner. We declined graciously. How could we ever lose weight? Everyone fed us. We had already decided not to eat, but breakfast would be served in our room.

Bandung was cooler, as promised.

We had been spoiled for five months in India and East Africa. Both had been English colonies. In Ceylon they spoke Sihalese, but the Wanigatunga family spoke English.

Nita went to sleep in her new handmade nightgown. It was only basted and we hoped it held together.

Saturday, May 3

I had the roughest sheet I ever slept on. It felt like sandpaper.

I learned it was the only sheet like that. The other bed had smooth percale sheets. It was just my luck that I didn't know.

Achmat, our proprietor, stopped by to be sure we slept well and were happy.

There was a breakfast of juice, eggs, meat, banana, coffee, butter and jam and eight slices of bread. The bill presented for 50 rupials was 13 cents for two breakfasts. I paid it gladly.

I spent an hour reading about Indonesia. New York was 10,000 miles away. Indonesia is the same length as width of the United States, fifth largest in population in the world.

At the bank we met a Dutch lady. She drove us to Soeti Hotel for 600 rupials a night or $1.50. We took it.

We walked to the shopping district. It was Saturday afternoon and everything was closed.

We stopped at Hotel Baga's restaurant for a lunch of gado gado – peanut sauce over vegetables and soup.

All afternoon we relaxed and read.

Joke: I was asked to put English words next to the Indonesian menu. I went into the kitchen to locate the foods.

I did it correctly.

Muddy market areas were replaced with modern large buildings, orderliness and cleanliness was prevalent!

Bandung was the capital of West Java. Rice, chinchoma and tea were the principal exports. People were Sudanese. We saw architecture of the University of Indonesia and volcano 6,300 Tangkuban Prahu. There was a cool mountain area. Fumaroles.

In the evening, I went to Wajang Golek, a puppet theater. I was brought to the first row, first seat, a 1,000 rupiah seat, and charged 50 rupiah or 13 cents.

The puppeteer was deft with the head movements of the puppets. He played all the roles. The play went on all night long without a script

I went backstage. They were broadcasting it over the radio.

The Gamelan Orchestra performed the music.

After two hours, I returned to the hotel and brought Nita back to the theater to show her the puppet show. Vendors sold food, and people talked throughout the performance.

Mr. Jonkers and Jon, the brother of the director of the hotel, spent from 11:00 to 1:30 with us.

We sat in the ballroom and talked, drank orange soda and ate a plate of hors d'oevres. Then I danced. I went to bed at 1:30 but Nita did not return until 3:00. I was worried.

"Nita where have you been?" I queried.

"You know if you can't find me, Mother, I'm playing chess."

Sunday, May 4

I called the Soeti Hotel early to tell the Indonesian gentleman that we were at the Homann Hotel.

Alexander, who worked at the desk, made a date to take Nita to a movie.

We took Oblat, a small truck/bus to Lemang for 20 R.

Nita was crushed in back with 25 people. There were people holding on. I sat in front and sang songs with Elly.

Elly said, "Come meet my brother."

We found ourselves on the beautiful campus of Peiguruan Tinggi Advent, a Seventh Day Adventist school.

We met George Fisher, principal of the college. He told us the schools need books.

He supplied his jeep and Nootje, to take us up to the volcano. Nootje had hard luck; he had a tough time with the car and a bee stung him. When he arrived home, he got a flat tire.

We were excited about the tropical forests and huge ferns. We witnessed smoking sulfur fumes out of the volcanic crater. They explained that the powder at the bottom of the volcano was the material they used to make the delicate porcelain dishes.

When we returned, Mr. Hancock invited us for lunch. While it was being heated Mr. Fisher told Jan Hancock that Mrs. Oliver was making our lunch.

We had to go to her home. How much trouble we were! We had a luncheon from both families.

We spent the next couple of hours visiting with Mrs. Oliver and visited her clinic. That morning she saw 40 patients.

We visited a student who had a fever. His wife poured water over him to cool him off. He had chills, as the bed, mattress and blankets were all sopping wet.

Mrs. Oliver told me about the Baneo section, where people cut their tongues and licked the bodies of sick people. They covered the body with fresh blood. Sometimes several people helped out.

A mother brought her son into the clinic. He was contagious with small pox; it could spread to all those other people in the clinic.

It was an enlightening afternoon with Mrs. Oliver. She had a 25-year-old son. She had had eight miscarriages, was 50 and maintained good health. Her energy was great. She was in charge of the clinic and doctoring the neighborhood. She was responsible for the kitchen and diets for the sick patients.

We had never met missionaries before, people who spent their whole lives outside the states. We talked all night and had morning devotions and held hands around the table while saying grace. The Hancocks were a lovable family.

The father was Robert. Janet was the mother. Cherie, 14, was in the ninth grade and studying by correspondence school this year. She took typing, sewing and cooking. Next year she would attend the Advent boarding school in Singapore.

Lorene was 12 and in seventh grade. She was very good with Denise, the baby. They were all pretty girls and they had dolls and stamp collections. Cherie had a bell collection. The children gave up their beds for us, and they slept in sleeping bags.

We had good things to say about Seventh Day Adventists. School was organized on a work basis. In the mornings the students worked in the field and did landscaping. In the afternoons, and when it rained, they attended classes.

Saturday was their Sabbath.

They were vegetarian. They did not drink alcohol or smoke, and did not drink coffee or tea. That was O.K. by me. They ate healthy foods and, luckily, could obtain them.

Monday, May 5

Nita spent time with 4-year-old Denise, reading and making mud pies. Nita bathed her in a washbasin.

Lorene took us for a hike to see the waterfalls. It was the first time we had actually tramped through a lush, tropical jungle. The huge ferns were similar to those that existed in primitive days. We trail blazed for more than an hour. The perspiration streamed down our faces. Denise was carried part of the way and we had to push the dog up the embankment.

Janet had a happy first marriage, but her husband died of leukemia. Paraguay was her home for a little less than two years. She married Bob two years after her husband died. He was a loving father for this family.

In the evening, we played jotto. The trickiest word was "yacht." And Bob didn't believe it, even after he saw it. We all laughed. It was to bed at 9:30.

My attitude toward missionaries had never been positive. But we were happy we had this opportunity to befriend the family. They were real and easy to be with. They were Americans and our attitude towards Americans was not always good. But these people had high values. I believe their religion was a binding force in their family life. They had morning and evening devotions and handholding grace around the table. I liked it.

Nita said their humanitarian point of view was different from the religious fanatics we met. They did not feel that all people who did not believe as they did were damned.

Sunday, May 4

Ruth writes:
Dear Family,

Today we saw swarming locusts.

In Djakarta we stayed with Luz, who worked for the Philippine Embassy. She was used to a large family and lived alone, so she welcomed our company. We had comfortable quarters in her home.

We spoke to a betjack rider who pushed us in a cart to secure us "cheap lodging."

We were driven to the swankiest, largest hotel we ever saw —The Savoy Homann. Nita spoke to the clerk at the desk. Result is that we were established in a suite of rooms in the staff quarters of the hotel. They refused to take money from us. It was luxury living and gracious quarters.

Mr. Jonkers, manager of the hotel, became Nita's friend and chess partner. We sat in the dance hall Saturday night with the top brass of the hotel.

This was after my "cultural" venture into the puppet theatre. The puppeteer recites all the parts and he uses no script. There is singing and many unusual instruments.

Nita played with the hotel manager and she was happy that he won. She enjoys the challenge of a good chess player.

We took a mini bus to Lemang, 25 people crushed into a space for 8. Ellen, sitting next to me, taught us an Indonesian folk song. She took us to visit her brother.

She took us to Perguruan Tingjr Advent, a campus of the Seventh Day Aventists schools. The principal lent us his car to see the volcano.

Mrs. Hancock and Mrs. Oliver prepared lunch for us. The Principal's wife is sick with the flu.

Mrs. Oliver has a clinic and administers to the poor families.

We traipsed through lush tropical forests. Gigantic ferns reminded me of ancient times.

Love, Ruth/Mom

Tuesday, May 6

In town we bought $6.00 worth of presents. We wanted to buy batik and have a dress made.

We left Homann Hotel on Sunday morning and returned Tuesday at noon. We found the hotel in an upset state. They had the police and military on the search for us. Even the governor was notified of our disappearance. The campus had no phone and we could not contact the hotel as we had wished to do. However, we should have sent a note in yesterday.

We were not used to having people concerned about us. The generosity we were receiving was overwhelming, and regardless of our objections, meals arrived in our room several times a day. Now we signed the bills instead of paying them.

Mr. Jonkers insisted on preparing us a box lunch for our train rides.

Jan, the director, sent us folders and a banner of the Savoy Hotel Homann.

A policeman came to see that we were all right. I'm still overwhelmed at all the attention and concern for us.

Nita admits she was confused about the roles of Mr. Jonkers and Mr. Ahmat. We finally realized it was Mr. Achmad who sent us dinner and had the box lunch prepared for our train trip. He beat Nita in four games of chess. Good for him.

We were asleep at midnight.

Wednesday, May 7

The postal clerk helped me mail my purchases, after filling out four declaration forms for customs. The cost of postage proved more than the cost of the contents, so we decided to drag our packages with us.

Nita received a telephone call, something about cashing a traveler's check. Could something be wrong? The bank clerk wanted a date with Nita.

We were on the train from 10:00 a.m. to 7:30 p.m., nine and one half hours.

At first we were comfortable, then it became hot. Our fan did not work and Nita sat with the sun baking her most of the trip.

We had various companions in our compartment, but Hason Sjarif was with us at the end of the trip. He was originally from Sumatra. When we approached Central Java he pointed out the differences between Sudanese and Javanese. Homes were more primitive. The people were under a Communist government four years ago. He felt Communists accomplished nothing for the people.

Hasam was a shoe manufacturer.

At Djogjakarta we found the friendliest people yet. Everyone in our compartment, four of us, climbed into a horse and cart. The poor horse balked at the weight. Hasam's home was available. Much to Nita's chagrin, we were given a room with beds. It was windowless and airless. We much preferred a mat on the floor in the breezy entranceway where the rest of the family slept.

Nita begged me "Please, Mommy, I'm so tired. Let's stay in a hotel tonight. I can't socialize."

Sorry Nita. Buffeted about by people again. The whole family arrived and talked until late. Dawanto, 23, was a student at the foreign language academy in Bandung. He worked for the government tourist agency. He was studying English to become a tourist guide in Bandung. We spent time working on his paper: "Investigation of the Savoy Homann Hotel as a possible tourist hotel."

We rewrote as much as we could in the limited time into understandable English and incorporated our story as a human-interest twist. I hoped he passed.

Devi, 17, studied in Bandung. She spent time with us, but could not speak English. They claimed five children, but I counted many more in the family, three brothers and three sisters, at least.

We sat around after a bath and a handful of "aunts" arrived and chattered. I passed the pictures of our family around as my contribution to the discussion.

Chalk up another hot sleepless night.

Thursday, May 8

At 6 a.m. people expected us to get up.

We had banana fritters and rice and bean curd.

Devi took us to a batik factory. We selected seven and bought three cheap ones. I wanted the 3,000 Rupiah wall hanging. We saw the handwork and Nita tried her hand at making a batik. We watched the hand stamp method, which requires meticulous care and skill. Then we watched the dying and boiling processes. Wax must be scraped off dyed material and reapplied to get the colors.

My iced drink was unusual, avocado with coffee flavor. Nita's was blended from jakfruit and ice. Beware of ice. Poison— it might be unclean water.

Friends brought us to their home, a typical Javanese home. There was a huge room with a raised area and three separate small rooms with pallets and stored pillows.

We had another Javanese meal — soybean cake and rolled omelet, all good.

Devi and Dawanto rode on a motorbike and we trailed behind in a betjak.

We all sat in the train station for while. After they left, who should appear, but Hasam. We had been disturbed that we couldn't even thank the gentleman responsible for the kind hospitality we received. We were glad to see him. We were coming up in the world. Two different people saw us off to Surabaya.

I wrote on the train. Nita was already asleep. Djogjakarta was hot. We made a quick decision not to visit the famous temples an hour away.

We had several days travel yet to Den Pasar.

We ventured onward armed with the original Braman, whose letter I found in New Delhi, and Nootie's address, and now two friends of Dawanta.

We expected to arrive late that night after seven hour's of travel. We started at 3:30 p.m. arrived 9:30 p.m.

The train superintendent accompanied us to a nearby, cheap hotel. The dirty mattresses smelled dank and the room was airless. There was a great mosquito problem. I refused. It was 400 for both of us. Finally, a man in a car gave us a ride to a couple more hotels, all 1,000 each. We chose one. We entered a large room, with two large double beds, clean sheets and a clean floor. I felt contented.

We refused food, bathed, washed hair and slept well.

Friday, May 9

Nita slept till after 8:00. We had breakfast at 10:00. The cook and servant were talkative and told us to stay on two nights. It was our laziest day yet. I napped before lunch and from 3:00 to 4:00. I took pictures of children playing in the courtyard. I read and relaxed all day.

At 5:30 Justini told us to put our suitcases in the car and he drove us to Mr. Bramasthagir's home, after stopping to get directions.

Mr. Bramasthagir had received my letter, without any return address, and tried to answer it at the local GPO.

He welcomed us and he decided we would stay another day. We talked for a while before retiring.

Mr. Bram belied the stereotype of a "commandant." He was a slender man, sensitive and an intellectual. He read many good books in English.

Sudisarti tried to speak, but her soul was her eloquence.

She did all in her power to please. She had sweet children, relaxed. Only the 2-year-old demanded her attention.

She was a kindergarten teacher before her marriage. She had four children in five years (same as I had).

We had good discussions with Mr. Bram on communism and the States and Indonesia.

We spent almost 12 days in Indonesia, and never once paid for food or lodging.

In Djakarta, it was Luz from the Philippine Embassy who harbored us.

In Bandung, Mr. Achmat of the swanky Savoy Homann Hotel took us under his wing.

The Hancocks, an American Seventh Day Adventist missionary family, hosted us for three days.

In Djogjakarta, we were thrust upon a defenseless Indonesian family for a day.

Saturday, May 10

We slept under mosquito netting with the mosquitoes.

I relaxed and wrote letters and Nita traced designs from an Indonesian art book.

At 10 a.m. a jeep with Dwi and Yiyoto, two army men, arrived for us. We bought books and then they escorted us to the zoo.

When we got home Dwi beat Nita at two games of chess. That thrilled her. She said he played an "Army man's game. All attack!"

We relaxed in the afternoon and evening.

Amateur boxing was the popular sport. Mr. Bram took us and we spent three hours watching some good bouts. Then we went back home.

Our meals were delicious. I liked the cooking in this country.

Bed at 11:30 and up at 3 a.m. to catch a bus.

Sunday, May 11

We arose 3:00 a.m. and staggered on to the bus. It was still in the Surabaya bus station at 6:00. It was a long day's drive in an uncomfortable bus. The window was situated in the wrong place and there was no resting place for my head.

On the ferry we found there was an express comfortable bus for twice the amount of money, but no one seemed to know where we could get on it.

Friends Mentioned in Chapter 44

Luz Dayrit. She was a Djakarta Consulate from the Philippines.

Linda Urule. She was her niece.

Raden Achmad. We met him at the Savoy Homann Hotel. He beat Nita at chess. This thrilled her.

Hason Sjarif. We met on the train and he took us to his home for the night.

Darwanto and Devi Darwana.They were our guides and hosts in Jogdakarta.

Elly Perguruan Tinggi. She was at the Seventh Day Adventist school.

Mr. George Fisher. He was the principal of the Perguruan Tinggi Advent school.

The Hancock family missionaries. They included Rev. Robert, Janet, Cherie, Lorene, Denise and Bobby.

Mrs. Oliver. She conducted a clinic for the sick.

Dr. Bramasthagir. He was a military man who was intellectual and had a diversified library. He hosted us.

WOMAN SELLING STUFF ON STREET

BOY CARRYING WOOD

WOMEN LUGGING WOOD ON THEIR BACKS

FORTY-FIVE

BALI

The three and a half-hour bus ride from Gitabali to Denpasar was picturesque.
In every stream beautiful brown people bathed. In Bali women were often bare topped. However, most had drooping breasts.

A boy yelled out "Adi Yassi Hotel." I looked it up in my notebook and let him guide us there. He carried our bag and we followed.

Australians and Europeans stayed here. We fell asleep early.

Monday, May 12

We investigated hotels that were outrageously expensive.

Musicians played and we listened to gamelon music.

We took a bus to Guinjar.

Adjati, an Army boy, walked us to Dr. Sockarto's home.

We looked around the festival grounds. There was a huge figure of a dragon called Barong, Barong, a symbol of good that also represented good luck.

We located the Sockarto family. The father was in Holland studying. He was an archeologist, a specialist in inscriptions like calligraphy.

Toky, the son, also an archeologist, talked with us. We were given a room for the night, and a dinner of rice, fried peanuts, sate meat and bananas. It was a wholesome meal.

Toky was assigned to investigate the artifact that had been discovered in North Bali. It would be a three-day trip for him.

We walked back to the festival. It would take me the rest of the book to describe it. There were food stands everywhere, and card and dice games. A man ate fire and gymnasts did rope tricks. Activity and crowds were everywhere.

We met Michael, a tourist, a San Francisco painter, and Anne, working on the script of a film that would be produced in Bali. We shared the wonders of Bali.

Adjat bought front row tickets for us at the Samyan Tiga Temple for a drama. It was an excellent gamalin orchestra with perfect synchronization and young musicians.

The drama had the following actors — two clowns, two mustached men, an excellent actor as the old king, prince and princess, two lady orderlies and a witch doctor.

The story line was: the Princess had a dream of meeting a man and she wanted the witch doctor to help her, because her strict father did not permit her to meet men.

The clowns pretended they were statues in the King's throne room, and food was thrust into their hands. An excellent actor became a monkey and did antics all over the stage. There was much humor throughout the drama and much to enjoy regardless of the language barrier. It was produced in the Bali tongue, so our friends could not understand it either.

The audience was great to watch. There were nursing babies in hooded outfits and laughing children with smiling faces.

We went home at midnight, but two people from the house we stayed in returned to the play and remained until 3 a.m.

Tuesday, May 13

We were awakened at 5:00 a.m. by Toky, who said goodbye.

The family requested a photo. All six children posed for photos of the family at 5:30 a.m.

Adjat arrived around 8:00 a.m. We walked to the Elephant Caves. The Elephant God resided deep in the recesses of the mountain.

I bought a Bali hat, horse wood carving, rings and a belt.

Later that day, a truck gave us a hitch to a cockfight. Adi Yassa, the hotel owner, spent his money there daily.

Gambling with cards and dice occurred in back of the arena while the audience waited for each fight to begin.

In a large arena cocks were chosen and opponents decided. Knives were tied on the left foot of the fighting cock. Two at a time fight, usually to the death of one cock. It was usually bloody. Official bets were placed, then people bet among themselves.

After an hour we had had enough.

Walked, walked, walked. Then took a bus back to Denpasar to Hotel Adi Yassa.

From 2:30 – 3:30 we bathed.

Then we purchased records of the gamalin music.

I learned some of the Bali values and concepts:

Man is responsible for his own destiny. He can use his ideas to control his external environment and his internal impulses.

Man must create a scale of values according to his society and culture. These values require a mode of social organization in which man must contribute a minimum of time and energy to his work. But he is entitled to a minimum standard of living and satisfaction of his essential requirements.

Men must share a common promise and a common destiny. There must be a genuine atmosphere of tolerance for educated people to learn to respect themselves. Ask for more human rights worldwide.

Adjat, the army boy, took us to the Samyan Tiga Temple for a drama there.

Tuesday, May 13

Nita writes:

Dear Wendi and Lori,

This is a birthday letter.

The Indonesian post office is notoriously inept. The postal clerks take stamps off the letters before they are cancelled, throw away the letters, and then resell the stamps for some extra rice for their families.

We have another package, carvings, shadow puppets and batik materials that we are sending from Singapore rather than Indonesia.

Lori, I am buying a present for you in Hong Kong. It will be useful as well as beautiful. Wendi, I haven't decided yet on a present for you. Tell me if there is anything specific you want in the Bangkok-Hong Kong area. Otherwise it is potluck.

All the packages we've been sending are stuffed with presents for other people. Therefore, please don't show them to relatives or friends.

Bali is fantastical. The scenery is, in my opinion, on a par with that of Ceylon or Goa, but the people and the temples and the "artistic" atmosphere are unique in this part of the world.

In Djakarta, Luz, cultural attaché of the Philippine Embassy harbored us.

In Bandung, Mr. Achmat of the swanky Savoy Homann Hotel took us under his wing. He beat me in chess four times.

The Hancocks, an American Seventh Day Adventist family, hosted us for three days.

I even attended one of Robert's lectures on, "Why Christ is so late in his Second Coming."

They were a family of Californians who have been living in Indonesia for five years. Four kids and their missionary parents were the most broadminded missionaries believable.

In Djogjakarta, we were thrust upon a defenseless Indonesian family for a day.

In Surabaja, Mr. Bram hosted us. Mommy found a letter in Delhi he had written to an American couple that had stayed with him, and she wrote to him that we were coming.

Mr. Bram speaks English and took us to a boxing match. First the referee comes out and bows to each of the four sections of the audience. The fighter comes out and bows to each audience section and to the referee; then the opponent comes out, does the same thing and bows to the other fighter.

Finally, the two fighters come together and shake hands, hug each other and then bow to each one again before fighting. The end of each round is filled with more

311

hugging and at the end of the fighting they throw their arms around each other. The referee had a hard time separating them before he announced the winner.

At the zoo in Surabaja we saw an animal called Komodo — a relic from the dinosaur age. It looked like a 20-foot long lizard. His huge forked tongue kept lashing out. They ate small animals and sometimes men. Komodo Island, Indonesia, swarms with them. It is uninhabited by man.

We also saw a Kasuari, a Camel bird. He looks like a brilliant turquoise and red ostrich, but is even more ungainly, with a huge bright lumpy crown on his head and hanging jowl like a turkey.

One day Luz said, "I'm unusual, I guess, but I don't like those exotic western fruits like apples, peaches and pears. I much prefer the ordinary fruits like rambutans, duriens, seleks and mangosteens."

Duriens are similar to jakfruits. The odor turns many people away. I ate many in Goa. Selaks look like snakeskin on the outside and are crunchy and sour. Rambutans are my latest passion. It means "hairy fruit" and is scarlet and has a gray cream, smooth slimy golf ball on the inside. But it tastes sweet and juicy. I had my first mangosteen today. It looks like a pomegranate on the outside and a cross between a selak and a rambutan on the inside. The juice runs down the face.

O.K. how's life? I'm getting bored having to ask the same questions over and over. College? Orphanage? Dancing? School? Are you guys going to spend your vacation on the West Coast and meet us in San Francisco? Both of us would love it, if you would.

Lori, are you having a "Sweet Sixteen" celebration?

Wendi, are you still not going to break down and write?

Well, anyway, Happy Birthday

Love from your sister, Nita.

We took a bus and walked to the Natour Barong Dance. It was staged for tourists. It cost 600 R and I had none with me. Fortunately, no one asked us for money.

This dance for tourists was not well executed. The acting was poor compared to the performance we witnessed at the festival. The dancers were not proficient.

Nita met Matti, the tour guide, and they became friends.

Nita went off with Matti, who was the tour leader who brought the tourists to the drama.

Wednesday, May 14

Nita writes:

Ho hum. Another day, another proposal. This one was from Matti, a really nice 26-year old Balinese. He started out just liking me, but by the third kiss he was loving me, and by the fifth kiss — what else, but marriage?

He was an absolute sensitive gentleman. Motorcycling around the back roads was enjoyable, because the scenery was breathtaking. I could see the sunset on the

water and the fishermen in their long canoes for nighttime net fishing. We watched
the stars rising and I saw the Southern Cross again.
A peaceful, pleasant time. Matti had a delicate sense of beauty that is lacking in
Western boys. I wonder if I could spend my life in Bali? It is creatively, artistically
and culturally inclined. But is that enough?
I got front seat tickets on the bus for the next day.
Lucky, Nita

I spent the evening at Three Sisters and ate good mie-noodle dish and talked
with Frank from Australia, a pleasant gentleman. He had spent seven months in
Indonesia.

He told me about marriage rituals.

I learned there is a kidnapping, then a pre-marital "fake" search that goes on for
42 days before the wedding ceremony.

Adi Yassa, a landlord, became a guide for us.

In the gamelan orchestra the man who played the drum was the leader. Temple
music throws men into a stupor. Then they can walk on hot coals.

In Bali, there was a social system called Gotong-Rajong, or working together.
Everybody belonged to a small compound and lived like a single family. They all
shared in the work and profits of the rice paddies. The compounds were divided according to the water supply.

A compound meeting was held once a month with each family represented to
sort out compound difficulties. Within each compound there was neither wealth nor
poverty. Everyone was cared for.

It sounded like communism in action to me, but the Balinese I spoke to vehe-
mently denied this. In 1966 there was a purge and any friend of a Communist was
brutally slaughtered. The island lost thousands of people in the blood-letting.

The compound's nucleus was a belief in God. Everyone was Hindu, if not phil-
osophically, at least traditionally.

In my opinion, the main problem was that individuality was discouraged.
Because of the stress on "community," people did not question traditions.

They did not try to "do their own thing." Outside Den Pasar, a person not be-
longing to a compound, either by choice or because he was ostracized, would starve.
Alone, he could not work a rice paddy, and nobody would buy from a store that
was not stocked. Therefore, the westernization emphasis of "I am," was alien to the
Balinese. The people were happy living in a community.

Thursday, May 15

We rose too early, 4:00 a.m., in order to be at the bus stop. The trip in the bus
was from 6:00 a.m. to 6:00 p.m. Our seats were over the rear wheel and the bus
bounced us around deplorably. We played jotto, sang nursery rhymes and laughed
our day away. It was a pleasant time. Nita always was a good traveling companion.

But by the time we arrived in Surabaya I knew I couldn't go on by bus and not sleep all night.

We took a Betjak to the train. We debated — whether to stop at Djoga and see temples. Decision made and we headed for the other train station for the Djoga train. We took that train straight through to Djakarta.

At 6:30 the train left. We managed to stretch out and slept in hour snatches.

The train had many passengers who were going to a Baha'i conference in Djakarta.

During our trip from Den Pasar to Djakarta, Nita learned about a new religion called Baha'i. It originated in 1863. Its creator was a prophet called "Bab" and it has spread to every country in the world. It teaches the universality of all religions.

The crux is that all religions are one; all Gods are one; all prophets are one. The founder of Baha'i, the Bab, is believed to be the culmination of all previous prophets, the second Christ, the second Buddha, the second Mohammed, and Zoroaster. The religion strives continually for world peace and universal brotherhood.

One trouble is that it is totally non-political. It teaches respect even for unjust governments and laws. I considered this a great drawback, but the Baha'i say that this way the governments also respect them and thus make the movement more effective.

Bab arrived at the same time that Seventh Day Adventists proclaimed that Christ was due. I think that's interesting. Bahaullah left his son as another prophet and interpreter. He left a World Council of nine (the mystical number) men. Bahaullah was persecuted, and spent a lifetime in prison writing books for the Baha'i.

Some people think that because Baha'i originated in Persia, it is a faction of Islam. But that is not true. The Baha'i consider themselves part of all religions. They think that previous religions were good for previous days, but for today's world they are inadequate. The Baha'i not only teach all religions, but also have their own interpretations of holy works. The religion is very flexible and not dogmatic. It shows promise.

I switched seats with Nita several times on the train. Nita read the Bahai book. I ended up talking about Bahai religion with Paru. These pioneers are not missionaries. They don't preach. Intermarriage is encouraged. They believe in doing good now, not in the afterlife.

I said good-bye to Paru. He had his conference to attend in Djakarta.

Friday, May 16

Nita writes:

By the way, Wendi, Grandma wrote and said you really chewed her out for writing that letter. It was unnecessary. She is an elderly woman and feeling rejected and unloved. When she wrote that letter she did not do it maliciously. Please don't take it out on her. Please drop in on her often. You don't even have to talk. She'll feel bad knowing she is not in your confidence, but she feels worse if she doesn't see you guys at all. Remember, I went to her almost every weekend last year.

We can tell by Aunt Minnie's letters that she, too, is getting sicker and older. It is a terrible feeling. Please try to be patient with both. I'm a good one to talk. From a distance it is easy. But also I think that within this year I have changed a lot and can understand Grandma and be more patient with her from now on.

Love, Nita

We rode in the betjak from the Indonesia Hotel to Pan Am.

Our flight was arranged for Sunday evening on Thai airlines. We left our luggage at the hotel.

We arrived about 3:00. Luz didn't come home until close to 7:00 p.m.

I shopped in the market behind Tjikini, the peasant market, and everyone laughed at my feeble attempts at the language.

After dinner I conversed with Luz.

Saturday, May 17

We were up early and still we had a late get-away.

We visited the US embassy and USOS for information about Indonesia.

There was aggravation at the post office. "Man is sick. Come back Monday."

But we finally received our mail from: Mom, Minnie, two American Express cards, and Mr. Bram.

The bank had more money than they were supposed to have. It seemed the credit union wasn't paying off the loan as pre-arranged. I wrote them a letter about it.

We hitched to a museum with a Yugoslavian nun.

It was a good museum, but we were pressured for time. We spent an hour there. We heard gamalin music, and saw games, toys, dolls, and all kinds of interesting artifacts in the museum store.

We took a betjak to Gunning Agency and looked at books. I wanted to buy a Torah Kita, a beautiful photography book of Indonesia, but it was 2,500 R, or $8.50. Instead, I purchased Ramayama and a couple of small books on Javanese dance and Bali.

Back at home we rested and read and talked.

In the evening I went with Luz to Pasar Baru and I bought blouse material. Luz bought a leather pocketbook.

Sunday, May 18

I had a gassy stomach and diarrhea. I cussed because I had been eating only with Luz, not food from the streets.

We hung around all day and I read a "Time" magazine article about Constantine, a Philippine writer.

Luz told us horror stories about the war. Americans killed Philippines they were supposed to be helping.

We took a taxi to the airport. At 6:30, our Thai plane left.

It was an hour and one half to Singapore.

Friday, May 17

Letter from Dr. Harry

Dear Nita,

I was so glad to receive your pleasant and unexpected letter. It pleased me immensely.

At last you have overcome your desire not to write to me.

From your letter, I gather that your mother and you are having lots of fun. Naturally, you become popular everywhere and your sweet nature wins you friends easily.

I have been missing you terribly. You were stimulating company. Sometimes when I am alone in my bed I think of you and yearn for your warmth. How I wish you could be here again.

These days I am having a lonely time. The strike has been on for over one month now, and there is much hard work. Therefore, there is not much time to make new friends.

Yes, I received your beautiful present. I enjoyed it very much. It was really very sweet of you. But it was not my birthday.

When are you coming back to Delhi? Please do come. I'm inviting you. You can stay as my guest. We'll have a wonderful time together.

Write to me immediately. I'd like to hear from you.

Missing you very much.

Yours, Harry

Nita writes:

Dear Dr. Harry,

Singapore is a contrast to what we have been used to! Amusement parks like Coney Island in New York, exotic foods, many varieties of noodles and weird fish. Everywhere there are wide, smooth streets; millions of new cars; and huge modern department stores. It is overwhelming, even for a second visit.

Djakarta was too hot for comfort, so we worked our way, in uncomfortable trains and even worse buses, to Bali — the traditional Paradise Island.

In only four days, we managed to enjoy a huge brilliant Hindu festival with a hysterical all night long drama, a Barong and Keris dance, a rather bloody cockfight, a visit to some ancient carved caves, and a bunch of new friends. In between all that I went mad looking at the mounds of woodcarvings, paintings and other works of art.

We really weren't as touristy as I sound, though, because our Balinese friends took us everywhere we went.

From your letter you sound as if you're working too hard. What a crime! I've become very " enjoy life now," recently. It seems to me that if you don't take all you can out of life, you'll die without having lived.

I really cannot make a habit of writing. I have enough on my hands with an old aunt, a self-depreciating grandmother and an occasional word to my girlfriend and father.

As to your thoughtful invitation, I'm sorry, but I can only reply:

DEPARTURE
I have just seen you go down
the mountain:
I close the wicker gate in the
setting sun.
The grass will be green again
in the coming spring.
But will the wanderer ever return?
Wang Wei 699-759
Maybe in the occasional Blue Moon I'll write and tell you where in the world
I am.
Your friend, Nita

Friends Mentioned in Chapter 45

Adjati. He was an army man.

Dr. Sockarto. He was an archeologist and our host.

Matti. He was our tour guide for the dance drama.

Paru. He informed us about the Bahai religion on the train.

BARONG DANCE DRAMA

FORTY-SIX

SINGAPORE AGAIN

Sunday, May 18

Dear Wendi and Lori again,

I definitely do not trust Indonesian mail, so I'll send this from Singapore. Therefore, it will probably arrive late. C'est la vie.

I'm glad to be going to Singapore. It gets me one step nearer to my dream of Hong Kong. I'll go wild there.

I've decided to try to take Russian and Swahili at Marlboro next year. Wonder if it is possible?

Always love to you, Nita.

In Singapore we took a bus. An Indian on the bus got us a taxi to San Leong Street and waited with us until the landlady arrived.

We expected our arrival to be different from the last time, when we were hosted by Pan Am with the hotel chosen by them and bus service to the hotel, but this was a nightmare.

We were tired after bus rides and taxis to Jalon Besar and then sitting and waiting, just hanging around.

A girl from Penang spoke to us and offered her room to sit in. The place was filled; there was no room there. The girl told us mostly prostitutes lived there; we would be better off in another place, 92 Syed Alwyn Road.

This room had no window, but it had a fan. It was relatively quiet. It had a light, a mirror and even a table and two chairs. But best of all there was the cleanest squat toilet and a shower. We took two a day. It was such a pleasure.

It is funny, I recalled when we missed having *hot* water. Now we were so happy to have water.

Our Indian friend stayed with us all evening. He carried our heavy bag and hung around until we were settled in. He insisted on our taking a tour, and he paid for it. Now that we knew the bus went to our lodging we felt more confident.

Neither of us slept well. I had an upset stomach all day. Nita was nauseous all night.

I wondered if it was the ice in our drinks.

Monday, May 19

From 12:00 to 3:00 I was in a beauty parlor. No one spoke English. The beautician massaged my head for a long time — what a magnificent massage! The final result was like the style for a model in a magazine. She charged me S$11, which was less than $5.00 U.S. We gave them S$20, but she gave us a brush.

We went to the movies from 4:00 to 7:30 and saw "Dr.No" and "Goldfinger" with Chinese subtitles.

Then we discovered a Chinese festival. A theater was erected in the streets. We watched the sword dance acted and danced by two girls. It was all very dramatic.

One scene with blue lighting had men flying through the air like Peter Pan. It went on for at least four hours. We didn't stay that long.

We met the Indian fellow, who was on his way to us. He brought us a "Reader's Digest" as a gift.

We saw hundreds of food stands.

We had fried noodles in one and noodles in another, and watched fresh donuts being made without holes and ate one. We drank milk with it.

We watched a woman shape soft sugar into lollipops for children. Sometimes she made a straw and inserted it and blew it into a mold. She let children shape the sugar into a boat or a mouse.

We arrived back home around midnight.

Tuesday, May 20

A restaurant manager tried to fleece us. It was interesting to watch him in action double charging us for a meal. So we didn't eat.

We bought milk only. He doubled charged us for that, but we paid our 60 cents and left.

I told him that his attitude and behavior were unusual for us.

Pan Am discouraged us from going to Kuala Lumpur. People were trying to get out of that country, not in. We would have three hours freedom from 9:00 to 12:00 when stores and offices were open. All the rest of the time everyone was indoors, bound by curfew.

The Pan Am representative explained that Singapore was also having trouble with the Bank of China. It did not have enough assets.

We saw a run on the bank at 8:00 p.m.

We walked to Chinatown and discovered Pasar Malam, the night market.

Nita's comment was, "You can't be bored here."

She found many items she wanted, but we ran out of money.

I became weary about 9:00 and returned home to sleep.

I bought a box of preserved plums, but didn't like them. I chewed cuttlefish, the Chinese chewing gum. It had an unusual taste.

The baked goods in Chinatown were eye watering.

Nita discovered the Russian restaurant and we bought 30 cents worth of pastries. They tasted out of this world.

Our dinner was a smorgasbord of unknowns. Bean curd was the item we liked least. Dumplings, meats, cucumber and squid ... it went on and on for 45 cents. We felt like busting. There were two sauces, one brown and one red hot, to dip foods in.

We drank an orange juice and Nita commented, "These people know how to eat. None of the unwholesome soft drinks for them."

Wednesday, May 21

Nita writes:

My letter to Rajan Harry was so distant and impersonal. I really wouldn't blame him if he doesn' answer it. After his warm, human letter, mine is chilling.

I'm satisfied with my memories and the knowledge that he really cared very much for me. And to soothe my conscience, I did break down and write, which should have proven to him that I liked him more than average. If that's any consolation.

After days of looking I bought a Swiss watch today. I purchased a round gold face with a black band with a make I never heard of. Naturally. But I'm thrilled with it!

At Malaysia Hotel we secured our luggage that we had stored from our previous visit.

My massage energized me.

I thought the movie "Joanna" was very good.

Nita went to the chess club at the YMCA.

I straightened out accounts and papers and sorted mailing stuff.

Thursday, May 22

We started sorting and packing at 8:00 a.m.

We went to town and found people uncooperative.

I lost my temper.

"If you buy ... If you buy"... we'll help you.

Finally, I bought wrapping paper and was told post office employees would give us a hand.

Two employees watched us struggle with our packages, doing it ourselves. At the completion they told us at "that" counter they would do it for me.

Singapore post offices were not my favorite.

By 1:00 p.m., five hours later and $10 spent, we finished.

We cashed more money. There was a $7.00 airport tax again.

In the tourist center we met Allan Ward, my age. He traveled two years in interesting island areas.

We went together to the YMCA restaurant for a steak dinner for $.60. Chinese food would have been a smarter choice.

Back home we packed some more and Ganga Dhurhan came and took us to the movie, "Mad Mad World."

It was after midnight when we went to bed.

Nearly all packed.

FORTY-SEVEN

THAILAND

Friday, May 23

We were up at 6. We took a trishaw, loaded with luggage, to the bus stop to get to the airport around 8:15 a.m.

At the bus stop we met Peter Brauny, a German, who had worked as a mechanical engineer in Australia for two years. He guided us to our abode in Bangkok. He was an amiable, pleasant person.

We took Bus 40 to town then switched to Bus 18. Surprisingly, men gave up their seats for us immediately. Thailand was the first place this had happened. A young Thai boy paid our carfare and led us to the post office.

There we found newsworthy letters from Adam and Anne Harrison.

The prices in the tourist section were expensive.

A Bali bone carving worth 50 cents was sold as "ivory" for $5.00.

We decided to get some Thai silk when the price was reduced.

Temple rubbings would make good presents for friends.

Saturday, May 24

In the lobby of the Siam Hotel I met the Feinsteins and others on a Bnai Brith Tour from New York. I socialized with them for a while.

Mrs. Feinstein proudly announced, "We never discuss religion or politics when we travel."

I responded to that. "I always do. That way I learn more about the culture of the countries I visit."

I thought I had had my fill of movies in Singapore. But theaters in Bangkok were air-conditioned and comfortable. What else does one do in 98-degree heat?

Today we saw "Interlude" and the next day we would see "The Fixer."

My Thai friend might call and take us in his car. He was an electrical engineer, going to Japan the following week to study there for four months. I invited him to bring his wife along.

The young man from Tokyo that I met, Sasko, had a Fullbright scholarship from New York University. He enrolled in a course on television; he planned to film the hill tribes in Thailand.

Saturday, May 24

Ruth writes:

Hello Family,

Today is Saturday and we are in Thailand. Yesterday we were in Singapore.

Our stay in Singapore was four days and five nights and we avoided the airport tax by a few hours.

Singapore was a city to perform errands. We did what we came for. My hair was set and beautifully styled. I even received a head massage.

Our big job was mailing four packages and two packages of books at the cost of $10 postage. It took us five hours to sort, pack, obtain all the materials and wrap them.

There was less than $10 worth of goods in each package. Customs won't believe us, but it is true.

One must visualize Nita in action. She knows how to bargain. She bought her new watch to replace the one stolen in Nairobi.

We chose JAL airline because of their supplies in the toilets, soap, perfume and sanitary napkins. Nita eats two of their meals each trip.

We have a choice of 22 airlines that fly to Hong Kong. Our decision was Thai because we could get our dinner on the only evening flight.

Love, Ruth/Mom

Arriving at 9:00 p.m. in Bangkok presented lodging problems. We knew a place where we could sleep.

In Singapore we met Peter, who shared our taxi to the airport. When we arrived in Bangkok, he guided us to the Starlight Hotel, with two beds and air-conditioning, all for $1.00 per person per night. It was good lodging, but of course no one spoke English.

We received six letters. Several made us laugh.

We went to the Oriental hotel and used their Olympic pool, as per instructions from friends.

I located the weekend market. Nita would go crazy when she saw it. I didn't believe there were still fruits we hadn't tasted or goods we didn't recognize. The fragrance of fresh baked goods, frying food, roasted shiny-orange ducks, tiny birds and eggs attracted us in the many stalls along the streets and inside the market. We ate our 100-year-old eggs.

By our second day in Bangkok, we were getting around beautifully. We lived in an air-conditioned room for $1.00 a night. We swam in the Oriental Hotel pool.

We socialized and drank iced tea in the Royal Hotel, and I dipped in the hotel pool with my clothes on.

Nita socialized with a young man who invited us back tomorrow to swim and go to dinner in Chinatown with him.

323

We left the hotel at 8:45. As we walked to the corner, my handbag was snatched from my hand. The boy ran down the dark and deserted street. Nita chased after him and screamed and screamed, "It doesn't have any money in it. Please give it back."

A taxi drove up the street and caught up to the boy, but he jumped into the canal. He had a boat waiting for him there. He dropped the handbag into the boat.

By the time I lumbered to the end of the street and discovered it was a dead end with the canal, I saw Nita sitting on the steps crying.

I asked, "Do you have the pocketbook?"

"No, he still has it. He escaped."

He was too quick for us. Nita worried that our Pan Am tickets, passport and wallet were in it, but I had emptied all that out in the morning and left it in my suitcase.

There was much dialogue across the canal. A crowd formed on each side.

Finally a boat rowed across for us and we both entered. The rower talked while the people on the shack side held tight to "our man."

The handbag was handed to me. We rowed back to the other side and I opened it. Water poured out.

All those letters I had written were sopping wet. All the maps and travel folders were dripping.

A book borrowed from Clarence, our precious "Asian Stories" by Mentor Press, excellent reading, was now a wet glob.

I took my camera from its case. It rattled. He must have dropped it from the height at the top of the stairs to the canal. Besides water in between all the lenses, he broke all the focusing and automatic exposure parts. Then I cried, my new camera smashed to bits.

The photos of my hair in the sophisticated style were ruined.

An American, Charlie Sullivan, an Army man and lawyer who speaks Thai, appeared on the scene.

The Thai people begged us to prosecute. That boy had caused trouble before and a car of policemen had driven down the block to pick him up.

O.K., we agreed.

But first we had to find Nita's shoes. When she started to run she threw off her rubber clackies and ran barefoot. We located them and Charlie accompanied us to the police station.

The commander on hand wrote three reports of the case. I signed three duplicate statements. Charlie kept reading the Thai language to be sure I wasn't admitting to something else. The whole incident took about two hours.

The 18-year-old boy would spend two years in prison for this crime. Charlie begged for mercy for the kid. I wanted to ask the kid why he dragged the purse through the water. Did he know he was in all this trouble for 15 baht? 20 baht is $1.00 and that was all the money I had with me.

Charlie wrote up the statement for my insurance company. A full and accurate statement was signed by the police commander and on police stationary.

We arrived home around 11:30 p.m. in pouring rain and with the emotional impact of the evening hitting us full force.

Nita was dead tired. When we went into the Grand Hotel it was to find someone who spoke English and could guide us to an eating place. We didn't have any meals all day, just milk and snacks.

Nita hurt her foot running and continued limping for a day or so.

I would have to buy post cards and slides of the places we saw now and buy a new camera in Hong Kong. I liked my new Voitlander. Why did it have to happen?

Sunday, May 25

I typed my diary and letters at the Grand Hotel. We made friends with Swasd and Narong, who were employees. They encouraged us to use the swimming pools in the hotels. After we had a swim, our newest friends drove us to Chinatown for a meal.

Monday, May 26

We rose at 6:00 a.m. and later met Swasd and Narong. They were determined that we should see the countryside and be away from the city. They hired a boat and we had a canal ride to Thon-buri and Non-a-buri, 15 miles away. It was a wonderful morning.

In the afternoon, we hauled our blankets and other useless items to second-hand shops to sell them.

Back at the Grand Hotel we had a swim

Finally, we saw Thai dancing and heard singing.

We tasted fresh lychee nuts, which look like rambutans, but the flesh is very white.

Ruth writes:

Dearest Lori,

HAPPY BIRTHDAY ! SWEET SIXTEEN !

We have just enjoyed the greatest morning and we would like to share it with you. Bangkok is a happy city for us. Nita met Swasd and Narong who work in Grand Hotel. As a result we were taken out to Chinatown in Bangkok last night.

We walked past the huge movie posters depicting Chinese swordsmen with blood oozing from them.

We rode along a canal. On both sides were eating-places with interesting Chinese-style foods. We sampled various dishes.

We told the boys we wanted to get up early and see the Floating Markets. Tourists are only taken on expensive tours. The canal tour costs over seven dollars.

We were together a little after 7:30 a.m.

We got into another boat with Swasd and Narong and people stared at us, be-

cause no tourists ever go along this canal. It is the passageway the farmers travel into the floating market.

Houses were built on piles and one boy was bouncing on a mattress; another child was standing on his head. Several were in the water swimming. People were bathing and washing clothes in the canal.

The houses were built of teakwood—very expensive and built to last 100 years. The people appeared content and relaxed.

The floating market is exactly that. Many small boats congregate in this area loaded with their own produce. It is everything from fresh produce to fresh baked products.

Boats with people selling prepared foods, such as you buy in restaurants, stopped at various houses. There were other boats on which people brought food to sell to the shops along the canal. All shops had steps leading into the water.

We left Bangkok and were in Thonburi. (Buri means town.) Nita started her search for "A hat for my sister, Lori, who loves hats."

Nita bargained and paid more than the ones she had priced in Bangkok with the assurance that this one was superior and better quality work.

We took a bus to Non-buri. By now we were 15 miles from Bangkok, with delightful people and scenery to watch.

We took another bus back to Grand Hotel where we took another swim. Then I did some typing and Nita went home to catch up on her sleep.

Tonight, the boys will take us to the movies.

I want to see "Road Show." It is a Thai picture about two dancers.

The people were the most gentle, polite, and kindly of our whole trip. On buses they gave us seats. They were also quiet. On the bus I noticed no noise, no chatter of school children. Ninety four percent were Buddhists.

People were poor here. We have seen shanty towns and slum areas. But less begging exists than in other big cities where tourists abide. I also noticed how healthy the people were. Of course, Nita and I are giants among them. They wear size 3 and 4 and the "fat" ones wear size 5 dresses. We were taller than they were. But they radiate health. They have good posture and beautiful feminine bodies. The style in Bangkok was mostly Western dress, but we expect to see more sarongs up-country.

Bangkok was a city of tourist areas. However, with looking, we find Thai areas and the Chinese areas where we enjoy browsing in the markets, sampling the foods and bargaining for small items. We travel to Chiang Mai 600 miles away tomorrow.

We show your photo to everyone and everyone admires it.

Love you, Mom

Tuesday, May 27

We picked up a letter from Comfort and Robinson in London.

It made us feel guilty because we had not written to them. They were unusual people.

I sent off another $4.00 worth of letters. Am I foolish to do so?

Pan Am couldn't change the date of our flight to the next day. All flights were booked. So our flight remained Monday, June 9.

I tried to do something about the camera. What? The guarantee didn't cover water damage. I was unhappy about the damaged film.

I collected my knapsack and met Nita at 3:30 p.m.

While we waited for the window to open at the railroad station, we noticed a 12:00 noon train to Chiang Mai for the next day. Nita booked tickets for it.

We called the Starlight and reserved rooms for the night

Then we went to the film, "The Fixer" for the 7:00 p.m. show.

Back at the Starlight, the desk clerk never received our message, so he gave us an Army man's reservation. It was a lovely room.

We were glad to be at this hotel.

Wednesday, May 28

I was very upset to have no camera.

Nita said, "I like Thailand. I wouldn't mind living here."

It was a clean city! The floors of the railroad station were not strewn with trash because garbage pails were placed everywhere. People did not throw papers on the street. Yet there were no signs to keep the city clean (As in Singapore and New York, with fines for littering).

People were quiet. They were not loud and boisterous on buses. There was a tranquility about them. They had what they wanted from their own culture, but they seemed to absorb western dress and adapt it for themselves. It was a westernized city — the streets, the stores, the movie houses, but it all was new and nicer than the ones we had.

Tourism was a fact now. There were many hotels. The tour agencies planned expensive tours and only listed expensive hotels. No one told tourists about the two baht (ten cents) canal boat ride for ten miles past the floating gardens.

I was angry about the train agent who tried to sell us the second class $7.50 ticket and told me about the hard wooden seats in third class. I was sitting in a third class coach now on very comfortable cushioned seats. Four cars had wooden benches, but no one was sitting in them yet.

There was no begging on trains. People ate and drank at their seats or in the dining car. But the floor was clean at the end of our 17-hour trip. I repeat, these were a clean people.

Thursday, May 29

In Indonesia, many people tried to start a conversation with us. They were friendly people.

In Thailand, one young man who was a pre-med student sat down next to us. We chatted for a while. When the train arrived at 6:00 a.m., he took us in a cab so we could check out three different hotels.

He explained about the celebration for the rebirth of the Buddha and the pilgrimage up the mountain. We relaxed and read and mostly slept in our Thai Charong Hotel room from 7:30 a.m. until 1:30 p.m.

In the tearoom I met a family and a German agriculture man who was a dairy expert. The German government sent him here over two years ago. He liked it and recommended it.

He told me they needed teachers at the American school, especial the third and fourth years. He said I should see the principal, Mrs. Baldwin, on Monday, and also the U.S. Consul.

We switched to the Prince Hotel. I got a room for 40 Baht.

It was a luxurious place. I found Nita, who was resting, and brought her to our newest dwelling place.

Nita writes:
May 29
Dear Grandma,
We are in Chiang Mai, about 600 miles north of Bangkok. We arrived at 6 a.m. after a 17-hour train ride. It has been raining constantly. We are very glad because the past few days in Bangkok have been murderously hot and this rain is soothing.

Bangkok was everything we could want. The people were physically beautiful, extremely friendly and helpful. The men were absolute gentlemen; even in the most crowded buses they always us gave us a seat.

We made friends with two boys who work at the Grand Hotel, Swasp and Narong.

Narong is Chinese and the boys took us all around Chinatown and to a very hidden restaurant that was a part of a compound of restaurants, all of them in the open air. We had a windpipe and lung soup of some animal that was very good and some fish balls dipped in salad dressing. We enjoyed our meal.

The next morning very early, they took us in a taxi-boat for a two-hour ride along the canal (klong) to the section where only Thais go. The scenery was breathtaking along the canal.

The water roadways were crowded with small flat boats, high rounded boats, broad houseboats and other long flat swift taxi boats like ours.

Along the sides of the river were houses on stilts, each of them unique. Many of the oldest houses were made entirely of teakwood; because of their age they were faded. The most wonderful buildings were the temples, glittering golden and jade with fire looking dragon heads sticking out of the roof. We had a marvelous morning.

Friday, May 30

We took a bus and shopped for food. Our room had a stove.

We bought Thai cotton material and had a dress made for me. I was happy about it.

So this was Monsoon season. Rain and more rain.

On our arrival in Chiang Mai we met two men who lived on the Army base. Their names were Wayne and Mike. They invited us to their home. We made an arrangement. Nita and I would do the cooking and housekeeping in exchange for our room and board.

Wayne played the match game with Nita.

Afterwards he slept all evening, depressed, because he was insecure about his job. The flight he planned to take today was rained out. He wanted to spend the weekend with his brother.

We enjoyed the evening playing cards with Mike, his roommate.

Nita and I fought the stove all day. There was not enough gas to light the oven. We baked a cake, but no Pillsbury prizewinner. It tasted better than it looked.

Sunday, June 1

Friends of the men, Anne and Milly Evans, hospital workers, arrived for the pancake breakfast Wayne promised them. Nita prepared it.

We went to town with Milly and bought Thai silk for our dresses. I tried on my new dress; it was all wrong. It looked and felt like a potato sack with no shape.

I visited Prasert, a teacher, in the International School service, who proved to be interesting. Cornell University published the chronicle that Mr. Prasert translated.

Anne brought us to her home. We admired her decor and her wardrobe. The two had lived in Thailand for five years and loved it. Millie had a wardrobe the likes of which I had never seen. She had 50 pairs of shoes, each covered in Thai silk to match her dresses. Tailoring was so cheap that it was worth it to get clothes that way.

Nita left Anne's house and meandered, exploring the town.

So I was alone with Mike and we played cards for entertainment.

Nita returned and sat in the living room, quietly reading.

Then Mike and Nita took a walk together.

This was the first time in a long time that we were settled among Americans and speaking English.

Monday, June 2

As the German suggested, early in the morning I went to the American school and met Miss Baldwin, the principal, and spent time in Miss Franklin's class. The class listened as I related travel stories for an hour. In the higher grades I talked about the drug scene as I witnessed it. Then we played geography games.

The teachers in the faculty room invited me to join them for lunch.

Then it was off to the woman who made my dress. I was happy with the color of the dress, but not the shape. I asked the dressmaker to alter it to look more appealing on me.

Then I spent an hour in the USIS library. It had a fund of information regarding the country.

Nita happily played chess with Mike.

I had lunch with Mr. and Mrs. Paul and Elaine Lewis. What full, busy lives they had. They had two sons, who were learning the Thai language and doing mission work.

They were also teaching anthropology at the university and wrote dictionaries and translated hymn books. They studied the Akha tribe and Meau tribe, and they published a book with photos that was translated into German. They edited a combined AKHA and English dictionary. Cornell published it.

The most recent work was The New Testament written in AKHA language in 1968 by Paul Lewis.

Mrs. Lewis drove me to Prasert's home. He took us out to dinner. His wife, Bangor, had been a dressmaker for 16 years. Siri, their son, was with us.

Prasert invited me to stay in his home.

I had a satisfied night's sleep, one of the best so far.

Nita writes:

June 3

Dear Wendy,

Sorry for the long gap. We have been living in Chiang-Mai all this time, at the "Bungalo Workeow" with the Air Force.

We were living in a comfortable, large house of Mike and Wayne, two really nice men. The arrangement was we cook for them and in exchange have free room, board, and entertainment. Everyone was American around here except Papasan, the owner and general handyman of the compound.

Mommy and I have been relaxing, reading, listening to music, talking and playing card games. It's a wonderful break.

We also went to visit the Wat (temple) high on the mountain overlooking Chiang Mai

Mommy had a dress made of lovely Thai cotton, her second dress in eleven months, but it didn't turnout to please us.

We will probably be leaving Chiang Mai soon.

We will be in Hong Kong by June 10; after that our next address is GPO in Tokyo, Japan. We are having a wonderful time, but miss you.

Affectionately, Nita

June 4

Dear Daddy, Wendi, Lori and David,

I am at Chiang Mai at an American Air Force Base and they charge only minimal postage. We have been living here for almost a week now, resting, relaxing and trying to adjust to American living again. It isn't easy.

Today Mommy came back from an excursion to one of the Thai hill tribes. She brought some lovely hand-woven material for dresses, but I didn't find out much more.

We were introduced to Ajun (teacher) Prasert, a Thai professor, over 80-years-old. He was an absolutely fascinating character. In Berkley University he lectured on English philosophy and anthropology for a number of years as well as on other campuses.

Now he was in semi-retirement, only teaching at Chiang Mai University. He teaches the sciences, philosophy, anthropology and psychology in the university. He was building his own stereo and hi-fi equipment. He was making a detailed study of birdcalls, after having built his own reflector and recording devises. His home was a jumbled museum with a gem in every crack. Books were piled high all over every room.

Prasert lived 15 years in New York in the 1920s. He was married to a Jewish American woman for 8 years. What a home! Mostly library. An intellectual, intelligent human being.

Love to all of you, Nita

Wednesday, June 4

Siri arrived and took us to Lampuri. We entered the Wat and temple grounds. The Monk's school and museum had a large gong.

We saw Buddha's footprints and a drum that was sky-high and a carriage for the back of elephants and spears for fighting while on the elephant's back.

The young women in Chiang Mai were the most beautiful. Many of them were contestants in beauty contests and won.

Then Mike came home. Wayne called. He reported that five men would arrive from Taklee Army base and would need our beds. Nita and I had to leave.

We packed in the most uncomfortable, unceremonious way. And left.

Papason drove us to Anne's home, where we hoped to spend the night.

Anne said, "no room." She had Dr. Cavell, a pediatrician, for the night. We left Anne's house not very impressed with her American hospitality.

Papason drove us and we found Prasert and Siri at home. We told them that we were evicted from our local lodging. They welcomed us and invited us to stay in their home. Nita was in the guest room and I slept on the couch.

Ruth writes:
Dearest Wendi,
HAPPY BIRTHDAY!
Usually when trouble strikes an area Nita and I enter it to find out about it.

Perhaps you have read about the riots in Malaysia? Kuala Lumpur is the capital and as a result of the riots curfews have been inflicted. Now after a week they are opening up the offices and shops for three hours every morning.

If we did go there we would be house bound for the rest of the day and night. It doesn't sound like fun. So we decided to skip Malaysia.

On Friday, we take Japanese Air Lines (JAL) to Bangkok. That is an exotic spot and should be a source of great fun and adventure for us. We'll spend two to three weeks there because we cut short this part of our trip.

It was tough to pull ourselves away from Bali. We didn't begin to do it justice. Bali festivals and dances and art were enticing.

We keep thinking about losing the weight we have gained, but we haven't come to any country where the food is unappealing to us. Fascinating new taste thrills await us daily.

We rescheduled our plane ticket to take us all the way back to New York.

What are your summer plans?

Weeks have passed since I began his letter. There is a special type of male who attaches himself to us periodically. He must get kicks out of knowing us, but he is dull and even kills our sparkling personality and conversational ability.

I wrote to Lori about our day in Bangkok. What a difference. People can make or break the trip for us.

Swasd and Narong were delightful boys of 22 and 23. Narong was working in the hotel to support his four sisters.

His mother died 20 years ago. His father remarried and he died of a heart attack last year. So Narong takes over now.

They were gentlemen and well-mannered. Working in a big hotel does western-ize people; it was easy to talk with these men. But they seem to feel and know what we will like and enjoy and plan it out among themselves and we just go along with them.

How about Hong Kong? What would you like from there? I have to buy new cameras. Nita plans to buy Hong Kong out. I told her I'll cash in her plane ticket and she can live amidst that wealth of goods. You have to know how long she has waited and waited to get to Hong Kong. It is a shopper's paradise with bargaining for her, I hope.

Love, Mom

Thursday, June 5

After deep discussions, Prasert drove us to the station at 10:00 a.m. It was a two-hour wait for the train. Nita bought food for our 17-hour trip from Chiang Mai back to Bangkok, Thailand.

On the train Nita became involved conversationally with Chargoen. They argued politics. He was in teacher training school to become an English teacher. They played rummy.

Six hours later, Nita learned he was a champion rummy player. When she won a round it was because he "helped" her. They continued to play because it was a challenge to her. He continually was the winner.

We ate chicken and tasted lotus bud seeds. I walked through the train, held babies, and the conductor of the train fed me rambutans, sticky rice and tea.

I was invited to share dinner with the nine trainmen in the baggage car.

The conductor spoke English. He and another "youngster" claimed 60 years. It was hard to believe, as they had black hair and smooth skin. He let me sleep in second-class chairs.

Friday, June 6

Our train arrived in Bangkok at 6:00 a.m.

We had a hard time locating a bus home to the Starlight Hotel. We were given a room with bath and immediately conked out.

I put our records in order and let Nita sleep until 1:30.

Saturday, June 7

The temple rubbings Nita chose were artistic. We mailed them to California to give as gifts. I mailed Clarence his books and sent home pamphlets and a ballet dictionary for Lori.

I telephoned Tours Express as directed by Prasert, and Mr. Aman Pavel came to us.

He took Nita and me to a Thai restaurant in Bangkok. It was the only posh one we had been in. We enjoyed bowling and he was good. He got many strikes.

Nita renewed her friendship with Narong, the employee in the Grand Hotel. He brought her to Chinatown with his stepsister.

We drove back to Starlight Hotel and planned the next day.

Sunday, June 8

Early in the morning I stopped a car and asked directions to Pattayana Beach. The family's name was Crumley. The wife told me about the bus, but the husband suggested they were going to near there and I could join them.

I told stories of our trip to amuse them much of the day. It certainly livened up the day. They sat and sat and did nothing. I, at least, enjoyed the water and went swimming in Pattayana Beach.

Mr. Crumley was an ex-Air Force man and still worked for the Air Force. He recalled stories of his travels. Addie was his second wife. His first wife, a Panamanian woman, ran off with another man a few years ago.

Addie was Filipino and in her 20s. He had a good deal. She was an excellent housekeeper.

Nita writes:

Sunday, June 8
This is the last entry in this journal before I mail it.
I've loved traveling. Every minute was a new experience. My senses seem more acute. I was aware that things were happening to me that would probably never happen again.

I've the taste of vast popularity, of being considered beautiful, of feeling beautiful. Never again will complete strangers walk up to me, their eyes wide open with admiration, exclaim, "Oh, you're so beautiful!"

Soon I must return to the realities of America. Maybe I will retain some of my newly acquired flirtatiousness and poise? Maybe all of my discovered self-confidence will not disappear. I can only hope.

This past month, for the first time all trip, I have been looking forward to going home.

More and more I want to sit in a cool hotel lobby and read, rather than gain knowledge of the town.

I'm beginning to think, "Oh, I've done this already. I've seen coral gardens, temples, museums, shopping districts, markets and magnificent scenery. What is left?"

This feeling comes infrequently and I don't like it, because I am aware that we are reaching a wonderful part of the world.

I don't think anyone will ever realize what has happened to me this past year. I don't realize it myself yet. But I want to keep the freshness of my experience intact.

I think Mommy needs to go home sooner also. She doesn't have quite as much energy lately. But she, of course, would never let on.

Monday, June 9

Nita was still frustrated about getting her package mailed. It was too heavy to mail by a hair's breath.

Paul drove Nita to the airport. We stopped on the way and bowled. I couldn't concentrate on the game was anxious to get to the plane.

Tuesday, June 10

Errands for a change: Hair done in a beauty parlor and bought a zipper for my dress. Watch strap fixed. Cuticle scissors oiled and sharpened.

Chose material for a custom made dress.

Dress fitting. The red dress was altered and I was happy with it.

I was shot in the arm against Cholera in the clinic.

At the ear clinic I was told to do nothing. That cost me $5.00.

Paul and I talked. He had hopes for me to make something of myself.

Paul said, "You should write political ideas as well as your travels."

He took me to an Indian song recital.

Wednesday, June 11

Nita had taken the plane on June 9 to Hong Kong. I was leaving June 1. I took a motorbike ride to the bus and then the bus to Wat Po.

It took one half hour to find Amara at the museum. I was sorry she arrived. It was a miserable morning for me. She walked me in the hot sun for four hours. We saw Wat Po and the palace, then the zoo.

Amara wasn't satisfied with one restaurant and walked me to a more expensive one.

She ordered an extra dish, claiming she was still hungry. I couldn't see how she could be. I was full with a delicious dinner of Dim Sum, each item served in bamboo baskets.

The Jasmine tea was flavorful. But I did not plan to eat, knowing I was going to have dinner on the plane.

Amara did not fulfill my friendship desires.

I was half an hour late and nearly a wreck.

The day didn't improve. I had errands to do from 1:30 to 4:00 p.m.

I barely had time to check out of the hotel and race to the airport.

Paul wanted me to turn back and spend another day with him. He had spent about $100 on me. Why??

It was all business. He was interested in all the contacts I could give him in New York for his export business. He proved to be a good friend. He was helpful throughout our time in Bangkok. He had charisma and I liked him a lot.

He apologized for not being the romantic soul, while he was driving me to the airport.

At Bangkok airport I slipped into the passenger's waiting room. Ten minutes were left before flying time to Hong Kong.

My camera was stolen, thrown into a canal, so no photos.

Friends Mentioned in Chapter 47

Charlie Sullivan. He was an American in charge of the stolen camera.

Swasd and Narong Sutawasin. They were Grand Hotel workers. They took us on tours.

Mike and Wayne. They were U.S. Air Force. We lived in their home and kept house for them.

Ajan Prasert Choorat. He was in his 70s, a teacher. His house was on stilts.

Pauline and Elaine Lewis. They were Baptist missionaries. They taught at the International School.

Miss Baldwin. She was a principal.

Miss Franklin. I taught in her class.

Nsarinder Singh Aman Paul. He was an importer and exporter.

Amara Lepsprasopsook. She took me to museums and restaurants.

FORTY-EIGHT

MACAU

Ebrahim was told to go to Estoril Hotel. I looked it up and it was the most expensive. I begged to go to Belle Vista at half the price. But "No," it must be his way. We took a taxi and he overpaid.

The room décor was lovely; I can't complain. At $10.00 a day, it should have been. He insisted we eat in the hotel restaurant instead of exploring the town.

We had the Angeles special — African Chicken and spiced steak, both gourmet. He ate with a fork and knife in an antiseptic manner and left most of his food on his plate. I emptied my platter. He conversed all during the meal and time passed quickly.

He was told nightclub entertainment was at midnight. We entered the casino, but he let me know he was dead set against it.

"Gambling is a sickness," he insisted.

So I never put a coin in a machine. I watched two men collect 50 coins in jackpots. I cruised around.

Around 1:00 a.m. we retired, each to his or her own bed. His parents planted the "dirtiness" of sex in his mind. He wore his undershirt and shorts under his pajamas.

Thursday, June 19

I woke to a dark day. Luckily I had slept later than usual. It was raining. I suggested we go out. He insisted on eating breakfast in the hotel. We sat at the table for more than two hours while he told me the history of his family and his life. His brother nearly gambled away the family fortune. He would have made a good lawyer and I was sorry for him that he wasn't one.

I repeated "Let's take a bus ride and see the town."

"I won't go out in the rain." He was adamant.

We hung around in the casino again. Kids were swimming in a pool in the rain. I wished that I had my bathing suit.

He bought two tickets for the hydrofoil at 2:00 p.m. and I announced I wasn't going with him. He returned my ticket. He paid the hotel bill, and I offered to pay half but he wouldn't take it. Who is the devil who played with my fate?

Exit Ebrahim.

I said goodbye and walked away.

I took a bus as I planned. Sheridan and Louise got on the bus. Sheridan moved into the seat next to me. She said she was going to an English lesson and asked if I would help her with her homework.

Julia Tam's house was our first stop. She did beading in her spare time. All those sequins on fancy clothes were sewn, one at a time, by hand. Julia was making a white dress. I put on my pink dress and the girls hemmed it. I put on my nightgown and Sheri cut down the neck and the under arms to make it roomier and more comfortable for me. We left after I was invited to sleep there.

We went to Louise's home upstairs. Everyone I met was beading. The girls were studying English and I made two bead flowers. It took me ages and I earned 16 HK cents.

Louise and Sheri gave me a tour of the town and showed me the Buddhist temple and garden. The church looked impressive from the front, but it was a shell with nothing behind it. Sheri took me to her home, where we walked through a railroad-type flat. The people lived in what would be the hall. Three families were eating at different tables. Her mother and sister prepared dinner. It was The Dragon Day festival and a feast was served. I enjoyed the excellent cooking. Sheri took me to the factory where I saw more beadwork. Finally, we took a bus back to Julia's home.

Paul, Julia's husband, was a taxi tour driver, only for Westerners. Company arrived and I retired. They asked me to stay over the weekend or for another month.

Friday, June 20

I drove to school with Julia. Then I went back in a cab to Paul and we waited around until he drove to work. I spent most of the morning with him, driving back and forth to the pier, watching hydrofoils come in. There was very little tourist trade for him. A union organized the taxi system.

Chinese speaking drivers could only take the Hong Kong people. English speaking drivers could only take the Westerners.

There was a set rotating system and the drivers could not get out of order.

When the driver got a customer that was it. He could not get out of line. Even if it didn't pan out, like ours didn't.

Our American was a drippy guy who didn't like Taipei.

"Nothing to see there," he said.

He wouldn't go on the tour and yet claimed he would walk to see the town, but planned only to stay for two hours before his trip back. He was the worst kind of tourist. Paul drove him to an expensive restaurant. Paul gave up and drove us home for lunch at 2:00.

Paul took me on a personal tour of the island. I saw the gate at the Chinese border.

He showed me where to buy jade.

I had lunch with Julia and Paul. Then Paul left for work. Julia worked on her beadwork and I talked with her. I found out she earns 250$HK or about $60.00 a month teaching physics and chemistry. She pays 160$HK for the rent. She rents out rooms and does beadwork for extra money.

She had a year-old-baby living with her mother in Mainland China. Her parents were in Djakarta and heard such wonderful things about China they went there to live. Now they were sorry. I learned life there was very regimented. Many meetings constitute the main recreation. People conserve electricity and rise at dawn and go to bed at dusk. They grow food, but they export a great deal of it for money, especially to Hong Kong and Macau. Then they do not have enough to feed their own people.

Julia took me to a market and we bought meat and eggs. After we dropped the groceries off at home we went to the factory to find Sheri. She was in her home studying for the night's examination. Julia left and I stayed with Sheri until it was time to go to the hydrofoil.

Friends Mentioned in Chapter 48

Paul Tam. He was a tour taxi driver who showed me around Macau.

Julia Tam. She was chemistry teacher who also did bead work.

Sheridan Poon Shri. She spoke to me on the bus. She asked me to help her with her English homework.

Louise Lamu Put Mei.

RUTH AND SHERIDAN POON

LOUISE LAMU PUT MEI
AND SHERIDAN POON.

JULIA TAM,CHEMISTRY
TEACHER. I WAS A GUEST IN
HER HOME

FORTY-NINE

HONG KONG

Tuesday, June 11
Lufthansa offered us a ride in a large, empty plane.

I ate, read and rested and I spoke to no one.

Over the loud speaker at Hong Kong airport came an announcement for me to pick up a message from Nita.

To Ruth Kaufman
From Nita.
I am staying at Chungking Mansions Guest House "B" Block 9th floor. Bus No. 9 from the airport takes you there. Costs 10$HK per night.
Before you come to me, try others at B & C blocks. Doubt if you'll get a cheaper one.
Love, Nita

I arrived by 11:30 p.m.

It was 1:00 a.m. and Nita wasn't here yet. Where was she? The room was stifling. There was no fan nor air-conditioner. Cheap, yes. 10 HK $ = $1.50.

Nita was seeing a midnight movie with Eddie.

She sauntered in at 3:30 a.m. and we talked until 5:00 a.m.

Thursday, June 12
At the GPO I picked up letters. There was an extra good one from Nicholas about his travel experiences, and a letter from Mom.

Ruth writes:
Thursday, June 12
Dear Mother,
I am in the Mandarin Hotel in the baggage room typing letters. Hilton Hotel refused to lend me a typewriter. They offered to rent me a room, then they would rent me a typewriter

Nita discovered the chess club and Ron, an Englishman, and she was spending her evenings there.

Hong Kong was a little different from what I expected.

I thought hawkers would grab me.

We bought material in Thailand and a dressmaker Nita met was sewing it into clothes for us. I have traveled with only two dresses for four months. I gave a young girl in Goa two of my dresses because she liked them. I am looking for a replacement for my stolen-broken camera.

We keep busy.

Ear infections are common ailments in this part of the world. Nita went to a doctor in Ceylon and then Djakarta. She had bacteria behind a wax clot.

The doctor in Mombasa told me to keep my ear lubricated with oil and it would prevent the wax build up we get as we travel in airplanes. In Bangkok, my ear stopped up and the doctor told me not to put oil in my ear. Who to believe? My ears were cleaned out this week.

I also took another a cholera shot. Our last one on January 10 in Delhi expires in six months.

Our health is remarkable. We were careful to drink bottled water. However, the ice probably was scooped out of the canals. Each time we drink the iced drinks we toast, "Here's poison for you." You don't know heat — Bombay, Mombasa, Djakarta, Bangkok, and now the hot, humid Hong Kong.

I thought I would work on the slides and edit them into short talks. Then you could arrange an evening with friends of yours who would be interested.

You realize that I have spoken before several audiences already. I talked to a college class in Bombay, in New Delhi, Mombasa, and again in Chiang Mai, Thailand. I spent two days in the International School in the sixth grade classroom. I am able to speak for an hour just giving an outline of where we have been.

For your delicate sensitivities I can give a sober, sedate, dignified talk. The teachers asked me to return, so it couldn't be too bad.

Our Belgian artist friend, Nicholas, who borrowed $50.00 for plane fare in February, returned the money to us this week in Hong Kong. People prove honest and good in their relationship with us.

Our awareness that these are the last few months and the days fly by. We have until the end of June in Hong Kong, then Japan for July and part of August. We have six addresses of people we met en route.

Love, Ruth

June 12, 1969
Dear Captain Keith,

I know that I was only a tag-a-long to fill in a few dreary hours with your buoyant companionship. As much as possible I tried to stay in the background so you and Nita could form your own relationship.

I know that Nita told you she wouldn't write. I think you deserve better treatment than that, considering what you did for us for twelve days aboard your ship. Therefore, I am writing, knowing you would prefer a letter from her.

Did you ever hear about the original letter I sent the shipping company? The one in which I praised you? I sent the money they laid out for our visas in that letter. Did they ever receive it?

I sent a second letter of thanks also. I let them know when we received the health forms. Those health certificates arrived the very last day we spent in Ceylon. It was good timing.

More about our trip. We continue to manage to live with other people regardless of what country they live in or which language they speak.

Now Nita can spend time in her dream city, Hong Kong, now that we have arrived here.

We hope you continue in good health and good spirits. If we can be of service to you, please do not hesitate to ask anything of us.

When do you come into New York Harbor again so we can meet?

Again, sincere thanks to you. Every Humperdink melody is a constant reminder of the happy hours we spent in your cabin.

Sincerely, Ruth

Friday, June 13

Eddie took us 22 miles into New Territories to a beach. We spent the day there. Nita got painfully sunburned.

Very few people inhabited the beach, with its clean water in the morning at high tide. There were no sand flies or insects, so we could rest in comfort. We pulled a giant jellyfish out of the water on to the float to inspect it.

Eddie was a perceptive, bright man of 31, quick on the uptake. He had lived in Spain and spent five years in England. He liked Nita. He was pleasant company.

Saturday, June 14

I cashed Nicholas' money order for $51.00. I bought Lori a watch and Nita bought a dress and a pair of shoes.

I befriended Florence in the President Hotel. We went together to the Park Hotel and at the bar lounge socialized with Vietnam GIs. Florence introduced me to Chuck Recor. We saw the 1:00 a.m. show in a Chinese nightclub. At 3:00 a.m. we tried the locked door of our guesthouse in Chung King Mansions. Nita had the key.

So Chuck invited me to sleep in the second bed in his room in President Hotel. 7:00 a.m. Music woke us after four hours of sleep.

Sunday, June 15

Florence introduced us to her daughter, Doris, a chorus girl in a solo act. We spent the evening with Doris, whose stage name was Marquette Diamond. Both mother and daughter were depressed. They hated Chinese food and the people in Hong Kong.

"Everything is more comfortable and better in the United States," they kept saying.

Ebrahim came by and said, "You're Nita's mother," and we went to a movie together. He had become friends with Nita before I arrived.

Monday, June 16

Nita and I went our separate ways, engaging in identical activities.

We looked for material and a tailor. She found Sammy, a dressmaker, and had a pantsuit made.

I located a tailor in a dress shop that had dresses for me. I bought four; all looked good. They were $6.00 and $7.00 a dress. Nita admired the dress choices I made.

In the evening we went with Ebrahim to the Rex Theater and enjoyed, "How Sweet It is." Ebrahim was born in Aden. He was running an export business, which was supporting his mother, 11 brothers and two sisters.

He was unhappy about having to quit his Master's degree studies in Bombay. When his father died he had to take over the business.

He was depressed and needed bolstering up. He was a serious young man with no sense of humor at all. He was unhappy in Hong Kong. He did have friends here. He spoke Urdu, Gjudiat, Hindi, Arabic and English. He was bright, intelligent and apparently capable in business.

He told me a little about his family. His two sisters married multimillionaires and lived in Ceylon.

His father remarried and then died. He missed him. Of all the children, both parents loved him best.

Two stepbrothers gave him a squeeze play about shares in the business after his father died. He borrowed money and paid them off, yet he was still supporting them.

Tuesday, June 17

Nita bought two housedresses for $1.00. She sewed darts and pleats and cut the neck lower and they looked good. She was a capable seamstress.

I obtained the visa for Macao, but had misgivings about going with Ebrahim. He planned to leave in the afternoon instead of the morning, then he was anxious to race back. He bought hydrofoil tickets for the return trip.

Wednesday June 18

I brought my photos and Pan Am ticket to get the Taiwan visa.

I lunched with Nita. Then I went to Mytravel and Lloyds International to investigate charter flights.

I learned they were available only in summer. Philippine airlines ran a flight for $350.00 instead of the $465.00 from Hong Kong to Manila to San Francisco.

Ebrahim was polishing his shoes when I arrived. In 20 minutes, I packed and left with a shopping bag. I had more misgivings regarding this trip. The Chinese holiday was the next day and all lines were full. There were no seats were available.

I felt Ebrahim should have picked up tickets in the morning, but I purchased our tickets for the boat.

On the boat I sat in a comfortable seat. I was moved out of it by some of the crew, who pointed out the seat numbers on our tickets.

We have had several 12-hour crossings, but this three-hour ferry ride seemed forever. I wrote letters. I had no reading material and no one to talk to. We were the only two "foreigners" on that ship. Ebrahim went off by himself.

People sat in the gaming room and played mahjong. Two Chinese movies were shown and a strip tease entertained people.

In Hong Kong, it was not permitted to strip all the way, but on international waters it was permitted.

My first hydrofoil ride excited me. The boat was swift and close to the water. We sped home.

Back home I went to bed after talking with Nita a while.

Friday, June 20

I took the cable car up to Victoria Peak. It was a delightful experience, and I looked forward to the roller coaster effect on my way down. Bob Woods accompanied me. He was a delight. He had made the trip several times, but never before in daytime.

He said he had an air-conditioned office in Saigon that was little affected by the war. He was a fortunate soldier. Bob had a month's leave from Vietnam. He left Tokyo because it was an expensive town and he preferred Hong Kong. He walked alone everywhere and enjoyed the sights and sounds. His effervescence was a pleasure after Ebrahim's droopiness and dissatisfaction with the town and its people.

Bob loved the country and the people. He was thrilled with Hong Kong. He was spontaneous.

I needed Bob's shot in the arm. It was a pleasant three hours of walking and talking together.

Saturday, June 21

I cashed $200 to get us though Hong Kong expenses and have some money as a starter in Japan.

Nita picked up her ticket at Pan Am to leave Monday afternoon on China Airlines for Japan, and I booked a ticket for Sunday, at noon, on Cathay.

How much wasted time we spent trying to mail packages. Nita had knocked herself out for hours to get the package to be three pounds, and it weighed two ounces over, so we got smacked with higher charges.

What a labor of love, hoped the presents looked like something when we saw them all piled up on our living room floor.

It was after closing hour at the travel agency, but they were still open and gave me the visa for Japan.

I started to leave after trying on dresses, but decided to wait for Sammy.

Her father gave me a coke and I watched the family sitting around making costume jewelry for extra money. The money won't let up — dozens and dozens of necklaces. Nita told me that Sammy said they gave these necklaces away to friends. I couldn't believe it. Not when they made so many and worked so hard at it and needed the money so badly.

Sammy was the sole support of the family. Father retired because of ill health and appeared to do nothing. Four sisters lived at home and a married sister lived elsewhere.

Sammy worked hard with the dressmaking, working until 2:00 and 3:00 each morning, then rising for a full working day. How did she do it? She was pure genius, with her ability to make patterns and follow Nita's ideas, and her sewing was a re-fined job of the highest caliber.

At 7:00 p.m. she entered and I showed her that the bust area was too tight. After dinner she opened seams and altered it.

I was invited to dinner and drank both Chinese wine, sweet and good, and Chinese Taiwan beer. It was a delicious meal and I had no idea when it was cooked. The whole family worked at beads all afternoon while I was there. The youngest was painting a picture, copying from one in a book.

It was a friendly family and I approved of the constant busy quality and the many creative activities. Father had an enlarger and was a proficient photographer. I wondered why he didn't work at that.

We watched television. Various friends wandered in to join the family and I learned of Maggie's stamp collection. I took some of her duplicates and the following day gave her United States stamps. I gave her addresses to write to for a stamp exchange.

I arrived home around 11:00. Ebrahim called and I devoted a few minutes to him in his room, the poor mixed-up guy. I told him of my Macau experiences. He had a cold and was miserable. He had called me several times. He told me not to bother saying "goodbye" on Sunday morning, because he would be asleep. And I left thinking he needed a psychiatrist!

Back at our room I packed. Nita came in; then Eddie arrived. Nita decided she was hungry, and after debating where to eat we went to the Mandarin Hotel and Eddie called for noodles. At 3:00 a.m. we ate a huge plate of noodles and talked with a man from Vietnam. He was a nice guy. He got a kick out of me.

When he said " Vietnam" I replied " Lucky guy."

He was stationed in the North and saw too much action. "Don't shoot first" was his order. He wanted to know how else does one stay alive? He would like to have lived permanently in the Hong Kong area. He wasn't anxious to return to the United States.

At 4:00 a.m. Nita and I went to bed knowing we had an early and busy day coming up.

Sunday, June 22

Nita brought Sammy the letter, stamps and addresses for Maggie; our two old dresses for zippers; and Nita's blanket. Finally we got rid of that.

Nita and I walked through the markets of Mongkok. Her tailor was a good seamstress, and we bought Chinese style dresses for 17$HK, or less than $3.00 each. Hers was black and looked best on her. Mine was maroon and o.k. I still needed to lose weight.

Friends Mentioned in Chapter 49

Joe Luk Sing. He was my first friend there. He later moved to Singapore where we visited together.

Sammy and Maggie Chan. They were our seamstresses.

Ebrahim Adamphy. He took me to Macau. We stayed in an expensive hotel.

OCEAN PARK- MEN DEMONSTRATING HIGH UP

2 CHINESE GENTLEMEN

LITTLE GIRL

SISTER WONG, PRINCIPAL.
WE GAVE PEACE EDUCATION
WORKSHOPS TOGETHER.

CHINESE BABY

FIFTY

TAIWAN

Taiwan is a large semitropical island that lies about 100 miles off the southeastern coast of China, halfway between Hong Kong and Shanghai.

Sunday, June 21

Cathay Pacific gave us free drinks. It was the only airline that did. I had a Manhattan. Later, white wine was served with my meal of shrimp and chicken, also fruit to take along for the night.

Joseph Neal McBride, my seatmate, from the Boston area, was 25 years old. He proved to be a pleasant guy and the time flew. He was going to Taiwan for a week's training.

He majored in international relations, which he would use in his job in Vietnam.

At the airport I left my rucksack in bonded luggage for 25 cents. When I left Hong Kong each bag weighed 25 pounds and my camera case and pocketbook also weighed close to 10 pounds apiece. I don't know why I wasn't charged excess baggage. We bought alot in Hong Kong. We entered with about 25 pounds all together.

At the airport terminal they supplied umbrellas to get us to the terminal building. It was pouring. Angela at the tourist bureau desk found a room in Hotel Three Leaves for me at $1.50. I appreciated it and thanked her.

I left a message for Joseph, who called to find out where I was.

I met Chen Yao outside the building and he offered to carry my valise, shielded me from the rain and paid my bus fare. Then he escorted me to the hotel. We made a date for Monday.

Monday, June 22

I wrote a note:

Dear Nita,
Everything is moving along nicely in Taiwan, so far. You
enjoy Japan and eventually I will join you there.
Love, your Mother.

348

At the hotel, I settled in after making a date with Chen Yao for the following day. I took an afternoon nap. About 5:00 p.m. I wandered outdoors for a walk.

I discovered the most wonderful Chinese market, underground like the Isfahan ones.

I walked into a cinema. I paid 20 NT, or 50 cents. I had good seats for "Brotherhood, " a movie about the Mafia with Kirk Douglas. This was the 7:00 to 9:00 p.m. show.

As we exited the theater, I spoke to two girls. I asked where could I stay after tonight.

Ashun, the young Chinese girl said, "Stay at my house."

Kathleen Graves, an American, was with the Embassy. She would matriculate at Barnard College, New York, in September. She was to leave for New York the next day.

Ashun went crazy when I mentioned Marlboro. Her American boyfriend had been attending there since the March term.

I followed both of them around town. Kathleen bought sunglasses and we discovered an out-of-this world ice cream place. It had three in one scoops —mango, coffee and walnut.

They accompanied me back to my hotel and were in my room as Joe telephoned. Ashun gave him directions to come to my hotel.

The girls left as Joe arrived. He would like to have made love; we took a walk instead. He was a decent guy, about 25 years old.

Only partitions existed in this room, no walls to the ceiling. I couldn't sleep because of a mosquito so I turned on the light and read most of the night. I fell asleep with the light on.

Then I spent hours working out our finances. We cashed $849.50. But I had $70.00 and Nita had $75.00 after the tailor and Sammy were paid. So my expenditures were $692. Counting this we spent $273 a month for the last seven months. Not unreasonable. We were still within our $3.00 a day limit.

I packed and left my bags at the desk.

I stopped by the Sun Hotel and asked permission to use their typewriter. From 3:00 to 5:00 p.m. I wrote letters on their typewriter.

I had my nails manicured for fifty cents and, while I was at it, they combed my hair and made a tremendous styled bun.

Chen was waiting for me with Mr. Wang. Chen wanted to take me to an expensive restaurant and movie. I preferred to go with Mr. Wang to his home for dinner, which we did.

Mr. Wang's job was interpreter for Americans and he acted in that capacity all night. He had four children and the second one was a boy about David's age. His wife was a gracious hostess. She apologized because she didn't expect guests for dinner. It was a simple meal and you can guess what I was served — soup, rice and four other dishes. It was a feast.

We talked all night, because I had a 10:00 p.m. appointment to meet Ashun.

Mr. Wang offered to take me to lunch any day I called him at his office.

I rode home on Chen's motorbike and enjoyed that. I met Ashun and planned to see the Wangs and Chen again tomorrow to make it a more complete date for him.

I popped into a taxi, but not before thanking the hotel manager of Sun Hotel, David Chang. He gave me his card for any time I might need him. Can you believe this?

Kathleen and Ashun drove us to Ashun's home, where they parked me in the bedroom, not to disturb their party.

"You wouldn't enjoy what they are doing," Ashun told me. Three girls and one boy had a record player blazing.

Kathleen was perfect as a friend for Wendi. She was sentimental about Taiwan, which she had called home for two years. She had made many friends here. I'd written to my cousin, Marion Sheppard, and Clarence in Ceylon to tell him about the books he should receive.

If this continued, it would take me longer to reach Japan than I had planned. I wrote to Nita to tell her to go ahead and see the Japanese countryside. Leave your luggage with Kazumi or Pan Am and travel and enjoy yourself, I told her.

I wanted to go up country and still hadn't worked it out yet. Most people didn't speak English, but since when did that hinder us?

Tuesday, June 23: Time's flying

Ashun planned to see Kathy off at the airport and I listened to their plans.

I asked her to let me take the bus with them to get me out of town for the day. She consented. We took two buses and met Kathy. She hadn't slept and neither had Ashun. This was a very emotional day for both of them.

I saw the pirate book store and the books were printed beautifully. Every book you've ever wanted to read and were forbidden to take out of the country was in this shop. True, the authors got no copyright money, but I would have liked to send books off to friends.

We took the American bus through the American colony outside of town. The mountains loomed up all around. Everything was lush and green and beautiful. We glimpsed the Chinese architecture.

I said goodbye to Kathleen and left them.

I started walking and got a hitch from a man who had to go into the military area, so he dropped me off.

At the post office, I mailed the letter to Nita and bought more aerograms.

Children playing in a schoolyard were a delightful scene.

I followed teachers and children indoors and helped serve the vegetable soup to the 35-seated children. Each child was handed a face cloth to wash hands and face before and after eating. These Chinese are a clean people.

I took photos despite the poor lighting in the room. This teacher did not speak

English. We went into the large room where the children danced. The ages were 3, 4 and 5 year olds. Next week is graduation for the 5 year olds and they will perform these dances for their parents.

The pianist spoke English and acted as interpreter. They learned my age and I showed them pictures of my family. Chiang, at the piano, had two children in the class.

I wrote the words for "I'm a little teapot" and "An elephant carries a great big trunk" and Chiang was able to write the notes above the words and play it on the piano exactly as I sang it. She had an amazing ear and she never took piano lessons.

I spent more than two hours in the school. Chiang invited me to her home.

The school had a few displays of children's work.

As the children mounted the bus, I thought how important it was to send children home with "something they constructed" daily. We encouraged coloring, cutting and pasting.

The freedom of movement helps to develop the muscles necessary for reading and writing later. In this school they appeared to do none of this.

Chiang did tell me they had blocks for building in the kindergartens. Here, they had outdoor equipment and rocking horses indoors.

I watched the children put away the rocking horses, arranging them neatly without anyone telling them. No teacher stood over them to supervise.

Before we left, they picked up every crumb of paper in the room. They were most certainly not docile children, but had refined, good qualities. They each wore an apron over their dress or shirt.

Chiang and I walked to her home and her children lagged behind. Chiang's children were more mischievous than the others. We purchased ice pops. When we arrived home the children started temper tantrums to eat the pops immediately. Chiang gave in and they sat with a bowl under each pop to catch the drips.

I finally located what the "malodorous odor" was. Hot sulfur springs ran along the highway. The road to Chiang's home wound through mountains and the outrageous loud noises of the crickets provided a relief from the honking taxis in Taipei.

Chiang did not have household help; she did everything herself. I didn't go upstairs to see the bedrooms. She was embarrassed the house had not been cleaned for me. It had a cement floor, a medium-sized room with small couches and dining table and refrigerator. There was another room for toilet and a separate kitchen where she provided a feast in a few minutes. She would let me do nothing to help her.

She taught mornings and in the afternoon did housework and studied while the children took naps. Her son was 4 and her daughter was 3. She was proud of her daughter's unusually curly hair. The daughter was feminine and didn't like anything to cover her "pretty" dress.

Chiang was 30 and looked 20. She graduated at 19 and began work at this school after three years of Teacher's College. Now they required five years teaching education, and after 11 years of teaching, she returned to school to get the added two years.

I was only the second American ever to come into her home.

After her exam on Friday she wanted me to return and spend more time with her when she had less pressure.

I left her house about 2:00 to give her time to study before the children woke up.

I walked along the mountain road following signs to Yah Ming Park. I looked in on the International Hotel. I realized there was much military activity in this area. Several other people were walking. I walked alone and no one joined me.

I finally asked an American couple, "Where are we going?"

We arrived at the entrance gate of Yah Ming Park and paid 5 NT, about 12 cents. We walked and talked together. She was from the University of Colorado in Denver. She had studied Chinese for four years and planned to study here for about three months. Her boyfriend managed to connive an R and R at the right time, in the right place, to spend this time with her. We walked around the garden. When I stopped to take photos they went off and I did not follow.

I spoke to a woman who was on a tour.

She said, "Most of us came from Hawaii, and a few tourists from San Diego. Only one or two Caucasians. We are a peppy group."

In a month of travel they had been to Tokyo, Taiwan, Hong Kong, Bangkok and Singapore. All arrangements and handling of meals and luggage was done for them at a cost of $1,500. Not bad. They had days of going and going, but I saw their Taiwan program, and it had two free days out of the four.

Ted Ma, of K Travel Agency, invited me to have lemonade with him. He invited me to join the group.

First I asked permission, as he sat the group down and explained about the park. The property belonged to a rich man and he donated it to Chiang Kai Shek as a birthday present. Chiang donated it to "the people" to enjoy.

We talked a while, then we got into the tour bus and he used the microphone and instructed us as we rode. We took a different road back. We passed an extinct, smoking, sulfurous volcano where men dug clay and brought it to porcelain factories.

We passed mountains where trees were planted to spell Chiang's name on the mountainside, showing the people's love and respect for Chiang Kai Shek.

I was reading "Dragon Hotel" by John Ball, and I recognized the town of Peitou. Many hotels had hot spring baths. The water here was healthy for the body, not to drink. Further south there was drinkable spring water.

The tour driver let me out at the Peitou bus terminal. The bus there would take me to the railroad station in Taipei.

The tour group was going first to a porcelain factory and then a jade factory. I would have liked to go along but would not have made my 5:00 p.m. appointment on time. These factories were included so the tourists could purchase merchandise.

In Taipei, the bus stopped and everyone was told to get out. I refused. I didn't know where I was, and I told the conductor that I had been told that the bus went to the railroad terminal. Finally, she may have understood, and she told me to sit down. The bus drove further and then I recognized where I was. It drove into the railroad station grounds, and she let me off. Well, my obstinacy worked that time for my good. I arrived at my hotel on time.

I was relieved to see Chen Yao walk in. We discussed where to go and I was pleased to see that "Rachel-Rachel" was playing at the movies. We rode on his motorcycle and he parked it with a friend.

We strolled past Japanese fish restaurants and entered a narrow lane of eating houses. We walked the entire length and I decided which one I was ready to sample.

This was Taiwanese cooking. We passed a couple of Cantonese style, tiny bowls of food to be eaten with rice.

The snakes fascinated me as I peered into their cages and admired the huge ones. Chen didn't like to eat snake, so I skipped it for this meal. He didn't like frogs, so I didn't choose those either. He wasn't crazy about all the seafood so beautifully displayed.

They tied a piece of duck and vegetables to the package of soup, neat and compact. The soup flavor was sweet and pungent and I loved it. But the squid dish was scrumptious. Cost was 3 NT, less than 12 cents.

As we strolled past shops, we passed one display case. On scrutiny the case contained thousands of teeth. I guess pulling teeth is the first, not the last resort, of these dentists. I saw one dentist at work, but did not stay to examine his practice.

We walked to the movie house, purchased tickets, and then walked through another marketplace. Most of the food displays and fried food were new to me. We circled back and had watermelon. Not because there was room in our bellies, but to kill the spare time.

The movie "Rachel-Rachel" was my type of movie.

The insight into this lonely person was good. Joanne Woodward excellently portrayed her thoughts and her fearful attitude towards all new experiences. The constant conflict within her, because of her upbringing versus her basic needs, was brought out in the bed scene where she resorted to masturbation to put herself to sleep. The rejection of anything new, and the hurt she received from Nick, and again with her pregnancy, was vivid. It was a woman's film. Poor Chen was bored stiff.

We rode Chen's motorbike home. It was a long distance and I enjoyed the ride.

I planned to go to bed, but Ashun was in a miserable, unhappy, emotionally and physically upset mood. Kathy had been her best friend and was now gone. We talked to help her get over it.

Taiwan mosquitoes plagued me another night. What misery. The pests were sneaky and hid when I turned on the light. It was 2:30 a.m. and I was still awake.

Wednesday, June 24

Visitors to Taipei saw the "L" formed by East Nanking Road, which brought one from the airport, and Chungshan North Road, which was the center of the hotel and souvenir shopping area. At the upper end, just across the Keelung River, was the magnificent Grand Hotel. Below it for a mile there was an unbroken double row of curio shops, hotels, airline offices and compounds devoted to the American military forces.

I sauntered around town for a while.

Record shop loudspeakers blared and people jammed the sidewalks.

In downtown Taipei, young policemen directed traffic. They looked like Chinese counterparts of our own MPs. They stood ramrod tall in starched, sharply tailored khaki uniforms, spit-shined combat boots, white helmet liners and 45- caliber pistols holstered on their hips.

West of the main railway station, south of West Gate, were the small crowded shops. The overflowing family groups made it seem that the main occupation was not merchandising, but population increase.

In front of the first department store, I watched the swarming multitudes that lived in the buildings. They had a bland disregard for the straight-line functionalism of the architect and cluttered the structures with a jumble of clotheslines full of laundry. Bedding hung down from the balcony railings. Odds and ends of furniture, household utensils and other movable possessions were placed outside on the balcony. This created more living space within the crowded cubbyhole apartments.

Peddlers pulled their carts up to the edge of the sidewalk and sold slices of pineapple, guava, apple, watermelon and pears that had been peeled and skewered.

I turned up a narrow street, which housed one of the most remarkable trading places anywhere in the world. It was only 10 feet wide and paved with bare earth that had been pounded into a hard adobe by the passing of untold thousands of pairs of feet. The open-air shops and restaurants catered largely to poor people.

Despite the obvious lack of glamour, or even sanitation, the shopkeepers took pains to make their goods as presentable as possible. Many restaurant fronts displayed a large kettle containing the house specialty, steamed and bubbled. The small shops displayed varied merchandise. Heaps of live reptiles were coiled in cages. The customer selected a snake. It was skinned and made into delicious soup. The Chinese believed that snake is beneficial, especially during the winter. The street was filled with people chattering.

Two things in this unique street were of particular interest. The first was an open-air dental office. The chair was 1890s vintage. A foot-powered drill and a few operating tools were on display. This dentist had previously extracted and proudly displayed a showcase filled with teeth.

Thursday, June 25

Ruth writes:

Dearest Nita,

I hope Japan is proving all you hoped it would be.

Monday, June 30, I am taking Northwest Airlines. It will be a long ride for my money.

I'm still living in Ashun's friend's house. It is a luxury apartment, very spacious and even has two bathrooms with bathtubs.

You'd like Ashun and Ahhwa, her sister. Both attend the university. Ashun, a philosophy major, is graduating now.

The literature in this house is highly intellectual. She is very intelligent and so far I've spent too little time with her because she is studying for her final exams.

Mr. Wang introduced me to David Chang, the assistant manager of Sun Hotel. He permitted me to use his typewriter for hours of letter writing.

David spends his days off with me. We will traipse into the hills and go swimming.

Hope this reaches you in time.

See you soon.

Loving you always, Mom

Friday, June 26

Dear Henry,

In Bangkok, I made friends with a man who has a school where English is taught. I spoke to him about ways he could use you in his business of importing and exporting to help you get out of India. He plans a trip to India and I hope he finds time to interview you. Mr. Amanpaul runs a reputable business. I have misgivings about recommending you in such a big enterprise. If he can be a help to you, I hope you prove yourself responsible.

Thailand was a wonderful country and one of my favorites. People were flexible and adjusted to many western ways without losing the flavor of their own customs.

Hong Kong has many Indians living there.

I'm in Taiwan now and trying to learn more about this country. Nita went on to Japan without stopping here. We'll be separated for a week.

Hong Kong was Nita's dream city, but not mine. We spent enough money there to continue traveling for six more months. We have two months more of travel in Japan, the world's most expensive country, and only a few dollars left. Write to us in Tokyo and tell us what has been happening to you. Are you working and earning money?

How are your friends? Write to us, we talk and think of you often.

Your friend, Ruth

Friday, June 26

Ashun came home from her English examination and we conversed until David Chang arrived a little after 1:00 p.m.

He talked with Ashun and came away impressed with how unusual she was for a Chinese girl. I thought: They should get along well together after I leave.

We arrived at Green Lake by bus. In most of the boats were Americans who were on R and R from Vietnam. Chinese girls were lighting their cigarettes or bestowing other services in a feminine manner. The soldiers were made to feel like kings, seated at tables, drinking and enjoying themselves.

I inquired where we could change into our bathing suits. There were cages," but David took me into a hotel room. David didn't feel like going out, he would have liked an afternoon nap. But he didn't get one.

He decided to accompany me. The water was a comfortable, cool temperature. We swam together because he enjoyed it and didn't find swimming companions easily. His friends were married, and girls in China were taught to fear the water, and not taught to swim.

David rented a boat, and we took turns rowing until we came to the rapids. We would have portaged the boat to the other side of the rapids, but it began to rain, so we rode the rapids for a while. While we sat in the boat in the middle of the lake far away from other people David opened up about his feelings and opinions regarding Taiwan. He said fear is a constant with the people. They learned that they could not express their opinions for fear of it getting back to the authorities.

Chung Kai Shek was priming his son to take over when he quit. He appointed his son vice premier this week. Most important jobs were appointed by Chiang.

If you wanted to run a dance or a party you had to notify the police and get written permission. Why? The government feared that large gatherings would undermine it. Ashun could only invite five people at her home at one time.

Strikes were forbidden, though the man who told me this felt they were a strong force and had a purpose.

Naturally, the presses were controlled and censored.

All information sources about Red China were cut off and people were kept in complete ignorance.

People had trouble obtaining passports. ID cards were available on request; they were used for hotel registration.

My "alien registration" was a special form used by the hotels and I resented the way it was handled.

The dictatorships in Red China and Taiwan had a great many similarities.

Improvements: the arable land was being improved and landlord's holdings were limited and parceled out to people who would work the land.

Pedicabs were taken off streets the previous year; people had to drive taxicabs instead.

There were several coalmines along the way. The mines had shallow veins and men worked only with hand tools.

David had so much good about him. He was a good-looking man with a kind, smiling visage. His body was firm and his skin smooth. He said, "Rice eaters have smooth skins and bread eaters have rough ones."

He told me my skin was unusually smooth for an American. He had never had a woman who has such big breasts before. I am also the heaviest woman he had ever held.

He nursed with a wet nurse, but sucked at his grandmother's tits until he was 10 years old. Why? She didn't have milk, but he liked them. He still liked them and enjoyed them. It was a pleasure to watch his pleasure.

He said that his three brothers who nursed from his mother were all skinny, on the undernourished side, and the three boys who had wet nurses were heavier and healthier.

"Why don't your breasts hang after nursing four children like the Chinese do?"

He liked my dyed hair and said I looked like a young woman.

He was a natural gentleman, considerate and thoughtful. At the hotel I continued to pick David's brain and we held discussions for a long time. My respect for him as a person was high.

He was a geography teacher for two years and quit to take the hotel management course in Hawaii for three months. He had to work and he had less time for social life than he would have liked.

He was 35 and unmarried. He couldn't find anyone to suit him, and his parents were putting pressure on him to get married. I thought he could be happy for a while longer without it. I would like to have seen him with someone extra special — someone worthy of him.

The rainstorm chased us indoors after dinner.

We were happy to return to the room. A fuss was made about signing the registrar. He gave his correct address.

Friday, June 27

I awoke to drumming outside and watched people exorcising spirits of a woman who drowned. It went on for hours. The priest turned an empty chair around as the drummers kept the motion going.

Men were putting rocks into bamboo cages to build up the dam and make the lake deeper. I took a series of photos to show Jack, the engineer, who had been working on a dam.

Before David left for work he gave me all the information I needed to get to Wulai. The trip was through verdant mountains and past several dams.

There were souvenir shops, restaurants and bars on each side of the road, a constant reminder that this was an area for tourists. I passed through a gate and found myself looking at a spectacular gorge. Spanning it was a spidery suspension bridge. I discovered it swayed with each step. Tiny cars were being pushed by girl laborers along a narrow track.

The tribes in Northern Taiwan had migrated from Southern China and those in the south had come from Malay-Polynesia. They engaged in hunting, farming and headhunting.

With the coming of the Dutch and the flow of Chinese immigrants in the seventeenth century, the Aborigines were forced back into the central mountains. They continued to make stealthy forages to collect the heads of unwary Chinese farmers.

In time, the Japanese and Chinese squelched their resistance. They took to Christianity and to scratching out a marginal living on tiny plots of land on the tortuous slopes of the mountains.

It appeared that many of the men still could not accept the image of themselves as farmers, for farming was traditionally women's work. They were now faced with the gradual migration of their women to the lowlands, where there was the promise of a less arduous existence in Taiwan's expanding economy.

The performers were gaily costumed and had painted their faces with various bright colors. Most of them were young girls with curiously round faces. I took a photo of these tattooed aborigines.

I reached the end of the paved pathway and found the main attraction of Wulai. The high, lovely waterfall cascaded down the opposite side of the canyon. The scene was spoiled by shops with shelves full of souvenir items.

Miss Canada was on a tour and I walked with her back to her bus. The tour guide invited me into the bus to go back to Taipei and I had a free ride back to the university.

The tour dropped me off at Taiwan University and it was raining for a change. I located a hairdresser. I showed them my paper that asked them in Chinese to make it dark brown, not black. I paid 80 NT or $2.00 for the dye job and set and 10 NT or 25 cents for the manicure. My long hair required two bottles. It turned out black, not brown. I couldn't always win.

I went home to Ashun about 6:00 p.m. We were company for one another for nearly four hours. She was a cultured friend.

Saturday, June 28

I couldn't decide which books to buy and was still anxious about the excess weight it would cause for my airplane ride. I had enough trouble on that score. I went into the Oriental Hotel and spent hours in the office typing. I met Frank Wu, the manager, and a friend of David's. He was pleasant and conversed with me a bit. The morning flew by and I had to take a bus to meet David.

What to do? I pulled out 101 questions: What was there to see and do? Tanshui at the northern tip of the island was an interesting old seaport and fishing village.

I said, "Let's take a train because I have never been on one in this country."

"No, not the tourist express, which costs three times the price of the 'ordinary' train," David said.

Our tickets read Keelung, a seaport town. We pushed into the crowded train and stood between two cars. I could see the countryside through the crack. Still they served us tea. One waiter passed us with a tray over his head and another with a huge hot teapot. He only burned me once as he brushed past.

David told me the three ladies nearest us were talking about me. Would I talk with them? Of course. He told me they were curious about my age and decided I was young. They wondered why I took this train instead of the tourist express. He answered their questions and we gave them a briefing on me.

I forget that some people have no opportunity to meet and talk with tourists. I go out of my way to meet them.

There were many boats in the harbor at Keelung. We took a bus to Tamsui. We hiked around the town and climbed the rocks.

A fisherman popped up in the water from skin diving for a huge octopus. He held it up for my picture.

We watched men fixing and drying nets, and men working on their boats. The wind eroded sand stone rocks in the park. We stopped for watermelon three times. We also had an oyster and egg omelet but we could not abate David's hunger.

David Chang's ideas, his suggestions and his philosophy all clicked with mine.

He bought ice cream cones without asking. He wanted to climb mountains; he was an adventurous soul and much in my spirit. I climbed up on the rocks instead of taking the easier path around.

He suggested we go out in a fishing boat. I found myself in the position of veto-ing it for plebian reasons. His clothing would have been ruined in one of those boats. We weren't dressed for that activity.

On the way back to the bus at 7:00 p.m. we watched the fleet float out into the water. It was a pretty sight. At the bus stop people were sizing us up and talking about us. It was fun that he could eavesdrop and translate for me.

One beautiful scene was memorable, a village in the valley glittered with lights, and on top of the mountain a temple was outlined in lights.

David slept on the trip to his home. In Keelung I bought him a book. We had the house to ourselves. His aunt had a room and he had a room, but with the open wall system for air circulation there was little privacy. I requested we use the upstairs roof, set off by itself.

He told me he took his girlfriend up there for one night, but with all those Gods looking down on her from the altar, she became embarrassed and could not enjoy it.

Fortunately, they weren't my gods. This was the Ancestor Worship room.

Before we could get into the bathtub, we had to scrub down. That was new to me. Baths in these unlined bathtubs were a different experience. You couldn't slide around in them as in the porcelain lined ones we had. I washed my clothes and his shirt.

He asked me to make dinner. I made his thousand island dressing and poured it over the sliced tomatoes. I stirred fried rice American style using scallions and bok choy. He added pork and I put the green vegetables and eggs in. Together we made the meal, not Chinese, but edible.

We retired about 10:00 and talked for a while. Both of us dropped off to sleep for the night.

Sunday, June 29

David worked from 8:00 in the morning until midnight. I was on my own during the day. I came home to Ashun and we sat together for a few minutes while she got ready to leave.

I wrote about all the activities I planned but didn't do. I found that the cold I had really was enervating. After I spent hours at the typewriter, I did not have the energy or desire to do anything but take a bath and go to bed. I slept for hours.

Ahhwa, Ashun's sister, fed me wood ears and pork rump and my favorite green vegetable for lunch. She had friends in and one even spoke English, but I was laid so low I couldn't even try to be friendly.

After lunch I slept.

When Ashun returned she had a bite to eat and went to sleep.

She told me that the woman who was taking this apartment was the mistress of the man who owned the apartment. She looked like one — a stately, beautiful Chinese woman. She looked down her nose at the rest of us, but who cared.

Ahhwa returned and also went to sleep.

When I was ready to leave I left a note. I couldn't say goodbye.

I returned to Dave's Aunt's home. I lugged my suitcase there. We watched television and I tried to converse with her. When Dave came home a few minutes later he translated.

"I'm too tired and we just sleep tonight."

So we did.

He lay on his back all night and rested. He did not snore or twist and turn. Twice he spoke to me and I realized he was talking in his sleep. He had a history of always being sleepy. He didn't get enough sleep. Did working 16 hours a day do that to someone? He tried to take naps during the day, but could be interrupted for any little crisis when needed.

Monday, June 30

David went to work, and I turned over and read and slept. Eventually I had hot milk and potato salad for breakfast with Auntie.

Every day Auntie went out early in the morning to the bakery and brought back fresh rolls for us for breakfast.

She checked to see when I had an appointment with the dentist — 7:00 p.m.

I called Ashun and spoke to her. She was packing because she had to move out of the apartment. It was her last free day before work. So I didn't see her.

At the park a gentleman spoke to me. He mentioned he was with CAL — China AirLines, and I poured out my "tale of woe" about my excess baggage.

He was the supervisor at the airport.

I should use China Airlines and report to the airport about an hour before time, he said, and he would see to it I would have a seat on a plane.

I could not take anything out of the bonded luggage. It had to leave the country still intact. So I couldn't get out my sanitary napkins as needed, or my cold pills, or the camera to take pictures of the kindergarten graduation. But my luggage problems were solved and I could sleep soundly once again.

David took me to a very crowded, small restaurant. Only three items were served: egg rolls, absolutely the crispiest and best I have ever tasted, fried pork chops and a soup.

It was a filling and delicious meal. I really appreciated his efforts to find places to bring me.

It was hectic getting to the Palace Museum. When I got to the museum I looked around for a while, sat down and nearly fell asleep.

A guard warned me, "No sleeping, sit up."

I told him I was sick. A woman found a quiet spot for me to sleep on the next floor, and I slept for a couple of hours.

Later, I walked through the museum and was glad I came.

Labels were written in Chinese and English.

I was still uncertain about buying a lacquer tray for $10.00. I thought the engraving was exquisite.

I took the guided tour for a while.

The lighting was good in all the cases. The layout was well done, the organization was good and the items were displayed well.

The explanations of dynasties and what the articles were used for gave me better comprehension of the exhibit ... photographs of tomb excavations with a whole room of items taken from one grave.

The esoteric Buddhist room was most fascinating. Only the inner circle Tibetan monks used these materials. These were some items I would like to have brought back to America — that ivory coat, the skull heads and prayer beads.

Ready to leave. Rain for a change.

I went home to Auntie. She fed me a sandwich. She told me to take a nap and I slept hard again.

When I awoke her sister was there. The sister made a meal of melon and meat and the ginger flavor in the soup was delicious with chicken steamed and green vegetable.

After dinner Auntie took me to the dentist around the corner. I dreaded it. The hole in my tooth seemed gigantic. My only glimpse of dentists here had made them seem quite primitive. Not true. This doctor was a professional, and he spoke English. No need for any pain reliever. The protective coating remained where the filling fell out. No pain at all while he drilled with a water drill and cleaned it out and refilled it. Cost? 50 NT= $1.25.

In America I had hundreds of dollars worth of x-rays and fillings every year. My dentist asked how I could possibly think of leaving him for so long without dental help. In Isfahan I had one filing and in Nairobi a filling that fell out. My teeth were in better condition now than when I ate Western food.

Back at Auntie's I watched "Man from Uncle " on television and it was in English with Chinese titles.

Dave arrived and announced he had less than half an hour for a nap and was continually interrupted. He was very tired. We went to bed and I turned out the light. He asked what I would write in my diary about him. Very simple, I told him. I would write that he couldn't sleep, turned on the light and read himself to sleep rather than taking the natural way of making love to fall asleep. I must have fallen asleep while he was reading. I slept well.

Tuesday, July 1

According to my schedule I should have been in Japan for over a week now. I was glad it was a flexible schedule.

I woke Dave up. He had such a sweet way of reaching over and giving me a kiss. I loved that man. He was still tired and not ready to go back to work. He could have used two or three days straight sleep.

For breakfast Auntie bought fried bread and the long stick doughnuts and hot soybean milk. I explained I would type for a couple of hours and return in time for lunch.

I spent 9:00 to 12:00 at the First Hotel in the business office with the brand new typewriter. I wrote four letters and four pages of diary.

David and I took buses and taxis to Dave's friend's home. I philosophized a great deal of the day in my discussions with both of them.

I discussed the idea of conformity and inflicting a philosophy. Concepts are accepted by the public through the popular artists.

Unbelievable as the Christian crusades were, they happened.

We came home and ate with number two aunt, who really had herself a ball with her grand inquisition.

But I answered to her satisfaction. I always felt better for having people know a little more about me.

Wednesday, July 2

I went by bus to Yah Ming Park area to see my teacher friend. I spent an hour at the Kindness Kindergarten school. We walked to the swimming pool. It was filled with mountain water and cool. We had a little conversation, she liked her country as it was and she was a Christian. She was the sweetest young woman I had met so far. She wasd so good natured that I couldn't help wanting to do anything to help her and make her happy.

We came home and I conked out in sleep. I had a two-hour nap.

I left her when she went to the school to help them out.

I met David and he brought along a friend. We had a meat roll and shark's fin soup. The fuss made about it was worth it. He was going to take me for the snake soup afterwards, but I was full.

He brought me to a place to buy tourist jewelry. I settled for a few souvenir shell jewelry pins. We went home and watched television.

Auntie's friend, the doctor, arrived. We were two couples in the house that night.

Thursday, July 3

Dave and I went to town together. I went to the Kindness Kindergarten graduation. I took a seat about 9:00 a.m.

I'm glad I went, first and foremost because it made her happy to have me there. I enjoyed the performance and now I understood what the practicing was all about. It was an enactment of the Red Riding Hood story. The children acted it well. Dignitaries from the local government and teachers from another school came.

A puppet show of the King Midas story had Shi doing the work and a good job it was. The words were said by record; I wondered why the puppet show was performed at all. It didn't appear to be children's work in any area; teachers made the scenery and props and manipulated the puppets.

Several parents took photos and Shi presented me with a package of baked goods as I left.

During my absence at the graduation, a feast had been prepared. The two aunts must have been cooking all morning. The food was fragrant.

The food was brought up to our roof room. Each person lit candles and incense and bowed three times to their ancestors and left. Eventually the food was brought back downstairs to be eaten.

I admired people with this self-control. No one "snitched" a bit of the food set on the table and no one sat down to eat. We were waiting for someone.

I recognized Dave's mother, who had the same facial characteristics as David. She was a handsome woman. I was struck by her lack of contact and interest in me. I would say she was one of the "coldest cookies" we had met on the whole trip. Of course, I wanted to get close to her because of my feelings for her son. But she never made eye contact or smiled. She never asked questions about me even when Dave arrived. With her permission I took a couple of photos of her.

After the meal, we hurried out to Dave's friend's coalmine. I should have taken pictures here, forgetting it would be dark by the time we arrived at his father's coalmine. We had a drink and socialized a bit before we left.

Dave and I made a quick departure for the train. We walked up the mountains another hour to the coalmine. David's father was working on the broken rail and stopped long enough to wash, accept the money and chop (a seal for letters) Dave brought, and put food out for us. Then he went back to work on his broken rail.

The train didn't leave for hours, so we found a room in the hotel. It had good bath facilities and I was happy with the place. We went out for "hungry" Dave and back to the room for a good bath, and washed our clothes and had a good long night's sleep.

Friday, July 4

I was by myself all day. We rode early in the morning back to Taipei on the train.

In the afternoon I went to the beauty parlor for my hair and nails. They surprised me with a face make-up.

Sunday, July 6

David took me to his home to meet his family. We went into the room where his midwife mother delivered babies.

David wanted me to take the airplane to Koro Gorge. It cost $11.00. But we were invited by the Aunts to spend the day with them. Auntie and #2 Aunt and Uncle and grandchild took me to Monkey Mountain for Ancestor Day.

High up in the clouds was an architecturally artistic Taoist temple. They practiced rituals with incense, leaving foods for ancestors and burning paper money as a contribution to ancestors.

On display everywhere were ceramic lamps, carved wooden screens, piles of drums that doubled as end tables, batik prints, shell pictures and ornately carved chests, soapstone carvings and jade ornaments.

Ruth writes:
Dear Aunt Minnie,

I'm still in Taiwan. That is Formosa to Americans and Chiang Kai Shek took over the country 20 years ago when the Communists took over Mainland China. It was a small island, but in nearly two weeks I still haven't managed to tour the Southern area.

In my letter to mother I related the people who have befriended me. If I tell you that all I cashed is $21.00 in two weeks it explains someone is taking good care of me. I stayed at different people's homes and enjoyed it, as usual. Now I am with the aunt of my friend, she is 59 and her sister who stays with us sometimes is 61. They both remind me of the faces we see in the Shapiro family. One aunt will be in New York in September and I plan to have her meet you. Her daughters live in America.

Becoming Ruth

Nita is already in Japan and I will join her presently. By now she has friends there because she left with only $50.00 and we both know that Japan is one of the most expensive countries in the world.

Let me know what the family plans to do this summer. We are curious.

Love and best of health to you,

Your niece, Ruth

Monday, July 7

Auntie's sister and I breakfasted together. Auntie left and asked if I would be back in time for lunch.

I told her "No."

I kissed her goodbye on both cheeks and gave her a good hug. She left without realizing this was goodbye. Auntie was a good person. She reached out for contact with me and I understood what she had to say. It was a new experience for her to live with a Westerner, and my hairy arms and legs fascinated her. She commented that the bed had an "odor." Americans do smell. The Orientals do not.

I took the bus to the airport.

I left the suitcase at China airlines and got a reservation for the flight.

Dave brought me to eat mutton and it was good. At the table tears poured down and I felt so silly I couldn't control myself.

He presented me with a chop box for my inked signature.

He wanted to buy me jewelry, Taiwan jade, but I said it was too expensive.

I walked him back to work and tried to say goodbye in the park, but he insisted on coming to the airport.

At the airport I checked in. David arrived.

After giving me stamps and a letter to his Tokyo friend, David left. The plane was delayed.

Mr. Chao now offered to show me around. He said Pan Am should give me two bags for the price I paid. CAL gave airplane bags to customers who purchased tickets for $100.

Monday, July 7

I brought luggage to the airport. I met David, who took me to an excellent restaurant. I cried. He tried to buy me jade. I cried because it was painful to say goodbye to David. I didn't want him to see me off. But he insisted. He stayed with me at the airport.

Friends Mentioned in Chapter 50

Chen Yao. He shielded me from rain at the airport. Later on I rode his motorcycle.

Ashun Chiang Shu Shun. She graduated a philosophy major at college.

David Chang. He traveled with me and we became very close friends. His Auntie let me live in her home. We loved one another, ignoring the language gap.

Wang Shu San. This was an interpreter who befriended me.

Shi Hwo Chiang. She played piano at Kindness Kindergarten. For the children's graduation they danced and acted out Red Riding Hood.

CHIANG AND RUTH

FIFTY-ONE

JAPAN

Monday, July 7

I assisted Mr. Chen with his luggage as we boarded the plane. Mr. Chen sat next to me. We had conversation, which was a godsend because otherwise I would have cried the entire trip.

The air trip was much faster than I had believed. The meal was not especially enticing. Nita confirmed this. But CAL did not make a fuss about the weight of the luggage. At airport in Osaka I went through customs. The inspector never opened my luggage.

The tourist information desk could not locate a note from Nita. Later we learned that the desk had one information person and the Pan Am desk also had one.

I rode in the taxi with Chen to his hotel. Chen tried to switch for a double room, but none were available. There was a big conference in the hotel and the rooms were all occupied. We were located in a small room with one bed. Kimonos and slippers were laid out for us. We bathed, talked and did not sleep much that night.

No wonder Chen had a good marriage. He was a loving, physical man and liked the contact with his wife.

Mr. Chen had seven children, three boys and four girls. They were in high school or older. He would have liked all of them to be in his business in the Chinese way. We discussed a great deal. I tried to get insight into his thinking and his way of his life.

He invited me to his home in the Philippines.

Wednesday, July 9

We tried to locate Nita last night.

I called Kazumi and his father answered. He didn't understand Chen, so we still couldn't locate Nita. We called the hospital to find Dr. Kazumi, but that call didn't work either.

So this morning I had a Japanese man do the same calls for me and after a while I heard Nita's voice.

"Where have you been?" Nita asked. "I've been waiting for you."

She gave me directions to the home where she was staying.

I had breakfast, then packed and brought the bag down to check it with the hotel.

Chen offered me money. "No, thanks."

He gave me earrings for Nita and perfume for me. He made me feel like a high-class callgirl.

I took the train and found her. Our two weeks separation was good for both of us. She looked different each time I saw her.

Hiroko was at the information desk at the airport. When she realized she couldn't help Nita, she decided to invite Nita to her own home.

A friendly Japanese family welcomed me. Nita had become a vital part of this household. She was loved, cooked meals for the family, and enjoyed doing what she could for them. Hiroko gave Nita a kimono and slippers as presents and an aunt was making her a dress.

Horoko and her mother entertained me. Upstairs Nita told me where she had been the past two weeks, what she had been doing, and some of the people she had been seeing.

She had a busy life — full, rewarding and happy. It was really wonderful for both of us. We took our getting around for granted.

I met Nita at the post office and we mailed brocade.

I brought my luggage to Kazumi's home. After dinner we looked at his slides all evening. He selected a few for me.

Bed was laid out on mats on the floor. His house was typically Japanese. Leave shoes outside the front door. Use slippers in the house. Except on the matted bedroom we didn't use either shoes or slippers. It was confusing to me. The mother kept bringing me the slippers I left somewhere in the house to put on.

Our meal was served while we sat on a cushion on the floor. Each person had separate plates and bowls. It was different from the Chinese way of serving food.

Friday, July 11

Nita made pancakes for our breakfast.

I said, "Sayonara," to Mr. And Mrs. Tomita and left.

Finally, I bought a Ricoh camera.

We took a train to the Kobe youth hostel.

We cashed $100 into yen and $100 into cash. This should be enough to get us back to the states, I thought.

It was an hour train ride to Himeji. A bus took us to the hostel.

It was opposite an amusement area with interesting architecture.

The hostel room had mats, and we put our own sleeping bag down and set up our bed.

We met Eric Parker, an Englishman, 36, traveling and working for years in Japan, and Victor, Swiss, 26, who spoke seven languages.

Nita writes:
Friday, July 11
Dear Family,
Mommy finally arrived from Taiwan a few days ago and now we are about to embark on a two-week trip circling West Honshu in Japan.

Our first stop is Himeji where two friends of mine, university students, with whom I have been spending time in Osaka, will meet us.

Canaida and his friend arrived, also Eric and Victor, who are staying at the youth hostel. We all went to the Himeji castle, one of the best in Japan. This wooden castle is 375 years old. Figures of soldiers in ancient attire adorn it. Himeji is high on the mountain and we did a great deal of hiking.

In the afternoon my friends had to pack. Canaida was traveling to Hiroshima and Masakazu was going to Hokkaido.

Finally, secured a manicure. In Taiwan, it cost 25 cents and was good for weeks. In Japan, it cost $1.50 and was not half as professional. The color and shape were not satisfactory. I can't win all the time.

I'm in a beauty parlor waiting for Mom to have a manicure. My feet are tired from tramping around the castle and I'm glad to rest them. I thought Himeji would be a peaceful village, but instead it was a busy city.

Mrs. Masunaga, my hostess in Osaka, bought me a sleeping kimono and Japanese wooden shoes that make you feel like you're on a rocking chair. She's a doll. Usually only the older women wear kimonos anymore.

This youth hostel is a panic. There is a guitar and mandolin student orchestra staying here and giving concerts. There is constant music practicing.
More later,
Love, Nita

Sunday, July 13

We had breakfast with Eric at Himeji hostel. We hitched with Eric and Victor to Cemetery Park. We did some sightseeing and then we played cards. It was a hot day. Our friend with a car, Kazuhiko Nakayuama, arrived and drove us to Buddha. Buddha was skinny from fasting.

He drove us to the cable car for a scenic view of Mt. Shosha.

Eric and Victor were scroungers and would not help pay for our driver. I paid the ticket. We walked to a temple high in the mountains. We couldn't wait to scrap the men.

Our driver drove us home, picked up our luggage and drove us to the railroad station. He bought us noodles on the platform. The train left at 3:30 p.m.

Nita stood and I managed to sit, and napped for our hour ride. The train was speedy and smooth and clean. Food was sold in neat containers.

At Okayama hostel we watched television. Nita played cards and shoji. Cigarettes are called Peace and Hope. Candy also is labeled Peace.

Sunday, July 13

Nita writes:

Today we are going to Okayama after spending the afternoon with Eric and Victor. Victor is a crazy guy. He acts slow and dumb, but he must be brilliant. Although he graduated an engineer, he likes the simple life of a farmer.

The other day my two Japanese friends drove me to Kobe, the major Japanese harbor, then to the top of Mt. Rokko. It was a marvelous view with an observatory that rotates.

We returned to Canaida's house and played Shogi (Japanese chess) and Napoleon (Japanese bridge).

I tried to teach Mom.

Monday, July 14

Last night I played four games of Shogi with a Japanese hosteler and I won them all. Everyone was amazed because in Japan girls can't play Shogi.

At Okayama Hostel the girls in the next room ate and talked until late at night. All of them were up early and we were the last to leave at 8:30 a.m.

Nita and I looked haggard from lack of a good night's sleep. We took a bus to the train station. We left our luggage at Hotel Osaka and went to the travel agency. We found out Route 2 was our bus route to Hiroshima.

We took the bus only half way, then hitched. Our driver studied English for two years, but would not, or could not, speak with us. We drove in silence for five hours. Ridiculous!

We stopped and had a bite to eat and I watched Nita talk like mad with her driver. They told us that my driver had a brother and sister in Hiroshima. We figured that was who they were going to visit.

We were dropped off at the bus station.

Station Hotel sent a girl into the street to show us where to take the bus to the hostel. We met Kenji and walked with him to the hostel.

At the hostel we found our room had two beds instead of four. We spoke to two Peace Corps girls and bathed in the pool. We met other Westerners and spent the evening in discussion with them.

Nita played Shogi until "lights out." Music was played over loudspeakers. There were many rules and regulations here, but still I liked the hostel very much. We took a bath with four females in it.

Tuesday, July 15

We woke early to the pleasant strains of music.

The Peace Memorial Museum was on our schedule for the day. I was bothered by the fact of the bomb. I was very upset about the part America played in dropping it. I believed it was without justification.

Becoming Ruth

Nita didn't like certain aspects of the museum. We both felt that the actual horror was not portrayed well. She felt that the theme of Peace should have been stronger, and the positive note of Brotherhood should have been stressed.

We went through the Hiroshima Park and took pictures, but the camera gave me trouble all day.

Wednesday, July 16
Sharon Copeland, a Native American, became our companion. We spent much of the day in Hiroshima talking with her.

On Miyajima Island we climbed mountains and jabbered all day. What insight she had.

Ruth writes:
HIROSHIMA July 7-14 ,15,16
Letter to David Chang:
We saw the peace memorial and a park with swans. I am in Station Hotel and watching Japanese wrestling on television, in color, no less.

I read about the coalmine blast in Taipei that killed 24 and injured 61. That affects you with your father mining.

I notice all the new interests opened up to me since my contact with you. The last three places we stayed were youth hostels. Purchase a pass, if and when, you come to Japan. We sleep for 120 to 240 yen a night. This hostel has a swimming pool and I enjoy the hot baths also.

We have a huge kitchen and Nita is out buying food for our supper now.

We met Sharon Copland, who is a Native American and a college graduate. She has traveled by herself, is 22 years old and our companion all day. We enjoyed this young woman's ideas.

I have very mixed feeling about this country. Glad you adjusted to it. I'm not sure I can. I'm getting used to the changing shoes fetish, I like looking at the hatted children, like the hot bath, find the food good, but nowhere near the variety of Taiwan, where I was very spoiled by you. We have hitched twice and both times the drivers have gone miles out of their way for us.

Sunday, the boys took us sightseeing in their cars up Mount Shoshi ropeway. Everyone draws maps to show us where to go, or else they come down out of the hotels and take us to the bus blocks away.

The girls keep explaining the thinking behind the actions, why they dislike us, but go so far out of their way for us. Why they are embarrassed and ashamed that they don't speak English, yet have mental blocks learning the language. They explain the giggles when we approach with a question.

I can't fall into their ways. The trouble with the youth hostels for us was that we meet English-speaking people, and it was most natural for us to come together and share experiences in our own language. We have discussions and arguments.

371

Hiroshima is a sore area in my point of view. I believe it ranks as bad as Hitler's gas chambers.

Others say, "War is War. And they started it at Pearl Harbor."

Nita was disappointed in the museum because it did not end on a positive note of peace forever. No more war.

We decided to hitch from now on when possible, because we can see the countryside so much better and the trains cost money. We have to stand, and people keep the shades down, so we can't even see the countryside.

The materialism of this country baffled me a bit because it seemed contrary to the simplicity of the lives of the Japanese. The formality of the customs is alien to me, and the materialism is the thing I hate most about my own country.

Nita plans for us to travel from hostel to hostel for about two more weeks until the end of July. I still have Kyoto and Nara and Osaka to see before we reach Tokyo.

Nita wants to leave Tokyo immediately, but I doubt if I will. She will spend a few days in California and I want to be there for two weeks. Nita is anxious to get home.

Any chance that you could come to Japan on that tourist visa? Just to try to locate a job for yourself? And see me again before I leave?

How are "our" aunts faring? What have they to say these days?

All my fondest love to you, David.

Ruth

Thursday, July 17

One bus, another bus, then we hitched to the Shimonoseki hostel. We reached the hostel by 3:00 p.m., rested and slept. At 5:00 p.m. I bathed in the hot tub.

At dinner a special class of 15 children arrived. They were retarded, blind and some had cerebral palsy.

We climbed up a ropeway and the teacher explained about the castle that had soldiers in it. The view of the Japanese Sea and Pacific Ocean was magnificent.

The teachers brought candy for each child and distributed it on top of the mountain. They gave them sparklers. We had a lot of walking in the dark through tunnels.

The children were frightened. They received watermelon on our return.

This trip gave me the opportunity to dialog with the teachers. I accepted the invitation to visit their school.

Friday, July 18

I rode two buses to the children's school. The male teacher had nine children in his class. Two television sets with educational channels were in all the classrooms I peered into. A huge radio with two stereo speakers was available also.

The classrooms were decorated with hanging paper designs. Clocks made by the children, scales, birds, fish and plants. Pictures painted by children were well done and hung to be displayed.

Each classroom had ample closets with equipment. (I was reminded of the schools in Lhasa that had no children's work exhibited and had practically no equipment.)

A young group was standing in front of the room and relating experiences — our 'Show and Tell.'

I was glad to have the opportunity to learn more about the education of these Japanese students.

Sunday, July 20

We left the hostel at 8:30 a.m. It took us three hours to get from Shimonoseki, 107 km, to the Hamada Hostel.

The bus cost 50 yen so we hitched in a truck first. On the next hitch at 11:00 a.m. a man and his wife drove me to Hagi.

I walked until a girl selling textiles gave me a ride. I had a new experience as I rode in her bulldozer.

By 4:15 p.m I joined two boys in a car and they took me to Misaim.

The car stopped at 5:10 p.m at a farmhouse. The wife gave me food and tea.

At 6:00 a car drove me to Hamme and at 6:30 p.m. I arrived at the youth hostel.

They sent me to the public bath. Many women bathed with me.

One of the rules of all the hostels was that a bath must precede dinner.

This was a day to remember. I was lucky to find many helpful people who managed to get me to my final destination.

Sunday, July 20

At the Hamada youth hostel after dinner we watched slides of a festival. I played Go-na-ra-be and played a card game called Donkey. In America we play it quietly and slyly. Here they were noisy and aggressive.

Monday, July 21

In every youth hostel there is a corner devoted to beauty and nature.

There was the prettiest flower garden with fountains and colorful carp in the pond.

We left the hostel at 8:00 a.m. and walked through town. People stopped their cars for me.

We passed Mt. Sanbe in a luxurious car and had a beautiful drive of 100 km for two hours.

We managed four hitches from the Hamada hostel to the Matsue hostel.

Usually youth hostels in Japan empty out by 8:00 a.m. But today I spent day the day at the youth hostel watching the Moon Walk on television.

Everybody was engrossed in watching our man walking on the moon.

Nita had two male companions and played Go-no-ra-be and chess with them.

Tuesday, July 22

Hatsuyo, a restaurant owner, a sweet person, became Nita's good friend.

Hatsuyo arrived with her son, 11, and daughter, 6. We sat in her back yard and talked for a while.

She called the Matsue youth hostel and received permission for us to sleep there.

Three boys arrived, and we drove to a beach for swimming. I rowed a boat and swam, played chess and cards.

I took photos of school children on the beach as they played a watermelon game.

A group of 13 Americans had already registered. Ingrid was a graduate from Minnesota College and had been in the Peace Corps in Tanzania. Ingrid traveled with her 19-year-old sister for six months through the countries we had seen. They loved Kashmir and Chiang Mai best.

Once a person entered the youth hostel for the night, the doors were locked and entertainment was provided for the evening. Often it consisted of a meeting, songs and games.

Wednesday, July 23

Nita arrived at the Hori youth hostel at 2:00 p.m. and I arrived at 6:00 p.m. I had a bath first, then a delicious dinner and meeting, games and songs.

Nita and I managed to see some cultural events during our month in Japan.

Toshiro Mayuzumi's Nirvana Symphony won the 1958 Otaka Prize. We enjoyed that concert. Peggy Hayama sang Nangoku Tosa, an old Shikoku folk song.

It took us a long time before we attended Kabuki.

The Gagaku court musicians used instruments not seen anywhere else.

In Bunraku one person spoke all the parts and narration.

We saw several movies including the "1958 Ballad of Narayama,"

"Hidden Fortress," "Naked Sun," "Adulteress," "Child Writers," "Street in the Sun," and "Snowy Heron," which won a prize at the 1959 Cannes Festival.

We sat through one evening of Sumo wrestling.

The Tea ceremony from China in the 13th century began as a guessing game. Shiko, patriarch of the tea ceremony, aimed at spiritual accord.

The Japanese automobiles were covered with rubber mats on the floor and seat covers. White curtains covered the windows and dolls hung over the windshield. Their cars were a "home away from home."

We didn't see any old automobiles.

Heavy rains caused mountain landslides that destroyed bridges.

Many roadsides had the mountain covered in concrete to prevent this.

Japan had mountains everywhere; therefore, there were many tunnels.

Older women had stooped, crooked backs from working in the rice fields and their gardens.

We took a public sulfur bath with many children. I am tired of "I don't speak English."

Route 90 was a picturesque road. All roads were two lanes, but four lanes were needed. Passing was dangerous.

I saw no accidents, however. There were no traffic jams. Strange, considering the number of cars.

These were the cleanest, most honest people in the world.

Thursday, July 24
Hamada Hostel

I sat around reading "Japan Today" while Nita climbed a mountain with two boys and two girls. This time Nita was included and I was excluded.

There was swimming and boating near the hostel. I swam and baked in the sun for two hours.

In the evening after a dull meeting, we had no songs or games. Instead we had fireworks. The American youth hostel group was there with us.

Friday, July 25

At 5:00 a.m. six American girls were awake and gossiping. They were like little girls at a pajama party.

At 6:30 the music started. The girls pestered us to get up.

Breakfast was at 7:00 a.m. The day before, everyone had thrown away the seaweed that was on top of the egg on our plate. No one ate it this morning either. We were informed it was healthy for us.

It took six hitches to get to the next hostel. Two boys along the scenic coastal route knew our destination. Why did they drop us off on the wrong roadway, out of our way?

They knew our route and brought us to the train. We had a long walk back to our route.

The last two boys had difficulty finding our hostel. I finally gave them money and they telephoned for directions.

We arrived after 3:00 p.m. at a well-structured hostel. There was swimming and girls played card games – I Doubt It, Donkey and Concentration.

We learned a new kind of shogi.

Saturday, July 26

It took three rides to get to Kyoto. The youth hostel was full. We made three telephone calls to other hostels. They were all full. Finally, we found an air-conditioned room, at a cost of 240 yen each. That's less than $1.00.

Our evening entertainment was a lecture in Japanese on 'Industries in Kyoto' and a movie.

The air-conditioning shut off at 11:00 p.m. and the room became hot. Nita banged around the room and opened windows.

Ruth writes a letter to David Chiang:
July 27, 1969
Dearest David,
We have been traveling along the coastal route of Western Honshu, hostel to youth hostel for about three weeks. We must be seeing the most beautiful areas with mountains and inland seas; it is constantly breathtaking scenery. We love the bamboo stands that artistically shine their light green colors among the darker pine forests.

The finest youth hostels are undoubtedly found in Japan. I understand they are government sponsored.

Nita and I groan at the youth hostel song that blasts at us through loudspeakers at 6:00 a.m.

However, our Japanese roommates rise at 5:30 a.m. and gossip cheerfully like young schoolgirls at a party. We must be out of the hostel from 10:00 a.m. until 3:00 p.m.

Nita climbed a mountain with four kids and we went swimming with them.

I still have mixed feelings about Japan. It wasn't easy leaving the person I loved so much. When I arrived, I was in an unhappy state of mind.

The more we get to know the girls the more I like them. However, I still have found no one I can get close to in an emotional, spiritual way.

Nita disagrees with me on most points now. She has made close friends, she finds no difficulty hitching, and young people have much to share with her. My age seems to hinder me in relations here.

The most important thing I wanted to tell you was how much I miss your aunts.

Despite the language barrier, we established contact and I felt happy and relaxed in their home. I miss their smiles and laughter. I miss their imitation of me. I miss the excellent Chinese cuisine. I miss Taiwan meals.

Only after living in a Japanese home can one really appreciate how lucky I was in Taiwan. How many times I have heard, "Do not stand on ceremony." Well, here they do.

Please try to convey to your aunts how much they mean to me and how much I miss them.

Know that you will always have my fondest love.
Your loving friend, Ruth
July 28, 1969
Dearest Ashun,

Becoming Ruth

You creep into my thoughts more often than you can ever imagine. I miss the relationship we had. Because of our mixture of personalities, I feel we understood one another. This is not true, as far as I'm concerned, in Japan. People "stand on ceremony," and even when I think we understand one another, we don't. In fact, I miss you, think of you, and have very fond feelings towards you. Thank you once again for leaving me with these positive feelings in relation to yourself.

Nita and I are hitchhiking in the countryside and she finds it very easy. We traveled along the coastline of Western Honshu. The most beautiful country you can imagine, and living on less than a U.S. dollar for sleeping in hostels. I miss Taiwan cooking very much. These meals, despite the filling rice, do not satisfy me. But we are managing to stay within a very tight budget, fewer than five dollars a day for both of us. Don't let expense frighten you.

I'd love your opinion of the "freedom" in Japan. They appear as trained robots to me, and conformity is the watchword.

I think that with their training, authoritarian government is a natural and each one complies with all laws with no military or policemen in control. Amazing to me.

These are the most honest people I have ever met.

I will leave Osaka in a couple of days and move on to Tokyo. From there back to the U.S. Kyoto still has people wearing kimonos and obis, a beautiful dress. I have lived in a very formal situation in a Japanese home. Nita had the less formal, more relaxed home environment. People are kind, go out of their way in driving us to destinations, and I have managed to spend a day in a school before they closed for the summer vacation.

What do you hear from Cathy?

Yesterday I saw an anti-Vietnam demonstration in the streets, but I understand the hot issue now is the return of Okinawa. This was the first time I heard the singing of the International in 20 years. I thought it was a dead song.

We spent an evening in a small coffee shop with decorated walls of "Newsweek" and "Life" magazines. We listened to the music of Donovan while drinking lemonade. The boys, your age, were delightful and would have taken us to a Japanese movie, but hostels close the door at 9:00 p.m., which kills my nightlife. I have met no one here who even resembles David for the good qualities he possesses.

I have made no close relationship with anyone.

My love to you, Ashun.

Your friend, Ruth

Monday, July 28

I rose at 5:30 a.m. and joined the crazy Japanese.

A serenity overcame me in the Sinjin Temple. The Rock Garden and Golden Pavilion were conducive to meditation. In Zen there is no worship of images. In the

377

hall where the regimen of meditation is pursued are neither images nor pictures of Buddha, nor are there scriptures.

The Zen disciple sits for long hours silent and motionless, with his eyes closed. Presently, he enters a state of impassivity, free from all ideas and all thoughts. He departs from the self and enters the realm of nothingness, Nirvana. This is not the nothingness or the emptiness of the West.

It is rather the reverse, a universe of the spirit in which everything communicates freely with everything else, transcending bounds, limitless.

At 10:00 a.m. Nita and I meandered through Dairamu and Takashimaya stores until afternoon. These department stores have everything, and they are on a level with Macy's and the best stores on Fifth Avenue in New York.

We arrived at the hostel too late to cook so we ate bread and butter for dinner.

At the meeting we played a paper game. The paper was cut into four parts and the one with the longest strip won.

Tuesday, July 29

We left the hostel after several calls to Osaka hostels. We took the bus, a train, another train, bus and finally a hitch to get to another hostel. There is a park nearby with swimming, horseback riding, tennis and boating. I organized my four rolls of film. I'm very pleased with the pictures from both cameras.

It was a hot night and many mosquitoes came out fighting and biting.

Nita writes:

Dearest Lori,

Just heard you are staying with the Dixons as a mother's helper. Sounds great! Now that Lynn has grown up, it is probably an easier job.

This afternoon, Mom and I have been lazing around the youth hostel looking at slides and letters she picked up in Osaka.

We are out on a veranda facing a lovely bamboo forest and there are enough breezes to cool us down.

I'm crazy to see you again and hear what your year was like. You know a bit about what I've been doing from my letters, but I know nothing about what has been happening with you.

We are going to Tokyo tomorrow, July 30, from there to California.

We are completely out of money and have been hitchhiking because we don't have enough for trains.

Japan is hot. While we were traveling along the sea we constantly swam in the gorgeous blue water. Osaka has nothing but buildings and heat. I hear Tokyo is even worse. Help.

How is your dancing coming along? I can't believe you'll be a junior next year. I've been missing you. Is your hair long now?

Oh well, I'll see you in about a month.

Love, your sister, Nita

July 29
Dear Wendi,
We've been circling Western Honshu from youth hostel to youth hostel. Mommy has mixed feelings about the Japanese people. She just can't adjust to their totally alien culture. She gets impatient with their deliberate slowness and their non-comprehension of anything she says.
I, on the other hand, am very happy with the Japanese and am enjoying Japan immensely.
We're back to Osaka today after three days in Kyoto. I'm amazing really; out of over 200 temples and shrines in this ancient capital, I managed to see just one. I did, however, go to a rock garden with 15 rocks, arranged on raked gravel. If you look with your mind, the rocks are islands in the wavy sea, or the jutting scales of a dragon in the clouds. I contemplated it for three hours.
The Zen priest took us around to the gardens, explaining everything in detail. Later they had a ceremony with all kinds of instruments and three priests reciting the Bodiwathe. I was lucky to have participated.
Today as I was waiting for a train, a little old man in a gray beret came beside me and wanted to take my picture. Many people come up to me to take my picture. It's a funny feeling.
My love to you. We'll be together soon.Nita

Ruth writes to Debbie Greene, the concert pianist in Russia:
July 30, 1969
Dearest Debbie,
Your warm letter was welcome.
My wild enthusiasm has simmered down and in Japan my emotions are low key. We are staying in youth hostels, there are only teenagers and college young people. I am the only oldster who has to play the kindergarten games with them. It is the evening entertainment.
The kids get close to Nita and they talk, but "respect" holds them off from me. I haven't established a warm relationship with anyone in this country yet. It has been a little over three weeks so far.
My heart was left in Taipei and I wasn't ready to face Japan. It also is the hardest country to adjust to because the culture is very different.
Besides that, knowing I have to return to face the family and their problems is not easy.
We arrive in Tokyo tomorrow and I hope to meet a man, my age, who might take me to the Japanese theater and a restaurant for a 1,000 yen meal. The 180- yen meals consist of rice, and noodles and potatoes all in one meal. I planned to lose weight in this country, but impossible.

We take an August 7 flight to San Francisco. My cousins, Lucille and Dick Shoemake, live there.

My cousin, Marion, moved to Pasadena and wrote the warmest, most beautiful letter of welcome to us. She has four children and three were born on August 13. She invited us to the giant birthday party. She also has her eldest son arriving with fiancée to meet the family. Though crowded, she says she'll find room for us.

In Japan, we sleep on tatami mats on the floor most of the time and think nothing of a floor bed after this trip.

I have a few boxes of processed slides so I hope you have a projector so we can view them.

David, in Taiwan, gave us an introduction letter to Mr. Niko in Tokyo.

He has a car, and met us early in the morning and helped us move from one hostel to another. August is the busiest time in Japan. University students book the hostels for three months in advance. Mr. Niko drove us around and fed us a meal and despite his lack of confidence in the English language, he does talk to us. He even offered us a home with his brother and five children if the hostel did not accept us.

Did the package of temple rubbings from Bangkok arrive?

My best to you and love, Ruth

Wednesday, July 30

Today is a good day. I guess there must be days like this to counteract the others.

It was a terrible night. The one small spot of window screen gave no breeze and very little air. I slept in the top bunk. "Heat rises," and it did. Mosquitoes buzzed and dive-bombed around my ears. At 3:00 a.m. I rose and wet a cloth that I laid on my naked body to feel cooler and sleep.

At JAL I spoke to the public relations man and finally got across to him the purpose of my interview. My idea was to become a customer who liked Japanese Air Lines best of all. I wanted to be used in their advertising. When he comprehended he was very pleased. He gave me the address of the man in Tokyo and told me my best bet was using the JAL office in New York. He suggested I write my ideas in the "Global Courier" magazine, which I shall do. For my efforts and thoughtfulness he gave me a present of a bottle of perfume. I'm thrilled with it.

Thursday, July 31

We were on our own. We lugged 72 pounds of luggage to trains and the JAL bus that cost 400 yen.

The airport was spacious and well organized, but they could have used more escalators instead of steps.

At Pan Am I asked for airplane bags. The clerk told me they were for first class tourists only, not economy class. I spoke to the manager and told him other airlines gave them when the customer spent more than $100 in fare. We spent over $1,000.

We needed them leaving Japan because we bought so much stuff here. Without any further argument he gave us two airplane bags.

Armed with my perfume package and Pan Am bags, we left for Namba, where I found a man I could talk to. I bought my Sony TC 100 tape recorder, anticipating hours of listening pleasure. I would have liked to send tapes to every country and have my friends record the music of their country.

We were to leave on a noon JAL flight, which usually gave us a good lunch on the plane.

It was the bumpiest ride of all the airplanes. We both felt nauseous. A meal in a wooden box was mostly rice and two shrimp and one piece of fish. A disappointment!

It was a lousy trip. When we arrived in the Tokyo airport we had a tough haul of our luggage to a locker. It cost 100 yen a day for only four days. We luckily fit four pieces in one locker. The other way it would have been 200 yen in left luggage.

We received 12 letters at the GPO.

A man, Mr. Ike, took me to our hostel. I also befriended a man from Manhasset, a community near my home in New York.

We could only stay one night here. We would call for the Yoyiga hostel tomorrow.

Ruth writes:
July 30, 1969
Dear Jack,
It always gives us much pleasure to hear from you. We received the June 23 and July 19 letters together, yesterday with twelve others.

Glad you have a vacation. Enjoy it as long as you can. We will be staying in California for a while with friends and relatives. Then Nita plans to spend time in New York with her grandma, Aunt Minnie and Lori and her chess friends. She is anxious to get back and believe me she is independent now and can handle any situation. Nothing will phase her as soon as she sets her mind to a task she desires.

We're glad David spent weeks in Homestead camp. Did he enjoy the experience there?

Yesterday we picked up four rolls of slides that were developed. There are many good photos. What a pleasant surprise.

I have been through three cameras on this trip. The first, in Spain, had an underexposure problem and when that was fixed the man botched up the advance lever. So I have double exposures on my bull fight photos.

The Venice printing of the first roll of the Voightlander camera was water spotted. Otherwise the photos are good. That camera took good pictures for me. A thief threw it in the canal in Thailand. End of Voightlander camera.

Hong Kong Vitessa 500 has been taking good pictures.

Nita has been very unsympathetic to my taking pictures and hinders the taking of them in every way possible. Now she enjoys looking at them and admiring them. What a life!

We are about to meet Mr. Nito and learn about Tokyo.

Won't be long now that we will be together.

Your wife, Ruth

Friday, August 1

Mr. Nito arrived in his car. We drove to a coffee shop for ice cream. We passed the Olympic pool stadium, a magnificent structure, and I managed to get a photo of it. He drove us to the hostel and we left our bags there. Mr. Nito promised us we could stay in his brother's home, if we were kicked out later.

We drove to shopping area and had a Chinese lunch. It was a good day.

Saturday, August 2

JAL flight 002 arrived on August 7, at 10:00 a.m.

We managed to get around in Tokyo. Nita saw the movie "The Graduate." I went to the science museum but there was no English there.

Mr. Niko played shogi with Nita. He beat her consistently.

He was a champion Shogi player and taught bridge. He swam, skied, and played golf. He was a great athlete.

I like him because he was Japanese and liked Chinese food.

Mr. Nito took us to his brother's home. The brother was furious with us because we were not staying there that night. He wanted to "do the town all night long!"

Neither wives liked Japanese Theater. They were bored. Mr. Nito's wife was pretty and spoke English.

Home to "fun in the bath" and bed.

Tuesday, August 5

We slept in a new youth hostel nearby. There was no bath in it. We had to go to a public bath before our meals.

Then to the Ginga area and the Imperial Hotel designed by Lloyd Wright to withstand earthquakes. It was not a beautiful building and I thought the architecture unattractive.

They wouldn't let me type there.

Nita was on her own and bedded down on tatami mats with two Japanese girls.

Wednesday, August 6

I slept in the youth hostel again.

I attended the Kabuki Theater in the afternoon. The orchestra was on the stage. Lighting and backdrop pictures were projected on the back screen. There was smoke around the feet of the actors. Colored lights enhanced the singers.

The woman's chorus was behind the scene and the audience clapped when they sang.

In the evening I walked to Brother's home and met his delightful parents. The father, an excellent player, beat Nita at Shogi.

His mother brought a friend who played the hamisen, a musical instrument, and they sang.

We ate fish and chocolate for dinner. This was an enjoyable evening.

I was back home at the hostel at just under 9 p.m.

Diary entry:
August 6, 1969
My first night in Japanese surroundings was the Tomita home. Kazumi, the doctor friend we made on the tour, was my host.

A bath was prepared for me and I left my slippers at the door and entered the anteroom. I opened the glass doors and there was a sink. Steam emanated as I slid the door aside.

From the Chinese home I learned that one washes outside the bathtub and uses the bath for soaking and relaxing. So I squatted on the wooden stool, about eight inches high, and scrubbed with a washcloth. I poured basin after basin of water all over me, then stepped into the bathtub.

A Japanese bath is hot. As with most water situations, the faster, one plunges into it, if you can, the better. The sensations of the wooden slatted sides and bottom were sensuous and added to the sensation of relaxation and luxury. It was a small tub, but had depth that American tubs do not have. It also had the wooden surface that was a very pleasant contrast to our cold porcelain tile. I sunk to my neck and closed my eyes and got ready for bed.

One is supposed to get out. Soap up again. Wash again because the pores are open and the skin layers scrape off easily. Then back into the tub. Out of the tub and then a cool water spritz bath.

I stepped out of the door into my slippers and paddled off to my bedroom. There on the tatami mat was a foam rubber mattress and crisp sheet, and on top was a soft, downy light quilt and a new shiny sheet. A sleeping kimono was lying on the bed for me. Needless to say, I slept well.

The youth hostels all had baths with slight variations.

In Himeji, it was comfortable and I was alone in it, even though bands of people were housing with us.

We had one night in Okayama with a very, very hot outside tub. I was unable to step into it and looked underneath and saw the fire heating up the water. No bath that night for me.

In Hiroshima, there was a swimming pool, but who wants cold water when a hot bath awaits? We took baths all three nights. After climbing the hill to the hostel one needed a bath. Here was my first experience bathing with other girls in the room.

They laughed as I grimaced at the hot water. It felt good to stretch out and sink down to chin level and soak and soak until completely relaxed.

In Shimonoseki, we had another hill to climb. The first bath night I shared it with the schoolchildren, who were being bathed by mothers and teachers who accompanied the group. One little boy kept peeking at me and laughing.

It is a Japanese act of cleanliness to leave street shoes at the entrance and put on slippers. Sometimes there are boxes to house the shoes, sometimes lockers. There is the third pair of shoes, wooden clogs that are situated inside the door of all toilet-bath situations. The slippers are left outside the door and when you go out you pick any pair of slippers, not your own usually. Hence the germs in the bathroom supposedly remain there. What bothers a few of us is the fact that many different people wear those bathroom slippers in and out of toilets. What about germs on those?

Slippers are also worn on wooden floors within the home. On matted rooms the slippers are left outside the room. This requires thought for the newcomer to the country. I find more I have acceptance and less resentment about the system now.

However, in Mr. Nito's brother's home, where we walked barefoot, I felt more at home and at ease. I guess I liked the Indian system of leaving shoes outside the door and barefooting it around the house.

The Japanese squat toilets were the cleanest we had ever seen. Tiled floors usually surrounded them. The plumbing system worked well here. Most places had paper to use — back to Western ways.

The Hamada youth hostel had no bath. I was given a ticket and told to go to the public bath. It was my first experience in one. This one had a thin separation between the male and female side. There were many children being washed by mommas. I sat in the bath, a wooden one again, but larger than the home variety. I held a baby on my lap while momma-san washed herself.

In this bathhouse there was also a sulfur bath where three old women sat. One woman lent me a towel in the drying room, because I did not bring one.

August 6, 1969
Letter to David Chiang
Dearest David,
I haunt the post office for mail from you. It is fruitless.

Thanks to you, my opinion of Japan has altered. Mr. Nito, his wife, Hiroko and son, 8, and daughter, 5, are the most admirable family we could wish to meet. They gave us happy aspects of ending our long voyage on a very happy note. Mr. Nito takes us in his car, plays Japanese chess and Shogi with Nita. He also swims, plays golf and dances. He can be a real swinger of a man, but we have not spent those kinds of activities with him. Mostly we go shopping for gifts back home, and he also feeds us meals. He did not like the youth hostel deadlines so he moved us into his brother's room for two days so we wouldn't have to be in by 9:00 p.m.

His children spent time with us and they are bright and delightful. We taught them card games and they beat us the first time they played.

We take the JAL flight to San Francisco tomorrow at 5:00 p.m. August 7 and arrive August 7 at 10:00 a.m. That International Date Line plays tricks.

I bought the book you wanted and mailed it to you. From the little English in the index it looks like tough reading to me.

Mr. Nito bought a slide projector and tested it out on some of my pictures I developed in Tokyo.

I went to Kabuki; it was mostly singing. The loveliest part was that a few women sat in the bath and sang.

Nita saw the movie, "If." I recommend it to you. Just your speed, I think.

Your letters will awaken fond memories of the hours we spent together.

My love for you is unending.

Your Ruth

Thursday, August 7

I met Nita at the airport. We picked up our bags that we'd put into lockers and repacked. We measured out our 44 pounds and shipped that on our ticket. We carried the extra 25 pounds on to the plane.

Friends Mentioned in Chapter 51

Mr. and Mrs. Tomita and Kazumi. They were my hosts when I arrived in Japan.

Siminoseki. She was a young woman who invited Nita to live in her home. They were close friends.

Mrs. Masunga. She was our hostess in Osaka.

Sharon Copeland, 22. She was a Native American I met.

Mr. Niko. He hosted us in Tokyo.

3 JAPANESE WOMEN

FARM WORKER

AFTERWARD

August 15, 1969

Dear Jack,

Nita caught the bus to Kennedy airport at 6:00 this morning. Not exactly her hour to rise. With the time change, we had to work out a reasonable arrival, not at rush hour. She is looking forward to seeing her friends and Lori and Olga and Minnie and to spending a little time with them before shooting off to college for the year.

It wasn't easy leaving California. Originally she didn't plan to stay so long, but people are so wonderful she couldn't help herself.

First it was our cousins, Lucille and Dick Shoemake. Lucille is still as creative and energetic as ever. I don't think she has changed in these 20 years. Dick has his sense of humor; he is quick, clever and a delight. He had a cerebral hemorrhage a year ago and Lucille nursed him back from a dead piece of protoplasm into her husband again. She taught him how to walk, talk and use his muscles. He had total amnesia and had to learn how to think. His recovery is remarkable.

Imagine, we were the first guests in their home for four days. He didn't want us to leave. They still have their rock-hound interests, camping, fixing up the house. Lucille does ceramics and painting and he enjoys reading.

Then we were off to my cousin, Marion, in Pasadena. Her son, Buddy, and his fiancée arrived the day before us; they are in and out of the house. Mark is working here for the summer and attending night school. Gloria lives nearby and will be going to Hunter College next week. Howard stays on.

They all had birthdays on August 13; Buddy, 26, Mark, 21, and Howard 16. On his birthday Howard passed his driver's exam. The sad note that happened that day was Howard's dog ran into the street and was killed.

We added to Marion's joy by asking her to drive us to our friend we met in Russia, Debby Greene. Debby had a beautiful home. As I expected, she was happy there and we listened to Debby practicing piano for her concert with a violinist. Now Marion will return there with me Saturday evening for her big concert. Nita stayed on with Debby, I stayed with Marion.

We still have to see Elsie from the Russian trip.

I'm happy and will stay on for a while longer. We decided if we could manage all the other airports around the world we would manage New York, also.

See you soon,
Love, Ruth

THE FINAL WORDS

To all of our new friends,

After 14 months of traveling around the world, Nita and I arrived home. It was an unusual and glorious experience from start to finish. We made so many friends in each country that we have come to realize people are more outgoing, friendlier and much less fearful in other areas of the world.

Americans are concerned how people "react" to Americans. We do not feel that the friends we made reacted to us as Americans, but as fellow human beings. People let us live in their homes, fed us meals, shared their families with us and involved us in their lives. They enriched our experiences beyond all expectations.

If we have been reticent in sending tokens of our thankfulness or warm feeling for you it will take time for us to get around to the many, many people who befriended us. Meanwhile, we do ask that you correspond with us.

We can outline our voyage as follows: Portugal; Spain, one month; Italy, two weeks, (David in the hospital in Florence for nine days); Greece; Athens and Aegina Island for one week; Russia, three weeks studying Russian.

A train through Berlin brought us to London for 12 days.

Our Indiaman bus tour from September 22 to November 27 took us through Belgium, Luxembourg, Germany, Austria, Italy, San Marino, Greece, Turkey, Iran, Afghanistan, Pakistan and India. We do not recommend bus tours, although the camping aspects of this one made it feasible for us financially.

We spent three months in India, then on a ship to Mombasa for two months in Kenya and a couple of weeks in Uganda.

We hitchhiked and lived in youth hostels in Mombasa, Nairobi and Japan. We recommend both methods as the best way in these countries.

We took bunk class on the Haryana ship back to Bombay and became prisoners on board. If it were not for Captain Keith, we would not have survived this ship experience. His companionship was a godsend for us both.

We took a trip to Goa, where we saw Portuguese India, very different from what we had experienced in our three months in India.

Ceylon (now Sri Lanka) was a highlight because of the friends we made. Clarence doesn't forgive us for spending only two weeks there.

On to an overnight Singapore stop at the plush Malaysia Hotel that Pan Am paid for, then on to Djakarta, Indonesia. We spent three weeks, much of it on trains and buses, and reached Bali, but didn't stay there long enough. It is amazing we slept only three nights in hotels in Indonesia.

The hospitality overwhelmed us and I hope the friendships will be long lasting.

We traveled on to Singapore for four days and Thailand for three weeks; Hong Kong, two weeks with a two day stop-over in Macao; and Taiwan for two weeks. Nita skipped these two countries and I made some of my closest relationships there.

The political governments influenced our feelings about countries. But Nita did love Spain, despite the reactionary leadership. I loved the friendly people in Taiwan. Japan was our last country. We hitchhiked around Western Honshu and lived in youth hostels. We traveled around there for one month. The youth hostels in Japan are the finest in the world and are government supported. I would like to become involved in getting other countries, especially America, interested in building such hostels for world travelers.

Fourteen months of travel … and we would have liked to turn around and do it all over again, instead of returning home.

My friends, you have much to be thankful for. We cannot hitch in America. People live in fear here and avoid walking alone at night. Nita and I never experienced fear in your countries.

When we speak of the "villains" in our adventure story, they are usually people who did not fulfill our expectations, rather than people who harmed us physically.

The practical joker, Patrick, sent us to Murchisons Falls on a wild goose chase. There was Hussein, who dragged us around Uganda for three days and never found us a permanent lodging, and was very jealous if Nita socialized with anyone else. He was another "villain."

But the Zabuliwo family in Uganda welcomed us with such warmth and love that we recall our days in their home with great happiness.

Possessions bother me since my return to the States. We own too many material things. India had so little. There were no supermarkets or large department stores like those in America. People manage with much less. But this, in no way, seems to influence their ability to be happy and contented with their family life. I prefer the simplicity of the Japanese home — large empty spaces, as little furniture as possible and one area to display an item of beauty to be admired.

The pace is another admirable quality about your countries. Can you imagine what it is like to return after 14 months of no schedules, no time keeping, to suddenly have to rise at 6:30?

We actually have a sign-in sheet at school with the time of our arrival and our departure. Our teaching day is six and one half-hours.

Clarence Wanatungunda laughed at my rushing. So feel lucky you can relax and avoid the sicknesses we get from time pressures. Your family life is happier than those I see around me in America. We have more pressures that cause neurotic, emotionally upset behavior. It is true what you read about the unhappy marriages. I was hoping to find some answers to make mine a happier one.

We are back in the same routine we had before. Nita, the exception, will be off to Marlboro, Vermont, to college next weekend. Wendi graduated high school and temporarily will be working in a school with Down-Syndrome children. Lori and

David are still in high school. I spend my day teaching a sixth grade class. The additional pressures of housekeeping, chauffeuring, and doctor and dental visits leave little time for relaxation.

Lori and Wendi have me joining their ballet dancing class to "reshape" my figure. Wendi has a new graceful posture this year.

This past year's experiences give me much to think about and evaluate during the year. I hoped to gain important concepts for teaching and living. The ideas are all written down, and if I find the time to work on my journals I can finish the book about the friends we made and our adventures

I will encourage all the people I can to travel and see another way of living. I find that I prefer barefoot to shoes (until the cold weather). We are back to using silverware, instead of chopsticks. Hands for eating are still preferable to both.

Regarding my family life, Jack and I are still living together in the same house. Nita and I have been welcomed with hugs and kisses. The family is happy we are home again. Nita goes off to college. Wendy is prepared to attend the Marlboro College with Nita. She will be leaving the house soon. Lori beams that she has a mother once again. She has been improving in all her high school subjects. David is David. He's glad to see us and has missed us. We are a united family these days.

If you write to us we promise to answer as soon as possible.

All our love to you,

Ruth and Nita